Winning
Defensive Football

Richard Bell

ISBN: 978-1-60679-099-1
Library of Congress Control Number: 2010924204
Cover design: Brenden Murphy
Book layout: Bean Creek Studio
Front cover photo: U.S. Air Force Academy Sports Information Department

Coaches Choice
P.O. Box 1828
Monterey, CA 93942
www.coacheschoice.com

To the love of my life and my best friend—the real coach of our family: my wife, Marilyn. For 45 years in rain, shine, sleet, or snow, she has been there, sharing the joy of victory and the disappointment of defeat. The wins and losses have come and gone, but our love and friendship has continued to grow and become more meaningful with each season. The scoreboard has recorded the victories and defeats of each year, but in reality I've been undefeated every season with her at my side. Thanks for the memories, Marilyn. I love you.

Dedication

Acknowledgments

Throughout my life, both as a player and a coach, there have been so many who have gone the extra mile to provide me with assistance and positive reinforcement to enable me to achieve success.

My mom and dad gave to my brother and me the foundation of love, trust, work ethic, and a never-give-up spirit that enabled us to succeed far beyond our ability and talents. Although we were definitely not wealthy, we had a quality of life that wealth could never buy.

My junior high coach, Winston Faulkner, took a young boy who loved sports and gave me a sense of worth and value that has remained with me as a player and a coach. The example he set and the influence he had on all of us who played for him was one of the main reasons I knew that coaching was my calling.

The high school I attended (Little Rock Central High) had a tremendous program, which had attained unbelievable success under the leadership of Coach Wilson Matthews. The record he accomplished (111-15-1) in 11 years, 10 state championships, and a 33-game winning streak over his last three years at Central is still recognized as one of the greatest achievements in Arkansas sports history. His impact on all of us who played for him was unbelievable. He was a tough, demanding, in-your-face coach who took you beyond what you thought were your limits. To this day, when I've been faced with adversity, I think back to his words and actions to find the strength and courage to fight through it.

At the University of Arkansas, I had the privilege to play for Jack Mitchell (three years) and Frank Broyles (my senior year). These two quality coaches and their outstanding staffs gave me a chance to play, which I will always appreciate. Jim MacKenzie, Dixie White, George Bernhardt, Doug Dickey, Merrill Green, Steed White, and Wilson Matthews—I couldn't have played for a better group of assistants, whose knowledge of the game, their ability to teach, and talent to motivate have aided me tremendously over the years. I will always admire the success Coach Broyles achieved at Arkansas. Having had the opportunity to be a part of his program and then to observe it from a coaching perspective, I better appreciate what an unbelievable job he did with the Razorbacks. His attention to detail, astute knowledge of the game, ability to surround himself with outstanding coaches, and concern for his players all contributed to his outstanding record at Arkansas. Coach, it was a privilege to play for you during my senior year. I will always appreciate your willingness to help me and advise me throughout my career.

Thanks to Vance Ellis (superintendent) and Joe Shapes (principal), who gave me my first opportunity to coach at Walnut Ridge, Arkansas.

John McKenna at VMI saw something in a 24-year-old coach and asked me to join his staff, giving me my first experience of coaching on the college level. Coach McKenna will always be special, as he gave me a chance for which I will always be appreciative.

Coach Bobby Dodd, who is a legend in college football, invited me to join his staff at Georgia Tech. What an honor to coach for such a quality man and coach. His approach to the game and his innovative ideas has greatly influenced the game of football to this day. His offensive schemes, defensive alignments, practice approach, game preparation, player motivation, and recruiting techniques still are at the forefront of collegiate football. Needless to say, his influence on me was extraordinary.

Jim Carlen, who was the defensive coordinator at Georgia Tech when I joined the staff, took the head-coaching job at West Virginia. After his first two years at WVU, his defensive coordinator job came open, and he invited me to join him, giving me my first chance to be a coordinator. This began a 15-year relationship with him at West Virginia, Texas Tech, and South Carolina. I'll always admire the job Jim did at each of these schools. I know he never got the recognition he deserved in taking three losing programs and turning them into winners. His knowledge, his willingness to let his staff coach, his recruiting skills and up front, truthful dealing with the players I have always admired and made every effort to emulate. Jim, it was great being with you. The memories Marilyn and I have will always be meaningful.

It was a wonderful experience working with Steve Sloan at Duke University. He is a quality man and an excellent coach who truly did an outstanding job at Duke, although this never was realized in the win-loss column. The foundation he laid enabled Duke to achieve great success under Steve Spurrier's leadership.

It was fun working with Art Baker when we were both assistants at Texas Tech and then when he was the head coach at East Carolina. I only had a chance to be with you one year, Art, but what you accomplished with the Pirates enabled them to be a winner in the years that followed.

When I joined Ray Goff at the University of Georgia in 1989, I knew it would be a difficult task replacing the legendary Vince Dooley. I enjoyed my time with Ray and felt he did an excellent job in replacing Coach Dooley. The teams we put on the field in 1991 (9-3) and 1992 (10-2) were outstanding and achieved the success they enjoyed due to Ray's recruiting and leadership.

I only had the opportunity to be with George Chaump one year at Navy, but I came away from that time with a great respect for him as a coach and appreciation for his friendship.

Over the last 12 years, it was a real joy to work for and with Fisher DeBerry at the Air Force Academy. What he accomplished at Air Force over the past 23 years before his retirement after the 2006 season is miraculous. During this period, probably 90 percent of the games Air Force played, the opposition had better talent. Yet Coach DeBerry, year in and year out, through his philosophy, his leadership, his motivation, and his character consistently won because he instilled in the heart of his players that "what you believe in your heart, you can achieve on the field." Fisher, I have tremendous respect and admiration for the job you did. It was great to be a small part of it.

My thanks to all the assistants I had the honor and a privilege to work with: Bo Sherman, Clark King, Charles McGinnis, Weenie Miller, Fred Kelley, Dick Inman, Jack Fligg, Jim Luck, John Robert Bell, Jack Griffin, Bob Thalman, Dub Fesperman, Dick Bestwick, Jesse Berry, Bobby Bowden, Bill Hicks, Hayden Buckley, Bob Brown, Dale Evans, Tom Wilson, Jimmy Ragland, Marshall Taylor, Jerry Sullivan, Marc Dove, John Conley, Jess Stiles, Ted Unbehagen, Billy Michaels, Dave Fagg, Keith Colson, Bob Roe, Tim Clifton, Larry New, Jim Collins, Bob Sanders, Tommy Limbaugh, John Cropp, Tommy Bowden, Rod Broadway, Miles Aldridge, Don Powers, Donnie Thompson, Clyde Christensen, Kevin Gilbride, Dicky Clark, Frank Orgel, Steve Greer, Tim Kelly, Mike MacIntyre, Mike Drake, Ron Harris, Jake Gonos, Cal McCombs, Jappy Oliver, Tom Miller, Vic Shealy, Ron Burton, Dean Campbell, Brian Knorr, Bob Noblitt, Chuck Petersen, Jeff Hays, Ed Warinner, John Reagan, Paul Hamilton, Tim Horton, Larry Fedora, Sammy Steinmark, Dick Enga, and Pete Hurt. All are great people and good friends. It was fun being on the field with you. Thanks for some wonderful memories.

To long-time friends: Marshall Gazette, Jim Van Dover, Troy Green, Buddy Rotenbury, Bill Luplow, Jim Gaston, Harold Horton, George McLeod, Lloyd Woodman, Jim Clark, Albert Long, and Bill Hughes. Thanks for your encouragement, support, and friendship in school and throughout our lives.

I know I have left out some I should have named. Please forgive me, knowing that your friendship and brotherhood will never be forgotten. To each of you named and unnamed, thanks for the opportunity to coach with you.

To my lovely wife, Marilyn, who has allowed me to pursue my dreams in coaching, through many late nights, cold dinners, long separations, fun wins, and tough losses, your love, support, and encouragement have constantly lifted my spirit. I am truly blessed to have you as my wife, best friend, and mother to our children. Our love grows deeper and more meaningful with each day we share together. You are a special lady whose Godly life has truly blessed me.

Finally to my children—Michelle, Meredith, Murry, and Melinda—who loved, supported, defended, and stood with their dad in good times and bad, it has been a privilege to be your dad. I congratulate you on the quality lives you lead and Godly adults you have become. Words can never really express how you have encouraged and influenced me through the years. To your spouses, David, Dan, Chanda, and Ryan, thanks for bringing much joy and happiness into our family. Macy, Daniel, Benjamin, Taylor, Haley, Alyssa, and Kendyl, you are such special grandchildren, and will always have a treasured place in Coach and Mimi's heart.

Football and coaching has given me such fulfillment throughout the years. The wins, the losses, the burdens, the blessings, the tragedies, the triumphs, the obstacles, the opportunities, the setbacks, and the comebacks have all shaped me into the man I am today. The wins and losses have come and gone, but the relationships live on forever. To each person, I say thanks for the memories. It's been a fun run with outstanding players and coaches. Unless you have played or coached the game, you can never fully understand the bond and the brotherhood that was created between us and that will live on forever within each of us.

To be successful defensively in modern day football at any level, you must be very flexible in your base packages. No defensive coach in America is more qualified to help you coordinate the 4-2-5 defensive schemes with the base 50 defense than Richard Bell.

I am so excited he has elected to write this book because it will be so valuable to defensive coaches at every level as they attempt to match up with the demands and challenges that modern-day offenses are presenting. We are seeing a different offense each week during the season. Offenses are scoring at a record-breaking pace. Those with coaching responsibilities on the defensive side of the ball must be flexible from play to play and week to week. I am confident you will benefit from Coach Bell's ideas, which have withstood the test of time and game experiences.

Richard Bell has been recognized by the American Football Coaches Association as a national Assistant Coach of the Year. He has been the head coach of a university Division I program, and Richard has been a defensive coordinator at many outstanding and competitive programs across the country. His experiences facing so many different offenses make him well qualified to write this book. I guarantee you are going to benefit from many of Coach's ideas.

Many of Richard's former players have gone on and played at the highest level. Many have received outstanding awards and recognition. More importantly, Coach Bell's players have loved playing for him. I have not had a coach on my staff who had more respect from his players than Richard. He is the kind of coach we all would want our own sons to have the opportunity to have played for. His focus was always more on what was best for the welfare of his players in all areas of their lives. Richard's positive and consistent role modeling was just what players need.

Richard Bell is one of the best defensive coaches to have ever coached the game. He is even a better husband and father. I know you will enjoy this "ride" as he shares with you how to incorporate the 4-2-5 defense from the base 50 defense. Also, his suggestions for leadership and motivational ideas will really benefit your coaching. You are going to love reading this book, and you will be a much better and efficient coach as a result.

> — Fisher DeBerry
> Former Head Coach
> U.S. Air Force Academy

Foreword

contents

Dedication 3

Acknowledgments. 4

Foreword 9

Prologue. 12

Introduction 14

Chapter 1: Defensive Philosophy 17

Chapter 2: Leadership and Motivation. 22

Chapter 3: Defensive Communication System 32

Chapter 4: Tackling, Pursuit, and Takeaways 40

Chapter 5: Defensive Line Play. 57

Chapter 6: Inside Linebacker Play. 97

Chapter 7: Outside Linebacker Play 123

Chapter 8: Defensive Secondary Play 147

Chapter 9: Coverages: Cover 3, 2, 6, and 1 160

Chapter 10: Eighth Man in Box Principle. 199

Chapter 11: Gap-Fill Responsibilities 209

Chapter 12: Adjustments. 218

Chapter 13: Eagle, Under, and Hammer Fronts 240

Chapter 14: 50 Front (3-4). 268

Chapter 15: Six-Man Pressure From Eagle and 50 Fronts. 288

Chapter 16: Zone Blitzes. 296

Chapter 17: Nickel and Dime Packages 325

Chapter 18: Goal-Line and Short-Yardage Defense 342

Chapter 19: Defending the Shotgun Spread Offense 359

Chapter 20: Defending the Flex Bone Option Offense 381

Chapter 21: Game Planning 416

Chapter 22: Practice Organization 424

About the Author 431

Prologue

I have really enjoyed writing this book. To be honest with you, it has been much more difficult than I thought it would be. When I began, I felt a couple of hours a day could easily achieve what I desired to accomplish in relating ideas about defensive football. Once I got into it, I realized it was going to be more like five or six hours a day, if I was going to put together the caliber of book I desired to author. Yet, through the days when my mind was a complete blank, looking down at an empty page or in those moments when the words and ideas flowed with such ease, it has truly been a labor of love.

I really enjoyed researching years of notes, game plans, and scouting reports to come up with what you have been reading in the preceding pages. It was exciting to have the time without the pressure of a game or practice to research former ideas and schemes and discover how successful they continue to be, even after 20, 30, and 40 years. Unfortunately, football coaches can't take sabbaticals, but they could certainly benefit from such because I feel that time away from the game for a brief period would energize, excite, and provide some fresh ideas, and also allow time to review and refine old ideas and schemes that would be effective in the game today.

In the closing section of my acknowledgements, I spoke of how the brotherhood of relationships lives on forever. I could not write this book and be true to myself or fair to you as readers without telling you one very special, life-changing relationship that has transformed my life forever. Each of us has a spiritual dimension to our lives that we can develop to the fullest. We have an awareness of it, but sometimes we choose to be indifferent to it or ignore it completely, hoping it will go away. Throughout my life, I've always had a God-consciousness within me. It has always been very real to me, yet in high school and college it dealt more with a relationship-based on rules and regulations. It was a religion that was totally dependent on my performance, my effort, and my works in order to gain favor with God and attain the eternal life spoken of in the Bible. It was based completely on what I could do for God without any thought of what God could do through me. Early in my coaching career at Georgia Tech, some friends explained to me the difference between religion and Christianity. The words they spoke will never be forgotten. Religion is performance-based, depending totally on our efforts and good works with our eyes focused on ourselves, not on God. They explained that Christianity was not a religion but a relationship with a real live person: Jesus Christ. Jesus came into the world to do for us what we could not do for ourselves. Through His life, His death, and His resurrection, He has paid for every wrong we have done, we are doing, or we will do. The only thing we have to do is receive Him as Lord and Savior and allow Him to enter our lives and live through us. Christianity is not about legalism; it is about mercy and grace. This mercy and grace is focused on what Jesus has done for us, not what we have to do for

Him. I did invite Him into my life, and immediately the burden to perform and never knowing whether my performance was good enough was lifted. I knew a pardon, peace, power, purpose, and passion that I had never known before. As I began to walk with Jesus daily, every aspect of my life took on a new meaning. My roles as a husband, father, coach, and friend were now defined by the person of Jesus Christ living in me.

Players became human beings who were very special and unique, and I began to see the face behind the helmet and the heart behind the jersey. I pushed them harder to be all they were capable of being, doing it in a way of respect, not fear and intimidation. Instead of tearing down, I sought to build up because I saw that everyone played better when they had a strong sense of their worth and a powerful image of themselves. My hunger to win and to honor the Lord in my vocation increased unbelievably as He gave me a new spirit that would never give up, a new will that would never flinch, a new heart that saw every setback as an opportunity to come back, and a new passion that demanded me to stretch myself to the limit and beyond daily so that I could grow into the man God desired me to become. If you have not made this discovery in your life, I encourage you to investigate who Jesus truly is. He has changed my life, my marriage, and my coaching in an unbelievable way.

Now, you know who I am a little bit better. Many thanks for reading the book. I certainly hope that it has been helpful in giving you some ideas that will enable you to make your team better. I will be pulling for you this year and the years ahead to have great success. Make every effort each day to make this great game even better. We have a responsibility to those that have gone before us to honor them with our desire, dedication, and commitment to make these young men that play for us better competitors, better players, and ultimately better men.

Introduciton

The desire to coach had its start at an early age. My dad had coached immediately after college at Smackover, Arkansas, and even though he left coaching to work in the state government for the majority of his career, he never lost his love for teaching and coaching. We spent so many Friday nights watching the Little Rock High School team play, and then early on Saturday morning we'd head north to Fayetteville to watch our beloved Arkansas Razorbacks play all those Texas teams in the Southwest Conference. What wonderful memories I cherish of those special weekends, spending quality time with a wonderful Dad and enjoying the great game that has become such a part of my life as a player and a coach. Starting when I was eight years old, every day of football season, it was a nightly occurrence of diagramming plays, all of which I knew without a doubt had touchdown written all over them. The imaginary games I played every day by myself (of course with my Arkansas jersey on) against all the great teams of the late 1940s and early 1950s (Texas, Oklahoma, Notre Dame, Army) were won in the closing minutes because of a run, pass, or kick by a triple-threat running back by the name of Bell.

Once I began to play in junior high, high school, and college, my fascination for the game of football grew with each season I participated. I listened intently and wrote down feverishly the play, the defense, and the scheme we needed to execute that would give us the best chance to win. I was truly a student of the game.

However it didn't take me long to see that playing football (or any sport) was so much more than plays, defenses or schemes. The game of football parallels life more closely than any other activity. It demands you to play with pain, to work harder and smarter than your opponent, to get up when you get knocked down, to take your ability to another level with heart and spirit, and to never, never give up. I am firmly convinced it is 10 percent talent and 90 percent attitude. It is mind over matter; it is a band of brothers whose commitment to one another will never waver or flinch when obstacles are the greatest. It is the player who measures his worth to the team in how much better he makes his teammates play with no concern for personal recognition. As much as I enjoy the installation of game plans, I truly believe that motivation is as significant as preparation in the same matter that heart and will are the real key to maximizing your ability and talent.

The real reason for the book is simply to give back something to a game that has blessed me with more than I could ever have imagined. The coaches and players I have been fortunate enough to work with over the many years of playing and coaching have helped shape my life as a man and a coach. This book is a way of saying thanks to the many dedicated coaches and players I have been privileged to be around. Hopefully, there is a technique, a scheme, a defense, or a motivational statement that will help you as much as each of you have helped me. I love this game. As you face the opportunities and struggles you encounter as you walk through life, may you continually keep this thought in your mind: never let anything that doesn't have a heart whip you. I have lived by this simple statement many years, and time and again it has lifted my spirit, given peace to my soul, and provided the courage, boldness, and fearlessness to overcome when problems seemed insurmountable. Football is a heart game—so is life. Live it with all your heart so you can turn the impossible into the possible, the unbelievable into the believable. Live with your heart, honor the Lord, love your family, treat everyone special, make a difference, choose thanksgiving over bitterness, and have no regrets.

I hope you enjoy reading the book as much as I enjoyed writing it.

1

Defensive Philosophy

Football coaches look for athletes with exceptional talent and a hunger to play every down as if it's the last play they will ever play. Without question, players with this type of ability and unwavering dedication on every down will beat a team with good talent—even if they are highly motivated—9 out of 10 times. Most teams are not blessed with 11 players of this caliber, however, and it is up to the coaches to make the most of the players they have. A coaching staff should first lay out their roles as coaches. Just as coaches have certain expectations for players, the players also have expectations of coaches. Generally, players will not directly verbalize their expectations to coaches, yet most certainly they are watching and listening to determine:

- Can I trust these coaches?
- Do they care about me as a human being, or is my worth only determined by my playing ability?
- Are they consistent in how they treat all of us, or do they play favorites?
- If critical mistakes are made in games, will they share the responsibility?

With these and the many other questions that may exist, coaches need to confirm their sincere desire to be truthful with players, to build their significance not only as players, but also as human beings, to be consistent in dealing with them, and to share accountability if mistakes are made. It is important to always remember that players don't care how much you know until they know how much you care.

Coaches should define goals for themselves including:
- Take each player where he can't take himself.
- Teach players that they can "earn" anything, but they will be given nothing.
- Win each play, one down at a time.
- Do it right, do it hard, or do it again.
- Be a sound defense. Do what you do very well at full speed.
- Get your best 11 players on the field.

- Be positive. Your players are better than you think they are.
- Design the defense to play to personnel's strengths, not to their weaknesses.
- Stress individual techniques. To make the team better, each individual needs to get better.
- Always remember: you get what you demand. What is seen on the field is either taught or allowed.
- Get your players to do on game day what is coached in practice.
- Coaches are here to serve the players, not for players to serve them.

After coaches goals are outlined, player goals or expectations should be outlined. First, emphasize being the most physical and punishing defense on every play. Regardless of what circumstance or situation occurs, stress that mental toughness should allow no distractions. Second, emphasize working daily to be as good as possible. This goal would require that players not only work hard, but also work smart. Continually talk about using all their abilities—physical, mental, and emotional. Third, emphasize giving all-out effort on every play from snap to whistle. In every game, five to six plays will determine whether a team will win or lose. Because it is unknown when these "game-breaker downs" will happen, players should strive to finish every play. Fourth, emphasize playing with great enthusiasm. Enthusiasm is contagious; with it, performance can be elevated to an unbelievable level. Without it, regardless of talent, achieving goals will be difficult.

Defensive Mission Statement

To deepen the commitment of coaches to players and players to coaches, a mission statement is important to better define what achievement is being sought by the defense. Over time, players will often refer to their role as outlined in the mission statement. The following mission statement is a good example that defines objectives for the defense:

> The primary goal for the defense is to get the ball for the offense as near to the goal line as possible and as quickly as possible. Have a sense of urgency to achieve these two goals on every down. This objective will be accomplished through sound fundamentals, excellent techniques, swarming pursuit, a thorough knowledge of the defense, and a desire to play tougher, harder, and smarter than the opponent on every snap. Teamwork will be essential as the defense works together to get the ball. Work relentlessly to get to the ball with major emphasis on stripping the ball, creating fumbles, and achieving interceptions, sacks, and tackles for losses. These goals will be achieved only by playing together as a team, and knowing that the more opportunities the defense provides the offense for success, the greater chance to win the game. With reckless abandon, the mission will be singular: get the ball. By achieving this goal, the opponents will to play 60 minutes will be broken.

With one heartbeat, we will strive to accomplish our mission as we share the excitement, the enthusiasm, and the fun of competition every game day with our brothers.

Goals

The need for well-defined goals is essential for the success of every team. The team as a whole and the individuals that compose this brotherhood need direction to achieve their potential. Goals can be approached in several different ways to provide the framework necessary to give a particular team the best chance to win. A seasonal goal approach never changes throughout the season. Examples of seasonal goals include the following:

- Win.
- Allow 13 points or less per game.
- Get the ball to the offense inside the 40 (two times per game).
- Allow no more than three rush yards per play.
- Allow no runs over 15 yards.
- Allow no passes over 20 yards.
- Recover two fumbles per game.
- Make one interception for each 15 passes thrown.
- Limit opponents to less than 100 yards rushing per game.
- Limit opponents to less than 200 yards passing per game.
- Limit opponents to drives of 12 plays or less.
- Stop 70 percent of all third-down plays.
- Allow no scoring drives of 60 yards or more.
- Allow no touchdown after a sudden change.
- Do not take a penalty to sustain a drive.
- Do not allow opponents to move from inside their own 20-yard line.
- Win the two-minute drill.

Sometimes, game-to-game defensive goals are more relevant due primarily to the change of the opponent's offensive philosophy. For example, a shotgun offense using four and five receivers will require the defense to defend space, and the effectiveness of the horizontal and vertical throwing games will all contribute to an adjustment in goals. Some goals will remain constant, such as turnovers, stopping third-down plays, no penalties, keeping a team inside their 20-yard line, and winning the sudden-change situation. Yet some goals need to be adjusted game-by-game, depending on the type of offense faced from week to week. For example, when facing a team that will throw 35 or more times and is averaging 40 points a game, an adjustment in passing yards, points allowed, and such is necessary. In the same way, when playing a run-option-oriented offense, an adjustment in rushing yardage allowed is necessary.

General defensive goals that provide a better chance to win when accomplished include a combination of tangible and intangible goals. General defensive goals for your players include the following:

- Play together as a team (find 22 winners).
- Play hard on every down (swarm).
- Create turnovers (tackle well).
- Get off the field (three-and-out).
- During every practice, play hard, play smart, and play together.
- Play smarter, harder, and tougher than the opponent (this goal requires little talent or ability).
- Never assume. Believe, prepare, and work hard, but never assume.
- Allow no big plays.
- Be one of the top teams in scoring defense.
- Football is a heart game; prepare, and play with heart.
- Bring enthusiasm and excitement to every play.
- Know the defense, trust the defense, and always know where help is.
- Finish.

Common Defensive Principles

Little Things Add Up

Many times things are practiced which seem unimportant, but the cumulative effort of all these little things adds up to a successful effort. Repetition of techniques and ideas done correctly are one of the best learning processes in football. No one ever knows enough about football.

Nothing Should Ever Be Taken for Granted

Coaches should never assume that players know something and, therefore, not go over it. Players should never assume that they are not needed to stop a certain play. Players should go to the whistle. Players should never assume that they know enough so they don't have to listen to the coach. Players and coaches should never assume that the opponent will be an easy one.

No One Ever Does Anything to His Capacity

Every player can work harder, run further, and play smarter than he thinks he can. This axiom has been proven by some of the great distance runners. A lot of football players have limited ability but a great desire to excel. Very few football players have great ability and a great capacity to excel.

A Defense Must Be Consistent and Make Big Plays

Any defense must prevent the offense from scoring on big plays; this goal is achieved with a consistent, pursuing, coordinated team defense. Each individual must carry out the team defense. In order to get the ball back and to win the close game, a defense must have players who can make the big play (e.g., make interceptions, cause and recover fumbles, make key tackles) when the opportunity presents itself and still play consistent team defense.

Football Is Organized Confusion

War has been called organized confusion. Football is much the same. Players work hard on techniques, yet no individual does things exactly the same, and the situations in a game are not always the same as practice. Therefore, it is the team with the greatest unity that makes the fewest mistakes, that shows the greatest poise, and that has the least confusion that will win in the long run.

Every Score Is the Result of a Mistake

An offensive team can run 70 plays and only have three to four successful plays and still win the game. A defensive team can defend 70 plays successfully and only fail three to four times (sometimes only one time) and lose the game. Mistakes must be eliminated in defensive football.

2

Leadership and Motivation

Leadership and motivation are two keys that will determine the success of any team. With them, teams that are said to have less talent will continually pull off victories against opponents that, on paper, are said to be far superior. Without leadership and motivation, teams with tremendous potential will fall prey to losing to inferior teams with unpleasant frequency. A coach should seek to use the strengths of the leadership traits his team possesses, and to motivate these qualities to be displayed consistently so that the team performs above its talent level. In many situations, the talent level between teams is equal, but one team consistently performs better because its leadership and motivation is stronger. Some talented teams have the chemistry that enables them to play well together, but other teams with similar talent lack the commitment to compete at a high level in a tough ballgame.

Normal seasons are filled with highs and lows, ups and downs, victories and defeats, joys and sorrows—all of which work toward destroying the balanced, level approach the coach seeks to establish in order to give the team a chance to win each week. All these factors make it essential that strong leadership and solid motivational techniques are in place so that focus is not lost on what must be achieved each week.

Leadership must be taught; no one is born a leader. The number-one prerequisite for leadership is the ability to lead before expecting people to make a commitment to follow. The role of a leader can be lonely in the face of peer-group demands to follow their standards of conformity, compromise, and comparison. Sometimes, team members do not want to see leaders step up because of their unwillingness to make the necessary commitment needed for success. The leader must step out with no fear, knowing that one man with courage is a majority. Every decision is made with the team in mind, realizing that what makes him better must also make his teammates better. It is important that he has a real care and concern for each member of the team and is genuinely concerned about them as human beings who possess great worth and value. His integrity is respected, and his loyalty and commitment to his brothers is unwavering. He is not required to be the best athlete, but he needs to be one of the most committed players on the team. He must have the self-confidence and poise to make tough decisions and to confront individual and team issues that are not in the best interest of the overall group. An individual defined as a leader by his brothers and coaches is best described in the following poem by Edward Everett Hale:

I am only one, but I am one.
I can't do everything, but I can do something.
And what I can do, I ought to do.
And what I ought to do, by the grace of God, I shall do.

Developing Leadership Skills

Following are some proven ideas for the development of leadership qualities in football team members:

- Use questionnaires asking what his strongest leadership skills are and how he will make a difference.

- Have a one-on-one visit, and give the player the opportunity to discuss the role of a leader.

- Meet as a group with prospective leaders and seek their input on team policies.

- A number of great leadership books are available. Choose one of these titles, and in the off-season meet weekly for 30 to 45 minutes to discuss the leadership styles of the author. Give each player an opportunity to lead the discussion.

- Give players opportunities to talk with the team to develop the confidence of being able to relate as a leader.

- Define for the players what leadership involves and continually review with them the skills necessary to make a difference as a leader.

- Have seniors write letters to the team over the summer, expressing their thoughts and goals to encourage everyone in their preparation for the upcoming season. For sample senior letters, see Figures 2-1 and 2-2.

- Figure 2-3 contains some leadership statements or thoughts that can be given to the seniors prior to the start of the season. The purpose of these thoughts is to help the seniors become better leaders, and in the process make the team better by making the individual players better.

Team—

There is only will.

Strength alone is not enough. We learned that lesson last year. Being physically strong and talented is no guarantee. Being prepared and healthy isn't even enough. With pressure, these things will yield. However, a strong will can never be broken.

Heart is not even enough. Yes, heart is needed, but it doesn't guarantee results. Putting forth maximum effort and not quitting is admirable, but being admired is not one of our primary goals. Winning is the primary goal. Therefore, heart won't be enough; it doesn't guarantee victory. Will does.

There is only the iron will.

Will is the compilation of heart and strength. It's the coexistence of having a strong foundation with the energy to reach beyond. It's being prepared and knowledgeable and confident, but at the same time, it's the ability to give something extra when called upon. A piece of steel or raw iron can be a formidable weapon as is. It's heavy and can damage, but it won't win the big battle. A warrior can use this object to be successful, but it won't make him king. Instead, the piece of iron must be formed. It must be tested in fire, hammered, and folded—made stronger. Through time and effort, it's razor sharp; it's ready to dominate. So must a will be tested, pounded, and formed. A will is the compilation of every part of a man—the physical, mental, emotional, spiritual—everything. Everything must be tight, and it doesn't happen by itself. Start putting on your finishing touches. Form an iron will.

—Seniors

Figure 2-1. Sample senior letter one

Team—

There isn't much to say. Everyone plays and prepares for their personal reasons. You will have to live with yourself for the rest of your life if you didn't give everything you had, not me. All I want to say is: be ready for that first play. I am going to win my first play. How about you? After that, I will win the second, and so on. That's all you need to think about, the next play, and everything will fall into place. This team is going to be special, because everyone on this team cares. When you look at yourself in the mirror every day, don't forget to ask, "What have I done today to accomplish my goals?" You are the only one who knows, and you can't lie to yourself.

TEAM: Together Everyone Achieves More

—Seniors

Figure 2-2. Sample senior letter two

Champions Every Day

This is your team. Your positive leadership actions will determine the success of the team. A lot of people are counting on you to assume this responsibility.

Thoughts and Ideas About Leadership

- Being a senior does not make you a leader. It gives you the opportunity to become a leader. Expect no favors because you are a senior.
- Be an example. If you want to be an accepted leader, set a good example—on and off the field.
- Be first in everything. Leadership is like a piece of rope. It is easier to move the rope and keep it straight if you get in front and pull, rather than stay behind and push.
- Do not expect others to do that which you are not prepared to do yourself.
- Your teammates will admire and respect you for what you do, not just because you are a senior.
- Do little things well (be on time, first in line in drills, be positive). If you cannot be trusted to do little things well, you will not be asked to do big things.
- Encourage younger players, and have enthusiasm. It is contagious.
- Insist on discipline with your team, which is simply doing what is right. Nothing will ensure success more than discipline.
- Believe in each senior teammate. Know you can count on each other to do your best. Do not leave the leadership responsibility up to another senior.
- Outwork everybody on the team. If you want to leave your footprints in the sands of this team, wear work shoes. The only place success comes before sweat is in the dictionary.
- Remember that the senior who complains the loudest is generally the one who contributes the least. An excellent leader thinks positively, acts positively, and lives a positive lifestyle. A loser usually has a negative attitude and a negative approach to everything. Tolerate no "locker-room lawyers." If younger players are not positive, tell them to get right or get off the ship. Keep your coaches aware of the pulse of the team.
- There is no "I" in the word team. Make everyone understand it makes no difference who gets the credit as long as the team is successful. Give everybody else the credit, and eventually the real credit gets back to you and the seniors when you are successful as a team.
- You must play the best you ever have at any time in your career for the team to be successful.
- Finally, as a senior, you must realize love can carry you when nothing else can. We are already a close team. Let's continue to build on this positive factor. "God so loved . . . that He gave." Notice the order of the words: love, then give. Love your team and teammates, and give the best that is in you to be a strong leader of this team.
- Seniors before you have left a great legacy and foundation for you to continue. This legacy is a responsibility. Your team will be only as good as you want this team to be.
- Seniors, you will make the difference.

Figure 2-3. Player handout

Motivation

Motivation is a fascinating part of football. The coach should continually strive to get the team to improve daily, to overcome limitations, and to play at a level that is better than their ability, if they are to achieve success throughout a season. How the coach provides this motivation is made more difficult by the fact that players are all different. Following are some principles for the coach regarding positive motivational techniques that should be strictly followed to overcome the differences that exist in the personalities on the team:

- Get to know the players as human beings. They are all unique and special, so you must take time to discover their worth and value.
- Let them know; show them that you care about them (birthday, brothers/sisters, girlfriends, family).
- Be truthful and up front in your dealings with the individual and team. Make integrity the foundation of your relationship with each player.
- Always remember you are dealing with people's lives; don't play games with them. You may fool some groups, but one group you won't fool is your players.
- Be understanding, yet be tough.
- Be consistent. Don't worry about being liked; worry about being respected. Don't adjust to them; make them adjust to the standards of the team.
- Demand accountability. They are responsible for their actions.
- Help the team members to excel, as men and as players.

Once the players understand the depth of the coach's concern for all aspects of their lives, they will listen to his words and actions that prepare them to play. Every part of the coach's preparation is motivational, whether in team meetings, position meetings, or practice. The key is to keep them excited, enthusiastic, and passionate about the challenge they are confronted with each week. Furthermore, the coach should be creative and not afraid to try something new. He should think like a player and use motivational tools that will turn them on. The following motivational tools for coaches can be very beneficial:

- *Teach enthusiastically:* Enthusiastic, knowledgeable presentation of the game plan creates excitement in the players.
- *Practice preparation:* Organized, quick-moving, intense practice gets the juices flowing in anticipation of the game.
- *Stress visualization:* Whether in a meeting room or the stadium, give the players time throughout the week to visualize what they must accomplish to win the game. Example: If power G is a play that must be stopped, the linebackers need to visualize the proper press, inside or outside fit on blockers, and perfect finish.
- *Use a questionnaire:* Know each player as an individual. Have them fill out a questionnaire with information on family, high school attended, athletic and academic goals, girlfriend, etc. This way, you can relate to them in a personal manner when visiting with them one-on-one.

- *Be sure that players know one another:* Make it the responsibility of the players to spend time with five different teammates each week, developing relationships. Build the brotherhood.
- *Use motivational sayings:*
  ✓ Physical toughness will make your opponent weak; mental toughness will make him crack.
  ✓ You can't punish others until you first punish yourself.
  ✓ It's very easy to be ordinary, but it takes courage to excel.
  ✓ Perform your best when you're feeling your worst.
  ✓ Go beyond where you think you can go; go where your heart takes you.
- *Use motivational quick points:*
  ✓ POP: Performance Over Potential
  ✓ SYL: Stretch Your Limits
  ✓ PMA: Positive Mental Attitude
  ✓ WIT: Whatever It Takes
  ✓ SSS: Strong Shall Survive
- *Use inspirational stories:* Relate stories that feature individuals who overcome unbelievable circumstances, emphasizing that "If you believe it, you can achieve it."
- *Emphasize the following points in each practice:* Fumbles, strips, and interceptions.
- *Plan an "attitude emphasis" for the first two minutes of meetings:* A designated player or players are given a word ("heart") or saying (CTE, "Courage to Excel") to talk about as it relates to them and the team. It is best to let players know prior to the meeting (day before if possible), giving them the opportunity to prepare. The preparation enables players to truly express their thoughts on the subject in a meaningful way.
- *Create team-building exercises:* Form groups of six to eight players from all different positions. They are assigned to a coach to develop team unity through a series of questions on which they all elaborate. Following are example questions for the groups:
  ✓ Why do you love football?
  ✓ What factor most impacted you last year?
  ✓ What do we need to accomplish as a team? How do we get there and what is your role?
  ✓ How do you relate to the team motto?
  ✓ Define toughness and how you perceive yourself when it comes to toughness.
  ✓ Who are the playmakers on this team, and why?
  ✓ What are our team's strengths and weaknesses?

- *Give a Lunch Pail Award:* This award is given in spring practice or each game to the player who best demonstrated the "Bring your lunch pail/blue-collar/hard-hat mentality." This is a player who will compete on every play, every day, who has come to fight regardless of how long it takes to win.

It's exciting to light a fire under a team that enables them to rise up each week, regardless of the quality of the opponent (underdog, favorite, toss-up), and play with a heart, a will, and a passion that makes RTL ("Raise the level" or "Refuse to lose") come alive.

Regardless of age level, players are looking for words, statements, activities, and rewards that will inspire, encourage, and motivate them to greater success. Following are some motivational sayings that can be posted in team/position meeting rooms, locker rooms, or anywhere the players will notice them:

- A player who makes the team great is better than a great player.
- If you want something you've never had, you must be willing to do something you've never done.
- If opportunity comes, take it. If opportunity doesn't come, make it.
- Attitudes are contagious. Is yours worth catching?
- Hustle requires no talent, just heart.
- It's very easy to be ordinary, but it takes courage to excel. Behind all upsets is a great desire to win.
- The more I sacrifice, the harder it is to surrender.
- A champion is someone who gets up—even when he can't.
- You're only as good as your last play.
- Practice the way you plan to fight.
- If you believe it, you can achieve it.

Winner/Loser Statements

- A winner is sensitive to the atmosphere around him. A loser is sensitive only to his own feelings.
- A loser becomes bitter when he's behind, and careless when he's ahead. A winner keeps his equilibrium no matter which position he happens to find himself in.
- A winner goes through a problem. A loser goes around it and never gets past it.
- When a winner makes a mistake, he says, "I was wrong." When a loser makes a mistake, he says, "It wasn't my fault."
- Winners train; losers complain

At the conclusion of each week's game preparation, the coach finds himself in front of the team, waiting for his last comments before taking the field. Even when the coach has used many motivational techniques during the week, the pre-game motivational talk is the last chance to place an exclamation point on the team's preparedness to play. Figure 2-4 is an example of a pre-game motivational talk by the coach.

Context: In the week leading up to the game, the team has been confronted with adversity. Adversity can come in many forms and sometimes in multiples, such as a practice injury to a key player that will keep him from playing, suspension of a player for breaking team rules, and mid-term exams which are mentally and physically draining. Any number of these situations can take away from the mental, physical, and emotional edge needed to compete at a high level.

Pre-Game Talk

The key thing is to put away all distractions that keep you from being 100 percent committed to what must be done to win when the ball is kicked off. Never let adversity and difficulties control you; always remember you control the circumstances you are in by the attitude you take. It's not what happens to you, it's what happens in you. Your opponent probably feels that the adversity our team has faced this week will weaken us. That will be a big mistake on their part. They are a team, but we are much more than that: we are a brotherhood that grows closer and stronger when confronted with difficulties.

Many who have gone before us have taken obstacles and turned them into opportunities. Learn from these examples. A man by the name of Mark Wellman, a paraplegic, had a dream to scale El Capitan, a 3,200-foot granite cliff, located in Yosemite National Park. Mark's legs had been paralyzed since a fall in 1982 from another Yosemite peak. Yet, he had a hunger to accomplish his dream of being the first paraplegic to make the vertical climb up El Capitan. This plan was no small feat when you consider the Empire State Building is 1,414 feet tall. Wellman's goal was like climbing two Empire State Buildings stacked on top of one another. Yet, he set out with a friend, Mike Corbett, to accomplish this momentous task. To the amazement of all, they achieved their goal, battling gusting winds and 90-degree heat. It took nine days doing 7,000 push-ups (on ropes placed by Corbett) climbing six inches at a time. In a newspaper article, Mark said, "I'm tired. I have pains where I didn't even know I had parts. You have a dream, and you know the only way that dream is going to happen is if you just do it…even if it's six inches at a time." What an unbelievable accomplishment. What an example of taking all the adversities and turning them into advantages to achieve a goal.

You have a goal to win this game. Make up your mind to let no circumstance, no difficulty, and no problem keep you from achieving your goal. "What lies behind us and what lies before us are tiny matters compared to what lies within us." Just remember: yard by yard, it's hard; inch by inch, it's a cinch. Leave no doubt that nothing can discourage or defeat the heart of this team.

Figure 2-4. Example pre-game talk

The Winning Edge:
Axioms From Jim MacKenzie

The author had the opportunity to play for Coach MacKenzie during his final year at Arkansas. Coach MacKenzie's knowledge of the game, demand for excellence, and ability to get his players to play above their talent with heart and toughness, was not only beneficial to his players on the football field, but throughout life. His tragic death at an early age while the head coach at Oklahoma was a tremendous loss to the game of football—and a loss to the young men who missed the opportunity to play for this outstanding coach who could truly make men out of boys. Coach MacKenzie's winning-edge axioms can provide any coach with standards of leadership and motivational tools that will enable the team to play at a consistent, peak level. Following are some of Coach MacKenzie's winning-edge axioms:

- Play the percentages.
- Avoid losing first. Focus on defense, then the kicking game, and then do what you can offensively. Four or five games a season are lost, not won. Don't give anything. Make the opponent earn it. Mistake-free football wins.
- Play field-position football (Figure 2-5).
- Every coach knows more than he can teach. If you try to share all your knowledge with your players, you will overwhelm them. A confused player won't play well. Therefore, focus on:

✓ Simplicity

✓ Confidence

✓ Consistency

- Don't coach caution into good players by overcoaching.
- Nothing is accomplished without enthusiasm.
- Look for and recognize your mistakes in coaching.
- The little things are done by the winners. Everyone takes care of big things.
- Having a good team just gives you a chance to win.
- Physical conditioning precedes mental toughness. Discipline precedes morale. Both are necessary to win.

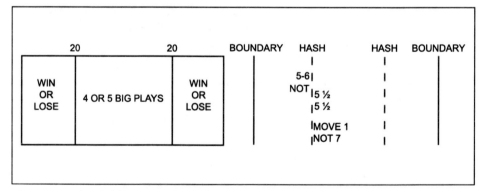

Figure 2-5. Play field-position football

- Players, not coaching, win.
- Be yourself, not an actor. Players recognize phonies.
- Play like you practice. Make second effort a part of your personality.
- Know the rules, players, and coaches.
- Game of critical situations.
- The kicking game is one third of football. Big breaks occur in this phase of the game.
- Prepare for the psychological lifts and let-downs.
- Know what to expect of your offense, defense, kicking game, and personnel.
- Always have a plan, and believe in it. Don't compromise or lose your guts. Everything must be planned. Nothing good happens by accident. Your plan will keep you from overlooking the little things.
- Form a team of winners. Surround yourself with players and people to whom football means a lot.

3

Defensive Communication System

The communication system presented in this chapter provides a foundation for the defensive fundamentals, techniques, and schemes that are discussed in the following chapters of the book. A communication system is necessary so that all coaches and defensive personnel are on the same page, thus enabling the defense to execute successfully. The system outlined in this chapter is a tried and proven method to accomplish good communication and limit assignment errors or misunderstandings.

Defensive personnel do not line up in a conventional huddle. Everyone lines up in close proximity to their position and looks immediately to the sideline to get the defensive call from a coach. All players are responsible for knowing the hand signals so that they can assume the proper position and execute the correct technique in the called defense. The Will linebacker communicates the down-and-distance as quickly as possible, and then identifies the formation as the offense lines up on the ball. The Sam linebacker makes either a Larry or Roger call, which is a strength call that coordinates the defense with the set of the offense. The defensive secondary receives a coverage signal from another coach on the sideline. After receiving the coverage signal, the free safety double-checks everyone by repeating the signal of the sideline coach. Again, communication is a vital key to the success of the defense.

Gap-Control Theory

The defense is predicated on a gap-control theory. To effectively communicate gap responsibilities to all defensive personnel, everyone must understand the same terminology. Instructions in a game must be illustrated in quick, understandable ways that allow for no misunderstanding on what adjustments need to be made. This goal is accomplished by lettering gaps A to D from inside out (Figure 3-1). The gaps will be the same both to the right and left side. This naming is significant because everyone must know their gap responsibility to the flow (direction) of the ball, and away from the ball flow. The success of the defense depends on each player securing his assigned gap and defeating the blocker(s) so that he can disengage the blocker, get to the ball rapidly, and tackle the ballcarrier. Every player should have the mind-set (after checking and filling his gap) that, with relentless pursuit, he has the chance to be in on every tackle. The theory of defense is based on "a lot of hats on the ball," but the player should first control his gap area of responsibility. Eleven men must commit themselves to being three to five yards from the ballcarrier on every snap.

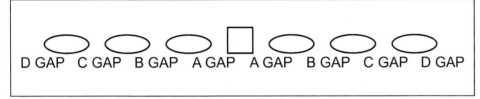

Figure 3-1. Gap identification

Defensive Alignments and Techniques

A technique is a description of a front-seven player's alignment, execution, and responsibility. Each technique is numbered for teaching and communication purposes (Figure 3-2).

Defensive line technique numbering:
- 2i, 4i, 7 are inside alignments on the offensive blocker
- 0, 2, 4, 6 are head-up alignments
- 9, 5, 3 are outside alignments
- 8 is a true wide alignment. (Example: Falcon on Eagle front plays an 8 technique.)

Linebacker technique numbering: A linebacker playing off the line of scrimmage in a two-point stance has the same technique number, but a zero is added behind the initial digit. (Example: 7 technique is 70; 5 technique is 50; and 3 technique is 30.)

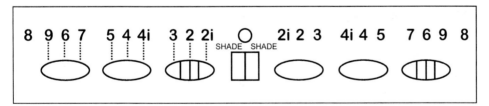

Figure 3-2. Defensive techniques

Offensive Personnel Groups

It is vital for the defense to have a clear and simple way of communicating the type of personnel and formation the offense has on the field so that they have an awareness of the formation they will be defending on each down-and-distance situation. This information needs to speedily reach the players on the field so that they can quickly mentally review the tendencies and tips from the scouting report to better anticipate what to expect from this personnel grouping. Coaches, either on the sideline or in the press box, need to watch and quickly communicate the offense's signals or jersey numbers that are coming onto the field to get a jump on personnel groups.

Offensive personnel are identified with a double-digit number to identify the personnel on the field. The first digit indicates the number of backs, and the second digit denotes the number of tight ends in the game (Figure 3-3).

21	Two backs, one tight end (two WRs)
22	Two backs, two tight ends (one WR)
23	Two backs, three tight ends (no WRs)
20	Two backs, no tight ends (three WRs)
32	Three backs, two tight ends (no WRs)
11	One back, one tight end (three WRs)
13	One back, three tight ends (one WR)
12	One back, two tight ends (two WRs)
10	One back, no tight ends (four WRs)
Zero	No backs, no tight ends (five WRs)
01	No backs, one tight end (four WRs)

Figure 3-3. Offensive personnel groups

Offensive Formations

Multiple formations are possible within each offensive personnel group. Therefore, it is vital for defensive personnel to identify the formation as quickly as possible. Figures 3-4 through 3-14 outline the formations within the various offensive personnel groups.

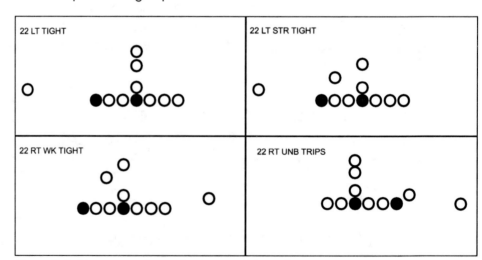

Figure 3-4. 22 personnel—two backs, two tight ends

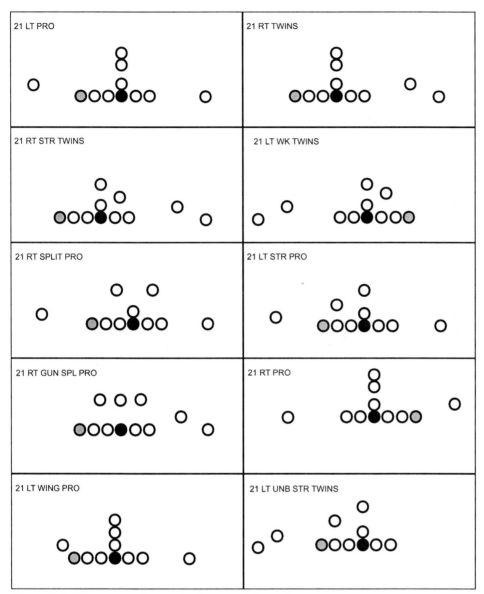

Figure 3-5. 21 personnel—two backs, one tight end

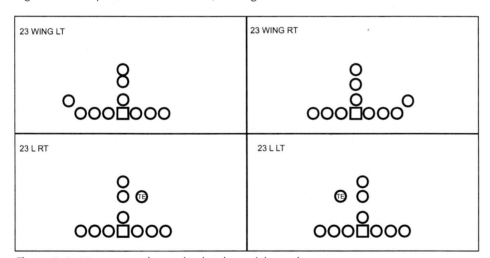

Figure 3-6. 23 personnel—two backs, three tight ends

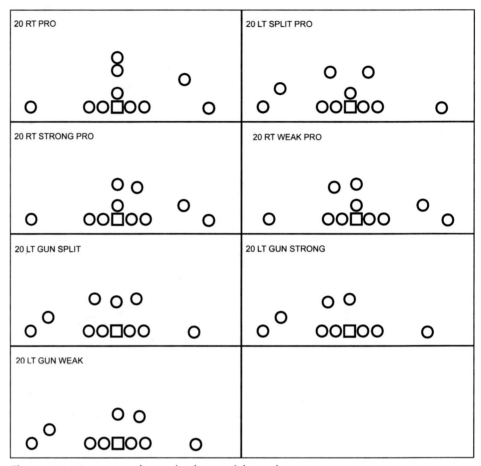

Figure 3-7. 20 personnel—two backs, no tight ends

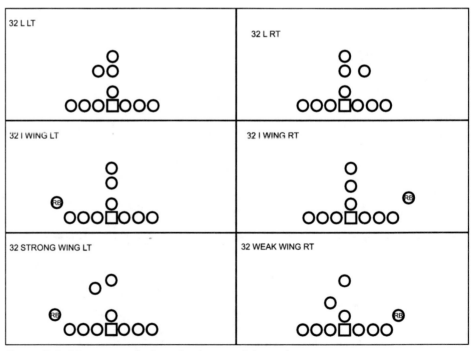

Figure 3-8. 32 personnel—three backs, two tight ends

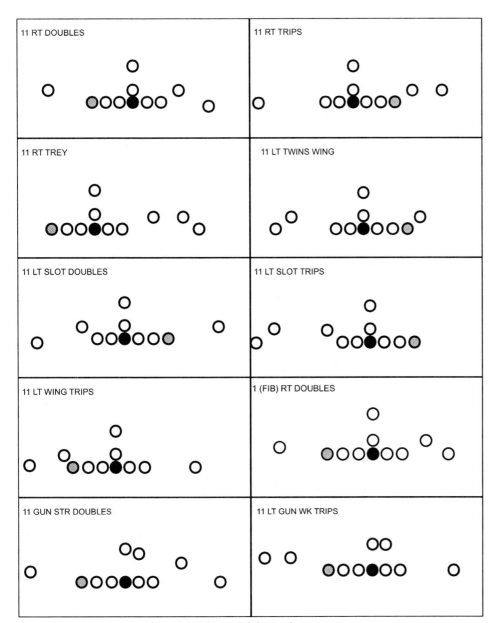

Figure 3-9. 11 personnel—one back, one tight end

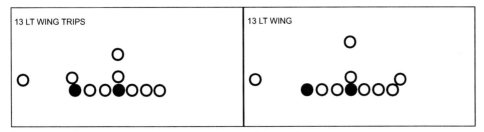

Figure 3-10. 13 personnel—one back, three tight ends

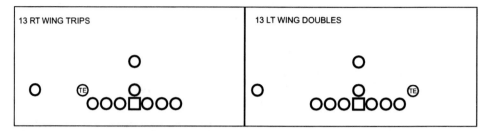

Figure 3-11. 13 personnel—one back, three tight ends

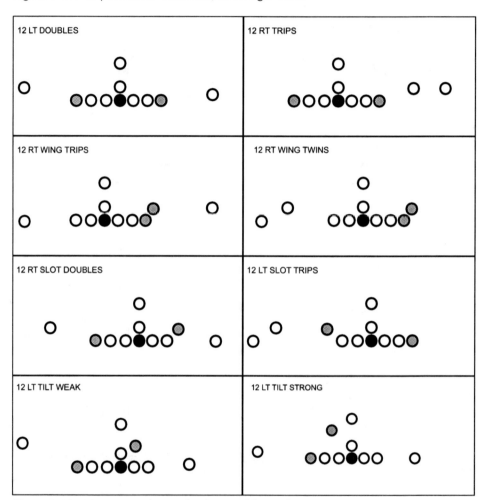

Figure 3-12. 12 personnel—one back, two tight ends

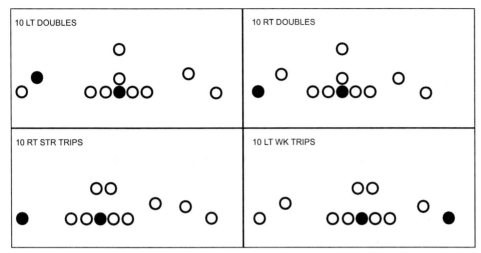

Figure 3-13. 10 personnel—one back, no tight ends

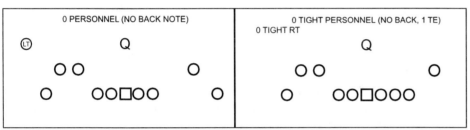

Figure 3-14. Zero personnel—no backs, no tight ends

4

Tackling, Pursuit, and Takeaways

Techniques and schemes are important to the success of every defensive football unit. To enable these schemes to be successful, several fundamentals must be executed to perfection on every down in every game. The importance of tackling, pursuit, and turnovers must be continually emphasized because these elements make the difference when two teams of equal ability play. The chance of winning will be greatly enhanced by solid execution of sound fundamentals as a team.

Tackling

The study and evaluation of tackling as it correlates to wins and losses is very important. More games are won or lost because of excellent tackling or missed tackles than because of any other factor. Missed assignments, the inability to get off the field on third down, red-zone defense, and so forth are all contributing factors in a loss. But, missed tackles have invariably been the biggest reason for a setback. It is important to not only record solo tackles and assist tackles, but also missed tackles. The need exists to tackle at 92 percent as a team for the best opportunity to play winning defense. Grading the entire defense on missed tackles will certainly increase the awareness of defensive players to the need of being an excellent tackling team. Proper teaching techniques and daily emphasis of tackling in individual drills and teamwork will definitely enhance the chances of winning. The fundamentals, tackling progression, the perfect tackle, and drills will improve skills in this area. Always remember that the perfect tackle should be stressed in practice, but the only ugly tackle in a game is a missed tackle.

Tackling Fundamentals

A correct tackle incorporates the fundamentals of the following factors:

- Approach
- Contact
- Finish
- Head and eyes

The most difficult tackle is an open-field tackle. The following is an example of a fundamental teaching progression or sequence:

- *Fit:* The tackler places himself in the ideal tackling position with knees bent, back flat, head up, arms wrapped, and hips rolled. Once this ideal position is assumed, a model to strive for is in place. The player should try to visualize this position.
- *Contact:* The pop is the coordinated skill of making contact in the correct position while rolling the hips, thrusting the arms, and utilizing the power of the lower back and legs. The tackler's arms are utilized in three steps:
  - ✓ As contact is made, the tackler thrusts his arms in an upward direction around the ball.
  - ✓ He wraps the arms around the back of the ballcarrier.
  - ✓ He pulls the ballcarrier toward him.
- *Finish:* The combination of the contact and the leg drive allows the tackler to finish the ballcarrier by placing him on his back. He should drive through the ballcarrier.

Once the fit, contact, and finish have been taught, it becomes necessary to concentrate on the approach. The single-most important skill to be learned is the breakdown as the tackler approaches the ballcarrier. He should gather his momentum, assume a good football position with the feet chopping, close the distance between him and the ballcarrier, and concentrate on the belt buckle. His point of aim should be the inside number on the side tackles. The approach is divided into five situations: straight on, side, boundary, open field, and desperation. He should keep his head up (eyes to the sky), keep his eyes open (see what he hits), keep his eyes up (if the eyes go down, the head goes down), explode with his eyes and hips on contact, never duck his head or close his eyes, and keep his head and eyes to the football.

Tackler Dos and Don'ts

- Keep the head up.
- Wrap the arms.
- Keep a wide base.
- Make initial contact with the chest.
- Don't close the eyes.
- Don't cross over.
- Don't duck the head.

Tackling Drills

In trying to stress the importance of being an outstanding tackling team, the need exists to use a variety of drills. However, the drills need to be meaningful and relate to what needs to be accomplished during the game. The emphasis is on being able to take what is practiced during the week and apply it to the game. It is important to use some creative ways to make players aware of tackling techniques without continually making them bang against one another. Most players love to strike someone, so use the drill time and team time to develop the correct skills to make the defense into a swarming, fanatical, and passionate tackling group. Always remember that tackling is what defense is all about. Nothing excites a defensive football team more than that solid, thundering thud that echoes throughout the entire stadium.

Mirror tackling drills place great emphasis on approach angle, proper head placement, keeping the head up and eyes open, explosion of hips, and running the feet through the ballcarrier without hard contact. Mirror tackling drills are illustrated in Figures 4-1 through 4-3.

Angle Tackle Drill (Figure 4-1)

The defender and ballcarrier align five yards apart in a five-yard square. On the "set" command, the ballcarrier runs at a 45-degree angle, and the tackler executes proper technique relating to press angle, head placement, keeping the head up and eyes open, hip explosion, and running the feet without any contact. This drill can be done with pads or without pads. The coach needs to position himself in front of the tackler so he can observe the performance of the correct techniques. The designated ballcarrier, which may be another defender, moves both left and right on the direction of the coach. The defender should run full speed through the ballcarrier. The tackler should be tight and close to the ballcarrier with no contact.

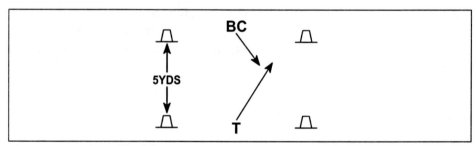

Figure 4-1. Angle tackle drill

Open-Field Tackle Drill (Figure 4-2)

As a general rule, place the tackler on the sideline and the ballcarrier on the hash mark. Alert the tackler and ballcarrier where the sideline is in the drill to make tackler aware of where his help will be coming from. On the coach's "set" command, the ballcarrier runs directly at the tackler and then makes his move two to three yards from the tackler. To prevent a long run or touchdown, the tackler should take an angle of approach based on where the sideline is located and where his help will be coming from, and thus eliminate the two-way go by the ballcarrier. Again, stress proper angle, head placement, keeping the head up and eyes open, hip explosion, and keeping the feet alive to and through contact. The coach can also have two tacklers in this drill so the first tackler will know where his help is coming from and take the proper angles. The second tackler will execute proper fundamentals and put great emphasis on being able to adjust his angle to the ball so he will be in good position to strip the football.

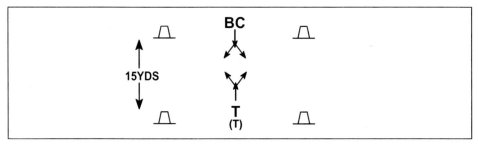

Figure 4-2. Open-field tackle drill

Leverage/Cutback Tackle Drill (Figure 4-3)

The tackler and ballcarrier align five yards apart in a five-yard square. On the coach's "set" command, the ballcarrier initially moves at a 45-degree angle, but on the second or third step, he executes a cutback move. The defender must be sure he presses at the right angle and adjusts his speed so that he does not overrun the inside number of the ballcarrier. The ballcarrier can move both left and right on the direction of the coach.

When in pads, all three of these mirror drills can become contact drills with the same emphasis on proper tackling techniques. A second tackler can also be involved with the primary emphasis on stripping the football. The defender involved in the strip will often get a better picture of finding the ball and adjusting to the ball by not actually stripping but visualizing the technique at full speed. The actual strip can come in team drills. In all contact tackling drills, high-speed hits occur, but no one goes to the ground.

In both the open-field tackle and the cutback tackling drills, the coach can instruct the ballcarrier to use a spin technique. Ballcarriers do this very effectively, so it is important to prepare defensive players for this technique by maintaining the proper base (feet shoulder-width), clubbing up, and grabbing cloth with strength and power.

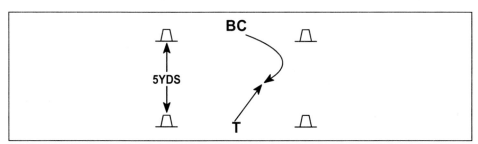

Figure 4-3. Leverage/cutback tackle drill

Popsicle Sled One-Man Tackle Drill (Figure 4-4)

The one-arm tackling sled (Popsicle sled) aids in the development of sound tackling fundamentals. This tool is great to teach proper base, head placement, keeping the head up and eyes open, explosion out of the hips, clubbing up and grabbing cloth, and running the feet to and through contact. A manager positions himself to the side where the tackler's head will be placed with a ball pressed against the sled. The players align five yards from the sled. The coach begins the drill with a whistle. On the whistle, the tackler approaches at the proper angle, hitting on the rise as he clubs up and grabs cloth while accelerating his feet on contact. He continues to drive until a second whistle tells him to take the sled to the ground. Proper techniques must be performed, or the sled will defeat the tackler just like a ballcarrier would. To prepare defenders for game situations, start the drill with a seat roll or shoulder roll to indicate to the tackler he is coming off a block and must regain a proper stance to perform the winning tackle.

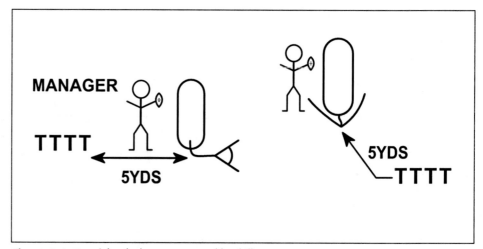

Figure 4-4. Popsicle sled one-man tackle drill

Popsicle Sled Two-Man Tackle Drill (Figure 4-5)

Putting two tacklers in the drill increases the repetitions. Again, have a manager align to one side with the ball pressed against the sled. Players align five yards from the sled, either directly in front or offset at an angle. On the first whistle, the first tackler presses to the sled at the proper angle, emphasizing the explosion out of the hips, clubbing up and grabbing cloth, and running the feet through contact. He lifts the sled off the ground and drives it until the second whistle, at which time he disengages from the sled, finds the ball, and then scoops and scores. The second tackler should adjust himself to the sled by speeding up or throttling down to maintain a five-yard distance from the sled. He then presses the Popsicle sled to get it off the ground, and takes the sled to the ground. A seat roll or forward roll can be used to start the drill just like with the one-tackler drill. This roll emphasizes the idea of exploding off blocks and accelerating to the tackle in the proper stance. Different drills using the Popsicle sled can be used that will maintain the players' interest and eliminate any monotony that may arise.

Figure 4-5. Popsicle sled two-man tackle drill

Press Tackle Drill (Figure 4-6)

The emphasis with the press tackle drill can be on all the points of the perfect tackle with particular emphasis on angles, the press of the line of scrimmage, and the tackler adjusting his attack point to the angle of the back and ball. The ballcarrier aligns at seven yards deep, and the tackler aligns at five yards deep. The tackler lines up outside the ballcarrier, as he needs to always be inside the ballcarrier to prevent the cutback threat. Stagger the bags so the tackler can always be pressing the line of scrimmage at the proper angle. The ballcarrier can hit any one of the three holes. He can cutback or fake into a gap and then dip out to the next gap. As the tackler presses the line of scrimmage, he should stay in a good stance so he is in position to reduce or expand to the back and ball. A full-speed collision with good tackling skills is required, but without taking the ballcarrier to the ground. This drill can also start with a seat roll for the defender, and a second tackler can be added to put emphasis on stripping the ball.

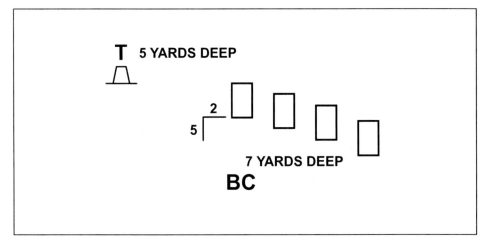

Figure 4-6. Press tackle drill

Goal-Line/Short-Yardage Tackle Drill (Figure 4-7)

Align the tacklers and the ballcarrier five yards from the line of scrimmage. On the command of the coach, the ballcarrier moves either left or right with a shuffle run or a crossover like a two-point wave drill. The two tacklers mirror the movement of the ballcarrier, keeping him inside and in front. The ballcarrier will plant and change direction. After his second or third move, the ballcarrier attacks the line of scrimmage at any one of the three angles indicated in Figure 4-7. Full-speed contact is required with the defense winning the collision battle (knock 'em back), but keeping the ballcarrier off the ground. The coach can give the directional moves for the ballcarrier if the ballcarrier is not providing consistent tempo in the drill. This drill is good for emphasizing leverage, explosion of hips, clubbing up and grabbing cloth while hitting on the rise, and accelerating the feet on contact. Remind tacklers that if the ballcarrier gets head-up on him, the ballcarrier has the tackler beat ("If he's even, he's leavin'").

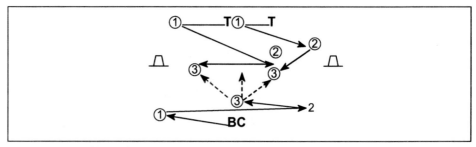

Figure 4-7. Goal-line/short-yardage tackle drill

Circuit Tackle Drill (Figure 4-8)

The circuit tackle drill is a 10-minute period that involves the entire defense. Each defensive position works on all phases of different tackling situations that will occur in a game. The defensive line, inside linebackers, outside linebackers (Falcons/Studs), and secondary occupy four different stations. Each group will have two minutes at each station and 30 seconds to rotate to the next station and coach. Groups rotate clockwise with a designated manager or coach keeping the time and blowing the whistle to move to the next station.

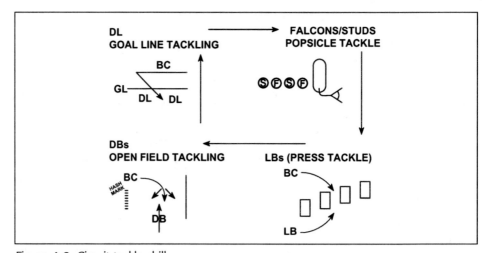

Figure 4-8. Circuit tackle drill

An Outline of the Perfect Tackle (Fit/Wrap/Strip)

The Approach

- Take proper angle to the ball.
  - ✓ Outside-in (contain)
  - ✓ Inside-out (pursuit)
- Sprint to the ball—close and breakdown, under control, knees bent, and tail down.
- Get a good base—football position, feet under armpits, and head and eyes up (eyes to the sky).
- Step on the ballcarrier's toes to prevent overextension; run the feet.

Making Contact

- Facemask on the ball—keep head in front, eyes up (never put head behind or head in back armpit).
- Pad under pad—hit on rise, climb up.
- Short six-inch explosion—uncoil out of hips, power punch (good explosion at point of contact, roll hips, explosive hips).
- Rip forearms up through the armpits of the ballcarrier.
- Climb up ballcarrier—hit on rise.
- Lock up—grab cloth, high numbers.

Follow-Through

- Maintain base with feet up under the body and shoulder-width apart.
- Accelerate feet through the ballcarrier.
- Drive the ballcarrier backwards to the ground.
- Keep feet tight and quick through contact.
- Tackle with legs—lose power without feet.

Tackling—Points of Emphasis

- Sprint to the ball.
- Take the proper angle.
- Step on the ballcarrier's toes to prevent overextension; run the feet.
- Get the face mask on the ball.
- Keep the head in front, eyes up.
- Get pad under pad.
- Hit on the rise; climb up.
- Use a short explosion, uncoil, and then power-punch.
- Rip up through the armpits of the ballcarrier.
- Grab cloth.
- Accelerate feet through the ballcarrier.
- No dead feet allowed on contact.

Key Tackling Words and Phrases

In tackling drills, the coach needs to communicate with quick, short, well-timed words or phrases what needs to be accomplished in the proper tackling progression. These words should be meaningful and convey the keys for tackling success that can be done in a fast, speedy manner to keep the excitement of the drill alive. Continually try to change it up, but always emphasize similar points, while making it meaningful in the effort to achieve the perfect tackle. Following are some suggested words or phrases:

- Punch, wrap, explode the feet, run through.
- Fit, wrap, strip.
- Punch, rip, climb (club up and grab), sink the hips, explode on contact, hit on the rise, run the feet, accelerate on contact.
- Gather, punch, kiss (the ball), club up, grab cloth.
- Run to and through, don't reach and dip, hit on rise, club and hug, eyes up and open, wrap and grab cloth.
- Dip, hit, lift.
- Eye target, close distance, sink hips, contact (chest-to-chest), club and grab, roll hips, buzz the feet, finish.

Another point of emphasis is limiting the collision yardage. In some games, plays occur where a first down is made just by inches in a critical situation, or a score is made by the slightest margin. It is imperative that the defense wins its share of these battles by winning the "knock 'em back" instead of allowing the running back to fall forward and make the first down or score. It is best to do this more through visualization and in scrimmage situations rather than a 1-on-1 drill where putting body-on-body can be a wear-and-tear on the players.

Pursuit

The goal of every defense should be to have the desire and dedication to be the best pursuit team in the country. The defense wants to have the reputation among opponents that it looks like it is playing with more than 11 players because of how passionately the defense flies to the ball. Nothing can discourage the morale of an opposing team quicker than to see 8, 9, 10, and 11 players three to five yards from the ball at the end of a play for a minimum gain when they thought they were going to get something big. Pursuit has nothing to do with talent, but everything to do with heart, soul, and spirit. How this deepens the brotherhood, the *esprit de corps* of a defensive unit, is immeasurable. Pursuit demonstrates in actions the accountability a band of brothers have for one another. Seeing on the field (or the video) the willingness of a brother to sacrifice his body for his teammates deepens the trust 11 guys have for one another. The effect this camaraderie has in a game or in a season is unbelievable. A player making a commitment to play all-out on every play gives him a chance to make one big play per game. If the defensive team commits to this kind of effort, they have the potential to make

11 big plays in each game. This phase of the game allows any player, regardless of ability, to have a tremendous impact on the outcome of a game.

When coaches make their team believe in pursuit, defensive success will jump tremendously without question. To accomplish this goal, it is important to grade each individual position player and the team on their pursuit. Individual players and the defensive team should score 95 percent or better to have the opportunity to win. Every offensive play is a potential touchdown, so relentless pursuit is needed on each down. In the same manner, coaches should sell the defenders on the fact that every offensive play is a potential big play for the defense. Excite them about the unlimited possibilities they can achieve if they play each down with unbelievable effort.

Generally, every player thinks that he plays hard and pursues every down, but often his standard does not measure up to a coach's expectation. Defenders need to know what is expected of them in specific terms regarding pursuit on every down. Once defenders know what is expected of them, the coaches can better define all-out effort on pursuit. Additionally, it also becomes easier to define a loaf.

What Is a Loaf?

- Change of speed
- Not turning and going to the ball
- Getting passed up by another player
- Laying on the ground
- Turning down a hit
- Not finishing with the mind-set to make a big play

What Is Pursuit?

- Pursuit is the most important part of defensive football.
- Pursuit is thinking more of effort than ability.
- Pursuit defines the value of a defensive player. A defensive player's value to his team can be measured by his distance from the ball at the end of a play.
- Pursuit means every play is a tackler's play to make.
- Pursuit is running to the ball with heart. Hustle and effort requires no talent, just heart.
- Pursuit is thinking more of the team than of an individual.
- Pursuit is all-out, finishing every play, roll call at the ball.

What Does Pursuit Do?

- Eliminates long touchdowns (the big play)
- Intimidates and discourages the opponent (especially the ballcarrier)
- Promotes team unity and team performance

- Helps to cover any possible mistakes in the defense (Example: What covers up missed tackles? People flying to the ball.)
- Creates take-away opportunities all over the field
- Allows the defense to consistently stop the run
- Keeps runs after a pass completion to a minimum
- Makes the entire defense play above their ability because of the effort they give

What Does It Take to Pursue?

- Pursuit is first a mental process ("If you believe it, you can achieve it"). Pursuit is 95 percent mental.
- The defender must visualize pursuing and making great plays (he must be a big play-maker).
- Great physical conditioning is necessary so that the defender can have great pursuit on each play (he must get to every play no matter where he is).
- The defender needs speed. He must think fast and react quickly. All players can improve their speed and quickness.

How Do Players Pursue?

- Play responsibility first.
- Take correct course to the ball.
- Escape and avoid blocks en route to the ball.
- Stay on the feet.
- Never follow the same color jersey (deepen pursuit angle).
- Perform responsibility either to squeeze or spill the ball so the rest of the defense knows where to support.
- Never assume the ballcarrier is tackled or that someone else on the defense will make the tackle (gang tackle, roll call at the ball).

Pursuit Drills

Every coach has his favorite pursuit drills. The main criteria for the success of any drill is a belief in it and the ability to sell the players on the reasons it will make them better and make the team better. Most coaches include a pursuit drill in their practice schedule. During the season, immediately after stretch is a good time to do a five-minute pursuit drill once a week. The emphasis on pursuit in a pursuit drill will continually remind players how important pursuit is to defense. Furthermore, every snap taken in 7-on-7 or during teamwork is a pursuit drill when the coach makes it a priority. Regardless of what pursuit drill is being practiced, the players need to believe in it, execute it, and finish it.

Perfect Play Drill (Figure 4-9)

To start the drill, the coach will call out the team he wants on the field. He will give the defensive call prior to them coming on the field. The designated team sprints onto the field and assumes their defensive alignment. This drill is a *full sprint*, and if the coach feels he's not getting the required effort, he will send them back to the sideline and begin again. If the initial sprint on the field is satisfactory, the team will align on the cones to execute the defense. A manager is used as a tight end so the strength of the formation can be set to either right or left. Two other managers align on the numbers, 10 yards deep to each side.

The coach gives the snap count and throws the ball to the manager to the side he wants the defense to pursue. The front five hit the ground from their three- or four-point stance and immediately get to their feet and pursue with the remainder of the defense in the direction the coach indicates. The entire defense sprints around the manager, circling him, and sprints back to their original alignment on the cones. Each position coach grades their position players on their execution and gives them thumbs-up or thumbs-down. If any of the coaches give a thumbs-down, the defensive team must repeat the drill. This pursuit drill is great to find out quickly who will play from start to finish. Some players may not execute the proper effort, but having them all repeat the drill unlimited times gets their attention in a hurry (if one fails, they all fail).

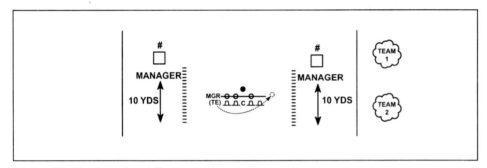

Figure 4-9. Perfect play drill

Angle Pursuit Drill (Figure 4-10)

The ball is placed in the middle of the field. Six stand-up dummies or cones are aligned on the sideline on each side of the field. The designated defensive team sprints on the field immediately and assume their proper alignment. The defense receives the call while on the sideline. The coach gives the snap count (using the upcoming opponent's snap count), and on the simulated snap, he gives the direction of the sweep. The defensive team sprints past the sideline cone they are assigned to pursue to on the play. Again, each coach will grade his player's position on alignment, effort, and angle he is taking to the ball. A thumbs-up or thumbs-down by each coach will determine the success of the drill.

Within the framework of the drill, several adjustments can be made to keep the pursuit period from becoming monotonous. First, all seven members of the defensive front hit the ground and then scramble to their feet to stress playing hard even when they get blocked. Second, two players (rabbits) line up about halfway between the numbers and the sideline. The coach throws the ball to one of the rabbits, and they sprint down the sideline at full speed, forcing the defense to take proper angles in their pursuit. If the rabbit drops the ball or the ball is overthrown, he should disregard the ball and take off without it. Third, align the defense on the 15- or 20-yard line, and once they have sprinted to their cone or taken the right cutoff angle to the rabbit, they turn and sprint into the end zone to simulate making a big play with a fumble recovery and celebrate the touchdown in the end zone. Fourth, the coach can drop back for a pass and throw to a linebacker or a secondary back, and they will return an interception for a touchdown. Fifth, if the defense does a great job on their initial pursuit, the coach drops and throws to a defensive back or linebacker, who tips the ball in the air, and then other players tip the ball a predetermined number of times before they all sprint back past the line of scrimmage.

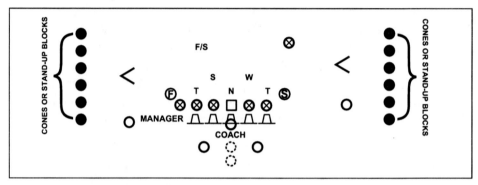

Figure 4-10. Angle pursuit drill

Standards for Pursuit Drills

Standards for the perfect play versus the run:
- Exhibit proper execution (get-off).
- Exhibit proper pursuit angle.
- Run full speed past the ballcarrier.

Standards for the perfect play versus the pass:
- Exhibit perfect get-off.
- Exhibit perfect drop.
- Exhibit perfect break on ball.
- Intercept at the highest point.
- Accelerate upfield on pass rush.
- Finish. Run harder than the opponent past the line of scrimmage.

Takeaways

In many games, the ability to strip the ball and take it away from the opponent's offense has enabled a team to regain momentum in what looks like a hopeless situation. An example would be when a team is down by a touchdown or field goal or leading by a slim margin, but the opponent is driving, and the defense is unable to get them off the field, and then it happens. The strip of the ball occurs; the defense recovers the fumble, and immediately the momentum of the game flip-flops. This shift usually doesn't just happen because of chance or "good luck." The stage is set by continually stressing to the defensive team that they are an attacking defense with takeaway ability on every play. Every team has some players who are naturals at being able to get the ball loose. But, the majority of defenders on most teams don't have this instinctive ability to strip unless it is continually emphasized through word repetition and daily practice situations. When "momentum" is standing at midfield trying to determine which sideline it will go to, "old mo" will definitely go in the direction of the team that strips the ball.

Strip Techniques

Punch

This technique can be done from the front, back, or side. Generally, its best results are from the back or the side. The same techniques are applied for both the punch and the rip, so valuable repetitions are gained regardless of which method is being practiced. The far arm wraps, and the near arm punches. The punch is like an upper cut in a boxing match: quick, powerful, and explosive. The punch must break the ballcarrier's vice-like grip on the ball. It is important that the far arm grabs cloth to secure the tackle if unable to get the ball out.

Rake

This technique is similar to the punch, but it usually occurs from the back. The near arm will come over the top and rake downward on the side of the ball with the far arm wrapping to secure the tackle if unable to get the ball out. The rake is a forceful downward move to break down the five pressure points the ballcarrier uses to secure the ball (fingers, palm, forearm, elbow, and ribs).

Rip

This technique occurs mostly in frontal or side tackles by the second or third defender to the ball. All tacklers should close on the ballcarrier at the proper angle with their head up and open. A good analogy is when the tackler presses to the collision area, he should have his dim lights on the ballcarrier and his bright lights on the ball. Increase the size of the ball with great visualization. The tackler should explode up through the pressure points (fingers, palms, forearm, elbow, and ribcage with speed and power). He is trying to separate the forearm from the rib cage, making the weakest part of the pressure points (fingers, palms, and wrist) vulnerable for the strip. It must be a reckless, violent rip to get the football out.

Fumble Recovery

When recovering a fumble and securing it without trying to advance it, it is best to grab the ball, lock it down with both arms, and cover it with knees and hips. Then, the player should get into a fetal position and protect the ball so it cannot be wrestled away in the pile.

Scoop and Score: When recovering a fumble with an attempt to advance it, it is best to approach the fumbled ball in a good football position and anticipate the opportunity to scoop the football. Try to get the ball in the center of the body, the player should bend the knees and scoop the ball (don't reach). It is important to try to straddle the ball when they pick it up rather than pick up the ball outside the framework of the body. When the ball is outside the frame, the player has a greater chance to be off balance, and the ability to bend down is hampered.

Strip Drills

Punch/Rake Drill (Figure 4-11)

Players are placed on the sideline in groups of two by defensive position. The drill is set up from the sideline to the hash mark. One player will assume the offensive position with the ball in the arm designated by the coach, while the other player is positioned behind him. The two move toward the hash mark with the defender trying to punch and rake the ball away from the offensive player. The two players reverse positions on the return to the sideline. Two repetitions are necessary to practice the punch/rake with the ball in both arms. A ball on an elastic cord with a wristband can be used so that if the ball is punched out or raked out it can immediately be placed back under the offensive player's arm. This using the cord prevents the ball from bouncing all over the field, and helps meet the goal of two strips from sideline to hash mark and the same on the return.

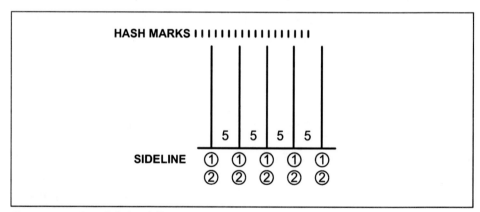

Figure 4-11. Punch/rake drill

Rip Drill (Figure 4-12)

The ballcarrier has two balls with one placed under each arm. Two tacklers are aligned five yards from the ballcarrier with their inside foot on the near foot of the ballcarrier. The ballcarrier will start either right or left at a 45-degree angle. The two defenders both think in terms of being the second and third man to the ball. Emphasize the car headlight principle, with the dim lights on the ballcarrier and the bright lights on the ball with the idea to increase the size of the ball as the tackler focuses on the strip. Other key points to emphasize include: visualize, rip, separate, and recover.

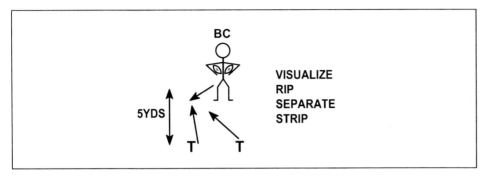

Figure 4-12. Rip drill

Fumble Drill (Figure 4-13)

Place the defenders in two to four lines, depending on the number of defensive players in the drill. Align them on the sideline or in a line on the field. The coach and the number of managers needed to cover each line will all have a ball. The coach will indicate the type of fumble recovery he wants to be executed: recover the fumble, or scoop and score. On the coach's command, the balls will be flipped out in front of each line so the defenders can either recover the fumble or scoop and score. Another option is to place the balls five yards in front of each line on the ground, rather than flip them. To conclude the drill, designate one of the defenders to recover the fumble and the other three to surround the player who recovered the ball, shouting, jumping in excitement, and pointing that it is their ball. Their job is to try and remove any doubt in the officials' minds regarding which team has recovered the ball.

Another fun, competitive, and good-tempo fumble drill involves five or six dummies on top of a ball. On the coach's command, two players will bite and scratch to secure the football.

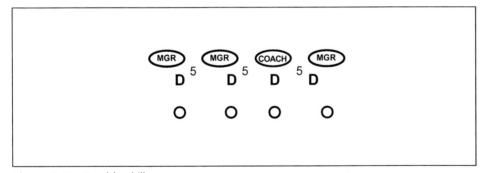

Figure 4-13. Fumble drill

Circuit Strip Drill (Figure 4-14)

The coach should schedule the circuit strip drill at least once a week for 10 minutes and practice creating takeaways. Each coach starts with his position players, and then the players move in a clockwise direction through all four stations. The four stations are rake it, punch it, rip it, and fumble drills. Each station lasts two minutes with 30 seconds allowed to move between stations.

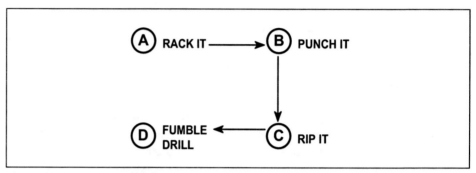

Figure 4-14. Circuit strip drill

5

Defensive Line Play

Philosophy of the Defensive Line

The defensive line has a tough, demanding job that requires uncompromising effort and winning execution. The physical requirements are the toughest of any position on the defensive team. The defensive lineman needs to be a total team player to accomplish what is expected of him. He is expected to smother the run, sprint to the ball with relentless pursuit, get penetration on short-yardage and goal-line plays, and pressure the quarterback successfully in passing situations. To meet these expectations, he must sacrifice both physically and mentally to play at a high energy level necessary for success for four quarters. He needs to commit to strength and conditioning that will be second to none.

The defensive lineman should have a determined attack mentality that will affect every play. It is essential for the success of the team that he makes a big difference by making big plays. He should be determined to never have a bad play, a bad practice, or a bad day. He should play at the same high level of consistency every day—regardless of whether it's rain, pain, sleet, or snow. None of these factors has a heart, and he should never let anything that doesn't have a heart whip him. No one ever said it would be easy, thus he should decide in the mind and heart that it will be worth it. He should accept the challenge of being a great defensive lineman because he knows that with powerful quests come powerful rewards.

Qualities of a Great Defensive Lineman

Pride: Pride in himself, his teammates, his school, the defensive scheme, and the coaching staff.

Aggressiveness: A reputation as a tough, hard-nosed, and aggressive football player. An aggressive reputation produces a mental edge on opponents.

Toughness: Toughness for a defensive lineman is not just expected; it is demanded. He must be willing to throw his body around, knowing that the key to his success is being able to practice and play with pain.

Essentials of Good Defensive Line Play

Pre-Snap Keys: Stance of the offensive lineman, line splits, down-and-distance, formation, the depth of the running backs (to determine run or pass). Must be attentive.

Alignment: Shoe-to-shoe, eyeball-to-eyeball, and nose-to-nose on the offensive line, ready to react.

Stance: Feet, shoulders, head, arms, back, and weight equally distributed.

Keys: Focusing and reacting to blocking schemes that tell whether the opponent is going to run or pass.

Assignment: Knowing and understanding the defense called and the proper techniques needed for a run or pass. Defense means knowing where help comes from.

Technique: Proper use of the body to defeat any blocking scheme, which puts the defensive lineman in position to make the play.

Contact: The ability to attack the blocker by delivering a blow in such a manner to defeat his block or gain position on him.

Escape: The ability to cause separation from the blocker, which enables the defensive lineman to flow to the ball.

Pursuit: An all-out effort to get to the ball.

Tackle: Contact, which punishes the ballcarrier and knocks him back.

Pass Rush: The best pass defense.

Hustle: Simply a desire or want to "get there" more than the blocker wants to keep the defensive lineman from "getting there."

Terms That Apply to the Defensive Lineman

Spill: Occurs on blocks coming from the inside. The defensive lineman will take on the blocker with his outside arm and leg, forcing the ball to bounce outside. He must work to get as much penetration as he can to keep any other blocker from getting to the second level.

Push/Pull (Lockout): Technique used to escape off a block. After initial fit, the defensive lineman will push (punch through) with his near hand and violently pull with his back hand on cloth. Gets the blocker's shoulders perpendicular to the line of scrimmage so the defensive lineman can explode off the block with quickness and power.

High Wall: To the backside away from a play. A technique used by offensive linemen to build a fence to cut down the pursuit of the defensive lineman. When the defensive lineman reads this technique, he must be ready to retrace his steps, rip through, and get to the ball.

Hug: For a defensive lineman in a contain or outside force position. This concept reminds the defensive lineman as he comes upfield to play with his eyes, take a picture, and keep proper leverage to prevent the quarterback from scrambling outside.

Penetrator: The first rusher on a two-man stunt. He will work the man on space, seeking to get penetration upfield to create an open window for the second rusher.

Flasher: The second rusher in a two-man stunt, who works tight and upfield off the penetrator. He is primarily trying to find an open window created by the upfield move of the penetrator.

Tilt (Noseguard): The noseguard aligns in a 45-degree angle shaded on the center. He is in a four-point stance and still steps with his covered foot. The pre-snap key is reading the guards, and the post-snap key is being able to beat the reach block.

Shade (Noseguard): The noseguard is shaded on the center in a squared stance. He is still in a four-point stance. He steps with his covered foot, and the speed of his hands will determine his success.

Second Level: This term normally is used in reference to linebackers. The defensive lineman is to work to keep any immediate blocks off the defenders at the second level.

Scoop: Block used by two offensive linemen to cut off a defensive lineman and linebackers from pursuit to the ball. Important for the defensive lineman to flatten out the scoop of the offensive lineman trying to get upfield so the linebacker can still press the line of scrimmage at the proper angle to take away the bubble. Key for the defensive lineman is to not get reached by the offensive lineman coming down from his backside.

Difference-Makers for Defensive Linemen

- Four key factors determine whether a defensive lineman wins or loses on each play. Three of the four take place prior to the snap of the ball. Therefore, the defensive lineman has a 75-percent chance to win on every play before the ball is snapped. He must prepare to win the battle before the snap. The four key factors are:
  ✓ Knowing the assignment
  ✓ Being properly aligned
  ✓ Being ready to play
  ✓ Having the ability

- Attitude is not just a word; it is a way of life. A defensive lineman should make these attitudes a part of his personality every day, and on every play.
  ✓ Attack: Attack mentality with a big-play hunger.
  ✓ Takeaway: Get the ball.
  ✓ Escape: Don't get blocked.
  ✓ Pursuit: Every play is his play to make.
- The defensive lineman should be an explosive player every time he puts his foot on the grass. He must:
  ✓ Explode on the snap.
  ✓ Explode off the blocker.
  ✓ Explode to the ball (they will clip him).
- The defensive lineman must excel in KTE (Know/Technique/Effort).
  ✓ Know: Stance, alignment, assignment
  ✓ Technique: Getting off, power stepping, hat/eyes/hand placement
  ✓ Effort: Separate, pursue, tackle

Defensive Line Pre-Snap Reads

Versus Run

- Offensive lineman with weight forward
- Big line splits
- Guard's weight back and the offensive tackle's and center's weight forward (trap/pull)
- Running backs leaning or pointing
- Offensive backfield set
- Down-and-distance

Versus Pass

- Lineman setting back
- Two-point stance, looking right at the defensive lineman
- Quarterback habits (walking to the line)
- Narrow splits
- Backfield sets
- Game situation

Versus Draw

- Lineman offering upfield rush
- Lineman popping up, and upon contact, pushing the defensive lineman upfield
- Running back crowhopping to the ball

Versus Screens

- Offensive tackle cutting the defensive lineman after a pass set
- Offensive tackle taking excessive drops (double drops)
- Offensive tackle slipping out under rush
- Back setting up then showing across the defensive lineman's face

Defensive Line Stance

Feet: Should be slightly wider than shoulder-width and under, weight on the inside balls of the feet, and heels out. The heels should clear the ground with the toes pointed straight upfield.

Shoulders: Parallel to the line of scrimmage

Head: Natural extension so the defensive lineman can see the stances of the offensive linemen in front of him. Head slightly up, looking through eyebrows.

Arms: Extended straight down from the shoulders, elbows straight, with the rest of the arm on the thigh, ready to shoot.

Hand and Fingers: All weight on the hand, all fingertips contacting the ground, eyes slightly behind the hand, and hands inside so the defensive lineman can lock out for separation.

Back: Flat, tail slightly up, and knees bent so they are ready to uncoil.

Weight: Equally distributed on hands and feet.

Eagle Front Stance and Alignment

- Lined up in a three-point stance, inside foot back. Inside hand down no more than heel-to-toe stagger.
- Aligned with the nose in the middle of the outside shoulder pad of the offensive lineman.
- Shoulders parallel to the ground.
- Head at natural extension so the linemen can be seen to either side of the center.
- Back flat, tail slightly up, and knees bent so they are ready to uncoil.
- Feet no wider than shoulder-width and up under, weight on the balls of the feet, and the heels clearing the ground.
- Weight equally distributed on hands and feet.
- Lined up as tight to the ball as possible. Crowding the football.
- Wide alignment with the nose on the outside of the shoulder pad.

Eagle Front Movement and Blow

Each defensive lineman:

- Keys the movement of the ball and helmet of the offensive lineman to initiate movement. Must concentrate on it.
- Attacks when the ball moves.
- Steps hard when the offensive lineman's helmet or ball moves.
  - ✓ If the helmet goes to the inside or comes straight ahead, the defensive lineman steps with his inside foot directly at the helmet. He steps upfield into the offensive lineman's charge, gains ground into the neutral zone, and then quickly brings up his other foot to a parallel position.
  - ✓ If the helmet goes to the outside, he steps with his inside foot directly at the helmet. After a lead step, he steps hard upfield with the outside foot into the offensive lineman and then quickly brings up his other foot to a parallel position.

Pre-Snap Tips for the Defensive Line

The defensive lineman should eliminate as many as possible of the "What ifs" and surprises prior to the snap of the ball. The defensive lineman should never be a spectator between downs; he should always be a participant with his eyes trying to discover a pre-snap tip or formation anticipation. The defensive lineman can accomplish this goal by reading the guard for depth off the ball, splits, and a heavy or light stance. He should always be looking for run-pass indicators to determine, prior to the game or in the game, where the moment of collision is going to occur.

Examples: With wide splits, the defensive lineman should go on the premise of what the offense can't do. Over split by the guard means no scoop. One guard with a heavy stance and the other guard with a light stance means some type of play with the pull of a guard—trap, power, counter, bootleg G. The defensive lineman should watch the center's stance, observe the position of his hands, and watch the position of the quarterback's hands under the center.

The defensive lineman should play hard, but play smart, using the following defensive weapons:

- Ears: Listens for offensive line calls, and such.
- Eyes: Splits, stance, depth off the ball, backs set.
- Mouth: Communicates and verbalizes where keys are coming from.
- Hands: How quick?
- Feet: How quick?

Pre-snap reads are very helpful to the defensive line. With 11 men on offense, someone is giving something away on every play. The defensive line should see whether the offensive guard or offensive tackle is "sitting light," whether the heels are up or down, or if the guard has a lot of pressure on his fingers. They should also look at the opponent's pass splits and the amount of distance between the feet.

Defensive Line Mentality

The way the defensive line is defined is the way the defense is defined. The defensive line sets the tempo for an attack mentality. For the defense to accomplish its goals, the defensive line must practice hard on every play because they are attacking on every snap. Blitzing a lot doesn't necessarily make a defense more of an attacking team than a defense that primarily only brings four defensive linemen on each down-and-distance. The attack mentality of the defensive team—rather than the blitzing frequency—is what determines how successful the defense is. Strive to have the front four defensive linemen attack on the run front. They should never slow down the attack and reaction style of play.

Many styles of defensive line play exist, including: eliminating the read, reacting to the run off penetration, and playing pass on every down and then reacting to the run. Defensive linemen should attack and react, yet with all the different blocking schemes that occur (influence, power scoop, pulling, T-block), the defensive linemen should see and feel what is happening to them as they attack upfield. The defensive line is a one- or two-gap unit, striving to achieve an explosive read as they attack and react on the run with penetration. The emphasis is on vertical movement upfield with head, eyes, hands, and feet placement. The key is being able to separate off the block with penetration while keeping the arm free in the gap for which he is responsible. It's always better to be slippery than sticky.

Expectations and Points of Emphasis for Defensive Lineman Success

Key: Attacking and reacting. Keys the man or the ball, depending on the offensive line stance or call. When keying the ball, tries to read the writing on the football. Sees the back tip of the ball. Sees the big picture, but focuses on small things (i.e., fingers quiver).

Initial Movement and Reaction: Initial takeoff is everything. Beats the offensive linemen out of their stance, and creates or establishes a new line of scrimmage. Beats them off the ball; when the ball moves, the defensive lineman moves. Hits on the offense's side of the ball. Punches and attacks quickly; employs quick hands and quick feet, and doesn't get caught with one foot off the ground. Attacks with the knowledge that upfield penetration destroys (distorts) the cutback lanes. Gets out of his hips; launches the eyes and hands at the same time. Comes out of his hips with forward thrust of the eyes and hands with vertical movement upfield. Always attacks with the eyes, hands, and feet. Attacks the blocker with exceptional vertical speed and excellent hand and eye placement. Explodes with the eyes and hands as he hits on the rise. Works hard to get all three correct, but knows that if he can win two out of three, he has a better chance to win. Gets his eyes to the jugular vein at the same time as his hands fit on the breastplate. The emphasis is that the tightest and quickest hands to the breastplate win the battle. The man who gets the first six inches upfield wins. Explodes out of the stance with good hat and hands, and with speed going vertical upfield. Keeps hands inside, eyes to the jugular vein, and elbows tight to the body. Never slows up helmet or eye speed. The defensive lineman is not attacking if he sacrifices helmet and eye speed to get his hands in place (he must punch quickly). The helmet goes north, not up. The feet should react to the blocking scheme. The eyes and upper body give the feet a chance to react properly. The staggered foot comes behind him, not with him (as support, not thrust). Both feet should be on the ground upon impact with the blocker. Gets the feet back on the ground quickly. Takes a short, six-inch power step with the inside foot. Resets the inside foot as quickly as possible while going forward in an attack mode. The power step is used to generate a powerful forward (vertical) charge into the offensive lineman.

Versus a base block, the first step may be just a quiver (pick and place). If the outside shoulder is threatened, he should take a shorter step, and then get it down so he can shoot again. He should not overstride with the inside foot. The first step is important and should be quick and placed with explosion. He shouldn't worry about the forward step; he just doesn't want to take on contact with his foot off the ground. He escapes off the block with a violent pull, getting rid of the blocker away from the area of responsibility. He snatches the blocker away from the area of responsibility; explodes off him with quickness, speed, and power.

Noseguard Zero Technique

Alignment: Shoe-to-shoe, eyeball-to-eyeball, and nose-to-nose with the center. Plays as tight to offensive lineman as possible and still remains able to key, react, and attack. However, should not be offside.

Stance: Four-point stance with feet parallel and shoulder-width apart. This attack technique is good for fast hands. Stays low, and gets off with good base.

Key: Keys the movement of the offensive lineman's hand and attacks on snap. Pre-snap read is the offensive guards. Reads the center on the snap. The center is the usual read, with pressure key from the guards.

Responsibility: The backside gap—attacks and controls it. Becomes a back-door player on flow, which enables the linebacker to run.

Execution: Steps with whichever foot is most comfortable, and follows with the other. Fires into the offensive lineman, and delivers a blow with the hands, then uncoils the hips and arches the back. After delivering the blow, extends the arms out to get separation. Keeps the feet moving with shoulders square, sheds the blocker, and flows to the football. Attacks the offensive lineman with an aggressive charge. Emphasis is on the hands more than the feet; fast hands is key.

- Versus the base block (Figure 5-1): Destroys the offensive lineman with the charge. Keeps the feet moving with the shoulders square. Doesn't pick a side until the ball is found.

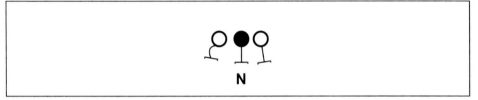

Figure 5-1. Versus the base block

- Versus the reach block (Figure 5-2): Destroys the center's block first, but may let the center's head hook him. Keeps the shoulders square, and squeezes through the backside, looking for cut back. Plays flat down the line of scrimmage. Plays reach first, scoop second. Punches, keeps the shoulders square under the center, and drives him down the line of scrimmage.

Figure 5-2. Versus the reach block

- Versus the scoop block (Figure 5-3): When the scoop occurs between the center and the backside guard, controls the center to the frontside. Flattens the center down the line of scrimmage with the playside hand on his helmet, and the backside hand punching through the backside pad with speed and power. If the center beats the noseguard to the frontside, keeps the shoulders perpendicular to the line of scrimmage with good hand placement ready to come in behind the scoop and flatten down the line of scrimmage. Beats the backside guard with quick feet; keeps the shoulders square, and drives the backside leg through with explosion. Never allows the center to come off the line of scrimmage. (Tries to turn the scoop block into a horizontal move on the line of scrimmage instead of a vertical move upfield.) Protects the linebackers so they can press the line of scrimmage and adjust their fit to the angle of the back and the ball. Backdoors the center, and pursues flat down the line of scrimmage, looking for the big hit.

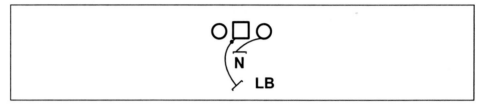

Figure 5-3. Versus the scoop block

- Versus the power block (Figure 5-4): Takes a quick, short lead step to the area-of-responsibility gap, and rips the backside arm and leg through. This action must be a violent movement of the forearm across the center's face. The aiming point is the heels of the center. Reacts to the ball, and flattens after initial penetration.

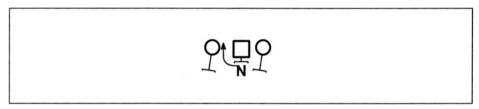

Figure 5-4. Versus the power block

- Versus the slip block (Figure 5-5): Takes a quick, short lead step to the area-of-responsibility gap. Reaches with the near hand, and grabs cloth on the center. Brings the backside arm in a swim move, and kicks the backside leg through. Reads on the run as flattens down the line of scrimmage.

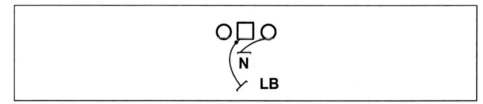

Figure 5-5. Versus the slip block

Coaching Points:

- Must protect the backside gap. Must hold ground on the double-team block.
- Must rush the passer in the proper lane. Must be a bull rusher, and look for the draw or a step-up by the quarterback.
- Must use good backdoor technique, and pursue flat down the line of scrimmage. Must look for the big hit on a cutback versus a reach block.

Noseguard Angle Technique

Alignment: Same as "O" technique, except back off the ball a little. Aligns between 6 and 12 inches; 18 inches is too far.

Key: Keys the guard's hip and sees the football out of the corner of eye. Keys the splits; looks at both sides. Bigger splits make it hard for guard to scoop.

Responsibility: The A gap—attacks and controls it.

Execution: When the guard or football moves, steps at a 45-degree angle with the foot to the angle side. The aiming point is the hip of the guard. If the guard goes away, stretches the lead step. If the guard goes toward, tightens the first step and gets farther upfield.

- Versus the reach block (Figure 5-6): If the guard goes away, the center will be trying to hook the noseguard. Flattens the center down the line of scrimmage, escapes, and runs to the football. Keeps the shoulders square. Keeps vision on the guard so as not to slow down.
- Versus the scoop block (Figure 5-7): If the guard moves toward and flat down the line of scrimmage, flattens him as the center goes away. Escapes and runs to the football. Keeps the shoulders square.
- Versus the down block (Figure 5-8): Attacks the V of the guard's neck. Squeezes him back into the hole, keeping the feet moving. Can also cross-face when ball flow commits. Can stuff the block and cross or squeeze and restrict, depending on the angle of the back and the ball. Must be able to cross when the ball passes the point of no return.
- Versus the pass set (Figure 5-9): Attacks and rushes through the A gap.

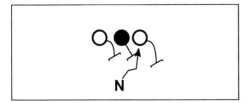

Figure 5-6. Versus the reach block

Figure 5-7. Versus the scoop block

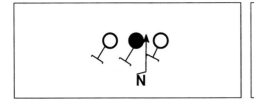

Figure 5-8. Versus the down block

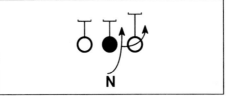

Figure 5-9. Versus the pass set

Coaching Points:

- Must key the guard and ball to get a good jump.
- Must pursue flat down the line of scrimmage on ball away and to.
- Must rush the passer in the proper lane.

Noseguard Rip Technique

Alignment: Same as "O" technique.

Key: Keys the guard's hip to the rip side. The guard is the visual key, and the center is the pressure key.

Responsibility: A gap to the rip side. Attacks and controls the A gap. Finds the ball.

Execution: Backs off the ball slightly. When the guard moves, steps with the foot to the rip side. On initial move, turns the shoulders and squares up on the second step. The guard is the key to how to react to the block.

- Versus the base block (Figure 5-10): Rips the backside arm quickly to the rip side. If the guard fires straight out, beats the center's block on the initial step. Finds the ball.
- Versus the reach/hook block (Figure 5-11): Takes a 45-degree step to the rip side. If the guard goes away and the center tries to hook, runs flat down the line of scrimmage in the direction of the hook.
- Versus the scoop away (Figure 5-12): Explodes low on the snap. Sees the guard coming, and feels the center go away. Flattens down the line of scrimmage and chases.
- Versus the double-team block (Figure 5-13): Explodes low as he would versus the base block. Sees the guard come at him, and feels the center. Drives hard into the guard, and penetrates the seam. Turns the shoulders toward the offensive guard, and creates a pile.
- Versus the down block away (Figure 5-14): Explodes low toward the guard. If the guard blocks down, stuffs him back and finds the ball. Cross-faces.

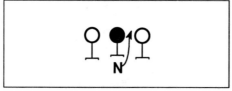

Figure 5-10. Versus the base block

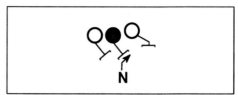

Figure 5-11. Versus the reach/hook block

Figure 5-12. Versus the scoop away

Figure 5-13. Versus the double-team block

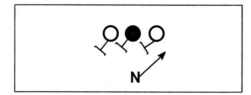

Figure 5-14. Versus the down block away

Coaching Points:

- Must key the guard's hip, and "get there" on the snap.
- Must rush the passer in the proper lane.
- Must close back fast and flat down the line of scrimmage on plays from rip.
- The rip move is good for teams that try to single block.

4 Technique

Alignment: Aligns head-up on the offensive tackle tight to the line of scrimmage. The head-up alignment is preferred with the 50 defense because it eliminates all the pre-snap reads and creates hesitation in the mind of the offensive line. It is taught much like the zero techniques. Teaches fast hands, but the cover foot should still be back.

Key: Pre-snap key is the offensive guard and the offensive tackle on the snap. Pressure key is the tackle; visual key is the guard.

Responsibility: B gap. Gets tight on the ball, and attacks the offensive tackle's inside breastplate. Keeps gap arm free, bench-presses, separates, and presses to the angle of the back and the ball. Reduces the run lane, and forces the ball to bounce on the cutback.

- Versus the base block: Attacks the tackle with eyes, hands, and feet with a vertical move upfield. Beats the tackle out of his stance, and establishes a new line of scrimmage. Emphasizes fast hands as he steps with the inside foot. Uses good push/knock back, and maintains inside leverage. Cross-faces when the B gap is no longer threatened. Sheds inside, and comes over the top.
- Versus the reach, hook block: Same as the zero technique noseguard.
- Versus turnout from the offensive guard: This block is difficult for the defensive tackle. Steps to the offensive tackle, visualizes or feels the man blocking him, and snaps his head back inside. Squeezes the B gap from outside-in to reduce the hole with the guard. Keeps the gap arm free.

5 Technique

Alignment: Aligns head-up on the offensive tackle tight to the line of scrimmage. The head-up alignment is preferred with the 50 defense because it eliminates all the pre-snap reads and creates hesitation in the mind of the offensive line.

Key: Keys the movement of the offensive tackle's helmet. The offensive tackle is the pressure key; the guard is the visual key. If the offensive tackle sets up or blocks out, keys inside to the guard. The guard provides a true key. If the guard blocks down, he closes; if the guard pulls, he works out. Same keys hold up when aligned on the guard, except the inside key is the center.

Responsibility: C gap. Contains pass rush, and trails when the ball goes away.

Execution: Steps flat with the playside foot, and keeps the shoulders square. On the first step, should be ready to punch with the hands and react to the offensive tackle's block.

- Versus the base block (Figure 5-15): Uses great takeoff, and attacks the offensive tackle's outside shoulder. Knocks him back, and keeps the shoulders square. Extends the arms, pulls the hips away, and pressures the offensive man's shoulders. At this point, he can either squeeze or shed the blocker and get in to pursuit. Bench-presses the blocker.
- Versus the reach, hook block (Figure 5-16): Uses great takeoff to beat the offensive tackle out of his stance. If the offensive tackle tries to hook, stabs him with the hands, keeps the feet moving, and keeps the shoulders square. Uses the escape technique and gets to the ball. The feet of the blocker determine the position of his body. If the blocker's head is outside, uses the hands to pull back over to proper helmet placement. If it is a wide reach, can go behind the blocker, which can be accomplished with a great takeoff.
- Versus the down block (Figure 5-17): Attacks with the helmet, hands, and eyes with a vertical move upfield. Gets the inside hand on the blocker, and pushes him down inside. Closes space, gets the eyes inside, and is ready to attack the first threat. Wrong-arms and spills all blocks from the inside.
- Versus the double-team block (Figure 5-18): If the offensive tackle and tight end block him, drops to a knee and uses up both blockers. Fights pressure, and doesn't allow the tight end to come off on the second level; grabs cloth. Doesn't get knocked off the ball. Attacks only one blocker, gets the shoulders thin, and fights to get the hips outside. Treats as a single block, stays up, and grabs cloth. Doesn't allow the tight end to climb to the second level. If knocked off the line of scrimmage, gets down. If using the spin move, makes the play.
- Versus the Y block (Figure 5-19): Squeezes the C gap, and expands the hole from the inside-out. If ball commits outside, cross-faces late. Fights pressure, and works the hips back into the hole. Squeezes the tight end back, or punches and cross-faces.
- To the split end (Figure 5-20): The number of outside plays to the split-end side is helpful in determining how heavy the 5 technique will align. A defensive end on air discourages plays to the split-end side.
- Flow away: Squeezes the blocker with the shoulders square to the line of scrimmage. Reduces down from the outside, and remains alert for cutback, counter, or reverse; trails with the eyes. Closes hard and flat, and expands vision while pursuing. If an opposite-color jersey comes toward him, gains depth to the angle of the ball.

Coaching Points:

- Must protect the C gap. Must hold ground on the double-team.
- Must contain the pass rusher.
- Must pursue with proper course on ball away.
- Must keep the offensive tackle off the linebacker to his side.

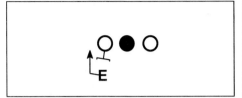

Figure 5-15. Versus the base block

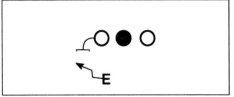

Figure 5-16. Versus the reach, hook block

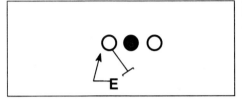

Figure 5-17. Versus the down block

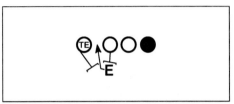

Figure 5-18. Versus the double-team block

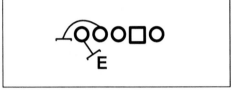

Figure 5-19. Versus the Y block

Figure 5-20. To the split end

Defensive End Angle Technique

Alignment: Head-up on the offensive tackle 12 inches off the ball—off the ball and not the man. Doesn't get cut off by the offensive tackle.

Key: Keys the guard's hip, and sees the football out of the corner of the eye. Concentrates on the guard and the ball without turning the head and looking; uses peripheral vision.

Responsibility: B gap. Attacks and controls it.

Execution: When the guard or football moves, takes a 45-degree step and angles with the foot to the angle side. Aiming point is the hip of the guard. After flat-stepping, crosses over with the trail foot, rips the backside arm through simultaneously, and runs. Attacks and reacts to the guard. If the guard goes away, uses a wider step; if the guard moves toward, tightens the first step.

- Versus the scoop block by the offensive guard (Figure 5-21): Takes a 45-degree step to the inside with the playside foot. If the guard comes toward, he will try to hook the defensive lineman. Punches the guard with the hands, and works outside.

- Versus the cutoff block by the offensive tackle (Figure 5-22): If the guard goes away, feels the offensive tackle moving inside to cut him off. Takes a 45-degree step, punches to the offensive tackle with the hands, and keeps the shoulders square. Flat-steps and punches to keep the tackle off. Keeps vision on the guard. Never gets cut off; the cutoff block is the critical block. If the 5 technique has a problem, forgets the disguise and puts the 5 technique in a position to get the job done. Takes a "success" or "ability" alignment.

• Versus the fan block by the offensive guard (Figure 5-23): Attacks the V of the guard's neck, and squeezes him back into the hole. Keeps the feet moving while driving him back. Doesn't cross-face on three- or four-man fronts. Stuffs the guard; doesn't run in. Keeps the shoulders square, and controls the outside shoulder of the guard. If the guard moves toward, the first step is tighter. If the guard goes away, the first step is longer. When moving, attacks the offensive lineman with the hands.

• Versus the pass set (Figure 5-24): Attacks through the hip of the offensive guard. The end has a two-way go on the guard.

• Keying the offensive guard: During movement, focuses the eyes on the offensive guard ("Key him"). If the guard pulls away, jumps in his hip pocket and follows him down the line of scrimmage (Figure 5-25). If the guard pulls toward, plants the inside foot, drives off it, and gets into the hip pocket of the guard (Figure 5-26). Stays square.

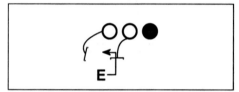

Figure 5-21. Versus the scoop block by the offensive guard

Figure 5-22. Versus the cutoff block by the offensive tackle

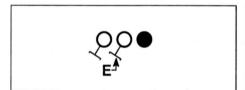

Figure 5-23. Versus the fan block by the offensive guard

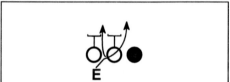

Figure 5-24. Versus the pass set

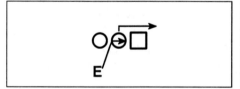
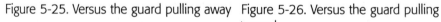

Figure 5-25. Versus the guard pulling away

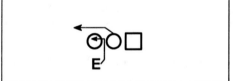

Figure 5-26. Versus the guard pulling toward

Keys for Movement

The ability to disguise a stunt will cause the offensive lineman to hesitate. The defensive lineman should take off with quickness and power to beat him out of his stance. He should be physical with the backside arm; rip the arm and shoulder across the blocker's face with explosion and speed.

5 Shade Technique

Alignment: Outside shade of the offensive tackle with the inside leg splitting his crotch. Plays as tight to the offensive tackle as possible and still remains able to key and react.

Key: Same as 5 technique—keys the movement of offensive tackle's helmet.

Responsibility: Same as 5 technique—C gap to trail away.

Execution: When the offensive tackle moves, attacks and reacts to his block. Steps with the covered foot, and follows with the other. Attacks and delivers the blow with the face, mask, and hands. Keeps the feet moving as he uncoils the hips and arches the back.

- Versus the base block (Figure 5-27): Knocks the offensive tackle back on the initial charge, and keeps the feet moving. Maintains outside leverage.
- Versus the reach, hook block (Figure 5-28): Destroys the offensive tackle's block first, and then escapes outside. Alignment will allow the defensive lineman to attack the tackle's outside shoulder. Fights to keep leverage to the outside.
- Versus the down block or inside release (Figure 5-29): Attacks the offensive tackle's outside shoulder pad. Becomes physical and knocks him off his path; gets hands on him. Squeezes and runs flat down the line of scrimmage. Snaps the eyes inside; spills the first threat.
- Versus the double-team block (Figure 5-30): Attacks the outside shoulder of the offensive tackle. If the defensive lineman feels pressure by the tight end, turns the shoulders into the tackle, and goes down on one knee. If the tight end comes off him, squares back up as the play is being run toward, and posts up with his head in the crack.

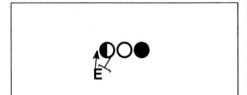

Figure 5-27. Versus the base block

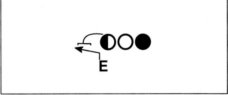

Figure 5-28. Versus the reach, hook block

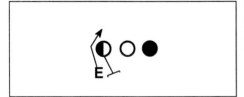

Figure 5-29. Versus the down block or inside release

Figure 5-30. Versus the double-team block

Coaching Points:

- Must protect the C gap. Must hold ground on the double-team.
- Must contain the pass rusher.

- Must pursue with proper course on ball away.
- Must keep the offensive tackle off the linebacker to his side.

Defensive End Loop Technique

Alignment: Same as 5 technique

Key: Keys the tight end.

Responsibility: C gap. Attacks and controls it. Loops from a 5 to a 7 technique. Aiming point is the face mask of the tight end. Doesn't cross the face of the tight end on the initial move.

Execution: When the tight end moves, steps with the foot to the loop side.

- Versus the base block (Figure 5-31): Takes a 45-degree step toward the tight end. If base block by the offensive tackle, squeezes back into him. Expects isolation; if option, responsible for the quarterback.
- Versus the reach, hook block (Figure 5-32): Takes a 45-degree step toward the tight end. If the tight end blocks out, and the offensive tackle hook blocks, stabs the tight end with the hands and keeps the feet moving. Uses the escape technique, and gets to the ball. Can't be hooked by the tackle.
- Versus the double-team or down block by the tight end (Figure 5-33): Takes a 45-degree step toward the tight end. Explodes into the tight end, and causes a pile if double-teamed. If down block by the tight end and no pressure from the offensive tackle, holds ground and makes the ball bounce. Once the ball clears outside, cross-faces the tight end and chases him flat down the line of scrimmage for the cutback.

Coaching Points:

- Must key the tight end to get a good read.
- All other coaching points are the same as 5 technique, except must keep the offensive tackle off the linebacker.

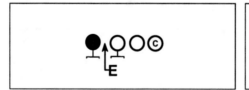

Figure 5-31. Versus the base block

Figure 5-32. Versus the reach, hook block

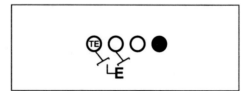

Figure 5-33. Versus the double-team or down block by the tight end

Ram Technique

Alignment: Ends align head-up on the offensive tackle, about 18 inches off the ball.

Key: Keys the offensive guard.

Responsibility:

- Frontside end: A-gap penetrator. Two-gap 45-degree step.
- Backside end: A- or B-gap penetrator, depending on the guard's block.
- Nose: Contains on wrap. Flasher.

Execution:

- Frontside end: When the ball or guard moves, takes a 45-degree step or flat-steps inside, and attacks the guard frontally. Walks him back with inside control.
- Backside end: Takes a 45-degree step inside, and assumes a three-way go on the guard. If the guard moves toward, goes under him. If the guard goes down, stays outside of him. If the guard sits, walks him back.

Example: Stack field thunder wrap (Figure 5-34)—Nose has a read call with the running back in the home position. Thunder wrap check.

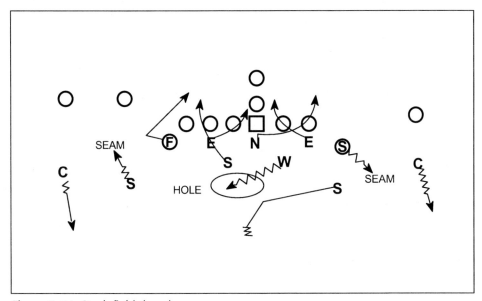

Figure 5-34. Stack field thunder wrap

Nose and End Technique G/2i

Stance: Three-point stance with the feet in a toe-to-heel relationship and shoulder-width apart. Down hand should be slightly inside of the back foot. Ankles, knees, and hips with power, producing angles of 45 degrees. Tail should be slightly up. Weight distribution should be 60 percent on the upfield foot and down hand, 40 percent on the back foot.

Alignment: Nose aligned in the middle of the guard's pad. Crowds the ball.

Responsibilities: Runs toward the A gap. Runs away, doesn't get cut off, and defends the backside A gap.

Keys: Keys the ball to the V of the guard's neck.

Movement and Blow (Figure 5-35): Moves on ball movement. Takes a six-inch step with the foot away from gap responsibility. Delivers a hard, double-hand shiver with thumbs up and elbow in. Inside hand to the inside pad, outside hand to the sternum. Punches, locks out arms, locates the ball, sheds, and tackles.

Execution:

- Versus the base block (Figure 5-36): Explodes hands and eyes to targets. Makes contact with a three-point strike—head, eyes, hands. Punches; locks out arms to create separation. Gets a knock back on the guard. Tries to create vertical push with initial contact, and keeps the feet moving. Locates and sheds the guard into the B gap; nose is A gap responsible. Creates a new line of scrimmage with penetration; knocks back. Penetration kills the running game because it changes the depth of the running back's cut.

- Versus the cutoff block (Figure 5-37): Attacks the guard; delivers a three-point strike to targets. Locks out arms in the direction of pressure. Escapes to the responsible gap and makes a play. Sheds the blocker with a rip technique, pursues, and tackles.

- Versus the scoop block (Figure 5-38): Attacks the guard, punches, and extends the arms on targets. Moves the feet, and maintains pressure on the offensive guard. Flattens out the guard's release; grabs cloth. If the guard releases to the linebacker, surfaces in the gap and makes a play.

- Versus the double-team block (Figure 5-39): Attacks the guard, and defeats the base block first. Doesn't try to play both because it is a 600-pound double-team. Punches and extends the arms on the guard, and if he feels pressure from the center, he should not allow movement. Stays low, and fights the pressure. Maintains the line of scrimmage, and attempts to split the double-team by turning the shoulders and hips to split the pressure. On any loss of the line of scrimmage, collapses the outside knee and shoulder to create a three-man pile.

- Versus the block back (Figure 5-40): Remains aware of the line splits and the depth of the guard. Takes a six-inch first step; shoots hands and eyes at targets. As he feels pressure from the center, he should lock out the inside arm. Keeps the feet moving, and squeezes the center's body to the opposite A gap. Stays behind the blocker until the A gap is not threatened. Holds position, locates the ball, and pursues; squeezes, slips, and runs to ball.

- Versus play away (Figure 5-41): Vertical move upfield with the hat, hands, and eyes. Doesn't get cut off—attacks/bench-presses/separates. Keeps the gap arm and leg free. Makes all plays in the A gap.

- Versus short trap (Figure 5-42): Explodes upfield with the hat, hands, and eyes. If no pressure from the outside, snaps the eyes inside. Closes/wrong-arms/spills the first threat. Traps the trapper. He is the trap squeezer; the linebacker is the trap stopper.

- Versus pass set (Figure 5-43): Attacks, punches, and extends the arms on the guard. Accelerates the feet, pushes the pocket, and executes a pass-rush technique through the responsible gap. Doesn't allow the blocking scheme to affect the pass rush.

Figure 5-35. Movement and blow

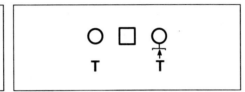

Figure 5-36. Versus the base block

Figure 5-37. Versus the cutoff block

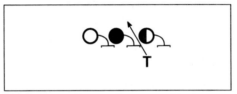

Figure 5-38. Versus the scoop block

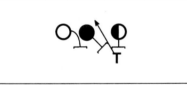

Figure 5-39. Versus the double-team block

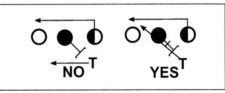

Figure 5-40. Versus the block back

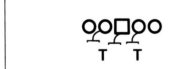

Figure 5-41. Versus play away

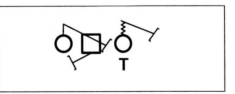

Figure 5-42. Versus short trap

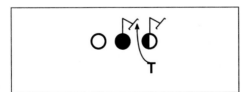

Figure 5-43. Versus pass set

Nose and End 3 Charge Techniques

Alignment: Aligns the inside foot just inside the offensive guard's outside leg. The offensive lineman on the ball may back off ball so he can get a power step.

Key: Keys the movement of the ball.

Responsibility: B gap to the rip side. Attacks it with shoulders square, and penetrates.

Execution: Steps with the covered foot, and follows with the other. As he charges, he should deliver the blow and keep the shoulders square. Keeps the feet moving, and reacts to the offensive lineman's block.

- Versus the scoop block (Figure 5-44): On the initial charge, knocks the offensive guard back, and keeps the feet moving. Maintains inside leverage on the offensive tackle with the shoulders square. Flattens the offensive guard's angle with penetration, and doesn't let him get to the linebacker. Worries more about the scoop block than the reach block. Can't afford to lose two people.
- Versus the reach, hook block (Figure 5-45): Destroys the guard's block first, and then escapes outside. Attacks straight up the field. Doesn't worry about hat placement, gets penetration, and establishes a new line of scrimmage. If the guard's hat is outside the defensive lineman, uses the hands to pull back over to proper hat placement.
- Versus the double-team block (Figure 5-46): Attacks the gap. Plays as a base block. Once he feels pressure by the tackle, he should drop the outside shoulder and leg to get upfield. Doesn't get knocked off the ball. Attacks one blocker, gets the shoulders thin, and fights to get the hips outside.
- Versus the influence trap (Figure 5-47): If no pressure comes from the outside, snaps the eyes back inside as he closes down and wrong-arms and spills the first threat. Defensive line is the trap squeezer; linebackers are the trap stopper. Doesn't allow this blocking scheme to affect the pass rush.
- Versus the down block trap (Figure 5-48): Gets hand on the down block, and forces the guard to release at a flat angle. Closes to the first threat, and spills him with a wrong-arm technique. "Trap the trapper."
- Versus the guard pulling inside (Figure 5-49): Steps inside and squeezes center with good hand placement. Keeps the pads parallel to the line of scrimmage. Works across the head of the center when the ball passes the point of no return. Can slip the center and get in the hip pocket of the guard.
- Versus the guard pulling outside (Figure 5-50): Snaps the eyes inside as he steps outside. Explodes into the offensive tackle with the shoulders square and good head, hand, and eye placement. Crosses the tackle's face when the ball is committed. Can continue penetration and get in the hip pocket of the guard.

- Versus the pass set (Figure 5-51): Attacks, punches, and extends arms on the guard. Accelerates feet, pushes the pocket, and executes a pass-rush technique through the responsible gap.

Coaching Points:

- Must protect the B gap.
- Must rush the passer in the proper lane.
- Must attack first, and react second.

Figure 5-44. Versus the scoop block

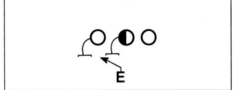

Figure 5-45. Versus the reach, hook block

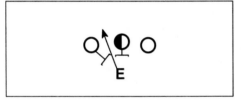

Figure 5-46. Versus the double-team block

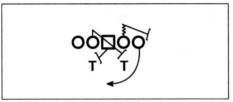

Figure 5-47. Versus the influence trap

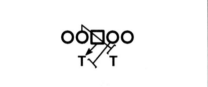

Figure 5-48. Versus the down block trap

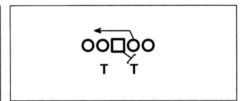

Figure 5-49. Versus the guard pulling inside

Figure 5-50. Versus the guard pulling outside

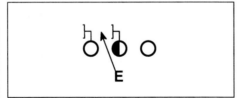

Figure 5-51. Versus the pass set

6 Technique

Alignment: Feet-to-feet alignment, head-up. Gets as much of the ball as possible without being offside.

Key: Pre-snap key is the offensive tackle. Keys the tight end on the snap of ball. Pressure key is the tight end; visual key is the offensive tackle.

Stance: Three-point stance with feet shoulder-width apart. Feet in a slight stagger with the outside leg back, the cover foot back, and the cover hand down. The down hand is aligned slightly inside the cover foot, not in the middle of the stance because this position causes the shoulders to turn. Hips and knees are flexed and ready to attack. Weight is distributed with 60 percent on hands and 40 percent on feet. Head and neck should be in a natural extension so he can key the tight end.

Initial Movement and Reaction: Initial key is the tight end's helmet. Moves on movement, takes an attack step with the outside foot. Attacks the tight end's chinstrap with the hat, and simultaneously hand shivers with the hands right below the shoulder pads. Keeps the thumbs up: hands/hat/hips. Locks elbows and separates, keeps the inside leg and arm free. Keeps the shoulders square to the line of scrimmage. Knocks the tight end back, and makes a new line of scrimmage. Keeps a good base and feet moving. Eyes stay focused inside, and finds the ball. C gap is the initial responsibility.

Frontside 6 Technique

Execution:

- Versus tight-end drive block (Figure 5-52): Attacks the tight end—hat/hands/eyes. Explodes out of the hips with pads low and the shoulders square to the line of scrimmage. Works for separation with eyes inside, and locates the football. C-gap responsibility—inside arm and leg free. Crosses the tight end when ball is definitely outside and past the point of no return. Uses push/pull to keep the tight end square to the line of scrimmage and to get a good squeeze on him.
- Versus tight-end reach block (zone) (Figure 5-53): Attacks the tight end: hat/hands/eyes. Pushes the tight end upfield with the pads low and the shoulders square to the line of scrimmage. Uses good push/pull technique on the tight end. Separates, and finds the ball. Slowly expands with the tight end, and keeps the inside arm and leg free. C- to D-gap responsibility. Doesn't get knocked back, and cuts off pursuit. Cross-faces to the D gap only when the ball has crossed his face and is on the line of scrimmage.
- Versus tight-end inside release (Figure 5-54): Attacks the tight end, and squeezes the tight end down. The key is to close space and not allow cutoff by the tight end. Closes the inside one hole, and keeps the shoulders square. Eyes move to the next key—fullback, the far offensive guard. Attacks the fullback, keeps inside leverage, and makes the football bounce outside. Spills all blocks. Cross-face blocks and pursues to the football once the ball

has crossed the C gap on the line of scrimmage (e.g., power play). Tight end should never be able to cut off on the release inside when the defensive lineman is tight. Fullback away and counter—attacks the pulling guard with the shoulders square. Spills the first threat, traps the trapper, wheels, and gets upfield with penetration. Keeps the second blocker from getting to the secondary level.

• Versus the power scoop block (Figure 5-55): Explodes on the tight end, and grabs cloth. Does not let the offensive tackle reach him. Locks on the tight end, and squeezes from the inside-out. Uses the push/pull technique with pad under pad.

• Versus tight-end outside release (Figure 5-56): With either the offensive tackle or fullback blocking from the inside-out, the tight end is the pressure key; the offensive tackle is the visual key. Once the tight end declares, snaps the eyes back to the inside. Attacks the offensive tackle from the outside-in, uses the push/pull technique, and keeps the pads square to the line of scrimmage. Keeps the outside arm and outside leg free to play bounce outside. Squeezes the C gap from the outside-in. If the tackle blocks inside, closes and remains ready to spill the first threat, whether the fullback or the guard.

• Versus veer read (Figure 5-57): Attacks the offensive tackle, and squeezes the tackle down. Closes the inside one hole down, and keeps the shoulders square to the line of scrimmage. Eyes to next key—the fullback. Attacks the fullback, and tackles him with the shoulders square. Hits the first thing that shows.

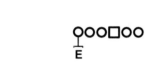

Figure 5-52. Versus tight-end drive block

Figure 5-53. Versus tight end reach block

Figure 5-54. Versus tight-end inside release

Figure 5-55. Versus the power scoop block

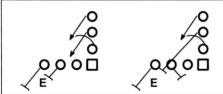
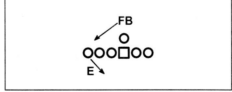

Figure 5-56. Versus tight-end outside release

Figure 5-57. Versus the veer read

Backside 6 Technique

Execution:

- Versus the inside zone (cutoff block) by the tight end (Figure 5-58): Attacks the tight end, squeezes, and keeps the shoulders square. Feels the flat zone scheme when the ball is going away. Shuffles down the line of scrimmage; physically and mentally chases contain. If the ball crosses the line of scrimmage, gets in the good pursuit lane. Feels the "high wall"— stops, retraces the steps, and rips through.
- Versus the tight end pulling inside (Figure 5-59): Attacks upfield. Keeps everything (quarterback, ball) inside the shoulder. Checks the quarterback for boot, naked, and so forth.
- Versus the tight-end set block (Figure 5-60): Attacks the tight end upfield— thinks draw. Punches the inside shoulder of the tight end. Keeps the shoulders square to the line of scrimmage, and squeezes the tight end to constrict the C gap. Physically maintains C-gap responsibility, but remains ready to jump outside if the ball bounces—sprint draw, power, delay away.
- Versus dropback pass (Figure 5-61): Attacks the offensive tackle. If reads pass, executes pass-rush moves. Keeps the feet moving, and pressures the quarterback. Keeps contain on the quarterback unless involved in a stunt— squeezes and constricts the throwing lane. Does not get driven by the quarterback; moves toward the quarterback if he gets driven by the quarterback. When the ball is thrown, runs to the ball.
- Versus sprint-out pass (Figure 5-62): Attacks the offensive tackle's reach block; reads the sprint-out pass technique. Keeps the feet moving, and separates from the tackle's block. Keeps outside leverage on the quarterback; remains outside and in front of quarterback, never even or behind. When the ball is thrown, runs to the ball.
- Versus draw (Figure 5-63): Tight end releases outside, and the offensive tackle pass sets to invite the end upfield. Same attack as versus dropback passes, but does not pass rush until the draw threat is eliminated. If draw, retraces steps, and squeezes inside.
- Versus bootleg pass (Figure 5-64): Keeps the shoulders square, and squeezes on flow away. If bootleg read, gets width first and depth second.

Coaching Points:

- Must be responsible for the C gap.
- Must attack upfield, and make a new line of scrimmage.
- Must stay in the rush lanes.
- Must read the stance of the offensive linemen.
- Must take care of home first, then pursue to the ball.
- Must locate the ball, and make plays.

Figure 5-58. Versus the inside zone (cutoff block) by the tight end

Figure 5-59. Versus the tight end pulling inside

Figure 5-60. Versus the tight-end set block

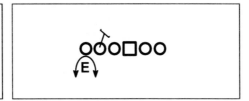

Figure 5-61. Versus dropback pass

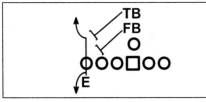

Figure 5-62. Versus sprint-out pass

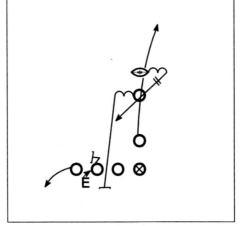

Figure 5-64. Versus bootleg pass

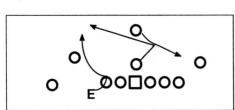

Figure 5-63. Versus draw

5 Technique to Split End

Stance: Two-point with inside leg slightly up, on the balls of the feet, with the knees bent, chest over the balls of the feet, and arms hanging relaxed in front. He can angle slightly inside for good read and attack on the offensive tackle.

Alignment: One foot outside the offensive tackle on the line of scrimmage. Deepens a yard versus an option team.

Key: Keys through the offensive tackle to the triangle (Figure 5-65)—near back, pulling guards, quarterback, and always the ball.

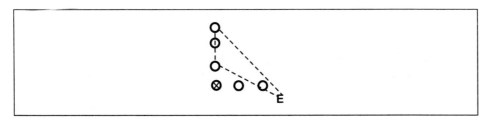

Figure 5-65. Key triangle

Responsibility: Forces everything from the outside-in.

Execution:

- Versus the option (Figure 5-66): Achieves great takeoff and gets upfield. If the offensive tackle disappears, snaps the eyes inside for the first threat. Attacks the quarterback, and forces him to make a quick decision. Attacks any pulling lineman with the near shoulder.
- Versus the near back kickout block (Figure 5-67): Attacks the blocker with the inside arm and shoulder. Wrong-arms and spills the block, getting upfield with penetration. Forces the ballcarrier to "run the hump" to buy time for pursuit.
- Versus the guard kickout block (Figure 5-68): Attacks the blocker from the outside-in. Squeezes, and keeps outside leverage. Doesn't run upfield. Remains ready for the ball to bounce outside.
- Versus the offensive tackle block out (Figure 5-69): Attacks the blocker from the outside-in. Squeezes, and keeps outside leverage. Plays all blocks from the offensive tackle as a turnout block. Doesn't run upfield. Remains ready for ball to bounce outside. Initial takeoff is everything. Beats the offensive tackle out of his stance, and creates a new line of scrimmage. Remains alert for the offensive tackle trying to reach block first, and then turnout block; maintains leverage and squeezes.
- Versus play away (Figure 5-70): Shuffles down the line of scrimmage, and looks for counter or cutback. Does not run upfield. Expands the view and visually checks for reverse; stays on the level of the ball. If reverse shows, keeps the ball on the near shoulder, and turns it inside.
- Versus cutback (Figure 5-71): If cutback, chases the ball.
- Versus dropback pass and draw: Same as versus tight end.
- Versus sprint-out pass away: Keeps the cutback lane tight. Never lets the quarterback reverse field when he gets contained on a sprint out pass away.
- Versus sprint-out pass toward (Figure 5-72): If the tackle reach blocks, he separates and widens, and gets upfield to take on the highest running back's block. Keeps the shoulders square to the line of scrimmage and the inside leg upfield. Never lets the quarterback outside; makes him pull up. Always contains by being outside and in front, never even or behind.
- Versus sprint-out pass toward with tackle turnback (Figure 5-73): If the tackle turnback blocks, he gets upfield, separates, and widens from the running back's blocks. Again, always remains outside and in front, never even or behind.
- Versus bootleg pass (Figure 5-74): Same as versus tight end. If the tackle pulls, he plays boot. If the tackle reaches and the guard pulls toward (the guard will usually pull deep), gets upfield and cuts off the roll action by the quarterback; never lets the quarterback outside. If he reads the bootleg, he should work for width first, and depth second.

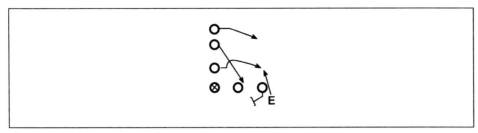

Figure 5-66. Versus the option

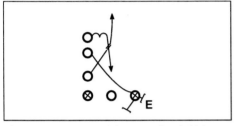

Figure 5-67. Versus the near back kickout block

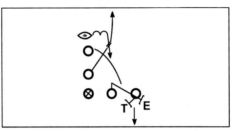

Figure 5-68. Versus the guard kickout block

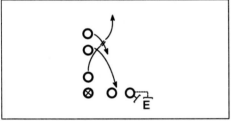

Figure 5-69. Versus the offensive tackle block out

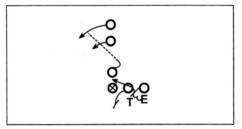

Figure 5-70. Versus play away

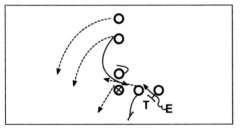

Figure 5-71. Versus cutback

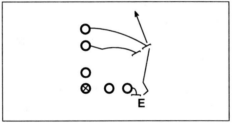

Figure 5-72. Versus sprint-out pass toward with tackle reach blocks

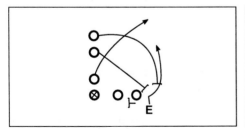

Figure 5-73. Versus sprint-out pass toward with a tackle turnback

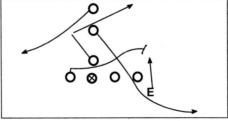

Figure 5-74. Versus bootleg pass

Pass Rush

Keys to Success on the Pass Rush

- Takeoff.
- Simplicity: Teach three to four pass-rush moves.
  - ✓ Defensive end: Rip, swim, speed, and finesse counter moves
  - ✓ Defensive tackle: Rip, swim, power, and finesse counter moves
- Repetition and mechanics: Footwork and hand technique
- Effort and desire: Keep the feet moving.
- Rush calls for the front set
- Pressure: Pressure is as important as sacks. The pass rushers must try to:
  - ✓ Move the pocket and destroy timing.
  - ✓ Bat the pass.
  - ✓ Cause an interception.
  - ✓ Cause a poor throw.
  - ✓ Keep leverage on the quarterback (scramble).
  - ✓ Maintain good distribution on the rush (compensate).

Combat Area

The combat area for pass rushers is from tackle to tackle and three to four yards on the offense's side of the neutral zone. Inside rushers usually face guards and the center in the combat zone. Once the inside rusher has penetrated beyond this area, he is in a no-man's land, and the pressure will increase. The offensive blocker's feet will usually get parallel at this time. The inside rusher should try to pull the blocker forward or counter move and penetrate past the combat area.

The outside rushers usually do not penetrate the combat zone. The goal for the outside rushers is to beat the blocker to the no-man's land. The outside rushers should not rush into the blocker. Once the outside rusher reaches the no-man's land, he should continue into the no-man's land if his initial movement hasn't been stopped, or counter move if his predetermined move has been stopped.

Critical Reminders

- *Pass rush starts with the eyes:* The rusher reads the blocker's set as he closes space on him. Is he too tight, too wide, too tall, or off-balance? He should adjust the pass-rush move on the run. During the rush, he should aim the eyes from one side to the other of the offensive lineman to both sides of the blocker. The rusher makes a move as the eyes pressure the blocker to both sides. He attacks him with eyes, hands, and feet with a good head-and-eyes fake, or foot fake with a dip and rip.

- *Never stop the feet:* When a rusher's momentum toward the quarterback has ceased, it is because the feet stop moving. This momentum drop mostly happens to inside rushers, but can happen to outside rushers. Once locked up and stalled with the offensive linemen, the rusher should do everything possible to get to the quarterback. This stalled or critical position should be practiced in order to teach how to get out of it.

Goals of Pass Rush

- Sacks
- Throwing the quarterback off his rhythm—sprint-out versus dropback
- Hurries
- Containment/leverage
- Getting into throwing lanes

Mental Aspects of Pass Rush

- Know down-and-distance tendencies.
- Know the opponent—quick setter versus deep setter.
- Make light and heavy stance calls.
- Inform the linebackers and secondary of the stance of the offensive line; throw arm up.
- Know formations for passing, and protections by formations; use film study.
- Versus pop-up blocks, don't take the path of least resistance.

Principles of Pass Rush

- Takeoff
  - ✓ Close distance quickly.
  - ✓ Collapse the blocker's arms. Don't allow separation.
  - ✓ Never allow blocker to set his feet.
- Plan
  - ✓ Have a pre-set plan.
  - ✓ Know the opponent's ability.
  - ✓ Know personal strong points.
  - ✓ Do change-up rushes.
  - ✓ Set up offensive lineman with different alignments.
- Target Area/Junction Point
  - ✓ Know where to go prior to the snap.
  - ✓ Get to target/junction point as quickly as possible.
  - ✓ Study film to get the best takeoff possible.

- Counter Moves
  - ✓ Each move should have a counter that does not stop movement toward the quarterback.
  - ✓ Counters should be executed quickly and naturally.
  - ✓ Counters should not take pass rusher out of rush lanes.

Teaching Progression

Pass Rush in a Passing Situation

- Pre-snap
  - ✓ Predetermined move
  - ✓ Stance
  - ✓ Alignment
  - ✓ Target/junction
  - ✓ Key: Use eyes.
- Post-snap
  - ✓ Takeoff: Four to six inches make a difference in winning or losing.
  - ✓ Close: How fast can he get on top of the blocker?
  - ✓ Explosion of hands: Use proper timing.
  - ✓ Grab cloth.
  - ✓ Shoulder turn: Flip the hips, and don't expose numbers.
  - ✓ Use proper pass-rush technique.
  - ✓ Disengage and accelerate feet; get hips around, and don't shuffle.
  - ✓ Sack and strip: Don't just sack, but rip the ball out.

Pass Rush in a Running Situation

- Pre-snap
  - ✓ Defensive line is in a run-stop mode.
- Post-snap
  - ✓ Recognize pass set.
  - ✓ Close the distance on get-off
  - ✓ Break down the blocker's position.
  - ✓ Use proper pass-rush technique.
  - ✓ Recognize draw or screen blocks.

Pass-Rush Lanes

Contain Rushers

- Widen alignment—can vary depending on move.
- Maintain three-point sprinter's stance.

- Always keep outside leverage.
- Always close at the quarterback's upfield shoulder.
- Never get pushed past quarterback depth. Don't allow him to duck under.
- Must redirect any inside move upfield when they have contain.
- Key ball for movement.

Inside Rushers

- Crowd the line of scrimmage.
- Key ball for movement.
- Never get frontal with a blocker; work the edge.
- Never get pushed wide upfield as it may disrupt the path of an outside rusher.
- Never get pushed across the ball. Spin back to maintain the rush lanes.
- Use different alignments to set up rushes.

Basic Pass-Rush Techniques

Bull: Good move when blocker is on his heels, off balance, or if he has overset. The rusher should drive the face mask at the blocker's chin with both hands going to his hands in an upward motion. The angle of the rusher's body should be pointed in order to destroy the blocking angle to blocker. Takeoff and explosion is key. He should be ready to swim or rip on brace up by the blocker. If he misses a basic move or the first portion of a combo move, he should go to a bull rush. The rusher should stay low, keep the head up, and move fast with a wide base. Bull rush is a good technique to use when the blocker is floating or is setting deep.

Slap: Slaps the blocker's hand between the wrist and the area between the wrist and hand. Breaks down the outside hand of the blocker using an inside hand slap or outside hand slap. The rusher should keep the slap tight to his chest.

Arm Rip: Upward movement of the arm, fist, and shoulder underneath the armpit and shoulder of the blocker, either to his inside or outside. The action should be aggressive in order to break any hold the blocker may have on the rusher. Quickness with the rip is key. Once it is set, the rusher starts the lift, pries off the blocker's hand, and removes his grip. Lifts elbow if the blocker's hands are low. Keeps the inside toe pointed to the quarterback. The rip enables the rusher to work under the pressure of the offensive blocker's hands.

Jerk: Pulls the blocker in either a vertical or a lateral direction. The direction of the jerk is usually determined by the type of pressure or body position of the blocker. Remains ready for a brace.

Swim: Crosses over the body of the blocker with the arm that is closest to him. It should be an upward and then downward movement. Flips the hands around, and uses an inside crossover step. The rusher should never expose his numbers. The key is patience. He can also give a head-and-shoulder fake opposite the swim. Uses the swim when the blocker is off balance. The minute he touches skin, the rusher swims over. The rusher should be explosive, be violent, grab cloth, swim, and break the elbow down. A good bull rush sets up this move.

Freeze: Head fakes and steps to get the blocker moving in one direction in order to execute a move in the opposite direction. The rusher should threaten the gap with his numbers low.

Club: The defensive lineman should use an arm to deliver a blow to lever the shoulder of the blocker, a club action in an attempt to knock him off balance. This technique is great for double moves. The second move must come quickly. As a general rule, the club doesn't help against a 300-pound offensive lineman. It's like hitting a telephone pole. Grab and pull may be more effective in that situation. The club technique is most effective when clubbing the blocker's hands, wrist, arm, or elbow. It will involve a club and rip move, or hips to the edge of the blocker, and then rip through to get hip-to-hip with the blocker.

Rake: The rusher uses his hands to knock the blocker's hands off him. Keeps the hands tight to the chest and high around the face. He must accelerate and get his hips around on contact. Uses an inside crossover technique.

Speed Rush: Widens the alignment, and sprints to a spot or target area; doesn't belly. Should have a pre-snap idea of how to rush. Remains quick out of the stance with an explosive first step. The rusher needs a great takeoff to close the space on the offensive lineman and force him to keep his feet moving. Gets on the edge of the blocker with speed. The rusher shouldn't block himself with poor approach to the blockers and poor angles. He must work hard to get even with the offensive lineman; he should get perpendicular to the blocker's pads. Makes a move when the pads get perpendicular to his. Reaches with the outside arm and snatches cloth on the upfield shoulder of the offensive lineman. Snatches the cloth; doesn't grab the cloth. Fast feet are essential with a quick shuffle and crossover. Gets the offensive lineman's hands and arm up, down, or pinned inside. It is important with takeoff for the rusher to get the cloth. Reaches and grabs cloth; jerks in and down. Violently rips with the inside arm under the pressure of the blocker's hands. Sinks the inside hip and shoulder, staying as low and tight as possible around the blocker. Drives the arm through the hip, and steps on the offensive lineman's feet. The rusher should speed up as he escapes off the blocker, and accelerate to the quarterback. He should never stop momentum toward the quarterback, keeping the feet alive to and through the rush because more than one move may be required.

Lift: With the outside or inside hand, depending on the move, attacks the forearm or elbow of the offensive lineman. Lifts the elbow area to the forearm. With the opposite hand, stabs down the middle of the chest, and rips through with the stab hand to the side of the lift. At the point of contact, locks out the arms, and drives the offensive lineman back. The lift gives a landmark and target without sacrificing speed. Concentrates on the arm to be lifted, and sees it through contact, keeping the feet moving at all times.

Rake: Uses the rake as a change-up when the offensive lineman is slow in getting his hands up, or the rusher has threatened the blocker upfield on the edge so that he has to punch hard at the rusher. Uses a hard rake down to eliminate his hands. The aiming point is the offensive lineman's forearms and wrists because he has less strength in these areas. As the rusher punches, takes both arms and rakes down on the offensive lineman's wrists or arms, then rips or swims over with the feet moving upfield to collapse the pocket. A great takeoff and speed to close the distance on the offensive lineman will be the keys to success.

Sprint-Out Pass: Must get upfield and meet the lead blocker with depth. If two blockers are used, gets to the second blocker at the proper angle. Versus a cut block, places the front hand on his helmet and the back hand on his pad. Sees the blocker, and reads through him to the quarterback. Bright lights on the lead blocker, and dim lights on the quarterback. Adjusts the angle to the move of the back. The rusher should be one to two yards outside and in front of the quarterback, never even or behind. Must be ready to attack with the hands and bounce with the feet. The hands need to be explosive to get the blocker's shoulders perpendicular to the line of scrimmage. May run through or bounce the blocker. Explodes off the block, and maintains outside and in-front leverage with the shoulders parallel to the line of scrimmage. Never want shoulders perpendicular to the line of scrimmage because it increases the blocking surface. Remains in the throwing lane, which forces the quarterback to pull up or turn back to the inside and into pursuit. Forces the sprint-out as quickly and deeply as possible to break down the rhythm and the timing of the route.

Scissors: Gets a tremendous takeoff at the proper angle, and closes the space on the offensive lineman. Keeps the blocker's feet moving, and increases the size of his hands with excellent eye concentration. Separates his hands, one down and one up. Aggressively chops or slaps the hands, wrists, or arm to create separation. The hands must be quick and tight. Stabs the offensive lineman in the chest with the hand going up. Snatches cloth, rips through either the inside or the outside, and accelerates to the passer.

Club, Chop, and Rip: This move begins with a strong club to the blocker's hand, arm, elbow, or shoulder with the rusher's outside or inside hand. As the club is finished, chops down on the same part of the body with the other hand. Then, finishes the rush by ripping up with the chop hand and pulling the hips through.

Chop Rip: This move begins with an aggressive rush to the edge of a blocker. As the rusher closes the distance between the blocker and himself, uses the hand that is nearest to the blocker, and chops down hard on his outside hand or forearm. As the chop gets to the bottom, immediately rips back up through the blocker's shoulder and remains ready to cut the edge that has just been created. This move must be used with speed. Must be ready to use a counter move immediately if the chop does not work.

Counter Moves: Counter moves are used when the rusher can't get to the quarterback in the lane he is in. The rusher dictates where the contact will happen, so in executing a move, he needs to know when the move has been taken away so he can immediately use a counter maneuver. As an example: if the offensive lineman opens his hips and kicks his outside leg back, this move is a good indicator to hit and counter back inside. The eyes determine whether the offensive lineman is playing outside, or is off balance, or has stopped the rusher's thrust upfield. When these situations occur, the rusher should use a spin or rip move to continue to press upfield. When using a spin, he should keep constant body contact and make a speed wheel on the inside leg. As the rusher wheels, he should drive his far elbow into the back of the blocker to propel him to the quarterback. This blow must be powerful and violent to escape contact from the blocker. It is important for the rusher to stay low in the spin, and pop the head and eyes around quickly to regain vision on the quarterback. He should come off the blocker with quickness, speed, and power. The rip is best used when the rusher is helmet-to-helmet with the offensive lineman or as a predetermined move that is planned from a pre-snap idea discovered on the previous down. The rusher should threaten the blocker to both sides with the eyes, use a good head fake, get eyes, hands, and feet in the gap to force the offensive lineman to freeze, and then explode to the opposite gap with a well executed rip, snatch, and explosion upfield. The key to success is never stopping the momentum to the quarterback.

Combination of Basic Moves

A successful pass rush is based on the rusher's ability to destroy the balance of the blocker. In many situations, the blocker's body position dictates the most effective combination to be used. Therefore, the rusher should take advantage of the position of the offensive blocker. At the same time, if the blocker takes away the rusher's predetermined combination, he should be ready to counter and use a reverse combination.

Power Swim or Rip: Attacks the blocker's chin like a bull rush. Must be ready to swim or rip on the brace up. Clears the hips on the swim move. Gets the outside shoulder raised on the rip move.

Slap and Swim: Brings the hand to the slap area on first step. Swims over with the opposite arm, escapes, and drives for the quarterback. The rusher can slap and swim to the outside. Uses an inside crossover technique.

Slap and Rip: Charges the outside shoulder of the offensive lineman, and tries to beat him before he can set up. As contact is made with the slap, rips with the other arm, and accelerates to the passer. Can slap and rip to the outside.

Stutter With Swim or Rip:

- Outside: As the rusher approaches the blocker, head fakes and steps inside. Delivers a blow with the inside arm, and escapes outside of him to the passer.

- Inside: Head fakes and steps outside. Delivers a blow with the outside arm or hand, and swims and rips with the outside arm, going inside the blocker and driving for the passer.
- Stutters and performs a wiper move.
- Stutters and goes to a bull rush.

Speed Bull: Gets upfield, and shows a speed rush. As the tackle bails and opens, attacks him with a good bull-rush technique. The rusher shouldn't bury himself and lose sight of the quarterback.

Counter Spin: A move to bring the rusher back to the quarterback when the blocker has gained upfield position and the rusher is too far upfield. Spins by pivoting off the inside foot, and throws the outside leg and arm around tight to check the blocker.

Combination Moves

Swap (Figure 5-75): The defensive tackle threatens the offensive linemen to both sides with his eyes. He then moves upfield, using a rip technique and no counter. Pads are down, and he is like a missile through the B gap. He takes a first step to be upfield with no directional step. He will be small in the gap with explosive penetration. The defensive tackle can't be soft. The defensive end widens his alignment to make the offensive tackle think he is going outside. He makes it look like a speed rush by selling the outside rush on the first step; the rush has no definite number of steps, as it may be one or three steps. As he pushes upfield and sees the defensive tackle clear the line of scrimmage, he will wrap behind the defensive tackle. He should be tight and quick off the butt of the defensive tackle. Pads will be down as he moves upfield and collapses the pocket with penetration in the face of the quarterback. He should play with the eyes, and find the open window.

Swap is better if a team is blocking the center away. It can be used as a delayed game or a speed game. Swap can be a double stunt or combined with wrap to be run together to create pockets in the protection.

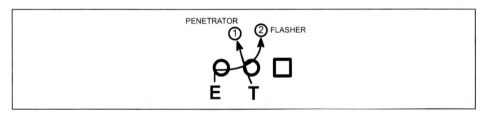

Figure 5-75. Swap

Wrap (Figure 5-76): The defensive tackle should sell his rush where he is lined up. He should move upfield, and then once the defensive end is beyond him in the gap, he should make his move. The wrap has no set number of steps. He should feel the defensive end in the gap after one, two, or three steps, and then start around the defensive end. He should be as low and tight to the end as possible. The most common mistake by the tackle is to take an extra step laterally. He should get upfield, and collapse the pocket from the outside. The tackle is outside force on the ball. Once the tackle clears one blocker, he should be ready to defeat another with a rip, swim, butt, or slip move. He should adjust to the run on the move.

The defensive end needs to get penetration with a good first step and a good rip. The key to both the wrap and swap stunt is to get gap penetration. If no penetration, both defenders are just going lateral. The end is responsible for B to A gap as he reads the offensive guard. He should attack the guard hard. If the guard steps to the end, he should go under him; if the guard blocks away, the end should get immediate penetration upfield. He must get behind the offensive line and get upfield in the throwing lanes. He must attempt to find an open window on the rush to put pressure on the quarterback. He will adjust to the run on the move.

The stunts can be run three ways:
- Quick: Versus man protection on a running down
- Delay: Versus deep setters
- Pick: Versus man protection

The key consideration is to know what is working according to blocking schemes.

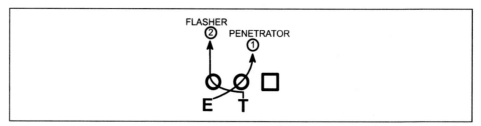

Figure 5-76. Wrap

Scissors (Figure 5-77): The two technique tackles go first. If a defensive call exists that puts both defensive tackles in the same technique, let the game plan for that week determine who has the first move. For both tackles, the aiming point will be the face mask of the guards. The tackle should work for an open window (daylight). The tackle will move to make the defensive ends right. As the tackle makes his move, he should visualize the defensive end's technique and adjust to his inside or outside rush. If he feels and sees color cross his face, he drives for width and penetration to contain the ball. If he feels or sees color outside, he immediately moves upfield, finds the open window, and collapses the pocket from the inside.

The defensive end widens his alignment to make the offensive tackle think he is going outside. On his initial move, he sells the outside rush, adjusting his rush according to the play of the offensive tackle. Since the defensive end can't be wrong and is trying to get the offensive tackle on an island, the end should force the tackle to move his feet and exploit the weakness in the outside protection as he reads on the run. All the components of a good pass rush should come into play to enable this maneuver to be successful.

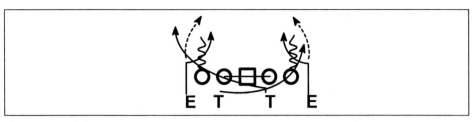

Figure 5-77. Scissors

Trio (Figure 5-78): The left tackle lead steps with his near foot. He will attack the gap unless the center turns to him, in which case he will rip through and cross-face. If the center blocks away, the left tackle should get immediate penetration in the nearside A gap. He must be tight on the center so he can beat the guard blocking down. He should accelerate as he clears the line of scrimmage, always ready to play the second blocker, and be that opposite color jersey in the face of the quarterback.

The right tackle will be as low and tight to the left tackle as possible. He moves to the B gap with speed and power. If he gets a down block from the offensive tackle, he should be ready to rip and cross-face to the outside. If the offensive tackle sets outside, the right tackle should immediately get upfield and work off the move of the defensive end. He is responsible for outside force, but if he feels and visualizes the defensive end outside, then he should redirect upfield into the open window. The defensive end will use the same concept and technique that he applied in the scissors stunt.

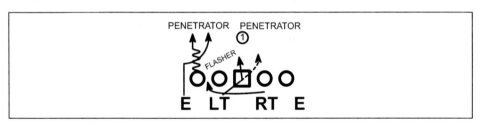

Figure 5-78. Trio

Weave (Figure 5-79): A combination of the wrap/swap is the weave. This stunt is good versus formations that create a two-man side to both sides—such as a 10 doubles formation or a 10 trips formation. Typically, the game plan determines what rush is used to the field or to the formation by the game plan from week to week. If a wrap or swap to both sides is wanted, a double wrap or a double swap is called.

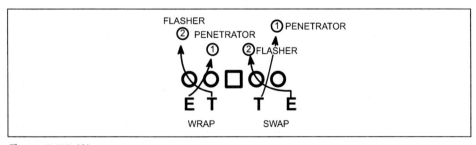

Figure 5-79. Weave

Points of Importance in Pass-Rush Game Penetration

- The best pass rusher should be on the right side. The quarterback doesn't see him as quickly.
- Be aware of offensive line cut blocks, especially on screen, flare, and three-step.
- In pass-rush situations (second-and-long, third down), the defensive lineman should take an ability alignment to enhance his chance for success.
- When attempting to deflect a pass, stress that one arm is longer than two. The pass rusher should mirror the quarterback, and time his arm extension with the quarterback's release.
- Most centers snap with the right hand and come up with the left hand.
- Club doesn't help versus a 300-pound offensive lineman. When used against the lineman's shoulders or body, it is like hitting a telephone pole. When the club is used, be prepared to club the hands, wrists, forearm, or elbow for most effective results.
- Losing contain on the quarterback will greatly determine the outcome of a game. The player with outside force responsibility goes for a point outside the quarterback, not in the face of the quarterback. He should know the quarterback's mannerisms, and anticipate his actions.
- Close; the rusher can't beat the blocker until he catches up with him.
- Relationship to the blocker is vital. If the rusher makes his move too far away from the offensive lineman, he gives the lineman the advantage.

Pass-Rush Lanes and Responsibilities

Lanes: Regardless of the defense called or pass-rush technique used, it is crucial that defensive linemen understand the concept of a balanced pass rush. Each pass rusher is assigned a general pass-rush lane with the freedom to adjust the lane to the quarterback's movement. A balanced pass rush will help put more pressure on the quarterback and prevent him from escaping the rush and running for yardage. Basic pass-rush lanes versus a dropback pass are illustrated in Figure 5-80.

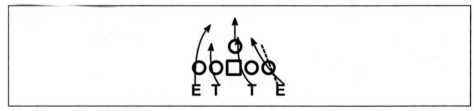

Figure 5-80. Pass-rush lanes versus dropback pass

1, 2, 3, 4, and Angle Technique: Pass-rush lanes extend from the ball to the offensive tackle's inside leg.

5, 6, and 7 Technique: Pass-rush lanes extend from the tackle's outside leg to the outside. The crucial responsibility is to contain the quarterback.

6

Inside Linebacker Play

Tempo Setter

Linebackers set the standard not only for the defense, but the entire team. The tempo that is demanded for them to prepare and play requires they be the toughest, most physical and punishing players on every play. The toughness is not only physical, but also mental, because they need to shut out any distraction that would keep them from playing at an intense, relentless level on every play. They know that they cannot allow themselves to ever have a bad day or a bad play. Whatever obstacle would keep them from performing at a high level should be dealt with and defeated instantly. The ingredient that makes linebackers special is that their effort is more important than their ability. They should approach every game with the attitude that they are as good as the opponent, and not one bit better, and, for that reason, the game must be won with great concentration, great anticipation, and great effort. Ability and talent will take them only so far, but at some point the heart, will, and spirit should elevate them to a plateau where ability will never succeed by itself.

Linebackers define pursuit as thinking more of effort than of ability. Top linebackers are difference-makers, because they have made a commitment to play better than their ability level. Their physical and mental preparation develops their poise and self-confidence so that they *want* the opponent to attack them in every critical situation. Their attitude is, "If you are going to run, run it at me. If you are going to pass, throw it at me. Give it your best shot, and, when the smoke clears, I'll still be standing victorious." Linebackers will always measure how well they play on the basis of how well they made their teammates play. Finally they know victory will require pain. They welcome it, because they have prepared themselves for it.

Pain is simply weakness leaving the body.
The question is never how much more can I take.
The question is how much more can I give.
When the body cries out, "I am finished,"
The heart, will and spirit demand him to push harder.
He listens and senses an inner peace that was not there before
And he suddenly discovers he no longer feels the pain.
He feels only the achievement of victory.
Expect pain.
Endure pain.
Conquer pain.
So now you can cause pain.

—Unknown

Basic Philosophy of Linebacker Play

Playing linebacker is the most challenging assignment on a football team. The linebackers are involved in every aspect of the game. They should have excellent coordination and cooperation with the defensive line and within the structure of the defense to stop the run. They should also have the same coordination and cooperation with the defensive backs within the structure of the defense to stop the pass.

The linebackers are expected to play the game from sideline to sideline. They may not be the biggest players on the field, but they are expected to be the most physical and punishing. They are expected to know not only their own position and job, but those of the players on either side of them.

Their assignments will require them to be the best conditioned, most observant, most studious, and most disciplined and physically tough players on the field. Linebackers should be the best and surest tacklers on the team. They should be the most aggressive defenders and display this aggressiveness by getting to the ball every time it moves. They should know their own assignments letter perfect, and also know the entire defensive concept to ensure a coordinated effort. Their thorough knowledge and understanding of the defense will be an important factor in the team's success or failure.

Linebackers cannot be satisfied with being average. Being average includes: being blocked, staying blocked, missing a tackle in a critical situation, slowing the runner up but still letting him make extra yardage, not carrying out an assignment, getting tired, not hustling, and permitting the big offensive play. Linebackers should never play or think in an average manner.

Things a Linebacker Should Know and Do

General

- If the system requires a defensive huddle to make calls, insists on the following. Looks into the eyes of every man in the defensive huddle, and makes sure they are looking at him. Maintains discipline in the huddle. Makes sure every man has heard and understood the calls correctly. Breaks the huddle sharply. Acts as a leader, and plays with confidence and poise.
- Knows not only own assignments on each defense called, but those of every position in the entire defense. If any teammate lines up incorrectly, immediately recognizes this error, and moves him into proper position before the ball is snapped.
- Knows the strengths and weakness of each defense. Anticipates what an opponent might do to a defense. Must be able to tell the coaches what is observed.

Situation

- *Down-and-distance:* Opponents call their offense by down-and-distance. Knows what to expect.
- *Field position:* Knows what the opponent does when coming out, in the middle of the field, in the red zone, or on the goal line. Will the opponent gamble, use regular offense, or employ trick plays?
- *Time remaining:* Many games have been lost because a team misjudged the time left to play in each half and what an opponent does during this time. In close games, the time employed intelligently by a team often determines the winner. Knows how opponents stop the clock to save time. Knows how many timeouts each team has remaining. The defense can determine whether or not the offense controls the time.

Tendencies

- *Formations:* What is the opponent's tendency by formation? Does he run to or away from the formation? Every formation has a favorite play (or plays) with which the defense should be familiar.
- *Personnel:* Must be alert for changes in personnel. Most opponents style their attack based on personnel.

Opponent's Offense

- *Huddle:* Knows where people line up in their huddle. This factor helps determine strength. Knows how long they stay in the huddle. Must be aware of no-huddle situations. Knows where the tight end is.
- *Alignment:* Knows if they run from a pre-shift formation. Knows if they like to go on a quick or long count, and in what situations they do so. Knows if they take unusually large line splits.

Special Situations

- Knows who and what the opponent calls upon in the clutch.
- Knows how the change of quarterback affects the game.
- Must be aware of a play being run at a new substitute after an injury to teammates.
- Watches for the home-run play after losing possession of the ball on a sudden change.
- Every time the opponent puts in a substitute, must be sure to recognize his number and position. This factor could constitute a change in the defense.

Takeaways

- Statistics have proven the importance of the takeaway. Takeaways are intercepted passes and recovered fumbles by the defense. The defense creates takeaways.
- Linebackers are in excellent position to go for the football. Backs are taught to protect the ball in traffic, but frequently they break away from defenders and look for daylight, and thus are vulnerable to being stripped. Receivers are often lax in putting the ball away after the catch, and they can be stripped. Always think in terms of attacking the football.
- The opponent will have the football an average of 13 times in a game. Each takeaway reduces his chance of scoring, and usually results in excellent field position for the offense. Takeaways are the result of hustle, desire, and concentration.

Big Plays

- Linebackers are in a better position to come up with a big play than anyone else on the defense.
- Must be aware of big-play situations. Four or five of these situations typically occur in every game.
- Must make things happen.

Missed Assignments

- Missed assignments come when a linebacker is negligent in one or more of the following areas:
- Uncertain of specific responsibility in a defense or coverage
- Lack of concentration
- Lack of discipline
- Lack of poise or ability to handle pressure.

Missed assignments cannot be tolerated and have a direct reflection on a linebacker's desire to be a champion and team pride. Nothing, other than lack of talent, will get a linebacker on the bench quicker than missed assignments.

Linebackers are the leaders of the defense and can never be uncertain or unprepared in a meeting, a practice, or a game.

Pass Coverage Tips

- Gang tackling is the most demoralizing maneuver in football, and is a must for all good defensive teams. The linebackers are the leaders in gang tackling.
- Must never take for granted that a man is tackled.
- Sprints to the cover area of responsibility, and breaks at the proper angle. Does not lose ground by breaking at the wrong angles. Reads the receivers.
- Plays the ball once it is in the air. If a linebacker doesn't fly to the football, he is admitting one of three things:
  ✓ Lack of conditioning
  ✓ Laziness or indifference
  ✓ Lack of commitment to leaving it on the field for his teammates
- Always plays the ball at its highest point.
- Must be in position to intercept a pass if it is deflected. Never quits.
- Goes up with two hands to break up a pass. Two hands are better than one.
- Remember: the defender has equal right for the ball once it is in the air. Must play it all out, but always play the ball, not the man.
- Aggressiveness is one of the hardest things to teach on pass defense. It starts in practice against teammates.
- Must be tough and aggressive. Some receivers are inclined to be timid. Must make receivers respect the linebacker position.
- At times, the linebacker has his man covered, but due to the type of pass thrown, it will be completed. A technique that is very effective is to slap at the ball and strip it from the receiver before he can put it away. In many instances, he will drop the ball. If he hangs onto it, the linebacker is still in a position to tackle him. Linebackers must perfect this technique when covering the receivers. Having quick hands is a great asset.

Goals for Linebackers

- Attack; don't catch.
- Play through the blockers, not around.
- Stay on the feet.
- Swarm the ball.
- Allow no missed tackles.
- Make it happen—big plays.
- Display effort, heart above ability, and talent.
- Get excited every second of every minute of every quarter; play with enthusiasm.

- PTS: Pursue, tackle, stay on the feet.
- SSS: Shock and shed, stay on the feet, swarm.
- Don't let the little things slide.
- Limit collision yards.
- Allow no cutback yardage.
- Force and create turnovers.

Linebacker Reminders

The following are some daily short statements that should be made to linebackers to remind them what it will take to achieve success:
- Play hard, play fast, and play smart.
- Outplay, outhit, outhustle, outfight, outsmart, and outheart the opponent.
- Play with heart, but also play with your head.
- Band together as one team, with one goal, going in one direction.
- Show respect.
  - ✓**R**esponsibility
  - ✓**E**xcellence
  - ✓**S**acrifice
  - ✓**P**ride
  - ✓**E**ffort
  - ✓**C**ommunicate
  - ✓**T**ogetherness
- Attitude is 10 percent what happens to you and 90 percent how you react to what happens to you.
- Never be afraid of failure; be afraid of being unprepared. Outwork the opponents.

These statements are short, but they can be easily said and are definite attention-getters. When players repeat them to one another or to a coach, it is a good sign that they're buying into the standard of excellence needed to win on the football field and in life.

Stance

Align in a two-point stance with feet parallel. Feet will be aligned armpit to shoulder-width apart with the weight on the inside balls of the feet. Width of the feet will vary according to ability to get out of a stance with quickness and explosion. If the stance is too wide, the linebacker has a tendency to false step to narrow his base. Must have a comfortable bend in the knees with shoulders aligned in front of the hips. Shoulders are over the knees, and knees are over the toes. Arms and hands are inside the frame of the body. Hands can be fully extended or rest on the inside of the thigh pads. Doesn't raise or lower to move from stance. Every move made should keep the blocking surface reduced by making the area between shoulder pads and knees as small as possible. Plays at the height of the stance; must never have to reset to take on a block or make a tackle. Linebackers are always one or two steps away from defeating a block or making a tackle, and by staying low they can be immediately pad under pad.

Pre-Snap Tips

Basically, a defensive player wins or loses on each play for the following four reasons:

- Readiness on the snap
- Knowledge of the assignment
- Proper alignment
- Demonstrated ability and effort

Three of these four factors take place prior to the snap of the ball, so the linebacker has accomplished 75 percent of the winning edge before the ball is snapped. The goal is to eliminate all the surprises before the ball is snapped. All thinking precedes the snap; then, the linebackers can react with confidence and speed. In other words, linebackers cannot be spectators between downs, but very active, alert participants. Must play with eyes, expand vision, concentrate, and communicate. Linebackers should break down the pre-snap reads into four categories:

- Line of scrimmage
- Backs
- Formations
- Down-and-distance

As linebackers read from front to back, they should closely observe the line of scrimmage as to line splits, distance off the ball, and heavy or light stance. A heavy stance is denoted by a lower helmet position, more weight on the down hand, and the heels raised higher to push off. A light stance can be recognized by a higher helmet position, less weight on the hand, and heels tighter to the ground. A heavy stance is normally a run alert. A light stance should increase awareness of a possible pass, a pull for trap, counter, draw, or bootleg. Figure 6-1 illustrates the relationship between stances and run or pass alerts. As linebackers read the backs, they should be alert for width alignment, depth alignment, and formation alignment. All teams have formation tendencies. Some formations seek to get a balance between run and pass, where others are very heavy run or very heavy pass. Down-and-distance has become more difficult to break down, as a majority of teams are currently seeking to get a balance in their run:pass ratio on various downs. A general breakdown of run and pass percentages by down-and-distance is:

- First-and-10: 60 percent run, 40 percent pass
- Second-and-medium (six yards or less): 60 percent run, 40 percent pass
- Second-and-long (seven yards or more): 70 percent pass, 30 percent run

- Third-and-short (two yards or less): 80 percent run, 20 percent pass
- Third-and-medium (three to six yards): 20 percent run, 80 percent pass
- Third-and-long (seven yards or more): 15 percent run, 85 percent pass

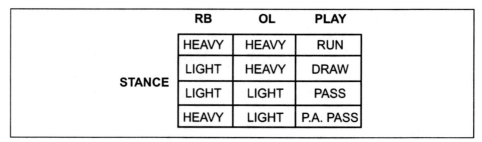

	RB	OL	PLAY
	HEAVY	HEAVY	RUN
STANCE	LIGHT	HEAVY	DRAW
	LIGHT	LIGHT	PASS
	HEAVY	LIGHT	P.A. PASS

Figure 6-1. Relationship between stances and run or pass alerts

Games can be won between downs. Emphasize this point to your players. Make the 25-second clock that little extra that helps to win big games.

Keying the Offensive Linemen

Linebackers are required to key both linemen and backs based on the offensive sets and the defensive calls. Keying either linemen or backs both have merit. With both methods, it is necessary to see the primary key and visualize the secondary key. Keying linemen and visualizing backs gives a better awareness of tips that will aid in quicker reaction to the offensive scheme—whether run or pass. Being disciplined when keying is essential for linebacker success. Linebackers help themselves when keying linemen for the following reasons:

- Allows quicker reaction to misdirection (e.g., counters and bootlegs).
- Provides better awareness of heavy/light stances, line splits, offensive line either on or off the line of scrimmage, and back alignment and depth
- Forces linebackers to align on air, thus requiring them to get run-pass reads off uncovered linemen.
- Enhances the importance of better communication before and after the ball is snapped.

Linebackers still key backs when they are in man-coverage situations. The use of line and back keys will make linebackers more aware of pre-snap tips and play anticipation, which enables them to eliminate even more surprises prior to the snap of the ball. The winning edge has been and will always be:

- Play hard, but play smart.
- Play with the heart, but also play with the head.

Keys From Various Fronts (Figures 6-2 through 6-5)

The linebackers' primary keys are the linemen on the line of scrimmage; the secondary key is visualizing the back. In other words, headlights focused on the linemen, and dimmers on the backs—play with the eyes. In the 50 under and over front, the primary keys are the guards to the back. In the Eagle (4-2), the 3-3 (stack), and the 4-3, the primary key is the triangle read—the Sam and Will read the guard and tackle to their side, and the Mike reads the center-guard triangle to the back.

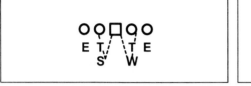

Figure 6-2. Eagle front keys

Figure 6-3. 50 front keys

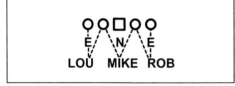

Figure 6-4. 3-3 front keys

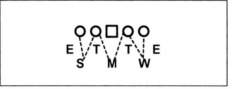

Figure 6-5. 43 front keys

Frontside and Backside Reads (Figure 6-6)

Frontside blocks include the base, reach, down, veer (down/down), pull (playside), pass, and turnout. The backside blocks are pull away, scoop, and pass. The block key and proper reaction to the key are outlined in the following sections.

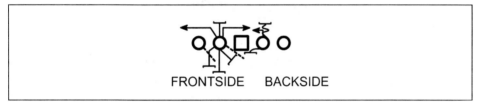

Figure 6-6. Frontside and backside keys

Frontside Blocks

- *Base:* Attack-steps, reduces the hole with the inside arm, and keeps the outside arm free.
- *Reach:* Presses the line of scrimmage at the proper angle, shocks and sheds with the inside arm, reduces the hole with the man, and keeps the outside arm free.
- *Down:* Attack-steps, presses the line of scrimmage, shocks and sheds with the inside arm, reduces the hole with the man, and keeps the outside arm free.
- *Veer (down/down):* Attack-steps, presses to daylight, takes the attack press to the angle of the back and the ball, and fills to daylight. Closes the B gap, and then expands outside. The veer block usually involves the option. If daylight appears inside the linebacker, he should play the dive. If daylight appears outside, he should play the quarterback.

- *Pull playside:* Reads the splits. Attacks the line of scrimmage, presses to daylight. If he encounters darkness, expands or reduces the attack point to daylight.
- *Pass-draw:* Keeps the eyes on the center or the guard, and keys their shallow set (i.e., flash) and high-hat read.

Backside Blocks

- *Pull away:* Reads the splits, and yells, "Pull." Must be ready to redirect and retrace steps, press the line of scrimmage, and get inside leverage on the back and the ball. If he loses depth, he may need to give ground to get around.
- *Scoop:* May look like a down block. Sees the split prior to the snap—tight on the scoop, wider on the down/veer. Reacts to the angle and helmet of the blocker—flattens on the scoop as he tries to get his helmet frontal on the defensive lineman. On the down block, he will place the helmet on the hip and butt of the defensive lineman. The scoop blocker's shoulders are perpendicular to the line of scrimmage. On the down block, his shoulders are parallel so the front number shows and allows him to climb to the second level. Linebacker should always begin press and be ready to expand or reduce the fit according to the shoulders of the back. The bigger the area the linebackers try to key, the less concentration they will have. Tell them to focus on the earhole, the number on the shoulder, or object on the helmet. They should reduce their focus and expand their concentration.

Keying the Backs

If the primary key for the linebackers is on the backs with the secondary key on the linemen, their headlights are on the backs, and dimmers are on the linemen. Linebackers' primary key of the backs occurs when playing man coverage (e.g., possible one-back sets or two-back alignments when counters are not a big threat). Linebackers are usually not as aware of line splits, heavy/light stances, pull of the lineman, and blocking angles when keying backs. Thus, they lose some anticipation reaction prior to the snap.

Rules Versus Different Backfield Sets

- *I backs:* Keys the tailback, and visualizes the fullback. If the tailback gets the ball, reacts to him and with him.
- *Split backs:* Keys the back to his side. The scouting report may dictate a cross keying adjustment.
- *Strong or weak backs:* Keys the back aligned in the normal fullback position unless in man coverage, in which case keys the assigned man and covers him. The game plan may indicate it is better to key the strong or weak back, so must be ready to adjust to tendencies.
- *One back:* Keys the single back.

Note: The bigger the area the linebackers try to key, the less concentration they will have. Tell them to focus on the earhole, the number on the shoulder, or object on the helmet. They should reduce their focus and expand their concentration.

The First Step Is an Attack Step

The attack step is about six inches and sometimes no more than a pick-and-place step, which gets momentum pressing the line of scrimmage. The linebacker must always strive for quickness with the first step, and then read and react without any false step. The initial step is tight and quick, so if the action of the ball or the blocking scheme forces the linebacker to redirect, he can do so without getting extended. He should always try to improve the quickness of the first and second steps. Must be ready to shock and shed off a block on the first step downhill, so as to get on and get off the offensive lineman before he is set or his shoulders are still perpendicular to the line of scrimmage. Speeds up the initial hit to gain leverage on the blocker.

Communication

The defensive team can never communicate enough. The source of information provided between teammates may be verbal or through hand signals to alert them to a vital tip that will be key in stopping a play. Alerts them to line splits with a wide or tight call. Alerts them to the types of stances with a heavy or light call. If no indication can be determined from their stance, gives a zero call. Linebackers should give some call on every play. Even if a mistake is made, he shouldn't let that stop him from making a call. He should put it in a memory bank because he will see that stance, split, or alignment again. Remember, it is a long game, and even if he doesn't get something until the fourth quarter, he still has something that may help to win on the last play. If unsure, thinks run. If nothing can be obtained from the stance, then turns attention to splits. The guidelines for splits should be tighter split = pass, and wider split = run.

The defensive line or linebackers can raise an arm and move it back and forth when they read pass, which alerts the secondary to pass prior to the snap of the ball. Or, the linebackers can give a verbal call to alert the defensive line and secondary to run or pass. An example of verbal calls can be deer = run (deer runs on the ground) and bullet = pass (bullet travels through the air).

The defense will average about 70 to 75 plays per game. With 11 men on the offensive team, someone is giving something away. Therefore, communication is a difference-maker when linebackers alert other defensive players to what they see prior to the snap.

Alignment Depth

Toes should be at least five yards from the line of scrimmage. Linebackers should not cheat forward on their depth, because the deeper they can play and yet handle plays straight at them, the more field they can cover. Linebacker keys tell them where to go; their depth and angle will get them there. With depth, linebackers can attack upfield as they move toward the ball rather than stepping flat and parallel to the outside. Depth enables linebackers to attack the line of scrimmage at the proper angle. The advantages of playing at five yards deep include:

- Having an attack mentality
- Getting on blockers quicker
- Playing through blocks at the proper angles in order to avoid taking on a 300-pound lineman straight ahead
- Using agility and quickness to beat blocks
- Getting through open windows due to the speed of the press
- Keying on the run
- Getting outside quicker after the initial attack step (If no ball threat and no back threat, they can redirect and get outside. Depth gives provides leverage.

Technique

Because the defense is an attacking scheme, the linebackers should have an attack mentality for the defense to succeed. The approach for the linebackers includes the following:

- Attacks; doesn't catch.
- Forces; doesn't shuffle.
- Runs through the blockers, not around.
- Attacks and reacts on run.
- Must be a great attacker, great reactor, and great adjuster.

The linebackers never want to take on blockers at the depth at which they line up. To stress this concept, coaches should emphasize PST and SSS.

- PST
  - ✓**P**ress the line of scrimmage.
  - ✓**S**hock and shed.
  - ✓**T**ackle.
- SSS
  - ✓**S**hock and shed.
  - ✓**S**tay on the feet.
  - ✓**S**warm.

For a linebacker, football is a game of angles, leverage, eyes, instincts, and trust. Trust knows where help comes from. The linebackers should realize that a blocker is assigned to them on every play. Thus, it is important for them to properly read with their eyes the angle of the back, because doing so helps them defeat the blockers and make tackles with leverage.

Discipline and the ability to think and play fast are a prerequisite for success.

- Linebackers must be disciplined with their:
  ✓ Key
  ✓ Alignment
  ✓ Depth
- Linebackers must think and play fast when they:
  ✓ Key
  ✓ Press
  ✓ Attack
  ✓ Shed
  ✓ React
  ✓ Redirect

Initial Step and Key

The linebackers' initial attack step is short and quick—pick and place. It is important to maintain a tight base so they can redirect without getting overextended. The offensive line and backs take the linebackers to their first step by providing them an immediate key for flow, attack points, and gap responsibilities. The defense is a gap-control defense with a big stress on angles and attack points. Yet with offenses using so much zone blocking, misdirection, pulling linemen, and split flow, the gaps tend to get cloudy and unclear. Therefore, it is important to coach them about angles, attack points, and expanding and reducing to open windows. The linebackers should know three things on his initial step and key:

- Whether he is a frontside or backside linebacker
- Whether the ball is tight or wide
- Whether the play is fast or slow
  ✓ High and fast—sweep, stretch, speed option
  ✓ Low and fast—dive option, veer option
  ✓ High and slow—power, sprint draw, draw
  ✓ Low and slow—trap, cut, fullback roll, midline iso

The offensive linemen and backs should take the linebacker to his first attack step. Then, the angle of the back and blocking scheme should take them to their commitment. Emphasis again is on great first-step quickness—attacking and reacting without any false steps. The linebackers' eyes should carry their feet to the hole. At this point, the linebackers should be adjusting their attack point to the angle of the back and the ball and finding daylight. The linebackers should press from their depth to their gap responsibility from the inside-out (or outside-in, depending on their instincts). Linebackers should trust their instincts. If daylight appears in their gap, they should run through it. If clutter appears in their gap, they should pitchfork to daylight and expand or reduce their press according to the back's angle. Physically or mentally fills in the A or B gap, depending on the angle of the back. If no blocking threat or back/ball threat as press is encountered, redirects with depth, keeps shoulders square, keeps inside-out leverage, and looks for back/ball to show outside. It is important to press the line of scrimmage with speed and quickness, and with the shoulders square to the ballcarrier. Must always be ready to make a speed adjustment to the angle of the back and space. Whether expanding or reducing with the back's angle, it must be done with speed. The linebackers should attack and find the bubble, and take away the soft spot the ballcarrier is searching for. Must attack upfield, and be ready to hit and shed the blocker on the first or second step. Linebackers should check and fill all holes in the direction of flow as they speed up or throttle down their press. Again, they should find the fit according to open windows and the angle of the back. The following points should be ingrained in the linebackers to be successful:

- Must strike upfield.
- Must attack with speed.
- If the gap is clear, must run through.
- If the gap is taken, must bounce to daylight and the angle of the back.
- Must finish.

Instinct is the most important trait that linebackers must possess to be able to play the position successfully. Again, instinct involves being able to feel the need to pitchfork to the anticipated angle of the back a step ahead of his move as the linebacker keys and feels on the run. The pitchfork to the angle of the back needs to be done with speed and power. The linebacker should use a good cat-and-mouse technique; the linebacker is the cat, so he should use those quick cat-like instincts. He should beat the ballcarrier to daylight, and trap the mouse while searching out the bubble or soft spot of the defense. He needs to beat him to daylight, and win the one-on-one collision battle with explosion and desire (e.g., "knock 'em back").

Attack Keys for Success

- Linebackers should never attack straight ahead. They should use a B-gap angle on plays toward, and an A-gap angle on plays away.
- Movement and attack of the defensive line is the key for linebackers. If the defensive line gets more horizontal zone blocks than vertical zone blocks, the offensive line is not able to climb as quickly to the second level.
- Linebackers must take an initial fast press. They should fast flow or cut flow according to the angle of the back and the ball.

- The cut play triggers an attack mentality: "knock 'em back." Linebackers must use a fast attack and fast press on the cut play because they have nothing to run to.

- When adjusting attack points to angles and space, linebackers should do it with speed, quickness, and explosion.

- On the cut, power off tackle, and sprint draw, linebackers should attack and penetrate the vertical break of the ball according to daylight. No ball, no penetration.

- Linebackers should call out backfield sets. If it is not called verbally, each linebacker should make sure to take note of it mentally.

- Press keys are determined by the angle of the back, where help comes from, and daylight or darkness. Press keys are: stay on the initial path, expand, reduce, fast flow, and cut flow.

- B-gap angle players on flow toward should play the B gap from the outside-in. They cannot be pinned inside by the down block or scoop of the offensive tackle.

- A-gap angle players on flow away should play the A gap from the inside-out. They must keep the arm free to the side of flow, and run through blocks, not away from or around.

- Pre-snap keys help anticipation; post-snap keys provide the edge to finish with success.

Attack Point and Angles

Many defensive coaches have contemplated the concept of using attack points and angles in connection with or without gap responsibility. Some coaches have eliminated talk about gaps, and others remain committed to the gap-control concept. Both attack points and gap-control concepts complement one another very well. Initially, the linebacker's first step should mirror the back's angle, which will fit him to the A, B, C, or D point. It is important to teach the plays that attack these gap points as illustrated in Figure 6-7.

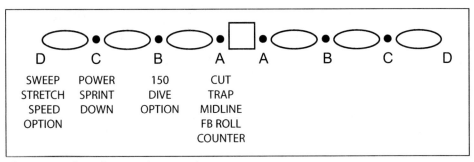

Figure 6-7. Plays that attack gap points

The step of the back should immediately tell the linebacker whether he is a frontside or backside linebacker. With the A point (or B point, etc.) reference tied in with the back's angle, linebackers can aggressively attack the line of scrimmage with a better anticipation of the play being run. He is considered a frontside linebacker if the back has stepped toward him in the B point or wider.

Anything inside the B point makes him a backside linebacker. After the first step, the back and the ball will seek to find the bubble or soft spot, so the linebacker should be ready to expand or redirect to the back's angle. The linebacker keys the linemen and visualizes the backs. If the linebacker steps to the "A" gap, he gets a great counter key because he looks through the offside guard's pull, and becomes ready to redirect with speed to the new angle of the ball. It is important that the linebacker trusts his key and reacts to it with speed and quickness. This trust will enable a linebacker to execute with confidence the proper attack point technique.

Technique Versus the Base Block and the Cut Block

Base Block

Linebackers should play all blocks as if they were base blocks, yet always expect the cut block. Success in defeating the base block requires the following techniques:

- Playing with your knees bent at all times—staying in the knees
- Keeping feet hot
- Attacking at the proper angle
- Using good hand placement
- Leveraging the blocker—pad under pad

The linebackers should attack the blocker at the proper angle to break the momentum of the block with the hat, hands, and upper body. They should shoot the hands toward the throat or top of the numbers, to get a good fit on the breastplate. Should shoot the hands up, not out—through the man, not to the man—and grab cloth. Hands should be inside the framework of the blocker's hands with the elbows tight to the body. The quickest and tightest hands to contact win the battle. Hands need to operate above the eyes with the elbows tucked; hands below the chin are too low. Both feet should be in the ground on contact; the feet should accelerate upfield, not out. The blocker is most vulnerable at the moment of contact. The first player to move his feet after initial contact is the winner. Always remember: quick hands and quick feet, tight hands and tight feet are the key. Again, the quickest and tightest hand and feet after contact are victorious.

The linebacker uses the following progression:
- Attacks.
- Uses proper angle.
- Shocks the opponent.
- Grabs cloth.
- Bench-presses off.
- Separates and sheds/disengages and escapes.
- Swarms to the ball.

Clears the blocker with a lockout or push-pull technique to get his shoulders perpendicular to the line of scrimmage while the linebackers' shoulders stay parallel. Yanks and rips, or yanks and swims as the linebackers escape off the block. Explodes off the block with quickness, speed, and power. Clears the shoulders and hips. Remember: the flatter, the tighter, and the quicker the linebackers are, the better they are.

Cut Block

The blockers attempt to contact the linebackers below the waist on the cut block. The linebackers should try to make the area between their shoulder pads and knees as small as possible. They should keep their knees bent and punch the blocker down and out to create separation. The lead hand should be on the helmet, and the back hand on the shoulder pad. Attacks with the hands, and gives with the feet. The hands and feet should always be working upfield. Separates not only with the pads, but with the feet. Explodes off the block with speed and power, keeping inside-out leverage on the ballcarrier. If the blocker does get outside, it may be necessary for the linebackers to punch the blocker and give ground to get around. Once the blocker is cleared, regains the lost ground as the linebacker presses to the ball.

Coaching Points

Points of emphasis on linebacker technique versus the base and cut blocks include:
- Attacks with eyes, hands, and feet.
- Attacks and elevates the blocker.
- Doesn't let feet or hands die on contact.
- Keeps hands and feet inside the framework of the blocker moving upfield.
- Uses violent separation not only with shoulder pads, but also with feet.
- Push/pull on lockout—attacks the hard shoulder (power through), and pulls on the soft shoulder.

Bluffing/Disguise

Bluffing should be simple and effective. It is a tool used to help create uncertainty in the minds of the offensive team. The idea is to create doubt and confusion; make it a weapon that the offense needs to deal with. Allow defensive players to be creative with the disguise, so they will have fun with it and will feel comfortable about using it in a game. Bluffing should not be minimized by the coaching staff. Not only talk about bluffing daily in meetings and on the field, but have the players doing it in a 5- to 10-minute period apart from team time. During this period, they can execute the disguise, coaches can make corrections, and in the process they gain confidence in what coaches seek to accomplish. Once this goal is achieved, they will find a comfort level in executing a disguise in a game. Bluff alignment calls can be tagged onto the defensive signals to remind them of movement prior to the snap of the ball. The following words can be used to designate disguise alignments:

- *Up:* Aligns three yards deep.
- *Tough:* Aligns on the heels of the defensive line.
- *Bluff:* Lines up inside the defensive linemen, and threatens the line of scrimmage.
- *Quick:* Uses a quick move to line of scrimmage. Gets up and then gets back, or gets up and stays up.

The key in any disguise is not to lose key discipline on any pre-snap moves. It is important, with regard to when the ball will be snapped, to understand how the quarterback moves when under the center and when he is aligned in the shotgun. When the quarterback is under the center, he is constantly moving his head to make checks and so forth. Usually, when his head gets still and he looks upfield through the defense, the ball will probably be snapped in two counts. In the shotgun, the key is off the raised leg of the quarterback or his open hands. Another key is the raised head of the center just prior to the snap. In both cases, the ball will probably be snapped in two counts. These snap keys can help linebackers better coordinate their blitz movement and disguise. The surprise element of the bluff needs to be continually practiced, so the offense is never able to get a pattern on the disguise. As an example: quarterbacks generally are taught that if the linebackers are up on the line of scrimmage, they are showing blitz but are not coming. It is important for the defense to not only show blitz from that alignment, but show and come, show and not come, not show and not come, and not show and come. The defense should try to force the offense into a guessing game on whether linebackers are blitzing or not. Once they start guessing, the defense has created the uncertainty needed to be successful in the bluff package. Following are some thoughts to consider incorporating into the bluff package. Not all of these aspects will be used in every game, but when game planning, three or four that the coaches think will be most effective that week can be picked.

- Blitzing out of the fake look; dropping into coverage out of the fake look
- Emphasizing outside disguises over inside bluffs (Generally, outside disguises create more problems than inside bluffs.)
- Coordinating front disguise and secondary disguise—press, show man, four across
- Showing inside blitz, and coming with outside blitz—same side or opposite side
- Showing linebacker up on the inside, and blitzing strong safety or cornerback from the opposite side
- Showing outside blitz, and coming with inside blitz—same side or opposite side
- Showing outside blitz to one side, and coming with outside blitz on the opposite side
- Showing inside blitz to one side, and coming with inside blitz on the opposite side

If a disguise concept is installed into the defensive scheme, the team needs to work hard at making it a weapon for success. It should also fit into the overall defensive package. Points for linebackers to remember include:

- Seeing keys at all times
- Maintaining the same type of stance to eliminate the pre-snap read
- Being in good football position and ready to play, whether moving up or back
- Not being afraid of getting caught up inside the defensive linemen's stance (If the ball is snapped, linebackers should bounce back to depth, and key and react.)
- Not being distracted by worrying about the disguise (This maneuver is meant to help, not hurt, the defense. If a player does not feel comfortable in doing it because it is a distraction, the coach should tell him to just play, and not worry about it. Some players have a better feel for doing it than others.)

Man Coverage

When the linebackers play man coverage, it is imperative that they understand what the receiver is trying to do. Their goal is to accomplish the following:

- Getting the defender head-up
- Influencing the defender deep
- Making the defender move in the opposite direction of his final cut

A majority of the time, the linebackers will be covering the backs, but the techniques are the same for a back, tight end, or wide receiver. The linebacker works upfield, and establishes an inside position; he doesn't overrun the receiver's inside number. He realizes everything will be a speed move. It is important to be strong on one side of the receiver. The linebacker overplays the inside routes, and remains close on outside routes. He doesn't lose inside position on the release or the route of the receiver. He covers the receiver tight, so as to not be susceptible to head and step fakes. He collisions the receiver if possible—not a knock-him-down collision, but a slow-him-down, reroute collision; he doesn't miss the receiver in the open field. When playing man coverage, the linebacker always concentrates on the receiver; he must be receiver-conscious, not ball-conscious. He keeps the focus low, so as not to be misled by head-and-shoulder fakes. He maintains great concentration at all times while looking for any transitional tips:

- Chopping feet
- Putting the hand brake on
- Dropping his hips and butt
- Keying the body lean of receivers

If one of these indicators is read, the linebacker gathers to transition quickly into coverage on the break. He plants and drives on the receiver, and determines whether or not to intercept, deflect with the far arm and wrap with the near arm, or run through—explode through the break.

WINNING DEFENSIVE FOOTBALL

If the linebacker doesn't see intent by the receiver to break, he should prepare to lock on the inside hip and run with him on the deep route. He must be in position to collision all second breaks if the receiver accelerates out of a short-route indicator. Once the deep route materializes, he quickly determines phase relationship with the receiver. The phase will be decided by whether the receiver can be touched with the near hand. If out of phase (he can't make a touch with hand), he immediately turns and runs to regain position on receiver. On the linebacker's wheel to catch the receiver, he doesn't turn his eyes back to the quarterback. Eyes to the quarterback will slow down the defender and create a bigger separation between him and the receiver. He doesn't panic, and maintains poise with the back to the ball. He must remember that he is not beat deep until the receiver catches the ball. He sprints to regain position on the receiver and gain ground on the ball. The goal is to catch his eyes, not his feet. He concentrates on the receiver's hands and eyes. When the receivers hands go up to catch the ball, the linebacker throws his fist through the receiver's pocket, and knocks the pocket open.

If the linebacker is in phase, then he squeezes into the receiver without contact to take his speed away. He touches the receiver with the near hand low, and touches him often to reduce the receiver's concentration on the ball. Establishes a focus point on the receiver—typically that point is the inside earhole. If the linebacker has him covered, opens inside and reads back to the quarterback. This move turns the defender into a receiver as quickly as possible, and then two receivers are fighting for the ball. If still running with the receiver with the back to the ball, looks when the receiver looks. Simply raises head and eyes when looking for the ball. Doesn't turn the body, as this slows the defender down and creates separation. When the defender does look, he wants to look up, not back, because the ball has been released by the quarterback. If the ball can't be located, pops head back to the receiver and plays through his hands. Destroys the pocket, or rips down the receiver's inside arm to break the timing of the catch. When in position to intercept the deep ball, must have square shoulders, attack at the highest point, get two hands on the ball, and drive for the football; doesn't float into the ball. Remember: the bigger the area the defender tries to key, the less concentration he will have. He must reduce focus, which will expand concentration.

Pass Coverage

Pattern Read Pass Coverage

Linebackers need to be aware of these factors in their pattern read pass coverage:

- Knowing down-and-distance
- Knowing where he is on the field
- Knowing that receivers are numbered from the outside in from both sides, with the widest receivers being #1 followed by #2 and #3 (Figure 6-8)

- Knowing how the offense will attack—horizontally, vertically, or a combination
- Knowing the width of the widest receiver—determines the curl area

When linebackers pattern read, they drop over receivers. Must see the receivers and the ball, be inside and underneath, and keep eyes on a swivel, not head. Defenders landmark receivers, not spots on the field and read on the way into the width and depth of the drop, according to the release and route of the #2 or #3 receivers. Adjusts the drop on the run, and either expands or tightens the landmark as he pattern reads the receiver. Focus on the following route combinations:

- *#2 vertical:* Reroutes and reads to #1; seeks a peek. Looks for the under route from #1 or delay by #3 from the inside-out.
- *#2 flat, to the outside:* Expands to #1 coming inside—slant, dig, and under routes. If no inside threat, settles and looks for routes coming inside-out first, then outside-in.
- If somebody is underneath, somebody will be behind—levels routes. Works from the depth of the drop to the front of the drop. Wheels underneath the inside routes on a pattern read. It is like a centerfield turn in baseball. It is important to be tight in the turn and gain speed and depth in the wheel, and get the head, eyes, and hands around quickly to relocate the quarterback and the flight of the ball. The success of underneath coverage will be based on the following factors:

  ✓ Getting an accurate read on the release and route of the #2 and #3 receivers
  ✓ Increasing the distance moved before the quarterback releases the ball (Linebackers should try to get one more yard in their break.)
  ✓ Adjusting drops according to the routes being run
  ✓ Tightening the coverage on the look of the quarterback

If no threat of a new #2 or #3, and no under route, gets depth to the look of the quarterback, fast breaks on the quarterback's eyes.

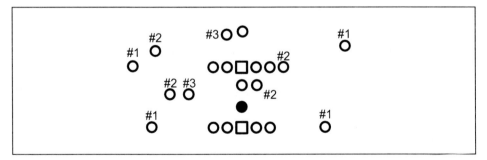

Figure 6-8. Receiver numbers

Spot Drop Pass Coverage

With spot drop, linebackers need to understand alignment of receivers, spacing, the attitude of the quarterback, and over and under threats. They should drop over receivers. They should know where the #2 and #3 receivers are prior to the snap of the ball. Eyes should be constantly on the quarterback. Reads the routes off the eyes and shoulders of the quarterback. Gets quick depth with an explosive open, drop step, crossover, and sprint technique; gets a 12- to 14-yard drop, and adjusts off the look and set of the quarterback. Depth gives the defender leverage on the routes and the quarterback's ball release. Stays inside and underneath the receiver, and pins his inside hip; doesn't be even or above the receiver. Reroutes the receiver by drop or by collision. Once depth is gained, then speeds up or throttles down according to the feel of the route being run. Keeps the throwing lanes or windows tight by the drop. Any question on the break of the quarterback's eyes, then breaks inside and looks for work.

Blitzing

Blitzing is an integral part of both run and pass defense (Figure 6-9). When used intelligently, it is an extremely effective way of destroying blocking patterns or putting pressure on the passer.

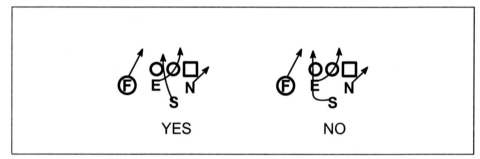

YES   NO

Figure 6-9. Correct and incorrect blitz techniques

- *Alignment:* It is important to hide the blitz, and yet it is imperative to be in a position to get off on the snap of the ball. Alignment must be such that the blitz is hidden but allows for maximum get-off.
- *Key:* Keying the ball.
- *Get-off:* This technique includes not only acceleration on the snap, but taking the most direct route. If blitzing with a lineman, it is imperative to drive over the heels of the lineman and not "round" the attack.
- *Neutralization—pass-rush techniques:*
  ✓ Shoulder dip: A linebacker usually takes on a back when blitzing, thus starts with the concept the linebacker will overpower the back with a hard charge shoulder blasted into the back's chest. Desire to get the passer is the prime factor in the pass rush, and the shoulder dip fits into this aggressive attitude.

   ✓ Leg over: When a back decides to cut a blitzing linebacker, the linebacker can use a leg over to give him a chance to pressure the passer. The key is for the linebacker to keep his feet and keep moving.

   ✓ If a run develops: The linebacker should get low and prepare to take on blockers or flatten down the line of scrimmage if the play goes away.

- *Escape:* Using the hands to throw the blocker is the primary technique used. Can also start on an inside rush route to try to force the back to take an inside blocking position and then grab and slip to the outside. This technique would be used when rushing up the middle.

- *Hands up:* The hands-up technique is a must when the quarterback takes his left hand off the ball as he gets ready to throw. This technique will impair the quarterback's vision and will upset his timing.

- *Coaching Points:*

   ✓ When blitzing inside backers, the secondary has primary pass coverage on the backs. It is important for the blitzing linebackers to eliminate any threat that may attempt to release inside for a pass. Failure to eliminate any threat will create coverage difficulties for the secondary.

   ✓ Searching out the draw: Never pass up a potential ballcarrier. Always secure any threat until certain he does not have the ball.

   ✓ Blitzing the assigned gap: In a gap-control defense, blitzes are designed to secure all gaps. Must not freelance. Should be prepared to adjust blitz path if a blocker seals an inside gap.

   ✓ Staying low: Attacks assigned gap with bent knees; should always grab grass in practice.

   ✓ Reading on the run: Plays recognition during a blitz is of the utmost importance. Must be aggressive, but should not be a blind hog. Reads.

- *Flow read blitzes:* Many blitzes are made with a flow call. Flow tells the linebacker that he will only blitz if the flow is toward him. If flow goes away, he plays base technique.

- *Bluff is used three ways in the blitz package:*

   ✓ Bluff without a designated blitz call tells the inside backer to show blitz but come out before the ball is snapped. The linebacker should use his imagination and develop a feel for how long he can maintain a blitz fake. Coaches should give him a key to help him. The 25-second clock may be a great key for offense or quarterback tendencies.

   ✓ Bluff with a designated blitz call tells linebackers to show the blitz and run it from that position.

   ✓ Bluff can also be used in conjunction with slide or stem:

      ❑ Slide bluff: Lines up in base and slides or moves to a bluff off the stem call.

      ❑ Bluff slide: Lines up in bluff, and slides or moves to base alignment off the stem call.

Blitz Technique

By bluffing and showing a disguise look, the defense can eliminate any pre-snap read for the offense that would indicate blitz. Linebackers should accelerate out of their stances on the snap and get downhill. It is important to get quickness with the first step at the proper angle. He emphasizes get-off and angles. He feels the width of the gap as he reads the ball flow. He reads on the run as he blitzes with the eyes—great vision. He attacks the assigned gap with bent knees, stays low, and goes hard and quickly. He must be relentless. A blitzer should always remember that a gap may move, but it never changes. The linebacker doesn't blitz to get blocked—he attacks daylight (space or open window); he doesn't attack the man. When the window moves, the linebacker moves. He anticipates the ball in the assigned gap. If run, he gets big in the assigned gap and makes the play. He gets penetration on the blitz, and must be ready to spill the gap. He blitzes the gap, and flattens in or flattens out, according to the ball's angle. On ball away, he pursues with the mind-set of being the first one "there" when the roll is called at the ball. He pursues with the heart. When he gets penetration on a pass, he sees the quarterback. If the quarterback is in his vision, he closes the distance, gathers, and grabs cloth. He doesn't try to knock the quarterback out; the linebacker merely secures him, because immediate help will come. He prevents the scramble. If the quarterback is out of his vision, the linebacker closes on him, wraps him up high, and goes for the throwing arm to create a fumble. If the offensive line stops penetration or can't get to the quarterback, then the linebacker mirrors the passer's release, gets big in the rush lane, and gets his hand up. He should remember that one arm is longer than two when playing through blockers. When blitzing, he should make something happen that is positive for the defense. Very few times will a stunt go unblocked. He must be ready to whip blocks, dominate the assigned gap, and make plays—he allows no stalemates.

Following is a quick, ready-to-use list when on the field and teaching the blitz technique, or in a blitzing period:

- No pre-snap read is needed.
- First step quickness with vision.
- Maintain the proper angle.
- Attack daylight.
- If the gap moves, the linebacker moves.
- Anticipate the ball.
- Run—get big.
- Pass—get small and slip.
- If the ball is away, flatten in and flatten out.
- Pass rush with quarterback vision.
- Maintain relentless pursuit.

Five-Man Rushes With an Inside Linebacker Blitz

Five-man rushes with a linebacker blitz can be called in a variety of situations:
- Field: Wideside or the boundary
- Formation strength: Strongside or weakside of the formation
- Back: Toward the back (tilt), or opposite the back (numbers)
- Formation with the tight end: Toward the tight end or away (split side)

Crash: When the crash linebacker blitz is called, a swap, trio, or twist stunt by the defensive line on the opposite side of the blitzer can be called. Tilt crash is a blitz toward the back, and numbers crash is a blitz away from the back.

Tilt crash (Figure 6-10): Crash blitz toward the back

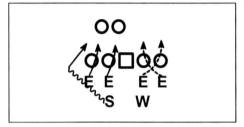 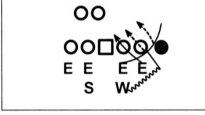

Figure 6-10. Tilt crash (toward the back)   Figure 6-11. Numbers crash spy (away from the back)

Numbers crash spy (Figure 6-11): The linebacker can blitz either inside or outside the offensive tackle. He can also call swap for the defensive linemen on the opposite side of the blitz.

Crash echo (Figure 6-12): The defensive end goes upfield with speed, and the linebacker blitzes off the defensive end's butt. The linebacker reads the offensive tackle on the move. If the offensive tackle blocks down, the linebacker goes outside the tackle and stays inside the block of the back. The defensive end stays outside the block of the back. A wrap, swap, or trio line stunt can be called on the opposite side of the crash echo.

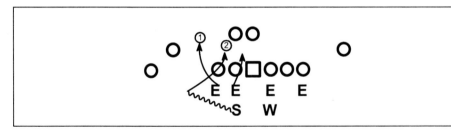

Figure 6-12. Crash echo

Weak blast trio (Figures 6-13 and 6-14): Like with crash, wrap, swap, or trio can be called for the defensive linemen on the opposite side of blitz.

Blast pick (Figure 6-15): The linebacker has outside force on the ball. He should keep his shoulders square on the tackle to prevent the quarterback from scrambling. Wrap, swap, twist, or trio can be called for the defensive lineman on the opposite side of blitz.

Twist attack (Figure 6-16): The linebacker needs to give the twist time to develop before blitzing. Takes a drop or shuffle step first. The linebacker has a two-way go on the center, meaning he can go into either A gap.

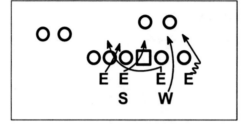

Figure 6-13. Weak blast trio

Figure 6-14. Weak blast twist

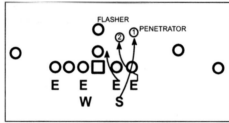
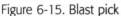
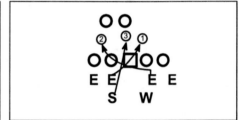

Figure 6-15. Blast pick

Figure 6-16. Twist attack

7

Outside Linebacker Play

Solid performance by the outside linebackers (Falcons and Studs) is necessary for a defense to be a dominating and successful unit. The players who play these overhang, or edge, defender positions must be versatile and fundamentally sound. They must have no weaknesses, must be masters of all techniques, and must be playmakers on the field. It takes an elite player to play one of these positions. These players should have the physical ability to play the run like inside linebackers and be proficient cover players who can defend like defensive backs.

Mentally, the outside linebackers should be committed to understanding both the fronts and secondary of the defense, and how they fit into both aspects. The position requires playmakers who are great students of the game.

Outside Linebacker Basics

Characteristics

- Recognized leader on the field
- Mentally and physically tough
- Plays with great emotion
- Playmaker
- Versatile
- Fundamentally sound and technique conscious

Fundamentals

- Plays with the knees bent and the feet underneath the hips.
- Learns to stay on the feet.
- Learns to unlock the hips. (Hip flexibility is crucial.)
- Plays with the hands.
- Plays fast—reacts.

Expectations

- Must be on time for everything.
- Must be prepared for all meetings and practices.
- Must learn assignments so as to play fast.
- Must trust coaches and teammates.
- Must always put the team first.

CASKREPT

The linebacker must know the following elements on every play:
- **C**all—both in the huddle and at the line
- **A**lignment—must be exact
- **S**tance—must allow to execute
- **K**ey—both man and backfield action
- **R**esponsibility—area to defend
- **E**xecution—technique used
- **P**ursuit—proper angle to ball
- **T**ackle—end the play

Tackling

An in-depth discussion of tackling fundamentals and techniques is presented in Chapter 4. However, the following list is a review of the basics:
- Eye the target.
- Close the distance.
- Sink the hips.
- Contact chest-to-chest.
- Club the arms, and grab cloth.
- Roll the hips.
- Buzz the feet.
- Finish.

Dos and Don'ts

Do	Don't
Get aligned early.	Be late in alignment.
Concentrate.	Daydream.
Stay low.	Be erect.
Hit a blow.	Catch.
Move feet.	Let the feet die.
Shed.	Lean.
Get to the ball.	Loaf.
Tackle.	Miss tackles.

Winning Tips for Falcon and Stud

- Must concentrate—this is the single-most important asset.
- Must recognize the play—it is essential in order to anticipate assignment.
- Must not get cut off—should not waste steps.
- Must deliver a neutralizing blow to the blocker.
- Must play square across the blocker's head.
- Must never miss a tackle. Must wrap up and use the legs.
- Must never take for granted the tackle has been made.
- Must tackle through the ballcarrier.
- Must do everything possible to get in on every play.
- Must take pride in staying on the feet. Must stay off the ground.
- Must always take the proper pursuit angle.
- Must sprint intelligently into pass coverage.
- Must read the quarterback and break on his throwing motion.
- Must catch the ball twice when making an interception: once when catching it, and again when tucking it away.
- Must disguise the final alignment; must keep the quarterback guessing.
- Must never tip off a blitz.
- Must never be late on the snap of the ball when blitzing.

General Rules Pertinent to Outside Linebackers

- Must never be offside. If the defensive man jumps offside and doesn't make contact, he should get back before the ball is snapped. He must always check alignment.
- Must make simultaneous contact with the offensive man if he jumps offside. Should not hit him late, as this move would be a nullifying penalty.
- Must fall on fumbles in heavy traffic areas. Must scoop and score a fumble in the backfield or in an open area.
- Must recover all passes that don't cross the line of scrimmage. The referee can decide whether it is forward or lateral.
- Must not make a late hit after the quarterback has thrown the ball, or when the runner is down or out of bounds. Must be the nastiest "legal" player.
- Must defeat the opponent with upper body strength since crackback blocks below the waist by wide receivers are a penalty in college.
- An eligible receiver who is forced out of bounds during a down may come back inbounds and make a legal catch.
- Once a pass has been tipped, pass interference is no longer possible.
- A player must have the required number of feet inbounds in order for a catch to be legal.
- No pass interference can be called on the offensive side of the line of scrimmage.

Techniques and Keys on the Tight-End Side

9 Technique (Figure 7-1): Aligns the inside foot on tight end's outside foot and 12 inches to a yard off the ball. Lines up wide enough so as to not be hooked. Two-point, parallel, or outside foot slightly back, with knees bent, back flat, and in good hitting position. Keys the hat of the tight end; visualizes the near back and the ball.

8 Technique (Figure 7-2): Angles inside at a 45-degree angle, and aligns one yard off the ball and one yard outside them tight end. Adjusts width and depth according to the scheme and ability. Keys through the tight end to the near back and the ball. Plays blocks similar to a 9 technique. Must not be hooked, and forces the D gap with an attack mentality.

Figure 7-1. 9 technique   Figure 7-2. 8 technique

6 Technique (Figure 7-3): Reads the tight end's chest for initial responsibility. Aligns head-up on the tight end (his feet will mirror the feet of the tight end). Secures the C gap. If the tight end blocks down, the linebacker comes off his hip for C-gap responsibility. Plays inside-out on outside runs.

Figure 7-3. 6 technique

7 Technique (Figure 7-4): Aligns his outside eye to the tight end's inside eye. Secures C-gap responsibility. The tight end can never release across the face to the inside. Plays inside-out to the ball going outside. Reads the tight end's chest for initial responsibility.

Jet Technique (Figure 7-5): Used for a better angle on an outside rush.

Figure 7-4. 7 technique   Figure 7-5. Jet technique

Techniques and Keys on the Split-End Side

5 Technique (Figure 7-6): Aligns inside foot slightly inside the offensive tackle's outside foot. Keys through the tackle to the near back for initial responsibility.

Attack 5 Technique: Aligns inside foot back with the inside hand down. Keys the ball, and attacks through the V of the neck of the offensive tackle.

Jet Technique (Figure 7-7): Used for a better angle for an outside rush.

Hip Technique (Figure 7-8): Aligns five to six yards off the line of scrimmage two to three yards outside the defensive end. Usually used when aligned into the boundary. Keys through the offensive tackle to the near back for initial responsibility. Plays as deep as possible while still remaining able to react back to the line of scrimmage. Depth provides leverage.

Walk-Away Technique (Figure 7-9): Aligns seven yards off the line of scrimmage. Splits the difference between the offensive tackle and the wide receiver. Keys through the offensive tackle to the nearback for initial responsibility. Doesn't cheat on depth because depth provides leverage.

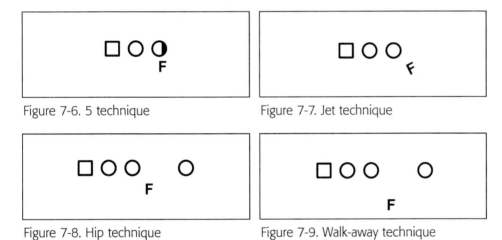

Figure 7-6. 5 technique   Figure 7-7. Jet technique

Figure 7-8. Hip technique   Figure 7-9. Walk-away technique

Triangle Technique (Figure 7-10): Aligns seven yards off the line of scrimmage. Aligns according to the width of the #2 receiver. Keys through the offensive tackle to the nearback for initial responsibility. If the wide receiver is closer to the tackle, the triangle technique stays outside at 1x7. If the wide receiver is closer to outside receiver than tackle, the triangle technique stays inside at one to three yards and seven yards deep. Keys through the offensive tackle to the near back for initial responsibility. If the #2 receiver is closer to the #1 receiver, aligns in the midpoint between the tackle and #2 receiver, but closer to the tackle than the receiver. If the #2 receiver is closer to the tackle, assumes an outside alignment on #2 one yard outside at the initial depth of seven yards.

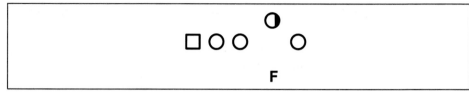

Figure 7-10. Triangle technique

Playing the Base Block

- Must stop offensive movement.
- Must stay in the knees (knees bent) in order to play with the hands.
- Must take a six-inch attack step.
- Must get number-on-number, feet-on-feet, and hat-on-hat with both feet in the ground on contact.
- Must put the helmet under the chin; bite his throat—low pad wins.
- Must shoot the hands at eye level (or above) and grab cloth.
- Must break the momentum of the block with the pads and helmet.
- Must keep the hands inside with the elbows tight—no strength exists with the hands inside and the elbows outside.
- Must have the quickest and tightest hands to the breastplate to win the battle.
- Must not let the feet die on contact. Keep the feet alive and tight through contact—no dead feet.
- Must make the first movement of feet after contact.
- Must attack—shock, bench, shed, swarm
- Must escape off the bench
  - ✓ Push and pull (lock out)
  - ✓ Yank and rip
  - ✓ Yank and swim

Base Alignments for Falcons and Studs

Figure 7-11 illustrates the base alignments for the various types of offensive formations that the outside linebackers will face. The Falcon always aligns to the strength of the formation, except in hammer and flex (hammer and flex are explained in detail in Chapter 13). Anytime the ball is on the hash or within three yards of the hash, strength is to the field. The Stud always aligns to the weakside of the formation or opposite of the Falcon. The Stud should do a great job of disguise and always start from a cover-2 shell. The Falcon's alignment versus a double width formation is determined by the alignment of the inside receiver. If the inside receiver is closer to the tackle than the #1 receiver, he stays outside at one yard outside and seven yards deep. If the inside receiver is closer to #1, he aligns one yard inside at seven yards deep.

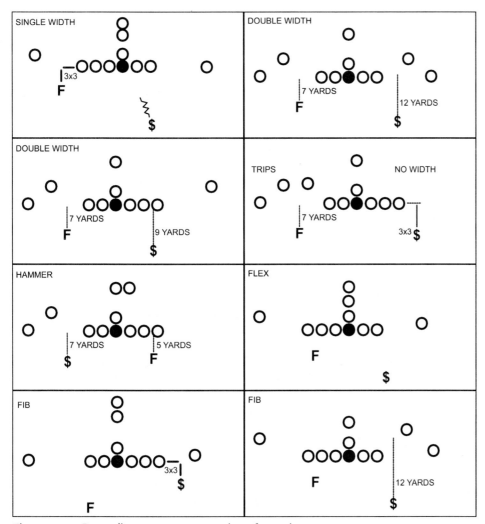

Figure 7-11. Base alignments versus various formations

Communication With Eighth Man in the Box

Anytime the outside linebackers are in the box, they should communicate by giving the inside linebackers an "I'm here" call. The Falcon gives the linebackers an "I'm here" call in the hammer defense or when motion changes strength. The Stud gives an "I'm here" call to the linebackers in cover 6 when they have a single receiver and no tight end to their side (Figure 7-12). When in coverage, the Stud gives a "combo," "robber," "cloud," or "bracket" call to the corner and Will linebacker before every snap.

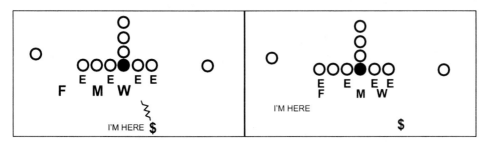

Figure 7-12. "I'm here" call

Run Techniques

Fit: Technique used by the Stud versus single-back zone-blocking schemes.

Force: Aggressively attacks the lead blocker, making sure to attack the outside number of the lead blocker and force the ballcarrier back to the inside to where help comes from.

Spill: Anytime safety support is behind the outside linebacker, aggressively attacks a leader blocker. Puts the outside number on his inside number and gets upfield, making the ballcarrier run east and west and into the unblocked defenders.

Stance

Field: Feet no wider than armpit-width, the outside foot back, and the inside foot up (heel-to-toe stagger); hips low, toes pointed toward the goal line, knees bent, and hands held low (defensive back stance)

9 Technique: Feet no wider than shoulder-width; no stagger with the feet; 45-degree angle with butt to the cornerback with the knees bent, hips low, and hands held high.

Dog: Upright stance with weight on the inside forward foot and with the outside foot back; hips are low, knees bent, shoulders square, and hands held low.

Keys

Falcon and Stud Keys

9 Technique 50 (Figure 7-13): Keys the tight end to the near back.

8 Technique (Figure 7-14): Keys tight end and offensive tackle to the tight end side. On the split-end side keys through the offensive tackle to the near back.

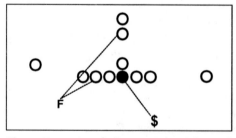 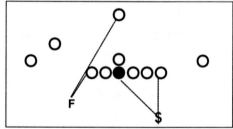

Figure 7-13. 9 technique on the tight-end side

Figure 7-14. 8 technique on the split-end side

Stud Keys on Uncovered Lineman (Figure 7-15)

Robber Technique: Keys the uncovered lineman for the run or pass. Versus pass, gets his eyes on the release and route of #2.

Combo Technique: Keys the uncovered lineman for the run or pass. Versus pass, gets his eyes on the release and route of #2.

Cloud Technique: Keys the uncovered lineman for the run or pass. Versus pass, gets depth and makes sure get to the deep half of the field.

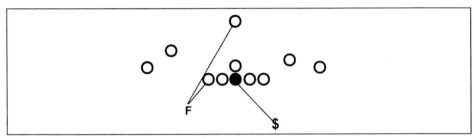

Figure 7-15. Stud keys on uncovered lineman

9 Technique Run Support

Perimeter Support (Figure 7-16): Responsible for outside force and contain. Attacks the V of the neck of the backfield blocker. Attacks with the hands and pads square, and keeps the outside leg back. Meets the blocker as quickly and deep as possible. Reduces the running lane, and forces the ball to cut back or bubble to the outside. With no width or safety support, spills the blocker by ripping through the inside numbers of the lead blocker, and makes the ballcarrier bubble to the outside.

G Scheme (Figure 7-17): Attacks the pulling lineman before he can get his pads turned upfield. Attacks low, and spills the ball outside.

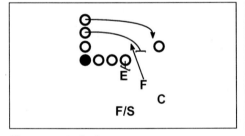   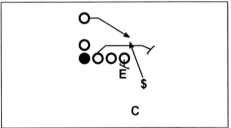

Figure 7-16. Perimeter support   Figure 7-17. G scheme support

Power (Figure 7-18): Attacks the fullback as deep as possible and forces/contains as required. With no width and safety support, spills the ballcarrier to the outside.

Lead (Figures 7-19 and 7-20): On the tight-end side, squeezes the out block by the tight end; makes sure the ball does not bounce outside. On the split-end side, anytime an outside linebacker has an "I'm here" call, attacks the lead back with the inside number on the back's outside number, and forces ball back inside to the inside linebacker.

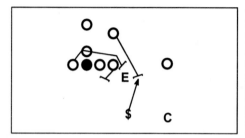

Figure 7-18. Power support

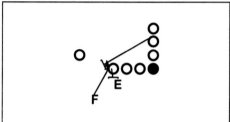

Figure 7-19. Lead support on the tight-end side

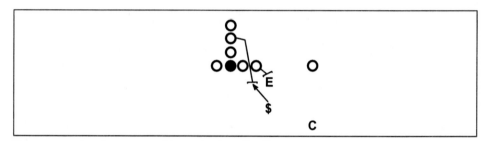

Figure 7-20. Lead support with an I'm here" call

Run Techniques When the Tight End Blocks

Tight-End Turnout (Figure 7-21): Attacks the tight end from the outside-in with the hands, hat, eyes, and hips. Keeps outside leverage with the outside leg free; keeps the shoulders square, and squeezes. Pushes and pulls to square the tight end's shoulders for the squeeze. Does not jump inside; stays outside for the ball to bounce. Reduces the hole with the tight end. Defeats the tight end and works inside once the ball has passed the point of no return.

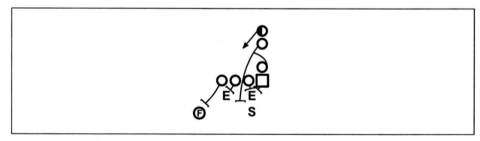

Figure 7-21. Tight-end turnout

Tight End Blocks Defensive End With Lead Guard or Tackle (Figure 7-22): Attacks the line of scrimmage. Leverages the blocker with the hands, hat, eyes, and hips. Reduces the hole from the outside-in. Keeps the shoulders square with the outside leg free. Makes the ball cut back or bounce deep. Attacks the pulling linemen before they get their pads turned upfield. With no width and safety support, spills the ballcarrier to the outside.

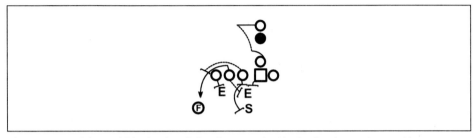

Figure 7-22. Tight end blocks the defensive   end with the lead guard or tackle

Counter (Figure 7-23): Recognizes counter action as quickly as possible, expands vision with flow away. Attacks as tight to the defensive end as possible. Attacks the pulling linemen before they get pads turned upfield, and cuts the cutter. Reduces the hole, and spills the puller. Creates a car wreck.

Flow Away (Figure 7-24): After one to two steps, shuffles and moves around a "picket fence" to get downhill on any cutback threat. Doesn't take off running without knowing where ball is. Expands vision, and reads for different color coming back—remains alert to stop the reverse. Feels and fits on the cutback.

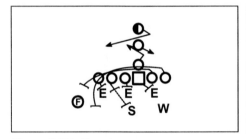

Figure 7-23. Counter

Figure 7-24. Flow away

Lead Option (Figure 7-25): Gains the line of scrimmage. Keeps outside leverage on the lead blocker. Plays in the knees—knees bent, shoulders squeezed, with good hands and feet to defeat the lead blocker. If cover 3, takes the pitch player. If cover 2, takes the alley player (quarterback outside; pitch inside). If cover 6 (quarters), takes the pitch player. On the lead option, the lead-option blocker overrides the veer call.

Dive Option (Figure 7-26): Gains the line of scrimmage. Plays in the knees with the shoulders square. If cover 3, takes the pitch player. If cover 2, takes the alley player (quarterback outside; pitch inside). If cover 6 (quarters) and tight end down, takes the quarterback. If the tight end arcs, takes the pitch.

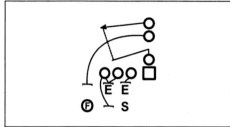

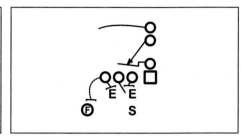

Figure 7-25. Lead option

Figure 7-26. Dive option

9 Technique on Tight-End Side

Base Block (Figure 7-27): Attack-steps. Attacks with the hands, hat, eyes, and hips. Squeezes from the outside-in. Keeps the outside leg and arm free and the shoulders square. Presses the blocker back into the hole; doesn't get turned. Gets big in the hole; reduces the hole with the blocker. Crosses the tight end's face when the ball has passed the point of no return.

Down Block (Figure 7-28): Attack-steps, and squeezes the tight end down. Punches the tight end with the inside hand, and finds the near back and the ball. Keys the first threat inside keying the back to the line of scrimmage. Reads the angle of back as he squeezes inside. Never replaces more than one hole down. If the back is tight, uses the back to squeeze the hole. If the back is wide, gets number-on-number and presses the blocker upfield, keeping the shoulders square. Must be ready to two-gap as he reads the angle of the ballcarrier. Spills all blocks—if he wrong arms, it's hard for the tight end to be wrong.

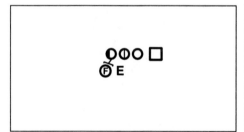
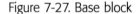

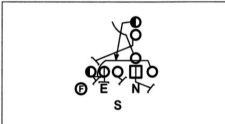

Figure 7-27. Base block

Figure 7-28. Down block

Hook or Reach Block (Figure 7-29): Attack-steps with the hands, hat, eyes, and hips. Steps, presses, and knocks the tight end back. Presses the tight end upfield. Keeps outside leverage with the eyes to the inside. Gets the tight end turned with a good push/pull technique. Plays with the eyes, and keeps the run lane tight with penetration upfield. Stretches the sweep with penetration, and squeezes the running lane with depth upfield.

Counter-Tight End Down Block, Back Away (Figure 7-30): Attack-steps. Squeezes inside; gets the eyes inside for first threat. Spills any blocks from the inside; creates a wreck. Wrong arms and spills. Traps the trapper. Aiming point is the inside knee and the inside number. Forces the ballcarrier and second puller to bounce outside with depth; stretches the counter. Wheels and gets penetration upfield.

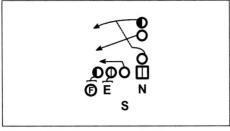

Figure 7-29. Hook or reach block

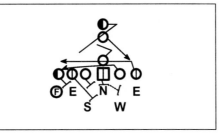

Figure 7-30. Counter

Inside Release With the Ball Away and Cutoff by the Tight End (Figure 7-31): Attack-steps. Attacks with the hands, hat, eyes, and hips. Squeezes from the outside-in. Presses the blocker as he anticipates a "high wall" technique. As a fold player, he may have to give ground to get around the block.

Option With Cover 3 and 2 (Figure 7-32): Attack-steps. Reads the block of the tight end.

- Down block: Responsible for the first ball threat.
- Base block or veer block: Becomes the alley player. Takes the quarterback outside, and the pitch inside. Slow-plays the quarterback to buy time for pursuit.

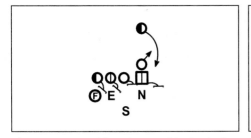

Figure 7-31. Inside release with the ball away and cutoff by the tight end

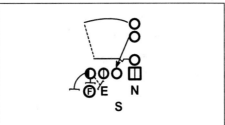

Figure 7-32. Option with cover 3 and 2

Option With Quarters Coverage (Figure 7-33): Acknowledges the "veer" call from the safety. Reads the tight end for option responsibilities. With the tight end down, is responsible for the first ball threat. With the tight end outside, has pitch responsibility; stays outside and in front of ball, never even or behind.

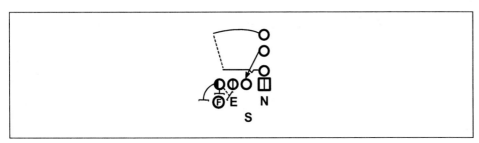

Figure 7-33. Option with quarters coverage

Crack by the Wide Receiver When in the Walk-Away Alignment (Figure 7-34): Recognizes the run. Attacks the wide receiver from the inside-out. Good helmet, eyes, and hands placement. Grabs cloth; maintains a strong push/pull technique. Presses the back; two-gaps, keeps the lane tight, and turns the ball inside.

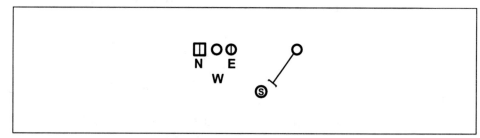

Figure 7-34. Crack by the wide receiver when in the walk-away alignment

Stalk Block—Funnel (Figure 7-35): Recognizes the run. Attacks the receiver with number-on-number. Reads his head:

• Head goes down to cut block: Uses a good cut-block technique.
• Head stays up: Leverages him, and presses him back.

Hits and sheds quickly as he reduces the running lane from the outside-in.

Cut Block (Figure 7-36): Recognizes the run. Presses the line of scrimmage, and attacks with the hands and good knee bend. Front hand on helmet; back hand on the shoulder pad. Bench-presses off the block. Quick releases off the block with the hands and feet. May have to give ground with the feet to get around the block.

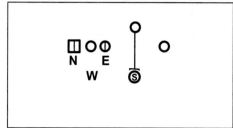 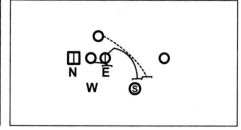

Figure 7-35. Stalk block   Figure 7-36. Cut block

6 or 7 Techniques Versus Run

Drive Block (Figure 7-37): Same as the 9 technique, except keeps inside leverage instead of outside leverage on the tight end.

Down Block (Figure 7-38): Same as the 9 technique. On all kick-out blocks, bounces everything outside.

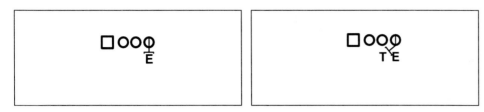

Figure 7-37. Drive block   Figure 7-38. Down block

Hook Block (Figure 7-39): Same as 9 technique except keeps inside leverage on the tight end. Does not cross his face until the ballcarrier is outside of the 9 technique.

Outside Release (Figure 7-40): Respects the hook block, and then gets the eyes back inside for the kick-out block or recognition of the pass.

Figure 7-39. Hook block   Figure 7-40. Outside release

5 Technique Versus Run

Drive Block (Figure 7-41): Keeps outside leverage on the offensive tackle. Must not be driven off the ball.

Down Block (Figure 7-42): Reads the quarterback for the run or pass. Keeps outside leverage on all inside-out blocks. If option shows, his responsibility is the quarterback.

Hook Block (Figure 7-43): Keeps the outside pad free. Must not be driven off the ball.

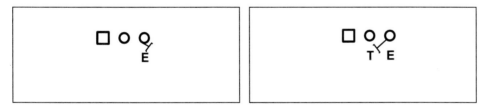

Figure 7-41. Drive block   Figure 7-42. Down block

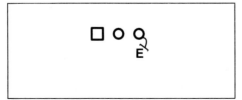

Figure 7-43. Hook block

Pass-Drop Techniques

Buzz Drop, or No-Vision Drop (Figure 7-44): Technique used in cover-6 quarters when playing robber. Uses a flat crossover run, and gets width quickly at a depth no deeper than six yards at the top of the numbers. Keeps the eyes on #1; must be aware of the split. First job is to cut the slant and drive through the hitch route by #1. Cuts the out, or stops the route by #1.

Once the three-step is cleared, gets the eyes back to the quarterback and looks for a new threat by #2. Runs with #2 through the zone; runs with the wheel route (Figure 7-45).

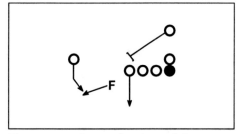

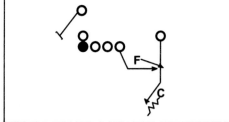

Figure 7-44. Get under slant of #1   Figure 7-45. Run with #2

Curl Drop (Figures 7-46 and 7-47): Drops to a depth of 12 yards over the top of the #2 receiver. If #2 is in a tight position, drops to a midpoint position between #1 and #2. Maintains vision with the quarterback, and feels the release and route of #2. Drop will either be a backpedal or a crossover run, based on how far removed he is from the drop. Breaks to flat on the release of the ball, or a "smash" call by the corner or #3 to the flat.

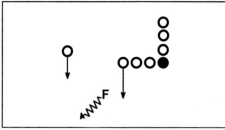

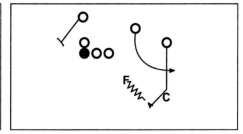

Figure 7-46. Drops to midpoint   Figure 7-47. Feels the release and route
between #1 and #2   of #2

Robber Drop (Figures 7-48 and 7-49): Aligns nine yards from the line of scrimmage on the inside eye of the tight end. Reads the uncovered lineman for the run or pass. Covers any vertical release by #2 by staying inside and over the top. On any under or out route by #2, turns and finds #1. Must be ready to cut off the slant and get under any dig or post route by #1.

Cloud Drop (Figures 7-50 and 7-51): Half-field drop by the Stud. Shuffles back and reads the uncovered lineman for the run or pass. Gets depth and stays inside and over the top of the deepest threat in his half.

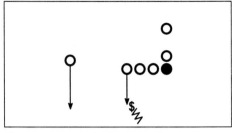

Figure 7-48. Vertical release by #2

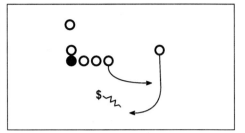

Figure 7-49. Out route by #2

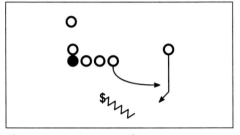

Figure 7-50. Out route by #2

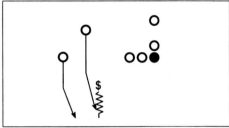

Figure 7-51. Vertical route by #2

Combo Drop (Figure 7-52): Aligns at a depth of at least 10 yards, and possibly deeper based on field position and splits. Shuffles outside, and reads the uncovered lineman for the run or pass. If it's a pass, reads the release of #2. If #2 goes vertical, stays inside and over the top of #2. If #2 goes inside, outside, or sits down, widens and gets over the top of #1.

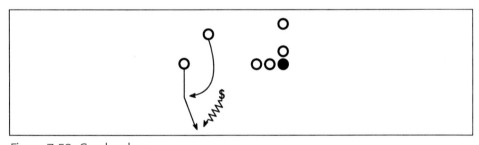

Figure 7-52. Combo drop

Key Drop (Only Versus Trips Set) (Figures 7-53 and 7-54): Aligns at a depth no closer than eight yards deep. Reads the release of #3. If #3 goes vertical or deeper than the inside linebackers, takes him. If no threat shows, brackets #1 to the weakside.

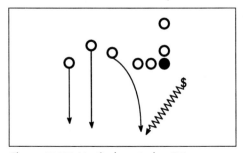

Figure 7-53. Vertical route by #3

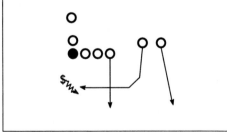

Figure 7-54. Crossing route by #2

Falcon—Alignment, Key, Run or Pass Reaction to the Tight-End Side

- Aligns 3x3 from the tight end—tightens on the run; deepens on the pass.
- Keys through #2 to the uncovered linemen.
- Knows the type of formation (21 twins, 10/11 doubles, 10 trips); the #2 receiver is a quicker flat threat.
- Knows the width of #1; knows the curl area.
- Bounce reads (bounces over his position) or freeze reads (freezes in his stance) for the run or pass.
- With lane #1 action: Attacks and builds a fence. Reduces the running lane horizontally and vertically.
- If the ball is off the line of scrimmage: Reads through #2 to the fullback's angle or the quarterback/tailback exchange to determine the run or pass.
- If the play is pass: Drop steps, crosses over, and sprints to 12 yards deep.
- Must find #1; takes a quick peek in the initial drop.
- Must make an aggressive drop; takes a quick four to five steps, and thinks three-step drop. Sprints out (drives out).
- Aiming point is five yards inside #1 at depth of 10 to 12 yards.
- Must be aware of #1 width and #2 release; keeps his head on a swivel.
- Versus #2 away (block, drag, vertical): Sinks through the curl area. Position helps the corner on the inside route by #1.
- Versus #2 flat: Keeps depth on the curl. Plays from the inside to outside portion of the curl. Holds the curl until he gets outflanked, and then shuffles for width.
- Doesn't jump #2 in flat. Jumps the quarterback's shoulders or thrown ball.
- Versus #2 vertical: Takes a peek at #1. If no under threat exists, moves to the landmark—the curl area is determined by the width of the #1 receiver.

Points for the Falcon to Remember in the Curl Drop

- Ball on the hash: Most out cuts are thrown into the boundary. Must be aware of #1 reducing his split for the out. With a wider split, thinks slant and digs inside.
- If into the boundary, don't have as far to go, thus can hang longer in the curl and jump #2 on the quarterback's shoulders or thrown ball.
- To the wide field, think more "in" cuts.
- If #2 takes a vertical route into the boundary, must be alert to run to the out. If #2 takes a vertical route to the field, thinks dig first and then "out" cut. Fit the curl by #1, and then the out.
- Hold the curl until outflanked by #2 or #3, then expands to the flat. Hold depth. Lose depth only on the quarterback's shoulders or thrown ball.

Falcon and Stud Pass-Rush
Teaching Progression

- *Focus:* Knows the game situation, down-and-distance, and opponent tendencies.
- *Get off:* Explodes on the first step off the ball or man movement.
- *Close the distance:* Does not reach; gets hip-to-hip, and gets toes and hips pointed toward the target, which is the quarterback.
- *Attack half the man:* Gets on the edge, and uses leverage and speed to close to the target, which is the quarterback.
- *Keep the feet moving:* Accelerates toward the quarterback; must never float or be flattened out.
- *Finish:* Gets the hands up in the passing lane versus the quick pass. Gets the eyes to the quarterback, and times the hands with his release. The rule is to get the hands up when the quarterback takes his hand off the football. Avoids leaving the feet, especially if he is the leverage rusher. Hits the quarterback high; doesn't stop progress to get the hands up in the air. If the quarterback's back is to the rusher, blind sides, and uses the strip technique with the outside arm.

Pass Rush Moves

Speed Rush: Beats the blocker with speed, and turns toward the quarterback. Drops the inside shoulder, leans in, and pulls through. Throws the outside arm toward the quarterback to help get the hips past the lineman's hips and toward the quarterback.

Slap and Rip: Slaps the shoulder of the blocker, and uses the same hand and same foot to get the hips pointed toward the target. Gets hip-to-hip with the blocker, and rips past.

Spin Counter Move: Once the rusher feels that he is getting deeper than the quarterback on his set-up, he plants the inside foot and drops the hips; throws the outside arm and elbow back toward the blocker; and spins back inside toward the quarterback. Every step made should be toward the target; does not give up ground and have dead feet, but keeps the feet moving.

Rush Techniques From Defensive Fronts

50 Defense Away From the 5- and 9-Technique Side

- Becomes the fourth rusher on the 4- and 6-technique side.
- Stays outside all out blocks by the offensive tackle.
- Spills all pullers and backs.
- Chases down all zone away plays, and reacts to the boot.
- Maintains responsibility for the quarterback on option.

Five-Man Outside Rusher/Blitzer on Perimeter Rush

- Makes a great first step. Prowls to get in a position to pressure off the edge.
- Contains the rush versus the pass.
- Spills anything off the down block by the tight end. Maintains responsibility for the quarterback on option.
- Chases all zone away plays, and reacts to the boot.

Five-Man Interior Rush

- Ensures position to rush from depth.
- Reads the block of the lineman inside of assigned rush gap. If he turns out, come under the block. If he reaches away, chase off his tail down the line of scrimmage.
- Keeps the feet moving and take an edge off the blocker; do not run down the middle.
- When approaching a back in the gap, attacks him, keeps speed, has a two-way go, and gets to his edge.

Zone Pass Coverage Principles

- Before the snap of the ball, determine the direction and zone to cover.
- Take a peek at the initial aiming point before the snap of the ball.
- After reading the pass, sprint toward the aiming point, keeping the eyes on the quarterback.
- Be aware of receivers in a position to threaten the assigned zone. Know what the #2 receiver is doing to help diagnose the pattern, but keep the eyes on the quarterback.
- When playing the curl-flat on the split-end side, know the initial aiming point is 10 to 12 yards deep in front of the widest receiver.
- Get to the zone quickly and sets up; listens for calls from the secondary.
- If the quarterback starts to run, play pass defense until he crosses the line of scrimmage. When the quarterback crosses the line of scrimmage, forces him back to the inside.
- When a pass is thrown in the short zone, gamble for the interception.
- Break on the ball; watch the quarterback.
- Develop the ability to cover a lot of ground while the ball is in the air. Break on a straight line to the ball.
- Intercept the ball at the highest point. Run through the ball.
- Don't enter the red zone unless the ball is thrown into it. The red zone is an area from the sideline to six yards inside sideline.
- Do not cover air; go only as wide and as deep as necessary to cover the area of responsibility.
- Intercept a tipped ball if hustling.

- Search any receiver who catches the ball. Attack him, and pull his arms apart. Keep the head up, and explode into him with the chest. Pull his arms apart, expand the chest, and drive through him. Keep the legs moving, and does not lunge.
- If responsible for the flat and all the receivers are inside, cheat inside to the next opposing player—cheat rule (e.g., sprint pass away).

Man Pass Coverage Principles

- Keep the eyes on the receiver at all times.
- If beat deep, keep the eyes on receiver and catches him. The receiver will run slower when his head turns to look for the ball. When he slows to go up or when his hands go up for the ball, the defender's hands should go up. Be alert for a "ball" call.
- Face guarding is legal as long as no contact is made.
- Never go in front of the receiver unless both hands can get on the ball.
- If timing is close, deflect the ball with a near-arm/far-arm technique. Wrap with the near arm over the upfield or outside shoulder, and drives the far arm through the pocket to bat the ball out.
- Have pride in one-on-one coverage.

Man Coverage Techniques

- Play the man first, and then the ball.
- Tighten on the receiver, and aligns head-up. Can even take inside alignment prior to the snap, depending on field position.
- Do not play a scared or loose man. The defender is not beat deep until the receiver catches the ball.
- Be poised; don't panic with his back to the ball.
- Concentrate on the receiver.
- The receiver will try to do three things to beat the defender:
  ✓ Get the head-up position.
  ✓ Convince the defender that he is going deep.
  ✓ Make the defender move in opposite direction of his final cut.
- Backpedal to establish an inside position.
- Always be inside the receiver, never head-up.
- Adjust the backpedal according to route and speed of receiver—speed up or throttle down.
- Establish a three-yard cushion and remains two yards inside.
- Do not lose inside position on the release and the route of the receiver.
- Maintains proper leverage at all times. Stay off the same plane of the receiver on a vertical move. Staying on the same plane gives the receiver an opening on both inside and outside moves.

- Stay in the backpedal as long as possible. Have confidence in the backpedal.
- Read the receiver's hips, hands, or numbers to enable good anticipation in the breaking area. Eyes on the "hip" area; must not take head-and-shoulder fakes.
- Be quick in the break. Gain speed as drive through upfield shoulder on the outside or inside break.
- Use the far arm for deflection and near arm to grab if unable to intercept the ball.
- If the receiver breaks down the cushion and forces defender out of the backpedal, turn the hips into the receiver and runs with him.
- Concentrate on the receiver's hands and eyes. He cannot catch the ball unless his hands go up.
- Do not peek at the ball until the receiver is covered.
- Have poise when his back is to the ball. Have confidence in the "ball" call by the other defenders.
- When the hands go up, the defender's hands go up in the same relative position and rake the receiver's arms down.

Man coverage is an individual battle within the framework of the team defense, and is between the defender and the receiver. The defender needs to be intense, accept the challenge, and win the battle.

Skills and Drills for Falcons and Studs

Mirror Drill (Figures 7-55 and 7-56): Mirrors the first move by the offensive player. Uses a high or low block protection, and keeps the outside arm and leg free.

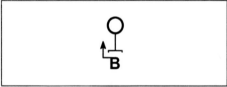
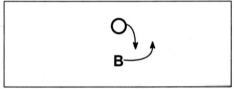

Figure 7-55. Mirror versus base block   Figure 7-56. Mirror versus reach block

Rapid-Fire Drill (Figure 7-57): Four blockers and a ballcarrier line up two yards apart. On command, the ballcarrier comes forward. The blockers attack the defensive linebacker's alternate shoulders. The defensive linebacker tries to beat each block with his shoulder and forearm blow, and then executes the tackle on the ballcarrier. This drill is done in rapid-fire succession.

Recoil Drill (Figure 7-58): The defender plays off high or low blocks by four offensive players. The next blocker starts when the defender gets off the previous block. May end with an accelerated tackle. Can substitute bags for blockers before progressing to blockers.

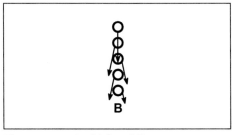

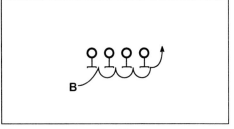

Figure 7-57. Rapid-fire drill   Figure 7-58. Recoil drill

Open-Field Tackle Drill (Figure 7-59): The outside linebacker pass-drops to his curl responsibility and reads the quarterback/coach. When the quarterback turns to throw to the receiver, the outside linebacker breaks toward the receiver and covers as much ground as possible. The receiver catches the ball and turns upfield to run; the Falcon/Stud breaks down and makes the tackle.

Shed Tackle Drill (Figure 7-60): This drill teaches the Falcon/Stud to take on a block with pad under pad, and keep the outside arm and leg free. The Falcon/Stud gets separation from the blocker and tries to stay square. He must not be driven off the ball. After getting separation, he finds the ballcarrier and makes the tackle.

- On first sound, the blocker attacks the outside linebacker.
- On second sound, the runner picks a hole and runs.

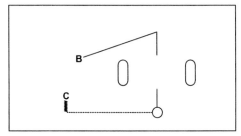

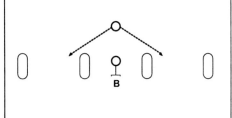

Figure 7-59. Open-field tackle drill   Figure 7-60. Shed tackle drill

Ball Reaction Drill (Figure 7-61): This drill teaches the outside linebackers to break on the quarterback's throwing action and catch the football. The coach signals the linebacker to backpedal, and then throws the ball in one of five directions. The linebacker breaks to the ball and makes the catch.

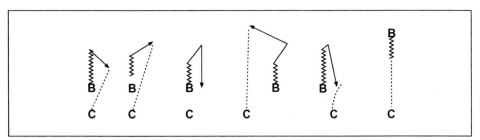

Figure 7-61. Ball reaction drill

Pass-Drop Drill (Figure 7-62): The outside linebacker reads the coach's eyes as he drops to a zone/area between two stationary receivers. The outside linebacker breaks to the thrown ball and makes the catch. The coach can throw to either side. The coach can call different coverages. The players rotate after each throw.

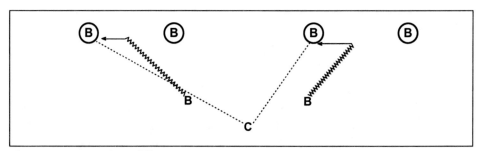

Figure 7-62. Pass-drop drill

8

Defensive Secondary Play

Defensive secondary players who are aggressive and confident contribute greatly to a successful defense. Aggressive play against both the running and passing game is a result of a secondary player executing his assignment with great confidence. Confidence along with aggressiveness is the foundation of successful secondary play. Secondary players should also have several other basic qualities, including: the ability to run well, the ability to change directions quickly, a great work ethic, and the ability to be a dependable tackler. Speed is essential in order to match up with receivers on deep routes. Quickness or change of direction is important for the defensive back to drive on a receiver's cut and give the body momentum to make plays on the short passing game. Good work habits promote improvement of the defensive back's overall performance. Tackling is a big part of defense against both the run and pass game. The secondary player should gain leverage on the ball before he makes contact. The tackle starts with leverage, then good eye contact, and then explosion into the ballcarrier and arm wrap.

Defeating blockers is another skill at which secondary players need to work hard. Whether to play the block with his hands or his pads is a decision he will need to do on the spur of the moment. The key is to avoid being knocked off his feet. As long as he is on his feet, he has a chance to make plays. Making plays is what defensive football is all about.

Goals

The secondary player should want to win, believe he can win, and commit himself to do what is necessary to win. He should set the following types of goals for accomplishing what he commits to:

- Short-range goals: Things to do in the present to compete well
- Intermediate goals: The hurdles along the way that need to be overcome (If a problem exists, find a solution.)

- Long-range goals: Where the individual players and team want to go, and what they want to become in the future

Establishing personal goals is recognized as possibly the strongest of all forces for motivation. Goals should be demanding, challenging, and realistic. Success in the athletic world is achieved by athletes who continually set higher standards for themselves. It is also far easier for a player to reach goals set for himself than it is to reach goals set by others. Players should try to develop a deep belief that personal goals can and will be reached. The clearer goals are visualized, the more desire is kindled for greater effort.

Attitude

- More athletes fail through faulty mental attitude than in any other way.
- Attitudes are habits of thinking. It is within every player's power to develop the habit of thinking thoughts that make up a winning attitude.
- The foundation for the proper attitude consists of developing the habit of thinking positive thoughts.
- When a player tells himself constantly that he can do something, he usually will. If the player tells himself constantly that he can't do something, he usually doesn't.
- A desire to win and a desire to prepare to win are important ingredients of a winning attitude.
- Before a player can reach the heights of athletic greatness, he must first learn to control himself from within. He can be his own master by controlling his emotions.
- An athlete with a good attitude is coachable. He welcomes criticism, constantly wants to learn, and avoids criticizing teammates.
- True success depends on teamwork. All players should put the good of the team ahead of anything else.
- Whether a winning attitude is created is up to each individual.

Secondary Philosophy

The importance of a good defensive secondary cannot be overemphasized. A closely-knit, consistent tackling secondary who thrives on dominating the offense is indispensable to success. He starts by being offensive-minded. He must be alert for interceptions and make the sudden change from defense to offense, then block and return the interceptions for touchdowns. He must cause and recover fumbles, and block kicks or make long punt returns that will give his offense good field position.

Primary Goals for the Secondary

Maintain the Perimeter: The goal of the secondary should be to prevent a long run or pass, and to combine with the rest of the defense to prevent an opponent from driving the length of the field and scoring. A good secondary should never allow a long touchdown run since two ingredients are necessary to stop the score: full-speed pursuit to the ball and flawless tackling.

Intercept the Ball: The secondary should not want to intercept the ball, but *will* it. He plays with aggressiveness. He must be confident and relaxed; he hopes the ball is thrown so it can be intercepted. He must not be afraid to take calculated risks and chances. The secondary never lets the ball go into the body, but catches it with the hands. He should remember that the quarterback will normally throw the ball perfectly only five or six times a game. The quarterback may hit a certain percentage, but when one poorly thrown ball comes along, the secondary intercepts it and turns the ball over to the offense.

In order to have an effective passing game, the opponent needs to accomplish a number of requirements, including:

- The quarterback must have time to throw. The defense must rush and harass the quarterback.
- The quarterback must be able to read the defense's coverage. The secondary must disguise its intentions.
- The quarterback must throw the ball accurately and on time. The secondary must reroute and disturb the receivers.
- The receiver must run an accurate route. The secondary must react correctly to the receiver's route.
- The receiver must catch and hold onto the ball. The secondary must be effective in stripping and punching the ball from the receiver.

Fundamentals of Secondary Play

Square Stance

- Shoulders and hips must be square to the line of scrimmage.
- Comfortable: no false steps and no unnecessary movement.
- Tight base: feet no wider than hips.
- Toe-to-heel relationship: Use greater stagger if preferred, but keep the weight on the balls of the feet, not on the heels.
- Forward foot in front of nose, with weight on the front foot.
- Shoulder over the knees and knees over the toes.
- Bend at the knees; do not drop head to set low.
- Be quick out of the stance.

Cocked Inside Stance

- Keep the outside foot up, with weight on the up foot.
- Body cocked in at a 45-degree angle.
- Belly button should be on the ball.

- Maintain tight feet and tight base.
- Keep weight on the balls of the feet.
- Have a relaxed and comfortable bend in the knees.
- Arms should hang relaxed and loose, comfortable inside the framework of the body.
- Be quick out of the stance.
  - ✓ No false steps from the stance
  - ✓ No unnecessary movement (no wasted motion)

Backpedal

The backpedal gives the defensive back a chance to see what the offense is doing by looking at routes and the quarterback. The backpedal should be a controlled movement with emphasis on good technique and leverage. A defensive back cannot run as fast backward as a receiver can forward, so he shouldn't try. Control in the pedal helps maintain leverage and helps prevent false steps or unneeded body movement. It allows the defensive back the ability to break effectively into the transition part of his backpedal. The defensive back should do the following when backpedaling:

- Think of the backpedal as three phases: Walk, pedal, and run.
- Push with front foot, and reach back with back foot. Be sure the first step is back. Start with short, quick steps. Do not overstride.
- Reach back with each step and pull the body over the feet.
- Take comfortable strides, slightly clearing the grass; feet work off the top of the grass. Keep the feet close to ground. Speed is only gained when the feet are in contact with the ground.
- Keep the knees bent so the feet can extend past the hips; comfortable bend in the knees—stay in the knees. Coming out of the knees will lead to having no power to explode on a break or turn.
- Maintain tight feet within the hips—don't backpedal from a wide base.
- Keep a slight forward lean with the shoulders ahead of the hips.
- Keep body weight down, and tuck the chin. Keep the chin down; stay low, and play low.
- Shoulders must be square to the receiver.
- Be relaxed with arms in normal running manner and elbows tight to body. Fast hands help create fast feet.
- Pedal on the balls of the feet, not the toes or heels (light feet, not heavy feet).
- Backpedal about three quarters of full-speed potential to allow an instant break on the ball or receiver.
- Turn to sprint on deep routes. Break on the ball/receiver on short routes.
- Stay loose in the hips.
- Always stay coiled until ready to run full speed.

Backpedal Reminders for Defensive Backs

- Receivers close distance too quickly in zone or man because of lack of concentration.
- Exaggerate the first two steps.
- On the backpedal, keep the feet within the hips; any good sprinter has narrow stance.
- Slipping is a result of overstriding in the backpedal.
- Quick hands save slow feet.
- At all times in practice, whether drills or teamwork, exaggerate the acceleration of the feet and the pump of the hands and arms.
- Keep a tight base at all times in the backpedal.

Weave

The weave is used to maintain a desired position. The secondary should:
- Know the necessary angle to take.
- Push off the opposite foot in the needed direction.
- Keep the shoulders and hips over the knees so as not to slow down the backpedal when adjusting to the receiver's route.
- Stay in the backpedal, and retain the desired position.

Transition: Speed Step

The transition game is everything. The speed to make the transition is as much mental as it is physical. It is a combination of making the right decision and reacting on that decision with speed and technique. When transitioning, secondary players should use the following guidelines:
- Be quick out of the backpedal into the break or turn.
- Accelerate off the plant or turn.
- Get the feet down and out of the ground as quickly as possible with emphasis on short, quick steps.
- Run in and out of the stance; don't hop.
- Maintain short steps in which the feet do not stop. Don't allow the feet to widen outside of the shoulders or overstride.
- Accelerate the feet and arms.
- Don't let the feet die in the break; never stop the feet.
- Don't raise the body coming out of the backpedal.
- The power and speed of the break come from the hips and knees. Stay in the knees with the knees bent. A straight-legged backpedal provides no power to accelerate.
- Keep the eyes up. Don't drop the head on the plant.
- Break at sharp angles. Plant and drive; sharp angles create faster breaks and better leverage; rounded angles lose leverage.

Rollover or Turn Rules for Secondary Players

- Tuck the toe of the foot opposite the direction of the rollover.
- Eliminate the false step.
- Keep the hips low with the rollover or turn.
- The foot on side of the rollover or turn is the directional foot. Gain ground with the step.
- Accelerate out of the transition. Drive for leverage.
- Snap the elbow around on the side of the directional foot.
- Be quick in the turn, and gain speed and depth.
- Get the head and eyes around with quickness so as to adjust to the look of the quarterback and the release of the ball.

Transition Reminders for Secondary Players

- Plant the toe—speed step/speed break.
- Keep the butt down, shoulders over the feet, and the feet close together; use fast feet.
- The feet must never stop. Punch and place.
- Get the feet down and out of the ground as quickly as possible. The key is short, quick steps with the feet under the body.
- Emphasize:
  ✓ Plant foot and stop foot
  ✓ Directional foot
- Stress the snap of the hips at the target and acceleration of the move.
- Accelerate out of the backpedal into the break; get acceleration off the plant.
- Gather, tuck, accelerate, and retrace.
- Keep the weight over the feet to eliminate the long stride.
- Make a change of direction on one step and accelerate full speed after the plant. Be quick in the break and be quick in the turn.
- Feet must never stop moving; don't let the feet die in the break.
- Break in position of the backpedal. Stay low, and play low.
- Explode out of the break; sprint out of the break. Gain speed; don't simply maintain speed.
- Emphasize that all breaks off the backpedal coincide with a particular pass pattern to be covered (e.g., out, post, dig, smash, fade).
- When settling:
  ✓ Get the butt down.
  ✓ Keep the shoulders over the feet.
  ✓ Keep the feet tight and close.
  ✓ Move quickly.

- For the speed break:
  ✓ Take two short steps; don't stop the feet.
  ✓ First step: break the backpedal, and begin the drive forward.
  ✓ Second step: begin to step forward with speed.
- *Key point:* In practice drills, whether in pads or shorts and whether in 1-on-1, skeleton, or team, explode through the break—never squat on the break. Always finish coverage by driving past receivers.

Turn Rules for Secondary Players When Covering the Deep Ball

- Deploy a directional foot and an acceleration step.
- Emphasize a pivot foot instead of a plant foot.
  ✓ Zone: Open inside with the foot away from the receiver.
  ✓ Man: Open outside with the foot to the receiver.
- After the pivot, the directional foot is vitally important.
  ✓ Gain ground with a step.
  ✓ Don't open too much; step in the bucket.
  ✓ Don't open too little; move across the receiver's body.
- Don't slow down in the turn; acceleration is the key.
- Accelerate out of the transition, and drive to leverage.
- Stay in the knees (knees bent) to ensure having the power to explode when opening the hips to run; keep the hips low.
- Snap the elbow around on the side of the directional foot.
- Don't try to look and turn at the same time.
- Gain ground on the receiver in the turn.
- Get vertical as quickly as possible. The key is to get vertical with width because there is always a tendency to separate.

Shuffle

When playing man coverage, the secondary needs to backpedal, whereas zone coverage affords definite merit in using the shuffle technique as well as the backpedal. With both techniques, emphasis should be placed on the same fundamentals so success can be achieved with the backpedal and the shuffle. The shuffle is very effective in three-deep zone coverage, read cover two, and quarters coverages when reading off the release of the #2 receiver. The same transition principles are emphasized in both techniques:

- Drive off the back foot.
- Make short, quick steps.
- Keep the feet alive through the transition.
- Never allow the feet to die in the break.
- Accelerate the feet off the plant.

- Keep the eyes up through the break.
- Plant and drive at sharp angles.

Shuffle Technique

- Cock inside at a 45-degree angle, and align at a depth of seven yards.
- Key through the #2 receiver to the quarterback and uncovered linemen.
- Initial step is with the back foot. Reach back to gain depth and keep weight on the balls of the feet.
- In the shuffle, keep the knees bent, the shoulders over the knees and the knees over the toes. Relax the chin. Execute a tight shuffle (skate), not a wide shuffle. Overstriding can cause slipping.
- Stay in the knees so as to be ready to explode out of the shuffle. Read the eyes of the quarterback or the route of the receiver.
- Keep the feet tight to ground so as to stay tight in the turn on both the shuffle and backpedal.
- Be on the balls of the feet at all times, never on the heels.
- Keep the elbows tight to the body.
- Transition speed is the key in the shuffle just like the backpedal. Maintain width while working for depth.
- Plant on the back foot, and break at a sharp angle according to the route of the receiver and the release of the ball.
- Always stay coiled until reaching full speed. Gain ground with width to get in the path of the vertical release to slow up the receivers.

Tackling

Every defensive position should tackle well. It is especially critical for the secondary because they are the last line of defense to prevent the long run or the long touchdown. Their skills will be tested because they must get good run-pass reads off the offensive lineman, fit off the defensive line and linebackers in order to plug, and keep run gains down to five yards or less. Then, they must be ready to win a 1-on-1 situation in the open field against a very good running back who may break past the first and second line of defense. The secondary's importance can never be underestimated in shutting down an opponent's running game. As is often said on defense, "The only ugly tackle is a missed tackle." It is the secondary's responsibility to not only take pride in defending the pass, but also take pride in being tough and aggressive when defending against the run.

Five Tackling Principles

- Take proper angle.
- Keep the head and eyes on the focus point.
- Avoid overextension.
- Be aggressive with the arms and hands.

- Maintain base and feet.

The perfect tackle is described in detail in Chapter 4.

Tackling Situations

- *Force player:* Plays the blocker first. Stands his ground and builds a wall. Comes off the block inside or outside to make the tackle.
- *Alley fill player:* Runs through the ballcarrier and maintains an inside-out relationship, which prevents the ballcarrier from cutting back inside. Explodes through the head on the flow side with the head up, clubs the arms, gets the hips through, and takes the ballcarrier backward.
- *Open-field player:* Knows when the ballcarrier has a two-way cut option in the open field. Keeps balance, tackles high, closes to the toes of the ballcarrier; closes space, keeps eyes on the belly, steps in direction of the cut, avoids crossing over, clubs with arms, and keep the feet under.
- *Backside cutoff player:* Uses the open-field concept. Uses the sideline to limit the two-way cut.
- *Goal line:* Squares up, and uses proper tackling technique. Must hold ground on first contact and not allow the ballcarrier to fall forward.

Basic Principles of Secondary Play

- Know the defense called, the alignment on the field, and the situations (e.g., down- and- distance) on each play. Communicate.
- Know the alignments, coverage adjustments, motion adjustments, and responsibilities on the run or pass.
- Know the keys and how to react to them. When in doubt, play pass.
- Do not try to do something that exceeds individual ability. Think and anticipate.
- Take care of individual assignment first. The rest of the team is depending on it.
- Keep poise; relax, and execute proper techniques.
- Keep the head in the game, pay attention to detail, and makes things happen.
- Stay in coverage on the quarterback scramble. Remain in coverage, and look for crossing routes. Quarterbacks have the ability to throw deep when scrambling.
- Break on the ball at full speed. Hustle at all times. Sprint to the football.
- Be a hitter, and physically intimidate receivers, blockers, and the ballcarrier.

Terminology for Secondary

- *Alert vertical:* This call is made in cover 3 or cover 2. Falcon and Stud read #3. The player away from #3 will carry the vertical, and the player toward #3 will reroute any vertical.

- *Alley:* The gap in the defense outside the end lineman and inside force defender.
- *Anticipation:* Mental alertness by the defenders.
- *Backside pursuit:* Applies to defender(s) farthest away from flow. Responsible for reverse, deep throw back, and saving a touchdown. Good angle to the ballcarrier.
- *Bail:* Technique used in zone coverage. Tight alignment to wide receiver and work out.
- *Banjo:* Two defenders playing inside and outside on two receivers with no deep help.
- *Boundary:* Space into the short side of the field when the ball is on the hash.
- *Bracket:* Two defenders playing inside and outside on one receiver.
- *Breaking on the ball:* Reacting and breaking on the quarterback's release of the ball.
- *Catch technique:* Technique used in man coverage from a press alignment.
- *Check:* Changing a defensive call because of an offensive adjustment.
- *Cloud:* Short zone pass term for corner force.
- *Collision:* Technique used to destroy the timing of routes.
- *Combo:* Inside/outside position on two receivers with help over the top.
- *Contain:* Technique used by a defender to keep the offense inside a designated area.
- *Crack:* Block by a wide receiver on an inside defender
- *Curl:* Zone area of the field 10 to 12 yards over a normally aligned #1 wide receiver.
- *Deep outside third (O/S 1/3):* Secondary player who is a security element of the defense. He is not a primary run support defender, except when crack block occurs, then he is part of the force unit. He must be aware of combination routes deep. He makes calls.
- *Delay:* A receiver delays for a count or two before releasing on a pattern.
- *Disguise:* Making coverage hard to recognize by alignment.
- *Divider:* Zone technique by the corner when two or more receivers are aligned in his zone.
- *Field:* Space to the wideside of field when the ball is on the hash.
- *Flat:* Zone area located five yards over the #1 receiver.
- *Force:* Technique/responsibility given to the defensive back when he is required to build a perimeter wall and turn the ball back inside.
- *Full flow:* To the side where both backs release to the same side of the quarterback
- *Funnel:* Funnel technique when the zone of responsibility is the flat area.
- *Gun:* Quarterback located behind the center at a depth of five yards.
- *Hash:* Field markings that divide the field laterally into thirds.
- *Home back:* Alignment of the running back lined up directly behind the quarterback.

- *Inside third (I/S ⅓):* Technique when the corner plays inside leverage on any receiver in his third zone.
- *Key coverage:* Call from the backside of the trips by the Stud or a free safety. He picks up #3 strong if #3 goes vertical or deep inside.
- *Keys/Reads:* Specific indicator on the offensive team when initial movement helps defenders quickly analyze the play as either a run or pass. The three keys are: eligible receivers, uncovered lineman, and the quarterback angle away from the center.
- *Leverage:* Either inside or outside position on a receiver.
- *Man:* Coverage when a defender is assigned to cover a single receiver on all routes.
- *Motion:* When a back or receiver moves prior to and until the snap of the ball.
- *Oskie:* Call made to indicate that the defender is about to make an interception. Defenders become blockers.
- *Press bail:* Technique when corners play an inside-third responsibility from a tight alignment to the receiver.
- *Robber:* Strongside technique with the Falcon or a free safety. The corner has the inside third, the Falcon is the buzz player, and the free safety plays robber coverage off the routes of #2.
- *Rock down:* Safety moves towards the line of scrimmage on the snap of the ball.
- *Seam:* Vertical route by the inside receiver that is on or slightly outside or inside the hash mark.
- *Shift:* The movement of one or more offensive players prior to the snap of the ball that is designed to alter the formation and/or strength of the formation.
- *Sink and settle:* Cornerback technique when, after keying the release of the #2 receiver, he plays over the top of #1 or settles over the flat zone.
- *Spill:* Technique when a defender takes on block with his outside shoulder, and forces the ballcarrier to bounce the run further outside.
- *Spin:* Safety moves back toward the center of the field and covers the zone in the middle third (M ⅓).
- *Split flow:* A two-back set when the backs release in the opposite direction of one another.
- *Tight split:* Tighter-than-normal alignment by a wide receiver toward the ball.
- *Tilt back:* Alignment of a back behind the offensive tackle—can be either strong or weak.
- *Trap:* Strongside coverage technique with the safety in the deep half, the corner in a funnel, and the Falcon in the curl.
- *Unbalanced:* Formation when one of the three receivers aligned on or near to the line of scrimmage is ineligible.
- *Upfield shoulder:* Receiver's deepest shoulder.
- *Wide split:* Wider-than-normal alignment by a wide receiver away from the ball.
- *X-ray:* Tight split by the X receiver.

Responsibilities on Each Defensive Play

- *Call:* Coverage, ball position, down-and-distance.
- *Alignment:* Best possible.
- *Stance:* Head-up, knees bent, weight forward; relax and execute.
- *Step, backpedal, and funnel:* Depends on responsibility.
- *Flow:* Direction of backfield and/or ball.
- *Run/pass key:* Discipline the eyes.
- *Eligibles:* Key for run/pass recognition; know if the unbalanced formation causes issues.
- *Responsibility:* Execution and pursuit.
- *Finish:* Finish the play.

Summary of Defensive Secondary Principles

- Deep defender's first responsibility is the pass. Never allow a touchdown.
- Keep the receiver in front. If necessary, turn back to the quarterback/ball, and sprint to catch the receiver before looking up for the ball.
- Intercept the ball at its highest point; always look the ball into the hands. Avoid waiting for it. Fight for the ball.
- When anticipating or upon interception, the call is "Oskie." Sprint to the nearest sideline with the ball, and the other deep backs should become blockers. Be sure to block the intended receiver.
- Keep the butt down and the chin out and over the toes in the backpedal. Stay in the backpedal as long as possible, until the receiver breaks down the three-yard cushion. When the cushion is broken, turn toward the receiver and run. Key the head and hands to determine the arrival of the ball.
- Most interceptions are made as the defender moves forward into the ball.
- A tipped ball should be an interception if defenders break on the throw of the ball.
- Communication is important. Talk to teammates, and help each other.
- Interference results when a defender plays the receiver rather than the ball.
- Always take the shortest route to the ball. Play through the receiver tough, and search him—pull his arms apart, expand the chest, and drive through him. Keep the legs moving; do not lunge.
- All receiver routes can be separated into three general categories. Be aware and alert to the following potentials:
  ✓ *Quick:* 3- to 5-yard cuts (slant, hitch, and quick out)
  ✓ *Intermediate:* 10- to 15-yard cuts (out, curl, and stop)
  ✓ *Deep:* Over 15 yards (post, fade, and post/corner)
- Look for a pass, particularly after the following situations:
  ✓ A timeout
  ✓ A penalty on the offense

✓A quarter change

✓Uncommon substitution changes

✓A sudden-change turnover

✓A big first-down run that creates a second-and-short situation

- Run to the ball regardless of how far away it is. The defense should have more men catching the ball in the secondary than the offense has receivers. Be in position to catch the tipped ball or block an intended receiver.
- Tackle the receiver immediately after a catch. Avoid giving up additional yards after the catch.
- When a receiver leaves a defender's area, he should watch for another coming into it. The defender should make everything happen in front of him.
- Always strip the receiver when he catches the ball. Active hands. Force fumbles.
- The defender needs to protect the secondary from blockers. Do not allow an opponent to get into the body. Play low and never be knocked down.
- Align to execute the defense first, and then consider the disguise.
- The closer the opponent gets to the goal line, the tighter the secondary must align and play.
- If the defender traps the ball, he should jump up, hold the ball over his head, and then give it to the official. Influence the call.
- With short splits or motion to short splits, think:

✓Crackback block

✓Outside breaking route

✓Crossing route

✓Reverse

- On flow away, think:

✓Bootleg

✓Play-action pass

✓Reverse

✓Pursue

Defensive Secondary Run Support Keys

- Pulling linemen
- Full flow of the backs
- Ball on the line of scrimmage
- Keys for recognition include:

✓*Sweep:* Pulling lineman, full flow, receivers blocking

✓*Option:* Full flow with the ball down the line, linemen attacking downfield

✓*Pass:* Ball off line, linemen retreat blocking

9

Coverages:
Cover 3, 2, 6, and 1

The discussion in this chapter is focused on zone and man coverages. The zone coverages discussed are cover 3, cover 2, and cover 6. The man coverage discussed is cover 1. Many variations of these zone and man coverages may exist. Therefore it is important to know the strengths and weaknesses of each coverage and how these strengths and weaknesses relate to scheme, and more importantly how they relate to available personnel. It is important to consider the strengths of the players when trying to implement individual skills or a particular coverage scheme, rather than their weaknesses. Get them comfortable, get them to believe, and get them to play fast with great intensity, and then the defense has a chance to be successful. Pass defense is really very basic: just cover the receiver, and don't take any decoys.

Whether in two-deep, three-deep, quarters, or man coverage, it is important to align four across to force the entire offensive reads to be post-snap, not pre-snap. Require the quarterback and receivers to do a majority of their adjusting after the ball has been snapped. As they try to sight adjust on the run, the defense has increased the possibility of offensive mistakes being made. It puts questions in the mind of the receivers as they attempt to adjust two-deep routes to three deep coverage, zone routes to man coverage, or three-deep routes to quarter coverage. Disguise alignments eliminate the quick answers and force the quarterback to take more time to read the routes, which buys time for the pass rush, and also disrupts the rhythm and the timing of the passing game. A quarterback given enough time to read his progressions and not feel threatened by the rush is capable of having tremendous success throwing the football. The key is to shorten his read time, force him to make quick decisions (not on what he sees, but what he *thinks* he sees), and put him into a panic mode.

Cover 3

Cover 3 is used in both the Eagle and 50 front defensive packages. This coverage deploys three deep and four underneath pass defenders. The three-deep consist of the corners and the free safety; each is responsible for their deep third of the field and stays deeper than the deepest receiver in their zone. The corners maintain inside leverage on their receivers. In the 50 package, the middle-third player will be the dimeback (Figure 9-1). In Eagle, the four underneath players will consist of the Falcon, Stud, and two inside linebackers (Figure 9-2). Also, this coverage always has a curl/flat player to the field and two hook/curl inside players and a buzz player into the boundary.

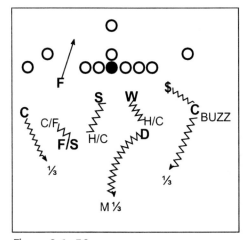

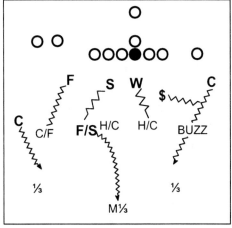

Figure 9-1. 50   Figure 9-2. Eagle

Strengths of the Three-Deep

- Free safety in the middle of the field
- Defends the deep zones
- Perimeter run support
- Five-under defenders with three-deep behind
- Cutback players
- Eight-man front

Weaknesses of the Three-Deep

- Three-step quick routes
- Out cuts
- Four verticals with both dropback and play-action passes
- Flood routes
- Four-under defenders with a four-man rush

The key to strengthen cover 3 is playing with great technique. The passing zones in the three-deep alignment are shown in Figure 9-3.

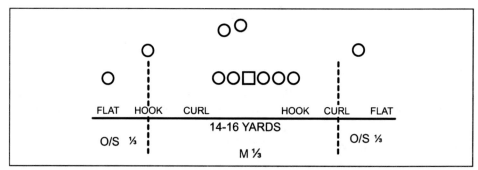

Figure 9-3. Passing zones in the three-deep alignment

For teaching purposes, it is advisable to show defenders four basic offensive formations (pro, twins, doubles, and trips) with different sets that relate well to the multiple sets that the defense sees from game to game.

- *21 Pro* (Figure 9-4): Two backs with one tight end: Can be I, split backs, strong or weak set
- *21 Twins* (Figure 9-5): Two backs with one tight end: Can be I, split backs, strong or weak set
- *11 Doubles* (Figure 9-6): One back, one tight end
- *11 Trips* (Figure 9-7): One back, one tight end
- *10 Trips* (Figure 9-8): One back, four wide receivers

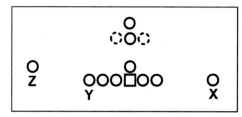

Figure 9-4. 21 pro formation

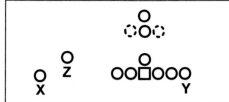

Figure 9-5. 21 twins formation

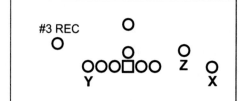

Figure 9-6. 11 doubles formation

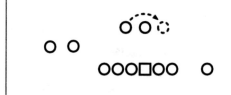

Figure 9-7. 11 trips formation

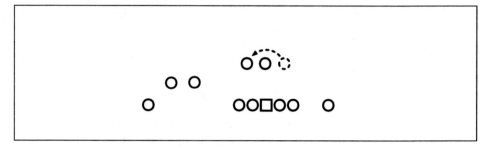

Figure 9-8. 10 trips formation

Cover-3 Alignment and Responsibilities

Corners: The corners align their front foot at seven yards and cocked inside at a 45-degree angle. They are one yard inside or outside the receiver, according to his width. They play one of two techniques: inside third or a divider technique. With a single-width wide receiver the corner plays an inside third, and with a two-receiver threat to one side he plays a divider. With the widest receiver lined up on the hash, he plays an inside third from an outside alignment.

Divider Technique: The corner takes his cushion off the #2 receiver threat. The deeper the receivers go (#1 and #2 vertical), the more inside the divider plays. If either receiver cancels out, he pushes inside or outside to the remaining deep threat. For example, if #2 cancels out, the corner becomes the inside third player. The corner maintains good depth as he reads the set-up of the quarterback so he can make a great centerfield turn back to the #1 receiver if the shoulder of the quarterback takes him to outside width.

Free Safety: The free safety aligns off the tight end, 10 to 12 yards deep in a parallel stance. He moves to the mid-point of his third at 18 to 20 yards depth, depending on the field position or the formation. He should see through the routes of the receivers to the set-up of the quarterback. He should always be inside and on top of the receivers, never even or underneath. Once he loses vision on the receivers, he should come out of his backpedal and open to his deepest threat.

Falcon: The Falcon is responsible for the curl/flat. He pushes to 12 to 14 yards deep and five yards inside the #1 receiver. He plays the inside portion of the curl and expands to the outside portion of the curl on the release of #2 to the flat. If no flat threat exists, he keeps inside position on #1 and forces the quarterback to throw through or over him. With #2 in the flat, the Falcon shouldn't jump him immediately; he should react to #2 on the quarterback's shoulder or the thrown ball.

Stud: The Stud aligns nine yards deep and one yard outside the defensive end. He gives the linebackers an "I'm here" call, which alerts them that the Stud is rocking down as an A- or B-gap filler on the run. The Stud should take on all blocks with his inside arm and shoulder, and squeeze the assigned gap from the outside-in. He rocks down as a buzz player to a single-width receiver. He drives for the inside numbers of the #1 receiver, and he should be ready to cut off the slant or drive through the three-step drop. He should fit up under the out of #1, and be ready to run with the wheel route of the #2 receiver

Check to Cover 6 Versus 21 Twins

The defense prefers to get a 3-on-2 look to the side of the twins. To get this look, the defense should check to six robber or combo to the twins and have the free safety read and rob off #2.

Strong Corner: Plays an inside third to protect the post; gets big on the post. Keys the #2 receiver. If the #2 receiver pushes vertical, squeezes back to #1. If the #2 receiver goes flat, keeps inside position on #1, and plays big on the post and the fade.

Free Safety: Aligns at 10 yards deep and one yard inside or outside the #2 receiver. If #2 is closer to the offensive tackle, he aligns outside. If #2 closer to the #1 receiver, he aligns inside. The free safety is the robber and reads off #2. If #2 is upfield, the free safety plays him on the UPS (up, post, and seam) routes. If #2 goes to the flat, he immediately looks to #1 to rob the curl. He should be aggressive in the curl and roll under the post. If #2 is away (not big with tight end backside), the free safety reads back to the #1 receiver to double on #1 with the cornerback. The free safety will be through the curl and under the post.

Falcon: Aligns over #2 at a depth of seven yards and one yard inside or outside the #2 receiver. Buzzes the flat, and drives the inside number of the #1 receiver. Cuts off the slant, takes away the three-step hitch/out with his body position. Reads back to #2 on buzz, covers him in the flat, and carries him on the wheel.

Backside Corner: Aligns in the guard/tackle gap at a depth of seven yards. Makes an "I'm here" call to the linebackers, indicating that the corner is the eighth man in the front supporting the A or B gap from the outside-in. If the tight end releases on the pass, the backside corner plays him UPS (up, post, and seam). If the tight end does not release and the quarterback's shoulder carries the corner frontside, the backside corner explodes for depth as he reads through #2 to #1 and gets position to play any deep threat. The corner should be aware that a big play will be made either by him or the receiver, depending on the quickness of his explosion for depth and his ability to overlap the frontside cornerback on the deep-ball inside.

Stud: If the offense aligns in an I or strong back set, the Stud makes a "socks" call to alert everyone that he is blitzing off the edge. He spills all blocks with a wrong arm and force the ball to bounce outside with depth. If the offensive backs are in split backs or a weak set, the Stud plays from the line of scrimmage, and when he reads pass, he will sink with depth and be ready to jump any flat threat, or squeeze the tight end from the outside-in.

Cover 3 Versus 11 Doubles—2x2 (Figure 9-9)

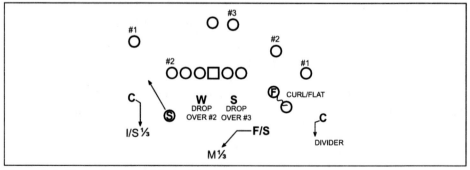

Figure 9-9. Cover 3 versus 11 doubles

Strong Corner: Plays a divider technique on the #1 and #2 receivers; depth provides leverage.

Free Safety: Gives a "stretch alert" call to make the secondary aware of the four vertical threats. Moves back to middle third, and leans on the two stand-ups because the Stud will carry the vertical by #2 as he rocks down. Keys the quarterback, and visualizes the release of the #2 receiver. Gets as deep as the deepest receiver, and adjusts backpedal to routes being run and the attitude of the quarterback.

Falcon: Aligns seven yards deep either inside or outside the #2 receiver, depending on his width. Becomes the curl/flat player.

Backside Corner: Aligns seven yards deep and one yard inside the #1 receiver, keys the #2 receiver (tight end). The corner becomes an inside-third player if the tight end is involved in protection. If the tight end releases, the corner plays a divider technique. If the tight end cancels out, the backside corner becomes an inside-third player. If the #1 receiver cancels, the backside corner pushes to the #2 receiver, who is the next deep threat.

Stud: Aligns at nine yards deep on the inside of the tight end. Bounces his read as he keys the tight end to the ball for run-pass indication. If the tight end (#2 receiver) releases, he is vertical and the Stud should be ready to carry him. The Stud plays #2 and takes a sneak a peek at the #1 receiver. If the #1 receiver is running an under route, the Stud drives on the under route of #1 while releasing the vertical to the corner, who squeezes to the next deep threat. If the #2 receiver is flat, the Stud plays though the curl and reads the set-up of the quarterback. Jumps #2 in the flat on the quarterback's shoulders or the thrown ball. If the tight end is away, the Stud plays out to the #1 receiver and mirrors his route from an underneath position.

Will: The Will linebacker drops over #2. If the tight end is upfield, plays inside and underneath.

Cover 3 Versus 11 Trips and 10 Trips—3x1 (Figures 9-10 and 9-11)

The defense plays either skate or sling versus a 3x1 trips set. This approach gives the defense two ways to play trips. The coaches should alert the secondary which way to play it by down, series, or quarter.

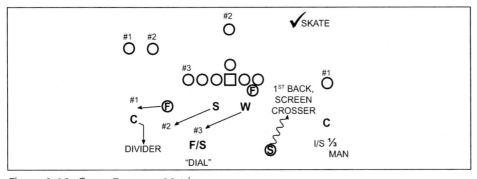

Figure 9-10. Cover 3 versus 11 trips

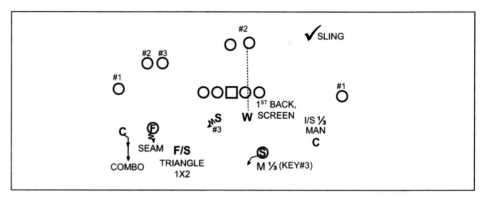

Figure 9-11. Cover 3 versus 10 trips

Skate

Strong Corner: Strong corner is the divider; reads the #2 and #3 box from the outside-in. If either cancels as a deep threat, the corner applies the divider principle to the remaining upfield receiver and #1.

Falcon: Buzzes #1. Walls from the inside-out. Falcon is responsible for the three-step, flat, and wheel by #2 or #3. Cuts off the slant by #1.

Free Safety: Aligns over the strongside guard, backpedals, and keeps inside leverage on #3. Reads the #2 and #3 as one person. Dials through #3. If #3 goes vertical, runs with him. If #3 goes to the flat, plays over #2 always from the inside-out.

Stud: Rocks down from depth and plays the first back, screen weak, or first crosser. Body helps the corner on any short to intermediate inside cuts by the #1 receiver.

Backside Corner: Plays inside man on the #1 receiver. Discourages the post by alignment. Stays strong on inside and deep route, and must be close on the out.

Sam: Walls #2 and cuts the slant, wheels with the dig, and carries the vertical. If #2 is outside, gets depth into the curl, stays alert for the new #2, and gets ready to fast break on the quarterback's eyes and shoulders.

Will: Walls #3 and cuts the slant, wheels with the dig, carries the vertical. If #3 is outside, expands with depth and width, and feels the route of #1 or #2. Must be ready to fast break on the quarterback's eyes and shoulders.

Sling

Strong Corner: Soft combo. Reads #2 and #3 as one person. Funnels #1 from depth, settles back under the corner route and the Yogi route, breaks up on the flat or bubble route. The corner will not run with #1 on fade with the #2 on a vertical, thus he settles so he can react to #3 on a flat or bubble route.

Free Safety: Strong outside-third player. Triangles the #1 and the #2 receivers. The release of the #1 receiver will determine the exit angle. If #1 releases outside of the corner, the free safety drives with width and depth to the outside third to overlap the fade. If #1 releases inside the corner, the free safety gets depth and must be strong inside for the post and over the top of the post corner.

Falcon: Becomes the curl player. Holds depth on the Yogi route, reroutes the #2 receiver on the vertical. Reads to #3, jockeys for position between #2 and #3 to discourage hot routes.

Stud: Becomes the zone middle-third player. Keys #3 and #2 as one receiver. Looks for a post route by #3 or #2. If no deep threat, gets depth and must be ready to react off the indicators of the quarterback.

Sam: Drops over #3. Cuts and carries the slant, wheels with the dig, and reroutes the vertical from an inside position. Cuts and carries all under or drag routes to the backside; the Will and the backside corner play man on #1 and #2 receivers.

Will: Mans on the back. Covers him on screen, flare, or flat routes. If the back blocks, the Will can either "read blitz" the back, or drop over his position for crossers or the inside cuts by the wide receiver.

Press Disguise

From the cover-2 shell, the corners can align in a press look to create the illusion that the defense is playing some form of press-man coverage. Prior to the snap, they open inside and shuffle for width and depth into the outside third into cover 3, combo, or robber off cover 6 or cover 2. The corners can also settle on the snap and still play man coverage with depth. This disguise can create confusion for the quarterback and receivers, give an extra count for pass rushers, and allow a blitzing linebacker an additional step to sack or put pressure on the quarterback. It can be effective against hitch screens, rocket screens, and three-step drops that many offensive teams use. The offensive answer to the press is to run fade or hitch-and-go routes, so the defense should be ready to collision all second breaks and to match the fade.

Cover 2

Strengths of Cover 2 (Two-Deep or Two-Shell Coverage)

- Gets a reroute of two to four receivers, and keeps them at linebacker depth
- Takes the wide receivers out of the game; gets receivers into the hourglass
- Eliminates the three-step passing game
- Provides a good answer for four verticals
- Five-under defenders with four rushers
- Six-under defenders with three rushers
- Hard corners on the perimeter run game

Weaknesses of Cover 2

- Dead areas at 15- to 22-yard pass routes
- Post-corner routes—outside levels route
- Level routes—a receiver in front and one behind
- Play-action pass—holds the linebackers
- Option routes
- Can't get the eighth man in the box for run support from the two-safeties alignment

Cover-2 Alignment and Responsibilities (Figure 9-12)

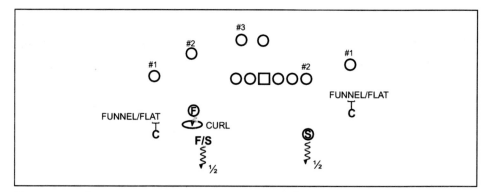

Figure 9-12. Cover 2 versus 10, 11, or 20 personnel

Corners: Square their stance, and pop their feet. Play 3x3, and force the receiver to adjust his desired route; reroute him with jam, open, sink, and squeeze techniques. If #1 releases outside, anticipate a three-step fade route. If #1 releases inside, anticipate slant-flat or post-corner threat. Locate the #2 receiver. If #2 goes vertical, carry #1. If #2 goes away, keep leverage on #1. If #2 goes to the flat, soft sink and read the quarterback. As they sink, the corners keep leverage on the outside receiver. On an inside release by #1 with no flat threat, match up with #1 from the outside-in.

Safeties: Soft pedal with good exit angle (width and depth). Read #1 to #2 receivers; know the release of #1. If #2 goes to the flat, play for width and depth. If #2 goes vertical, discontinue width and get depth. If a two-receiver threat, the safeties must be ball conscious; read the shoulders of the quarterback. Keep an inside-out position on the #1 receiver. Break to the ball with speed; both safeties play fast like two twins breaking on the ball.

Falcon: Curl to late flat. Drops over #2, reroutes #2 into the hourglass. If #2 goes vertical, seeks a peek at #1, and drives on the under route. If #2 goes to the flat, the Falcon gets width and depth into the curl, and finds the #1 receiver with his eyes on the swivel. Breaks fast on the quarterback's eyes and shoulders. If #2 goes away, anticipates an inside cut by the #1 receiver.

Cover-2 Combo (Figure 9-13)

The corners and safeties read the #2 receiver to their side on cover-2 combo. The defense will probably use more combo than a cover-2 funnel. The time needed to perfect the funnel technique in practice is difficult to plan for. However, the combo has good carry-over value to cover 6 so it is logical to tie it into cover 2.

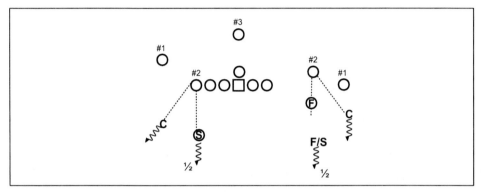

Figure 9-13. Cover-2 combo

Corners: Shuffle back, and read the #2 receivers. If the #2 receiver goes vertical, the corner will carry the #1 receiver until #1 becomes #2, and #2 becomes #1. If #2 goes to the flat, the corner should soften his shuffle, and settle as he reads the quarterback. Must be ready to sink under the post corner or react to the #2 receiver in the flat on the thrown ball.

Safeties: Read the #2 receivers just like the corners. If #2 goes vertical, the safeties have him UPS (up, post, and seam). If #2 goes to the flat, the safeties immediately key the release of #1. If #1 goes outside, they get width and depth to overlap the fade route from the inside-out. If #1 goes inside, they discontinue width and get depth to maintain an inside-out position on the #1 receiver. They take away the post first, and then the post corner. They should stay over the top of the receiver as the corner sinks underneath him to force the quarterback to put air under the ball on that 20- to 25-yard throw.

Cover 2 Versus Trips—3x1 (Figures 9-14 and 9-15)

Cover 2 is a good change-up coverage versus trips to give the backside cornerback help on the #1 receiver.

Strong Corner: Soft shuffles, and reads the #2 and #3 receiver as one. Funnels the #1 receiver with his body. If either #2 or #3 goes vertical, carries (stays with) #1. If #1 is nonthreatening, gets deep, squeezes to the next deepest threat, and looks for the ball.

Free Safety: Deepens the alignment to the trips side, and aligns inside #3 (ability alignment). Reads the #2 and #3 box as one person. If both push vertical, splits the difference and remains ball conscious. Either cancels out leverage on the remaining deep threat.

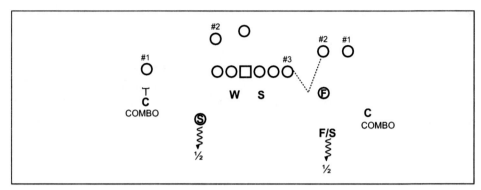

Figure 9-14. Combo versus 11 trips

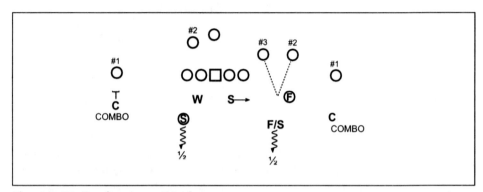

Figure 9-15. Combo versus 10 trips

Falcon: Aligns in a triangle between #2 and #3. Plays the curl at 12 to 14 yards. If #2 or #3 go to the flat, plays from the inside portion of the curl to the outside portion of the curl, and should be ready to drive to the flat threat on the quarterback's shoulders or the thrown ball. Alerts Sam to the #2 and #3 tight split. The Sam linebacker takes the shallow crosses, and the Falcon is responsible for the deep dig from tight alignment.

Sam: Drops over the #3 receiver. Cuts and carries the slant of #3, wheels with the dig, and runs with the vertical. Must be alert on the tight #2 and #3 split to cut and carry the shallow crosser.

Backside Safety: Half-field player.

Backside Corner: Funnel/flat player. Can also play from a combo.

Will: Spot-drops to the curl, and gets his eyes back to the quarterback. Must be ready to react to the screen or help on the shallow or deep crossers.

Cover-2 Macho (Figures 9-16 through 9-18)

Cover-2 macho is a five-under man with two-deep coverage (Figure 9-16). This disguise is usually used versus 10, 11, and 12 personnel, but it can also be used versus 20 personnel. It is best to use six defensive backs and remove either a lineman or linebacker, but still get a four-man rush.

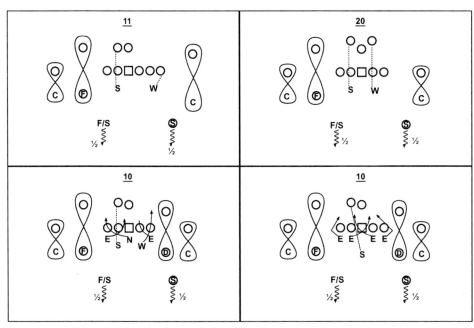

Figure 9-16. Cover-2 macho

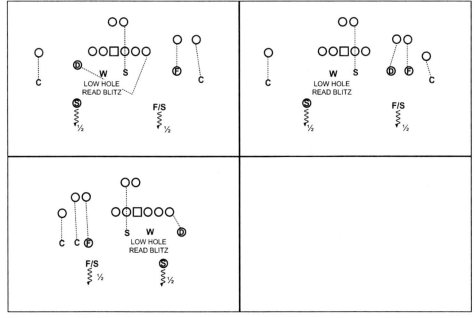

Figure 9-17. Macho versus trips

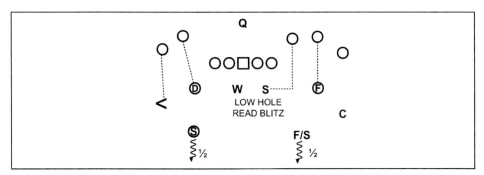

Figure 9-18. Macho versus empty

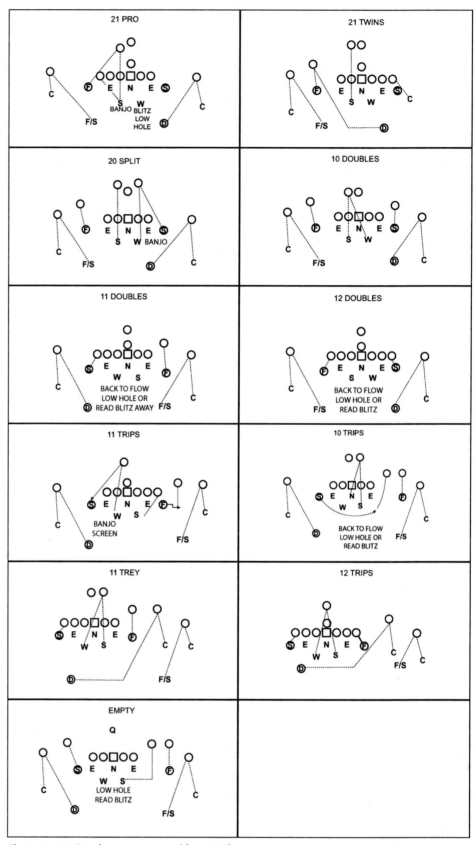

Figure 9-19. Bracket coverage with a 50 front

Corners: Deny the inside release by #1; run under the route, and always stay inside and underneath. Use the trail man technique; never on same level as receiver. Establish a cushion; corners have a tendency to be too tight. Key indicators are hips and numbers; should anticipate the break. Wheel under the inside or outside route; mirror the route. Stay strong on the inside, and close on the outside route. Always stay between receiver and quarterback. Peek only when the receiver is covered. Mirror his hands and eyes. The defense should be ready to substitute and play with either six or seven defensive backs versus empty (Figure 9-18).

Cover-2 Bracket With a 50 Front (Figures 9-19 and 9-20)

In cover-2 bracket, the defenders involved in bracket coverage are designated by the number (e.g., #1, #2, #3) of the receiver (Figure 9-19). The formation number is called first, and then the second number denotes which receiver(s) will be bracketed away from the formation. Bracket 11 indicates a bracket on the #1 receiver both to and away from the formation; bracket 21 indicates a bracket on #2 strong and #1 weak; bracket 22 indicates a bracket on the #2 receiver to both sides.

The defense will typically be in a 50 front to bracket, and utilize either a three- or four-man rush. A linebacker will usually be one of the four rushers (e.g., 50 tilt backer wrap bracket 11). "Tilt" alerts the linebacker to the offset back in the shotgun that he is the blitzer (Figure 9-20). If the quarterback is under the center with the back in a home position (behind the center and the quarterback), the linebacker to the formation side blitzes (or the linebacker to the side the back usually blocks to on protection blitzes).

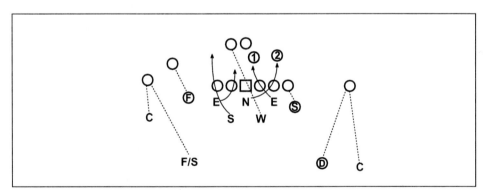

Figure 9-20. Tilt versus an offset back in shotgun

Cover-2 Backer With a Five-Man Rush (Figures 9-21 through 9-23)

Cover-2 backer is normally used with a five-man rush. Cover-6 cloud principles are used by the secondary. No middle drop defender will exist, but two wall players drop from the inside-out and wall the #2 receiver. The wall players deny and match up any inside or crossing routes by#2. If #2 goes outside, they expand, and they look for and wall the new #2. The two underneath defenders wall #2 and #3 versus trips.

Cover-2 backer is used in the fire-zone package with the Falcon and Stud, or the Sam and Will linebackers working together, or in a combination of the two positions to wall the #2 receivers to both sides, and take away all inside cuts from the inside-out. They should cut the slants, wheel with the dig, wall the crossers, and be ready to jump the #2 receivers on bootlegs when they run chip routes to their side. If the #2 receiver goes upfield, the linebackers sneak a peek outside to cut off any new #2 that replaces the original route with an under route.

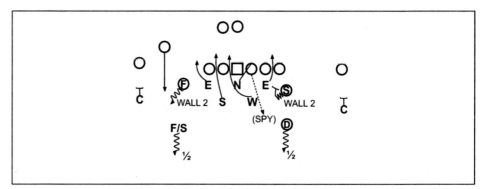

Figure 9-21. Cover-2 backer with a five-man rush

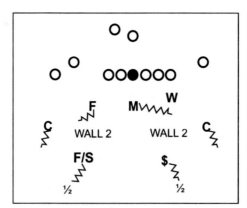

Figure 9-22. Cover-2 backer versus 11

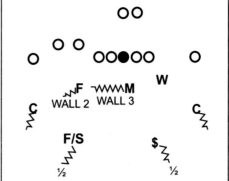

Figure 9-23. Cover-2 backer versus 10 trips

Cover 6

Cover 6 is a quarter-quarter-half coverage concept. It is a highly adjustable coverage that requires a call from the free safety and Stud on every play. They communicate the call to the linebackers, Falcon, and corners so that all positions play the same adjustment to the coverage. The base alignment is a cover-2 shell, and the adjustments are based on the number of receivers, alignment, down-and-distance, and game situations.

Strengths of Cover 6

- Fits well with a cover-2 shell concept before the ball is snapped.
- Uses robber coverage to both sides in a majority of formations.
- Discourages four verticals.
- Allows for multiple coverage without multiple techniques.
- Is an excellent way to get eight in the box on the running game and still maintain the coverage's integrity.
- Provides excellent coverage versus trips with the ability to adjust to the strongside or weakside throwing game.

Weaknesses of Cover 6

- Post-corner routes run to the weakside.
- Intermediate routes put the free safety and the cornerback in conflict.
- Three-step read routes by #2 in the 10- to 12-yard depth create hesitation about whether to carry or release.
- Level routes test linebackers' discipline to work from deep to short zones.

Cover-6 Adjustments

Combo (Figure 9-24): The combo call is made when two receivers are to a side. The free safety, Stud, and the corners combo the two receivers to their side. They read #2 to #1, and each will play inside and over the top of any vertical release by their receiver. Once #2 releases to the flat, the free safety or Stud should widen and deepen over the top of the #1, and the corner will ensure any inside release by the #1 receiver and be able to play the out cut by the #2 receiver. The Falcon or Will are underneath curl defenders.

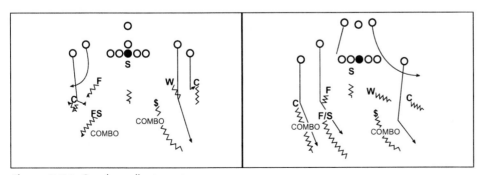

Figure 9-24. Combo adjustment

Robber (Figure 9-25): This call is made by the free safety and the Stud to tell the corner to play inside and over the top of the #1 receiver. The Falcon and Will are buzz droppers, and the free safety and the Stud play robber—play underneath #1 versus any inside, outside, or stop route by the #2 receiver.

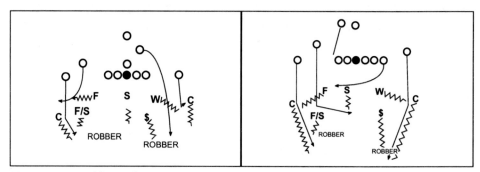

Figure 9-25. Robber adjustment

Bracket (Figure 9-26): This call is made by the free safety and the Stud to tell the corners to play man-to-man on the #1 receiver, and that he may or may not get help from the free safety or the Stud. This call also tells the Will that he has any crosser or #2 to the flat. The bracket is tied into an "I'm here" call by the Stud or free safety to the linebackers. If no run threat or back releases on the pass, the linebacker will drop toward #1 receiver weak and be under the dig, curl, or post, playing the low shoulder.

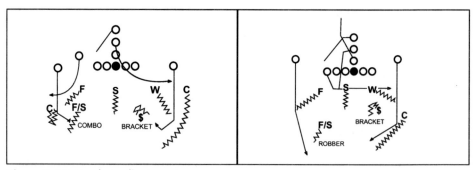

Figure 9-26. Bracket adjustment

Key (Figure 9-27): This call is made by the free safety and the Stud on the backside of trips. It tells the weak corner that he is man-to-man over the top of the #1 receiver, and he may or may not get help from the free safety or the Stud. The underneath dropper will be the same as bracket in that he has any #2 weak.

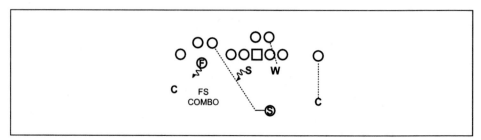

Figure 9-27. Key adjustment

Trap (Figure 9-28): This call is made by the free safety and the Stud to the trips side. It tells the corner to play cover 2. The corner funnels the #1 receiver. The free safety or the Stud plays to a half-field position and stays deeper than the deepest receiver in his half and midway between any two vertical receivers in his half.

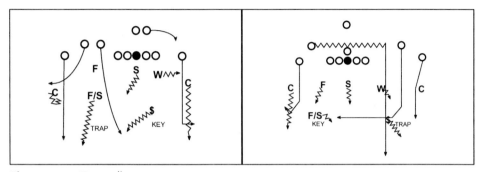

Figure 9-28. Trap adjustment

Tampa (Figure 9-29): The Tampa adjustment is made to the base coverage with dime personnel. The alignment is the same as typical cover 6, but with the dime aligned between the free safety and the Stud. Combo or cloud with the free safety and the Stud can be called, and the dime is always a deep-hole player who should carry any vertical through the middle of the field. The Falcon and Will are curl droppers, and the Mike will be a low-hole player whose responsibility will change week-to-week based on the opponent (e.g., spy, low-hole, screen player, hug rusher, middle dropper).

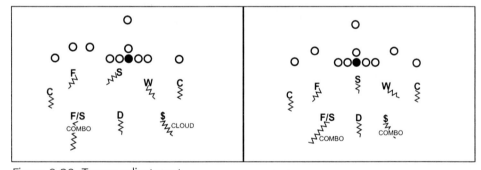

Figure 9-29. Tampa adjustment

Macho: Macho is similar to robber. However, the strong corner plays man on the #1 receiver on UPS (up, post, and seam). If the #1 receiver runs a nonthreatening route, the corner deepens and reads the #2 receiver for the post-corner route. The Falcon buzz drops to take away the three-step routes by #1 and carry the wheel by #2. The free safety robs the route of #2. If #2 goes vertical, the free safety has him UPS (up, post, and seam). If the #2 receiver goes flat or away, the free safety doubles on #1 and drives for width and depth to be over the top of the post as the corner plays aggressive on the curl or dig. The corner can now press the #1 receiver from a press alignment for man coverage or a disguise. The strong corner can play straight man or an outside man technique—man outside routes and zone inside routes.

Invert "Ike" (Figure 9-30): This call is used versus a 21/20 formation with a single wide receiver; or an 11/12 doubles formation for run support, and as a change-up for the weak corner and the Stud. It is similar to cloud support, but the Stud assumes the role of the funnel/flat player, and the corner plays a half-field technique from an inside-third alignment. The Stud uses a buzz technique to take away the three-step game to the #1 receiver and runs with the wheel route by the #2 receiver.

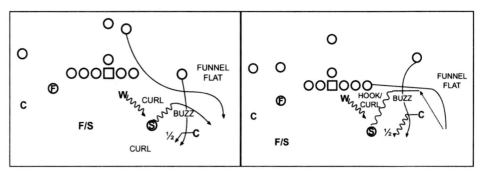

Figure 9-30. Invert adjustment

Cover-6 Robber Alignment and Responsibilities (Figure 9-31)

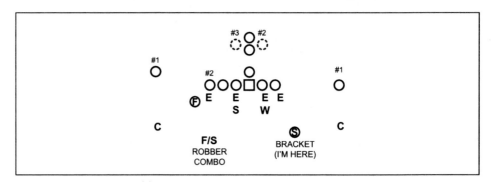

Figure 9-31. Cover-6 robber

Strong Corner: Aligns inside at 45-degree angle and seven yards deep. Keys through the tight end (#2 receiver to the ball). Plays an inside third and protects the post; gets big on the post. If the #2 receiver goes vertical, squeezes back to the #1 receiver. If the #2 receiver goes to the flat, keeps inside position on #1 and plays big on the fade and the post.

Free Safety (Figure 9-32): Aligns one yard outside the tight end at a depth of 10 yards. Keys through the tight end (#2 receiver to the ball). Reads for run or pass. If run, plays downhill and fits inside the Falcon; the free safety is responsible for the outside C and the inside D gaps. He should make the Falcon be right. If the tight end goes outside or inside, the free safety backpedals with his eyes on a swivel—keys #1 to ball. Plays aggressively through the curl and underneath the post. Some game plans call for the free safety to be a robber to the open end side, and be alert for the dig backside when the tight end runs a drag away from his original position.

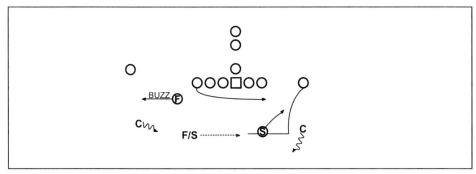

Figure 9-32. Free safety in cover-6 robber

Cover 6 Versus 3x1—10 Trips and 11 Trips (Figures 9-33 and 9-34)

Versus the 3x1, the strong corner and free safety read #2. If #2 goes vertical, the corner stays over the top of #1 and the free safety stays over the top of #2. If #2 goes to the flat, the corner settles and free safety plays over the top of #1. If #2 goes away, the corner keeps inside leverage on #1 and the free safety squeezes to the next deep threat inside. The Stud reads into coverage off #3. The Stud carries #3 on the vertical. If #3 drags or is slow to go, the Stud works back to a late bracket on the #1 receiver weak with the weak corner.

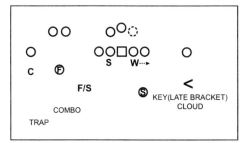
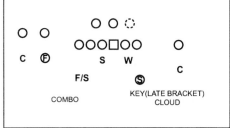

Figure 9-33. Cover 6 versus 10 trips (3x1) Figure 9-34. Cover 6 versus 11 trips (3x1)

Cover 6 Versus 20 (Figure 9-35)

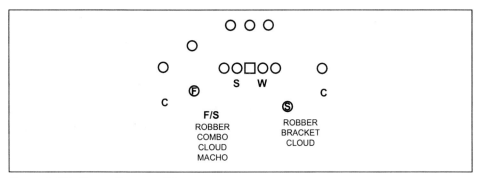

Figure 9-35. Cover 6 versus 20

Cover 6 Versus 2x2 (Figures 9-36 through 9-38)

In cover 6 versus 11/12 doubles (2x2), the Will aligns in a whip technique a majority of times. He will align in one of three positions: stack on the 6 technique, on the line of scrimmage outside the tight end, or in a normal whip position three yards outside the tight end at four yards deep. He should move around and disguise his alignment to confuse any pre-snap read by the offense.

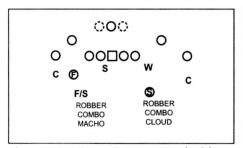

Figure 9-36. Cover 6 versus 10 doubles (2x2)

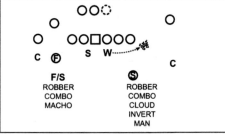

Figure 9-37. Cover 6 versus 11 doubles (2x2)

Figure 9-38. Three Will linebacker alignments

Cover-6 Combo Strong Alignment and Responsibilities

Strong Corner: Sinks and reads the #2 receiver with the free safety. If #2 goes vertical, the corner opens to the field and carries #1 on the fade route. If #2 goes to the flat, the corner settles, reads the quarterback, and gets ready to either jump #2 in the flat on the thrown ball, or sink under the post-corner with the free safety over the top.

Free Safety: Pattern reads off #2. If #2 goes vertical, carries him from the inside-out UPS (up, post, and seam). If #2 goes to the flat, plays over #1 and keeps inside-out position. Squeezes the post from an inside-out position and plays over the top portion of the post-corner; knows that the cornerback, who is sinking, will force the quarterback to put air under the ball. If both receivers go vertical, it is important for the free safety and the strong corner to carry out the read down the field so they can handle the fade/corner and the smash route.

Falcon: Keys through the tight end to the ball. Aligns three yards outside and three yards deep from the tight end. The Falcon is the force player from the outside-in; he reduces the D gap both horizontally and vertically. On pass, the Falcon has a buzz drop to the inside number of the #1 receiver. After his first five steps, he reads back inside to pick up the release of the tight end. If the tight end releases to the outside, the Falcon plays the flat and must be ready to run with him on the wheel. If the tight end goes up the field or away, the Falcon mirrors #1 to take away the three-step game. If no quick-pass threat, adjusts to the route of the #1 receiver; plays under the out cut and wheel with the dig.

Stud: Aligns seven to nine yards deep, and keys through the uncovered linemen to the ball. To the single-width receiver, he should get either a robber or bracket call. The Stud becomes the eighth man in the box with both of these calls. The Stud should make an "I'm here" call to alert the linebacker that the fit of the eighth man is on the weakside; this call enables the linebackers to slide strong (slide late to disguise). On robber, the Stud keys the #2 receiver. If #2 goes vertical, covers UPS (up, post, and seam). If #2 goes outside, blocks, or goes away; the Stud reads to #1, and gets in position to rob #1 on the dig or wheel under the post. He must be aggressive on intermediate routes inside. On bracket, the Stud can rock down because he can overplay the #1 receiver on the slant or three-step pass game. Once these routes are eliminated, the Stud gets his eyes on a swivel and fast reads off the quarterback's eyes as he gets depth underneath the route of #1.

Weak Corner: On robber, plays an inside third and protects the post; gets big on the post. Keys the #2 receiver. If #2 goes vertical, the weak corner squeezes back to #1. If the #2 receiver goes to the flat, the weak corner keeps inside position on #1 and plays big on the post and the fade. On bracket, plays man coverage on #1 and knows that it will be single coverage; help by the Stud will be a bonus.

Sam: Drops #3 to #2 receivers.

Will: On robber, employs a buzz technique. On bracket, covers #2 and remains alert to play the drag from the tight end.

Linebacker Buzz Technique

Versus a single-width receiver: The linebacker drives for the inside number of the wide receiver. Gets his head on a swivel and gets width; he must be aware of the release and route of the #2 receiver. Adjusts width and depth according to the release and route of the wide receiver. Cuts and carries the slant. If the #2 receiver goes to the flat in combination with a dig route, the linebacker plays through the outside portion of the dig—plays from deep to short and reacts to the flat route on the quarterback's eyes or the thrown ball. Must be ready to carry the wheel.

Versus double-width receivers: The linebacker gets out of the box and remains aware of the width of the #2 receiver. Aligns in a triangle, whether inside or outside triangle depends on down-and-distance, field position, and width of receiver. Inside alignment on #2 should be four to six yards deep. Keys through the offensive tackle and guard to the back. Must be aware of high hat or low hat reads. If he reads pass, the linebacker drives through, bangs across the #2 receiver to the inside number of #1. Cuts and carries the slant by #1. If #2 goes to the flat, the linebacker expands and drops; he must be aware of the dig by #1, playing from deep to short, reacting to #2 in the flat on the quarterback's shoulders and the thrown ball. Must be ready to carry the wheel by the #2 receiver.

Versus a nub tight end: Aligns in a 90 technique on the tight end. Gets width and depth, reacts to the flat, or carries the wheel. If no immediate threat, gets depth with his eyes on a swivel, and must be ready to fast break on the quarterback's eyes.

Will Linebacker Whip Technique

The whip technique is used versus a 2x2 set away from the formation, and versus 10 doubles, 11 doubles, and 12 doubles formations. It should not be used versus a two-back set, or the backside of a 3x1 set (trips).

Alignment: Versus a tight end, cocks inside at 45-degree angle, and aligns three yards outside the tight end at a linebacker depth of four yards. Versus a split end (10 doubles), aligns in mid-point between the offensive tackle and the #2 receiver at five yards deep; his stance is square not cocked.

Versus run: D-gap player. Spills the tight end versus the turnout block. Spills any blocks coming from the inside. Responsible for the quarterback versus the option. Responsible for the reverse on flow away. Fold player on flow away. Remember: a fence is over the outside hip of the tight end. The Will must go around the fence not through it as he checks for counters, cutbacks, and reverses.

Combo versus pass: Spot-drops, and splits the distance between #1 and #2. Sees the quarterback, and feels the release of the #2 receiver while dropping to a depth of 12 yards. If #2 goes vertical, Will sneaks a peek at the #1 receiver and must be ready to break on him with a smash route or under route. If #2 goes to the flat or runs a flare route, Will widens with his release, maintains depth, and breaks on #2 off the quarterback's shoulders or the release of the ball. If #2 is not a threat, blocks, or goes away, Will plays to #1's route. Plays the chip receiver on bootleg. Must be aware of the screen. Fast breaks on the quarterback's eyes and shoulders. If the quarterback's eyes are away, Will looks for a crosser on the break.

Robber versus pass: Drives to the inside number of #1. Takes away hitch and slant by #1. Must be ready to run with #2 on the wheel. Takes chipper on the bootleg. If #2 goes to the flat or flare route, Will maintains depth and breaks on #2 on the quarterback's shoulders or ball release. If no #2 threat, plays under #1.

Cover 6 With 50 Front and Eagle/Under Versus 2x2—10 Doubles, 11 Doubles (Figures 9-39 and 9-40)

The same calls are used within the framework of the secondary coverage when in a 50 front with cover 6 as in a 4-2 front.

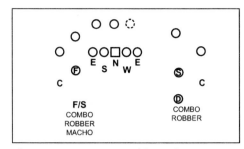

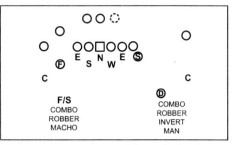

Figure 9-39. Cover 6 with 50 front

Figure 9-40. Cover 6 with Eagle/under front

The Falcon's alignment splits the difference between #2 and #3 and seven yards deep. Reads the #2 to #3 box. If both go vertical, reroutes #2. If #3 drags, the Falcon gets depth and anticipates a dig by #2 or #1. If #2 or #3 cancels out of their verticals, the Falcon should play over the remaining receiver and be aware of the high/low stack. If no immediate threat, he keeps his eyes on the quarterback and makes a play. The Sam drops over #3 and reads the release of #3 and #2. The Sam shouldn't be concerned about a reroute on #3 because the Stud needs to get a clear read on #3's route. The Will has first back weak, screen, and first crosser with late body help on inside cuts by #1. Weak corner takes a strong inside leverage on the #1 receiver and doesn't expect help from the Stud. Any assistance from the Stud will be a bonus.

Cover-6 Tampa From a Five-Across Look (Figures 9-41 through 9-47)

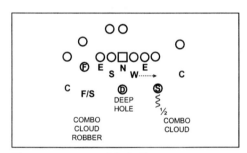

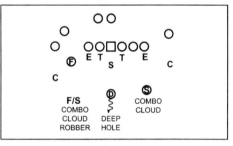

Figure 9-41. 50 nickel alignment

Figure 9-42. Eagle/under alignment

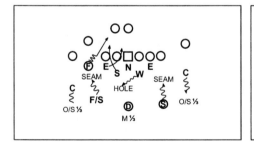

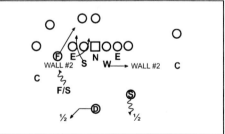

Figure 9-43. Tilt thunder Z spin (three deep coverage behind fire zone)

Figure 9-44. Tilt thunder two backer (two deep coverage behind fire zone)

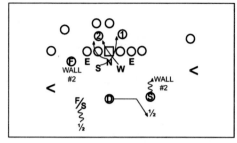

Figure 9-45. Tilt smoke two backer

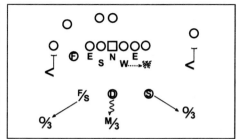

Figure 9-46. Cover 3 from a five-across look

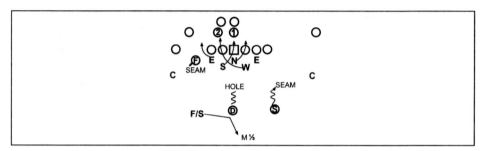

Figure 9-47. Cover-6 Y (tilt smoke 6 Y)

Cover-6 Game Tip Sheet With Corresponding Diagrams From an Actual Game Plan (Figure 9-48)

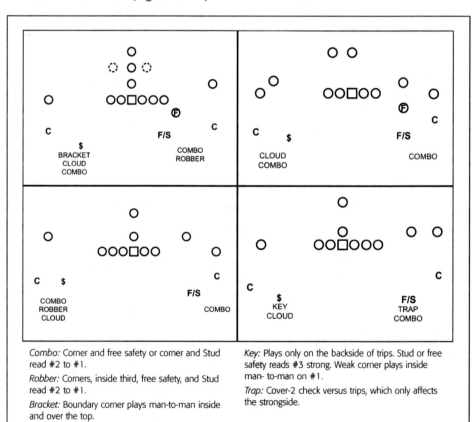

Combo: Corner and free safety or corner and Stud read #2 to #1.

Robber: Corners, inside third, free safety, and Stud read #2 to #1.

Bracket: Boundary corner plays man-to-man inside and over the top.

Key: Plays only on the backside of trips. Stud or free safety reads #3 strong. Weak corner plays inside man- to-man on #1.

Trap: Cover-2 check versus trips, which only affects the strongside.

Figure 9-48. Cover-6 game tip sheet with corresponding diagrams from an actual game

Flex or Hammer Call (Figure 9-49): Plays only versus a tight end. Does not call "robber."

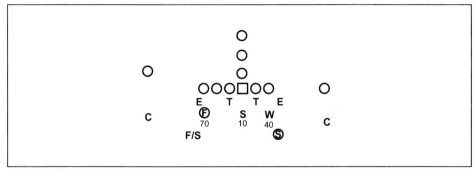

Figure 9-49. Flex or hammer call

FIB (Formation Into Boundary): Versus formation into boundary, the free safety aligns over the guard into the boundary (Figure 9-50). Plays combo. If motion to twins, the free safety slides over and plays combo.

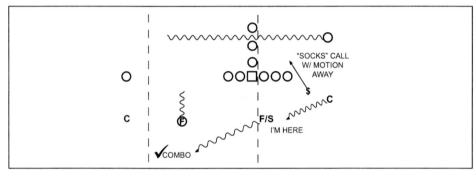

Figure 9-50. Formation into the boundary

Boundary Corner and Stud Versus Nub Tight End Backside (Figure 9-51): No wide receiver is outside the tight end. Combo versus tilt weak; locks man-to-man versus I, tilt strong, or single-back set. Boundary corner is the cutback player. If the tight end blocks, looks for #2 on a post route from the two-receiver side (formation side). Stud will make a "socks" call if the offense is in an I or tilt strong set.

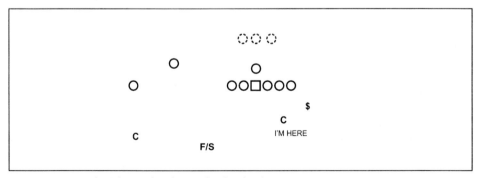

Figure 9-51. Nub tight end only on the backside

Game Plan Examples With Cover-6 Calls Versus Various Formations

- *Cover-6 Eagle Versus Pro* (Figure 9-52): The free safety plays combo unless the coach gives a "robber" or "trap" signal.
- *Cover-6 Under Versus Pro:* Plays combo unless the coach gives a "trap" signal.
- *Cover-6 Eagle Cloud Versus Pro* (Figure 9-53): Free safety plays robber. Play cloud to the weak side of the formation.

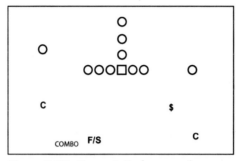

Figure 9-52. Cover-6 Eagle or under versus pro

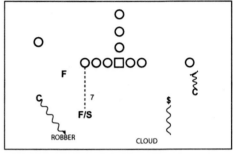

Figure 9-53. Cover 6 Eagle cloud versus pro

- *Cover-6 Combo Versus Twins* (Figure 9-54): Combo to twins unless the coach gives a "trap" signal. Does not play robber.
- *Cover 6 Eagle Versus 11 Doubles* (Figure 9-55): Combo to twins unless the coach gives a "trap" signal. Man-to-man on the tight end and the flanker.

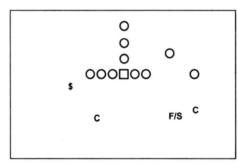

Figure 9-54. Cover-6 combo versus twins

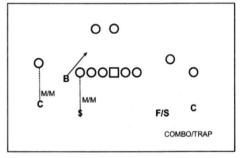

Figure 9-55. Cover-6 Eagle versus 11 doubles

- *Cover-6 50 Versus Doubles* (Figure 9-56): Combo or trap to the two standups. Man the backside of the 11 doubles.
- *Cover-6 Eagle or 50 Versus Trips* (Figure 9-57): Versus 11 trips check to two coverage.
- *Cover-6 Lobo Versus Doubles* (Figure 9-58): Same as cover-6 cloud, except to the field.

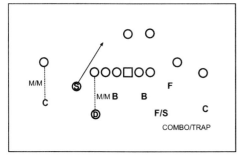

Figure 9-56. Cover 6 50 versus doubles

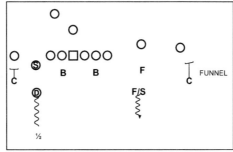

Figure 9-57. Cover-6 Eagle or 50 versus trips (check to two coverage)

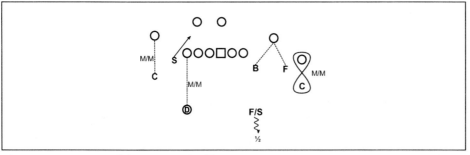

Figure 9-58. Cover-6 lobo versus doubles

Game Plan Calls Versus Various Formations

- *Versus Pro:* Plays combo strong, bracket weak; with a cloud call, plays robber strong; plays combo versus a pro set into the boundary; versus twins, plays combo, or could play trap as a change-up.
- *Versus Tight-End Trips With 12 Personnel* (Figure 9-59): Plays combo.
- *Versus Wing Trips* (Figure 9-60): Plays like tilt strong, combo.

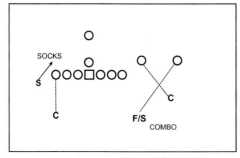

Figure 9-59. Versus tight end trips with 12 personnel

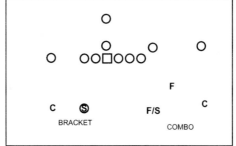

Figure 9-60. Versus wing trips

- *Versus Three-Wide Trips* (Figure 9-61): Cover 6 could be cover 2. In cover 6 versus trips play key coverage; change up will be cover 2.
- *Versus 11 Doubles* (Figure 9-62): Will mix combo and robber to both sides with a man coverage change up on the backside of 11 doubles.

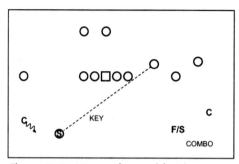

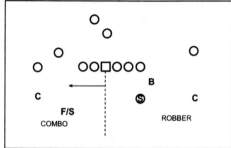

Figure 9-61. Versus three-wide trips

Figure 9-62. Versus 11 doubles

- *Versus Tight-End Trade, Shifts, and Such:* The free safety is the adjuster and makes calls.
- *Versus Empty:* If the offense shows empty and then shifts back to trips, tilts weak, makes zero check, and must be ready if the offense snaps the ball.
- *Versus a Three-Wide Look* (Figure 9-63): Combo to the formation side; bracket to the backside.
- *To the Combo Side in Any Formation:* Must be ready for the double post.

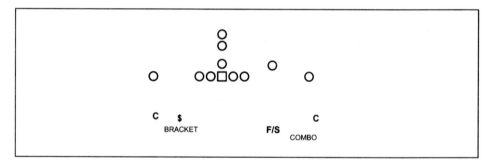

Figure 9-63. Versus a three-wide look

Summary of Cover-6 Calls by Formation (Figures 9-64 through 9-71)

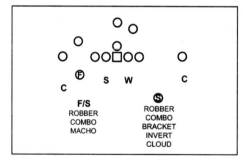
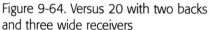

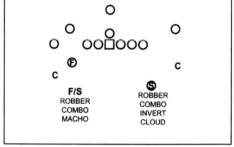

Figure 9-64. Versus 20 with two backs and three wide receivers

Figure 9-65. Versus 11 doubles

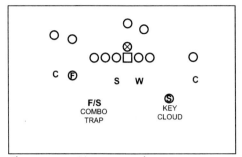

Figure 9-66. Versus 11 trips

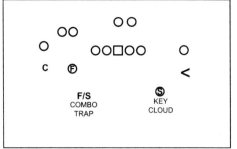

Figure 9-67. Versus 10 trips

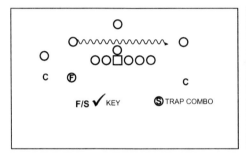

Figure 9-68. Versus doubles (2x2)
to trips (3x1)

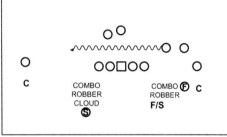

Figure 9-69. Versus trips (3x1)
to doubles (2x2)

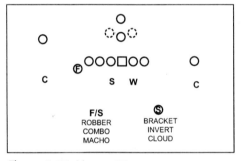

Figure 9-70. Versus 21 pro

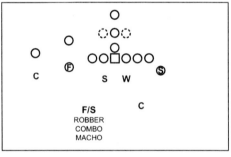

Figure 9-71. Versus 21 twins

On the backside of 21 twins, 22 pro, 12 trips, and 11 trey with either the two back or the one back in a home position, the Stud makes a "socks" call, which sends the blitz off the edge. The blitzer spills all blocks, runs down plays from the backside, checks for reverse, and reads on the run for the bootleg. If a back is set weak or in a wing position, no "socks" call should be made. On runs, the Stud spills all blocks coming from the inside, and on pass he gets depth to cover the back and a flat or wheel route.

Cover 1

The amount of man coverage that a team uses should be determined by how well their secondary matches up against the opponent's receivers and the ability to effectively rush the passer. The preference is to play a full man concept behind a four- or five-man rush, but to also take six- and seven-man blitzes into a majority of games to use when it is imperative to get the offense off the field in critical situations. The key to success in coverage—whether man or zone—is keeping pre-snap reads to a minimum, eliminating the quick options, forcing the quarterback to feel a sense of urgency, and attacking the pass protections at their point of weakness. Finally, it is important that the secondary have an attitude to go get the football rather than just cover people; he should aggressively attack the ball and make something happen.

Cover 1 With a Four-Man Rush From Eagle

Strengths of Cover 1

- Four verticals
- Play-action passes
- Bootlegs
- Screens
- Bubble routes

Weaknesses of Cover 1

- Stop routes
- Inside low-/high-level routes
- Crossing routes
- Rocket or jail-break screens
- Pick routes

Cover 1 Versus Two-Back Sets

Funnel Technique: The funnel technique is only used versus two backs (Figures 9-72 through 9-78). It involves the two linebackers and the Stud playing 3-on-2 on the two backs. The key is to predetermine the middle defender in the funnel . One of the two remaining linebackers is always the middle defender. The linebacker closest to the Stud is the middle man in the funnel. The middle defender always has the inside receiver if both backs move in the same direction. He is the low-hole player if the two backs split. The low-hole player helps on the inside back/receiver, is aware of the drag, and body helps on inside routes by the #1 wide receiver. Once the middle defender is defined, the remaining linebacker and the Stud have the first back outside or low hole. Good communication is critical.

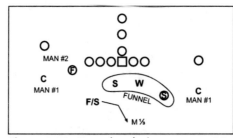

Figure 9-72. Funnel technique versus 21 pro

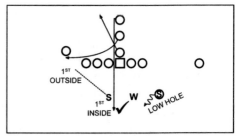

Figure 9-73. Funnel technique versus two backs to the same side

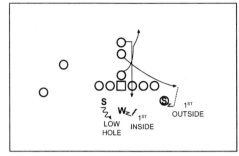

Figure 9-74. Funnel technique versus two backs to the same side

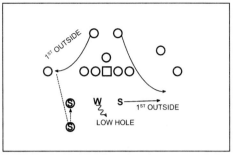

Figure 9-75. Funnel technique versus two backs that split

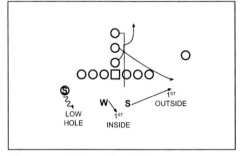

Figure 9-76. Funnel technique versus 22 set

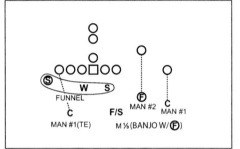

Figure 9-77. Funnel technique versus 21 set

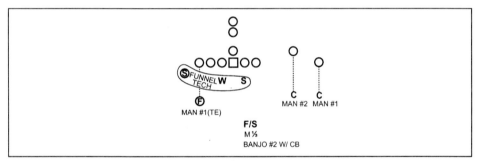

Figure 9-78. Funnel technique versus 21 twins with corners over to the twins side

Both corners can be moved over to the twins side to better match up with the two wide receivers.

Versus any one-back set, whether 2x2 or 3x1, the two linebackers banjo the single back. Once the back declares, the linebacker to the side he moves toward mans up on him, and the other linebacker becomes either a low-hole player or read blitzes. The decision as to whether the free linebacker becomes a low-hole player or blitzes should depend on the quality of the back, or crossing routes and screen potential.

Cover 1 Versus Various Formations (Figures 9-79 through 9-87)

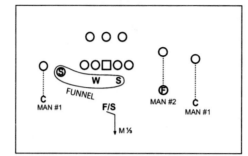

Figure 9-79. Cover 1 versus 20

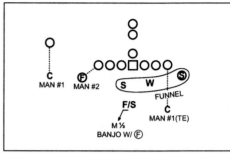

Figure 9-80. Cover 1 versus 22

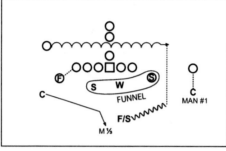

Figure 9-81. Cover 1 versus wide-receiver motion from pro set: bump secondary

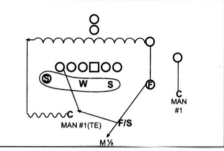

Figure 9-82. Cover 1 versus wide-receiver motion from twins: bump secondary

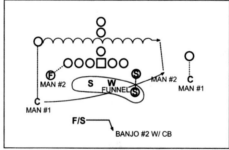

Figure 9-83. Cover-1 motion adjustment: corner runs with motion

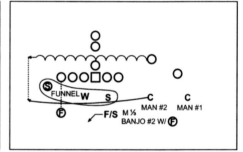

Figure 9-84. Cover-1 motion adjustment: corner runs with motion

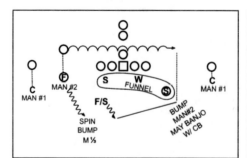

Figure 9-85. Cover-1 motion adjustment: bump secondary

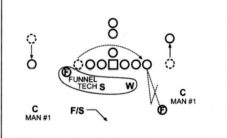

Figure 9-86. Cover-1 adjustment versus tight-end (Y) trade from two backs (Falcon and Stud trade with tight end)

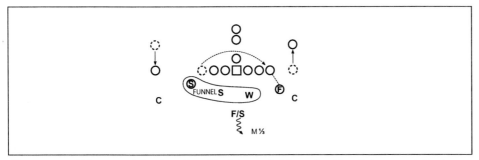

Figure 9-87. Falcon and Stud trade with tight-end (Y) trade—The Falcon and Stud trade so that the Falcon goes with the tight end. This adjustment allows the Falcon to man on #2 and the Stud to remain in the funnel technique with the other linebackers.

Cover 1 Versus 2x2 Formations (Figures 9-88 through 9-90)

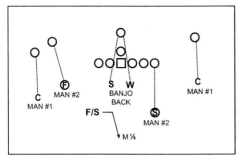

Figure 9-88. Cover 1 versus 11 doubles

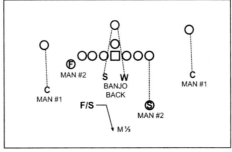

Figure 9-89. Cover 1 versus 12 doubles

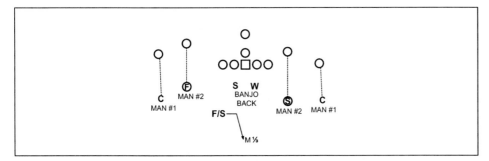

Figure 9-90. Cover 1 versus 10 doubles

Cover 1 Versus 3x1 Formations

- *11 Trips* (Figure 9-91): A "switch" call can be made between the Falcon and the free safety. The free safety mans up on the #2 receiver, and the Falcon has the #3 receiver. Most of the time, the Falcon and free safety will banjo the #2 and #3 receivers.
- *12 Trips* (Figure 9-92): With a nub tight end (single receiver to his side), the corner can make a "switch" call to the Stud. The corner is the middle-third player, and the Stud is man on the tight end, who is the #1 receiver on the backside.

- *10 Trips* (Figure 9-93): The free safety can make a "switch" call to the Falcon. Regardless of whether they switch or not, they banjo the #2 and #3 receivers.

- *11 Trey* (Figure 9-94): The free safety can make a "switch" call to the Falcon. Regardless of whether they switch or not, they banjo the #2 and #3 receivers.

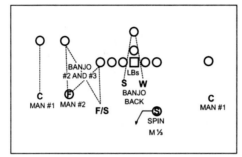

Figure 9-91. Cover 1 versus 11 trips

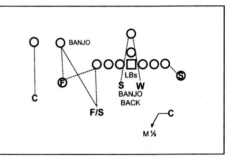

Figure 9-92. Cover-1 adjustment versus 12 trips with a nub tight end

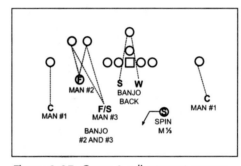

Figure 9-93. Cover-1 adjustment versus 10 trips.

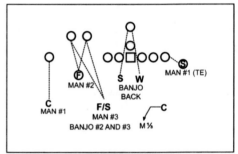

Figure 9-94. Cover-1 adjustment versus 11 trey

Cover-1 Motion Adjustments Versus 2x2 and 3x1 Formations

☐ 11 Doubles—Motion to 11 Trips (Figure 9-95)

Falcon: Goes from man on #2 to bump the free safety and becomes the middle-third player.

Free Safety: Goes from middle-third player to bump to man coverage on the #2 receiver. Free safety and the Stud banjo the #2 and #3 receivers.

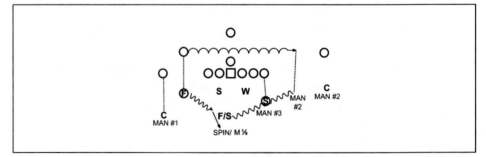

Figure 9-95. Cover-1 motion adjustment versus 11 doubles (motion to 11 trips)

☐ 11 Doubles (Figure 9-96)

Free Safety: Goes from middle-third player to man coverage on #3. Free safety and the Falcon banjo the #2 and #3 receivers.

Corner: Goes from man on the #1 receiver to switch with the Stud. Corner bumps the free safety and becomes the middle-third player; the Stud goes to man on the tight end. The free safety and Falcon banjo the #2 and #3 receivers.

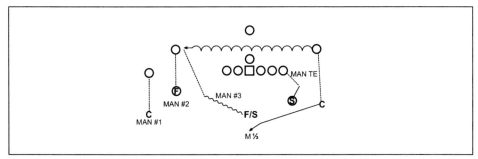

Figure 9-96. Cover-1 motion adjustment versus 11 doubles

☐ 12 Doubles (Figures 9-97 and 9-98)

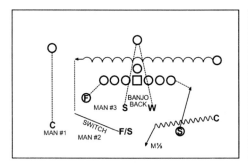

Figure 9-97. Cover-1 motion adjustment versus 12 doubles (corner bumps free safety)

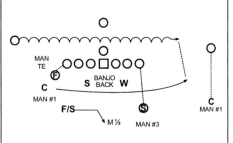

Figure 9-98. Cover-1 motion adjustment versus 12 doubles (cornerback runs with motion)

☐ 10 Doubles (Figure 9-99)

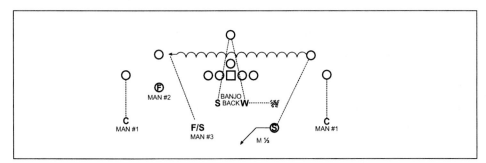

Figure 9-99. Cover-1 motion adjustment versus 10 doubles (Stud bumps the free safety)

❏ 11 Trips (Figures 9-100 through 9-103)

There is no secondary banjo versus motion to 2x2.

Corners: Man on #1 receivers.

Free Safety: Goes from man on #3 receiver with banjo to middle-third player.

Stud: Goes from middle-third player to man on the #2 receiver.

Falcon: Goes from man on the #2 receiver with banjo, to man on #2 with no banjo.

Sam and Will: Banjo the single back.

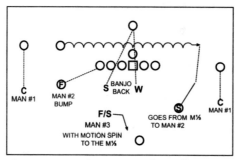

Figure 9-100. Cover-1 motion adjustment versus 11 trips

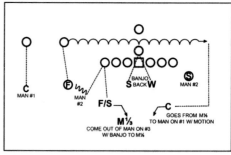

Figure 9-101. Cover-1 motion adjustment versus 12 trips

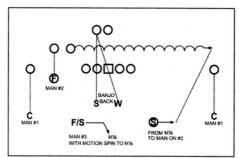

Figure 9-102. Cover-1 motion adjustment versus 10 trips

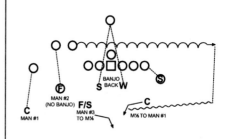

Figure 9-103. Cover-1 motion adjustment versus 11 trey

Cover-1 Tight-End (Y) Trade Adjustment Versus 2x2 and 3x1 Formations

Corners: Man the #1 receivers.

Falcon: Goes from man on #2 to switch with the free safety; plays man on #3; will banjo #2 and #3 with the free safety.

Free Safety: Goes from middle third to switch with the Falcon; plays man on #2; will banjo #2 and #3 with the Falcon.

Stud: Goes from man on #2 (tight end) to middle-third player.

Sam and Will: Banjo the single back.

❏ 11 Doubles (Figure 9-104)

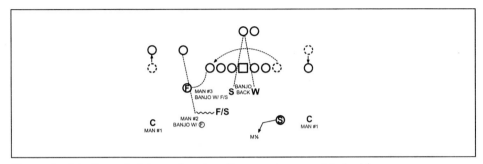

Figure 9-104. Cover-1 tight-end trade adjustment versus 11 doubles

Cover 1 With Five-Man Rush From Eagle

The only difference between a five-man rush and the four-man rush is the underneath coverage of the running backs. Otherwise, the secondary coverage is the same against the two-back, 2x2, and 3x1 formations. Figures 9-105 through 9-108 illustrate the linebacker coverages against the two-back, 2x2, and 3x1 formations.

20 Split Pro With Two Backs

The Will linebacker and the Stud banjo the two backs (Figure 9-105). The linebackers should make a "peel alert" call to alert the defensive linemen to not allow a running back to cross their face on a flare route.

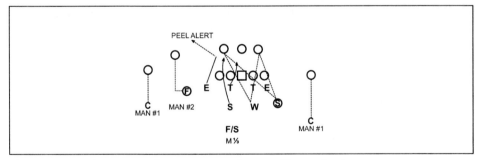

Figure 9-105. Five-man rush versus 20 split pro with two backs

Doubles 2x2

Versus a single back, the remaining linebacker is the man on the back. The defense gains an extra rusher but loses the low-hole player if the back releases. If the back remains in for protection, the linebacker can either blitz read or become the low-hole player. The low-hole linebacker plays for crossers, screens, and checkdowns to the back (Figure 9-106).

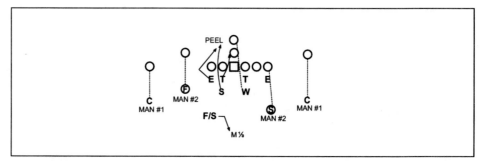

Figure 9-106. Five-man rush versus 12 doubles (2x2)

11 Trips—2x2

Typically, the free safety and Falcon switch on a 3x1 formation with tight-end trips (Figure 9-107), and banjo the #2 and #3 receivers with three stand-up wide receivers (Figure 9-108).

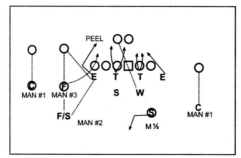

Figure 9-107. Five-man rush versus 11 trips with a tight end (3x1)

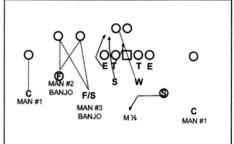

Figure 9-108. Five-man rush versus 11 trips with three stand-up wide receivers (3x1)

10

Eighth Man in the Box Principle

It is essential to have a simple, yet sound defensive scheme to get eight men in the box against both the one-back and two-back running game. The eighth man can come from either the defensive front or from a secondary player. It is equally important to have the eighth man in the box versus gap run plays and zone-concept run plays. Furthermore, the defense has to be very disciplined in its gap-fill responsibilities in order to neutralize the effectiveness of the run game. It is imperative that defenders know where their help is, that they trust the defense, and they have the proper fit whether it is inside or outside the blocker in the gap for which they are responsible. Most big plays of eight yards or more usually occur because of poor fits and mistakes on gap responsibilities. Thus, the primary key to be an efficient run defense is to be good in gap-fill responsibilities.

In both cover 6 and cover 3, either the Stud, Falcon, free safety, dime (50 front), or weak side corner (to nub tight end) can be the eighth man in the box. The majority of this chapter deals with cover 6, but cover 3 fits well into this concept also. Furthermore, the discussion includes two-back, doubles (2x2), and trips (3x1) formations. On every defensive play, the two linebackers must get either an "I'm here" call or an "I'm gone" call from the secondary. The "I'm here" call alerts the linebackers that one of the five players (Stud, Falcon, free safety, dime, or weak corner) will "rock down" for run support. The "I'm gone" call alerts the backers that, because it is a cover 2, cover-2 man, no rock down will occur by a defensive back.

"I'm Here" Call Versus Two Backs

21 Pro (Figures 10-1 and 10-2)

Versus 21 pro from a 50 front, the Will linebacker should be ready to fit into either A gap (pitchfork) off the nose, depending on the angle of the running back.

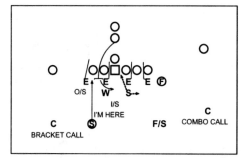

Figure 10-1. Versus 21 pro from an Eagle front

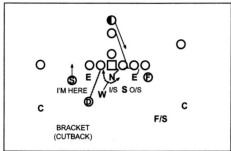

Figure 10-2. Versus 21 pro from a 50 front

21 Twins (Figures 10-3 and 10-4)

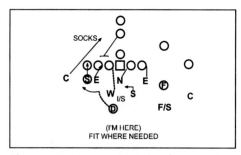

Figure 10-3. Versus 21 twins from a 50 front

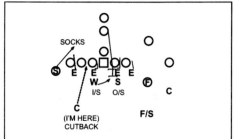

Figure 10-4. Versus 21 twins from an Eagle front

20 I With Three Wide Receivers (Figures 10-5 and 10-6)

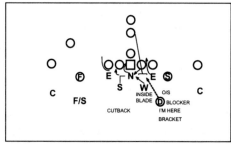

Figure 10-5. Versus 20 I with three wide receivers from a 50 front

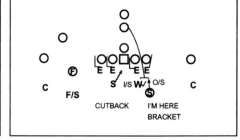

Figure 10-6. Versus 20 I with three wide receivers from an Eagle front

22 (Figures 10-7 and 10-8)

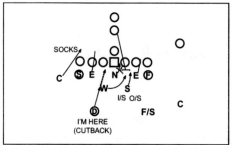

Figure 10-7. Versus 22 from a 50 front

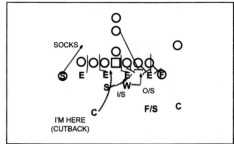

Figure 10-8. Versus 22 from an Eagle front

"I'm Here" Call Versus Single Back

All fits versus single-back formations are governed by the "one back, one gap" rule. A "base" call can be mixed with cover-6 invert and cloud, and cover 3 versus a strong running game from the 11 doubles and 12 doubles formations.

11 Doubles (Figures 10-9 through 10-11)

Versus 11 doubles with a tight end from an Eagle front (Figure 10-10), the standard adjustment is to play the Will linebacker in a whip technique. The Will backer is the D-gap player, and the Stud fits into either the A or B gap backside, depending on the alignment of the 1 and 3 techniques. The full explanation of the whip technique is in Chapter 6.

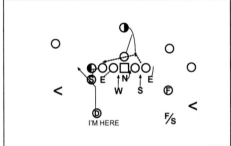

Figure 10-9. Versus 11 doubles (2x2) from a 50 front

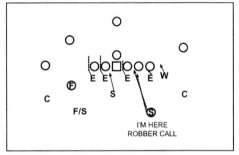

Figure 10-10. Versus 11 doubles with a tight end from an Eagle front

A change-up versus this formation is a "solid" call. The Will linebacker stays on his standard inside position, and the Stud and weak corner make an "invert" call. The invert is an inverted cloud with the Stud as the funnel and D-gap player; the corner plays a half-field technique from an inside-third alignment; and the Will must carry the #2 receiver (tight end) on a vertical move (Figure 10-11).

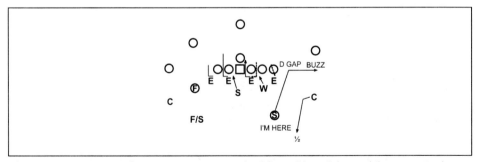

Figure 10-11. Invert adjustment versus 11 doubles with a tight end from an Eagle front

12 Doubles (Figures 10-12 through 10-14)

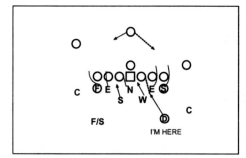

Figure 10-12. Versus 12 doubles from a 50 front

Figure 10-13 Versus 12 doubles from an Eagle whip

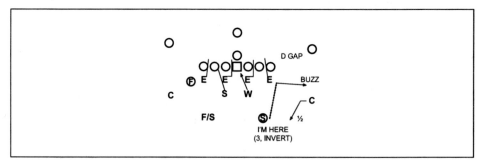

Figure 10-14. Versus 12 doubles from base, invert, or cover 3

10 Doubles (Figures 10-15 and 10-16)

The call versus this formation is "I'm gone" because only six gaps exist with the double split of the four wide receivers.

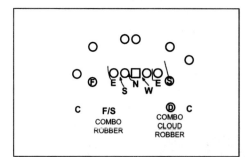

Figure 10-15. Versus 10 doubles with four wide receivers from a 50 front

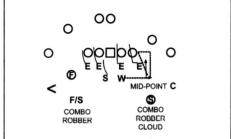

Figure 10-16. Versus 10 doubles with four wide receivers from an Eagle front

Linebacker Adjustment to Trips
(Figures 10-17 and 10-18)

The linebackers slide to the strength of the formation versus any 3x1 formation or four-man surface that is created by a wing or a tilt back. In an Eagle front, the Sam aligns in a 70 or heavy 90 technique, and the Will aligns in a stack 10, favoring his gap responsibility. In a 50 front, the Sam linebacker aligns in a 50 technique, and the Will in a stack 10. The Stud stacks over the outside hip of the defensive end in a light 50 technique. The linebackers slide back to their 30 alignment versus any motion or tight-end trade movement that creates a 2x2 formation. The linebacker's ability to adjust to a tight-end trade to the wing, a tilt back moving to the opposite side, or a wide receiver motion that creates a four-man surface is key to maintaining leverage and preventing seams the offense is trying to establish by variations they use prior to the snap.

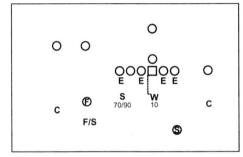

Figure 10-17. Linebacker adjustment to trips from an Eagle front

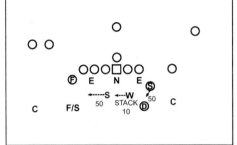

Figure 10-18. Linebacker adjustment to trips from a 50 front

"I'm Here" Call Versus Trips—3x1

11 Trips (Figures 10-19 and 10-20)

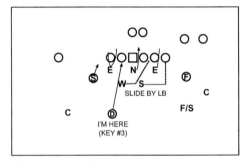

Figure 10-19. Versus 11 trips from a 50 front

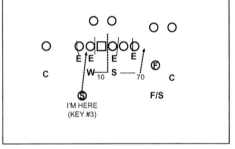

Figure 10-20. Versus 11 trips from an Eagle front

12 Trips (Figures 10-21 and 10-22)

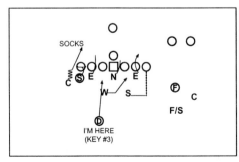

Figure 10-21. Versus 12 trips from a 50 front

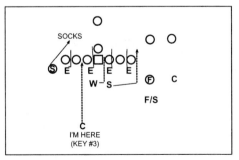

Figure 10-22. Versus 12 trips from an Eagle front

10 Trips (Figures 10-23 and 10-24)

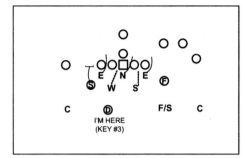

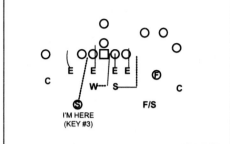

Figure 10-23. Versus 10 trips from a 50 front

Figure 10-24. Versus 10 trips from an Eagle front

"I'm Here" Call by the Free Safety Versus a Tight End

The Stud, dime, and weak corner all fit into the secondary fill principle. The free safety in six coverage (quarters coverage) is a rock-down player by his alignment versus 21 pro, 22, and 12 doubles. The free safety aligns 8 to 10 yards deep so he can trigger quickly when the tight end blocks, thus becomes a ninth player in the box. The free safety makes an "I'm here" call versus 21 pro in order to play bracket or cloud to the split end side. On bracket and cloud, the Stud or dime become either a buzz or bracket player (Figures 10-25 and 10-26). These calls are good versus a team that emphasizes throwing to the split-end side from the three-step drop and hitch screen.

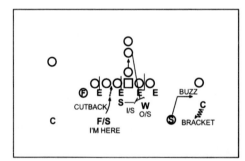

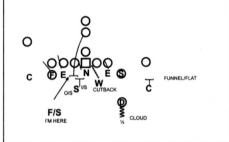

Figure 10-25. Bracket to the split-end side

Figure 10-26. Cloud to the split-end side

"I'm Here" Call Versus 12 Doubles

(Figures 10-27 and 10-28)

From an Eagle base wide 6 call, the wide call moves the defensive end to a heavy 9 from a 6 technique (Figure 10-27). Doing so allows the free safety to be an "I'm here" player. The Stud makes a cloud call. The linebackers slide away from the "I'm here" call. In addition, invert and man-coverage adjustments can take place from the Eagle front with a free safety "I'm here" call.

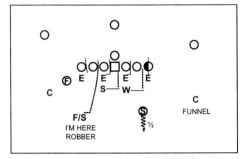

Figure 10-27. Versus 12 doubles from a Eagle base wide 6

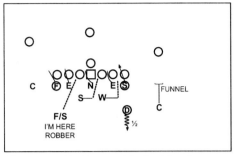

Figure 10-28. Versus 12 doubles from a 50 front

"I'm Here" Versus Formation Into the Boundary

(Figures 10-29 and 10-30)

From the Eagle front, the Falcon assumes the rock-down role and makes an "I'm here" call when the formation is into the boundary (Figure 10-29). The Falcon also makes a "robber" or "bracket" call to the strongside corner, which alerts the linebackers that the Falcon is the fill player from the secondary.

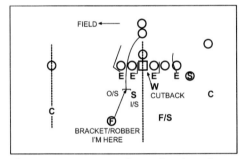

Figure 10-29. Versus formation into the boundary from an Eagle front

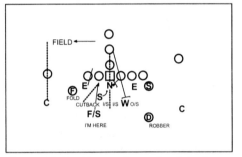

Figure 10-30. Versus formation into the boundary from a 50 front

"I'm Here" and "I'm Gone" Tips and Reminders for Linebackers

- With a nub tight end on the backside, the linebacker will get an "I'm here" call from the corner (Figures 10-31 through 10-33). The linebackers should slide toward the formation.

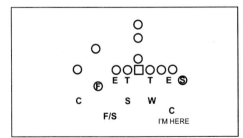

Figure 10-31. Versus 21 twins with a nub tight end on the backside

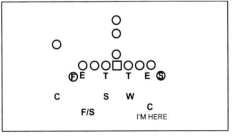

Figure 10-32. Versus 22 with a nub tight end on the backside

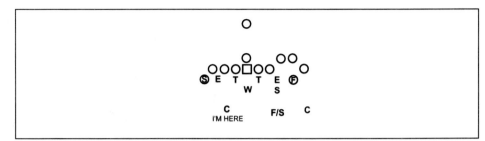

Figure 10-33. Versus 11 trey with a nub tight end on the backside

- With a single wide receiver to the backside, the Stud makes a "bracket" or "combo" call. If cloud coverage is called, no "I'm here" call comes from the Stud because he is a half-field player. The Stud makes an "I'm gone" call, and the free safety makes the "I'm here" call (Figures 10-34 and 10-35).

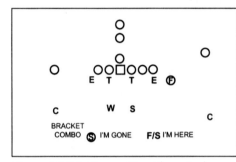

Figure 10-34. Versus 21 with a single wide receiver on the backside (Stud makes "I'm gone" call)

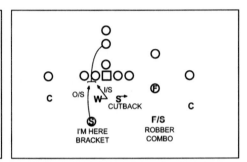

Figure 10-35. Versus 20 with a single wide receiver on the backside (Stud makes "I'm here" call)

- With the Eagle and under fronts, a lot of cover-6 cloud check or bracket check will be called to get double coverage on the single wide receiver (Figure 10-36). The free safety makes the "I'm here" call. This offensive team likes hitch and hitch screen to the single wide receiver (split end).

- With the formation to the boundary, the Falcon makes the "I'm here" call (Figure 10-37).

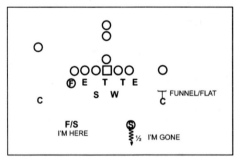

Figure 10-36. Versus 21 with single wide receiver to the backside (Stud makes "I'm gone" call)

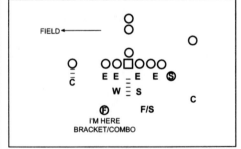

Figure 10-37. Versus 21 with formation to boundary, (Falcon makes "I'm here" call)

- With motion toward the wide field side, the weak corner will make the "I'm here" call to the nub tight-end side created by the motion (Figure 10-38). The Falcon makes an "I'm gone" call.

- Versus 21 tilt with motion toward the wide field side, no linebacker adjustment is made (Figure 10-39).

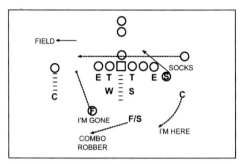

Figure 10-38. Versus 21 with motion toward the wide field side (weak corner makes "I'm here" call)

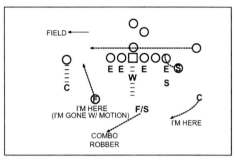

Figure 10-39. Versus 21 tilt with motion toward the wide field side (no linebacker adjustment is made)

- With under, flex, and hammer versus 21 and the single wide receiver is to the wide field side, there is no change for the linebackers (Figure 10-40). The Falcon aligns on the tight end side, and the Stud aligns to the wide field and makes the "I'm here" call.
- With motion to the wide field side, the corner makes the "I'm here" call, and the Stud makes the "I'm gone" call (Figure 10-41).
- With 10 doubles, only "I'm gone" calls are made by the secondary because all gaps can be accounted for with no tight end (Figure 10-42).
- With 10 doubles and motion to trips (3x1), the Stud makes the "I'm here" call (Figure 10-43).

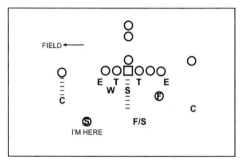

Figure 10-40. Under, flex, and hammer versus 21 with the single wide receiver to the wide field (Stud makes "I'm here" call)

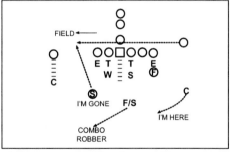

Figure 10-41. Under, flex, and hammer versus 21 with motion to wide field (Stud makes "I'm gone" call)

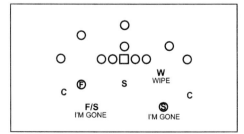

Figure 10-42. Versus 10 doubles (only "I'm gone" calls from the secondary)

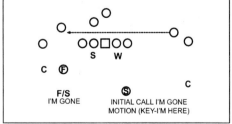

Figure 10-43. Versus 10 doubles with motion to trips (3x1) (Stud makes "I'm here" call)

- Against a 20 formation, the free safety and the Stud will set the coverage according to the alignment of the backfield (Figure 10-44 through 10-47).

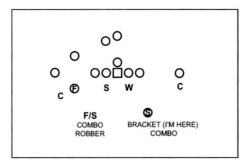

Figure 10-44. Versus 20 (Stud makes "I'm here" call)—bracket/combo trigger the I'm here call

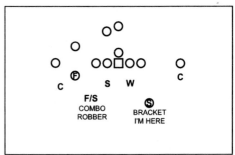

Figure 10-45. Versus 20 (Stud makes "I'm here" call)—enables the stud to be the "I'm here" player

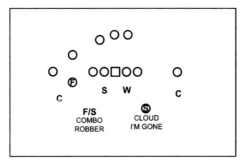

Figure 10-46. Versus 20 (Stud makes "I'm gone" call)—"I'm here" call in cloud coverage

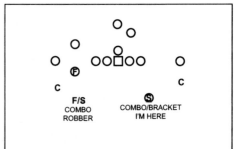

Figure 10-47. Versus 20 (Stud makes "I'm here" call)—similar to figure 10-44 and 10-45

Linebackers should remember that 90 percent of the "I'm here" calls will come from the Stud or the weak corner. A check at the end of the coverage call (e.g., cover-6 bracket check) alerts the linebackers that the free safety makes the call. If the formation is to the boundary, the Falcon or the Stud with hammer, flex, under is the rock-down player with the "I'm here" call.

Linebackers should not rely completely on a verbal call to indicate the "I'm here" or "I'm gone" player. Linebackers should establish eye contact with the defensive backs and see their hand signals to verify the support call:

- Tap chest = The defensive back who has the "I'm here" call will tap his chest, along with the "I'm here" call, when the linebackers look at him.
- Wave = It will be the same scenario with the "I'm gone" call when the defensive backer waves to the linebackers, alerting them that they are not the rock down players.

Fits will be key in winning the game. Linebackers should know where help comes from.

11

Gap-Fill Responsibilities

In order to successfully defend against the run, a defense should be a good gap-control team. Gap control simply means keeping a defender both inside and outside every blocker on each run play. It is important for each player to understand his role on each defense called so the defense can accomplish maximum success versus the running game. To accomplish maximum success, the defense needs to achieve three primary objectives:

- Force
- Spill
- Plug

It is particularly important for linebackers to know their area of responsibility so they can get the proper fit in the correct gaps. Linebackers should key offensive linemen and visualize the running backs. Linebackers should attack on the snap of the ball, pressing downhill to their gap responsibility while keying the angle of the back. The key to the linebacker's success is being able to adjust his press to daylight and the angle of the back and the ball. As he presses his gap and feels daylight, the linebacker should continue to attack downhill to the back's angle. If the linebacker presses and encounters darkness, he should be ready to expand (widen) or reduce (tighten) his press to the angle of the back and find daylight. On run plays, the offense is looking to attack the bubble in the defensive front, thus it is the linebacker's responsibility to take that bubble away by a fast execution of the following techniques:

- Key
- Press
- Adjust
- Shed
- Explosion

Linebackers should know where their help is coming from on every defense. This knowledge is important because it tells them how to fit in the hole and on blockers with the proper inside or outside technique. Linebackers need to remember the following keys:

- *Linebacker to the side of the "I'm here" call:* On flow toward the "I'm here" call, the linebacker to that side should stay inside the blocker with the rock-down player (secondary player) outside the block. The backside linebacker presses to the angle of the back and stays alert for a cutback by leveraging the ballcarrier from the inside-out.

- *Linebacker away from the side of the "I'm here" call:* On flow toward the awayside linebacker, the backer fits on all blocks from the outside-in. The backside backer stays inside the blocker and the ball, and stays alert for the cutback. The rock-down player plays downhill fast with a slow-to-go approach to prevent any cutback threat.

Other keys to good linebacker run defense are angles, vision, and leverage. The linebacker should concentrate on the angle of the back, expand his vision, press the line of scrimmage while adjusting his leverage to the ball, and finish strong.

Eagle Gap Fills Versus Two Backs

Eagle formation call versus flow strong (Figure 11-1): Will linebacker stacks and has the frontside A gap to the ball; Stud has the backside B gap.

Eagle weak call versus flow strong (Figure 11-2): Will linebacker stacks and has the backside A gap to the ball; Stud is a cleanup player, checking and filling all gaps from the outside in as he reads the angle of the back, searching for daylight; Sam has the frontside B gap.

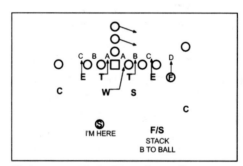

Figure 11-1. Eagle formation call versus flow strong

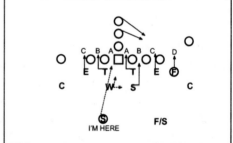

Figure 11-2. Eagle weak call versus flow strong

Eagle formation call versus flow weak (Figure 11-3): Will linebacker has the B gap to the ball; Sam has the backside A gap to the ball; Stud rocks down, and if he finds darkness, then he fills to daylight.

Eagle weak call versus flow weak (Figure 11-4): Sam is a backside B to A gap player with a cutback mentality, reading and fitting to the angle of the back; Will is the frontside A gap player—the angle of the back and ball will determine whether it is mental or physical fit in the A gap; Stud rocks down to fit to the angle of back from the outside in.

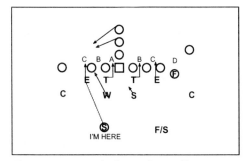

Figure 11-3. Eagle formation call versus flow weak

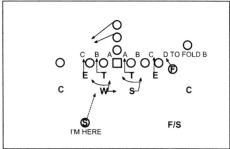

Figure 11-4. Eagle weak call versus flow weak

Eagle Gap Fills Versus One Back
(Figures 11-5 through 11-8)

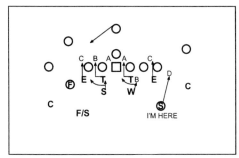

Figure 11-5. Eagle formation call versus flow strong

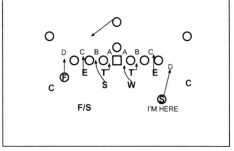

Figure 11-6. Eagle weak call versus flow strong

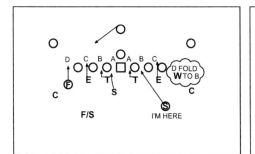

Figure 11-7. Eagle whip formation call versus flow strong.

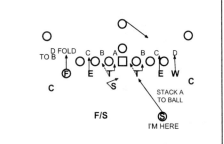

Figure 11-8. Eagle whip weak call versus flow weak

Hammer/Flex Gap Fills: Tight Call With Hammer

Hammer tight call versus flow strong (Figure 11-9): Linebackers slide when the "I'm here" call comes from the Stud. Hammer and flex fronts are explained in more detail in Chapter 13.

Hammer tight call versus flow weak (Figure 11-10): Will presses to the angle of the back, and spills all blocks to the Stud rocking down; Sam presses and stacks the A gap to the flow; Falcon checks the C gap, presses inside, and plays the backside A gap from the outside-in; Will has the inside of the B gap, Stud has the outside of the B gap, and fits to the flow.

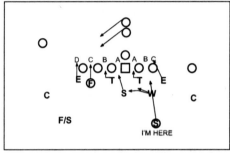
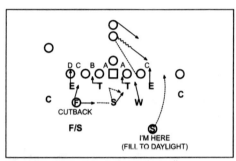

Figure 11-9. Hammer tight call versus flow strong

Figure 11-10. Hammer tight call versus flow weak

Under Gap Fills

Under tight call versus flow strong (Figure 11-11): The corner makes the "I'm here" call; he has the backside A gap/cutback to the angle of the back.

Under tight call versus flow weak (Figure 11-12): The corner makes the "I'm here" call; he rocks down, fits to daylight, and provides second-level gap security.

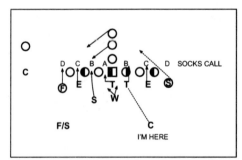
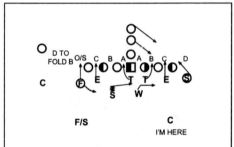

Figure 11-11. Under tight call versus flow strong

Figure 11-12. Under tight call versus flow weak

Gap Fills Versus Specific Run Plays

It is important for all defensive players to understand their role on each play so the defense can accomplish maximum success versus the running game. The vfollowing defensive responsibilities versus several specific run plays provide good examples of how the gap-fill concept is applied.

Versus Isolation Strong (Figure 11-13)

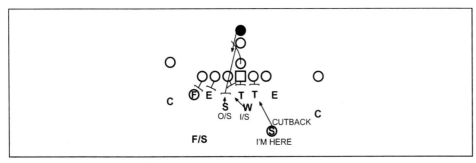

Figure 11-13. Versus isolation strong

Falcon: Squeezes, doesn't widen the 5 technique, reduces the hole from the outside-in, and doesn't run around the block.

Sam: Becomes the force player; fills the B gap from the outside-in, and plays downhill and through the fullback with inside arm and shoulder.

Defensive tackle to playside: Gets good upfield movement, and forces the tackle to block him.

Defensive tackle to backside: Attacks, and knocks the guard back.

Will: Presses, beats the center, and fills the B gap from the inside-out. Becomes the spill player.

5 technique backside: Squeezes, and reduces toward the hole.

Stud: Makes the "I'm here" call, rocks down, and looks for the cutback in the A or B gap.

Free safety and Stud: Act as pluggers

Versus Isolation Weak (Figure 11-14)

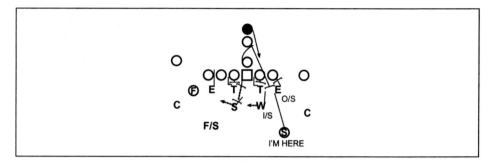

Figure 11-14. Versus isolation weak

Stud: Makes the "I'm here" call. Becomes the force player; takes away the outside portion of the B gap, and plays the fullback's block from the outside-in.

Will: Becomes the spill player; spills the fullback from the inside-out, and takes away the inside potion of the B gap.

Sam: Becomes the plug player; presses the line of scrimmage, and looks for the cutback in the A gap.

Versus Power G Strong (Figure 11-15)

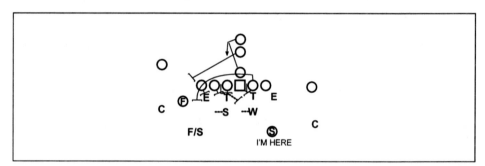

Figure 11-15. Versus power G strong

Falcon: Becomes the force player; squeezes from the outside-in, and sets the wall tight both horizontally and vertically.

6 technique: Attacks the tight end, and knocks the tight end back with his head and hands.

3 technique: Gets a strong push upfield, forcing the tackle to block on the 3 technique so he can't come off to the Will.

Sam: Becomes the plug player; stays inside the fullback kick-out block and outside the puller.

Will: Becomes the spill player; stays inside the puller.

Backside defensive tackle: Attacks, and knocks the center back to reduce the cutback in the A gap.

Stud: Becomes the plug player; takes away the A- to B-gap cutback threat.

Free safety: Should be a very aggressive plug player on all runs.

Versus Power G With a Tight-End Turnout Block (Figure 11-16)

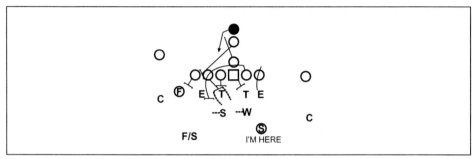

Figure 11-16. Versus power G with a tight-end turnout block

This blocking scheme has the tight-end turnout block on the Falcon, and the fullback leads on the defensive end.

Falcon: Becomes the force player; squeezes the tight end from the outside-in.

Defensive end: Becomes the spill player; closes down to the inside to spill the first threat, plays the fullback's block with the outside arm and shoulder, keeps the shoulders square, and plays upfield through the spill to eliminate the puller or to force the guard to take a new path either inside or deep to the outside.

Sam: Becomes the plug player; stays inside the kick-out and outside the pulling guard.

Will: Becomes the spill player; stays inside the puller.

Stud: Becomes the plug player; presses the line of scrimmage, and takes away the backside cutback lanes.

Free safety: When the free safety gets a run key from the tight end, he presses the line of scrimmage and becomes the outside-in plug player along with the Sam.

Will and Stud: Plug from the inside-out.

Versus Counter Strong (Figure 11-17)

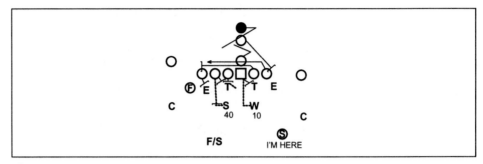

Figure 11-17. Versus counter strong

Falcon: Becomes the spill player; squeezes down to the inside and spills the first puller; stays up when he takes on the backs; takes on the linemen with the outside arm and shoulder through the inside knee; cuts the cutter and creates a pile; and eliminates the second puller with the pile.

Sam: Redirects, and gets inside the first puller and outside the second puller.

Will: Plays inside-out on the second puller, and makes the ball to bounce outside to the unblocked free safety and Sam linebacker.

Versus Counter Weak (Figure 11-18)

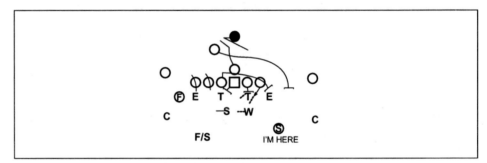

Figure 11-18. Versus counter weak

Defensive end: Becomes the spill player; spills the first puller.

Stud: Becomes the force player; rocks down, and sets the wall tight.

Will: Becomes the spill player; redirects, and spill the second puller (fullback).

Sam: Becomes the plug player; flows over the top to plug with the free safety and the defensive line.

Defensive tackle: Forces the double-team to keep the offensive tackle from coming off onto the linebacker.

Versus Sweep Strong (Figure 11-19)

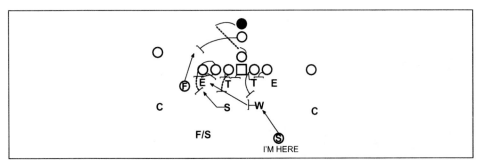

Figure 11-19. Versus sweep strong

Falcon: Becomes the force player; sets the wall quick and tight to eliminate the cutback area.

6 technique: Attacks the tight end with the head and hands, and grabs cloth; flattens the tight end to prevent him from getting to the Sam.

3 technique: Knocks the guard back, and gets the guard's shoulders perpendicular to the line of scrimmage to prevent the guard from getting to the Will.

Sam: As the plug player, slides over on the "I'm here" call and presses to the outside hip of the defensive end. Becomes the spill player when the free safety is the plug player.

Free safety: Becomes the plug player when the Sam is the spill player; fits where needed depending on Sam and Will.

Will: Beats the block of the center and the guard; keeps inside leverage with the Stud for the cutback.

12

Adjustments

Modern defenses are required to adjust to multiple sets; changing formations with motion, Y trade (moving the tight end), the shifting of backs from one back to two back or no back (empty), cluster formations, formations into the boundary, and misdirection (bootleg) passes. Because of this multiplicity of potential offensive sets, it is vitally important that defenses be able to place defenders in situations to minimize the thought process, and enable them to react quickly and play fast on every down. This chapter discusses the defensive adjustments required to successfully deal with these offensive strategies.

Y Trade Adjustments

Y Trade Adjustments From 3x1 to 2x2—11 Trips to 11 Doubles
(Figure 12-1)

It is important to combo/robber both sides of the formation versus a 2x2 set.

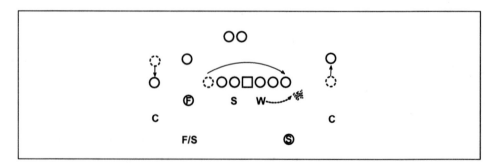

Figure 12-1. Y trade from 3x1 to 2x2

Stud: Still makes the "I'm here" call versus both formations for run support.

Will: Slides to whip alignment versus the 2x2 formation.

Y Trade Adjustments From 2x2 to 3x1—11 Doubles to 11 Trips
(Figure 12-2)

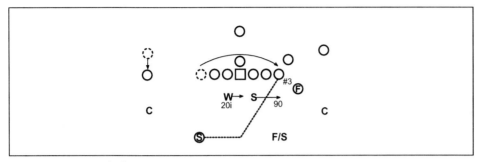

Figure 12-2. Y trade from 2x2 to 3x1

Stud: Makes the "key" call to read the #3 receiver, and the "I'm here" call to slide the linebackers.

Falcon: Moves to the 8 technique on the wing.

Linebackers: Slide toward wing trips (Sam 90 technique on tight end; Will 20i in center-guard gap).

Backside Corner: Mans on #1 weak.

Free Safety: Makes "combo" or "trap" call to trips.

Motion Adjustments

Motion Adjustments From 2x2 to 3x1—12 Doubles to 12 Trips
(Figure 12-3)

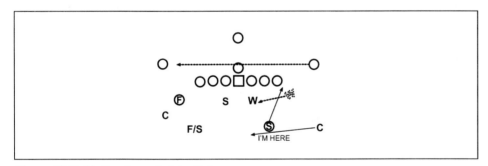

Figure 12-3. Motion from 2x2 to 3x1

Backside Corner: Goes from combo or robber versus 2x2 to a key call on trips (reading the #3 receiver), alerting linebackers to run support with an "I'm here" call.

Free Safety: Combo or trap versus trips.

Stud: Moves to the line of scrimmage with a "socks" call.

Will: Moves from a whip alignment to a 30 technique over the guard.

Motion Adjustments From 2x2 to 3x1—11 Doubles to 11 Trips
(Figure 12-4)

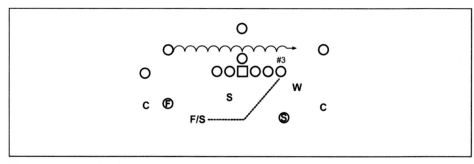

Figure 12-4. Motion from 2x2 to 3x1

Free Safety: Makes a "key" call to read the #3 receiver, and the "I'm here" call to linebackers for run support.

Stud: Makes a combo or trap call to the trips.

Will: Drops over the #2 receiver from whip alignment.

Sam: Drops over the #3 receiver.

Backside Corner: Man on the #1 receiver (away from motion).

Formation Corner: Plays the coverage called by Stud.

Falcon: Plays single back, screen, or first crosser.

Wak Corner: Man/man on the split end.

Motion Adjustments From 21 Twins to 21 Pro (Figure 12-5)

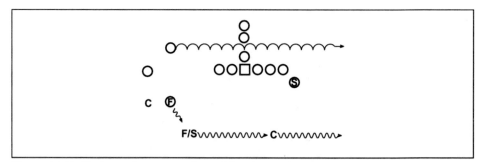

Figure 12-5. Motion adjustments from 21 twins to 21 pro

Stud: "Socks" call is off; plays combo/robber, depending on the call of the free safety.

Free Safety: Slides with motion and makes the combo/robber call.

Corner to Motion: "I'm here" call is off; slides with motion and plays combo/robber on the call of the free safety:

Falcon: Gets depth. Makes the "I'm here" call to the linebackers for run support, and the bracket call to the corner; goes from combo/robber to bracket with the corner.

Weak Corner: Remains alert for a bracket call from the Falcon.

Motion Adjustments From 21 Pro to 21 Twins (Figure 12-6)

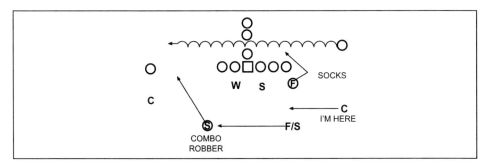

Figure 12-6. Motion adjustments from 21 pro to 21 twins

Free Safety: Slides with motion and gives a combo or robber call to the Stud and the corner.

Stud: Slides over the #2 receiver, and makes the "I'm gone" call to the linebackers, indicating a switch in run support.

Corner: Reduces down with motion, and makes the "I'm here" call to the linebackers.

Falcon: With no wide receiver to his side, he makes a "socks" call, and blitzes off the edge versus I backs or back set strong.

Empty Formation Adjustments

Instead of trying to match up each stunt, blitz, or coverage with the empty formation, it is best to use either a defend or pressure defensive scheme and adjust the approach by series or by quarters. The defense should be checked into the defend or pressure scheme by a call from the secondary, which is repeated by the linebackers. The term used to check into defend or pressure is flexible and can be easily changed from game to game, if necessary. As examples: "zero" can be used to indicate defend, and any state, (e.g., Utah or Texas) can be used to indicate pressure. Actually, any system can be used as long as it effectively communicates the check quickly and clearly.

Defend Scheme

When the defense is in a defend approach, all four- and three-man rushes can be used. The rushes can be called by the signal caller on any down when the opponent comes out in an empty formation. Change-ups should be used in the early part of the game to get a feel of what works best. The defend approach coverage is cover zero, which is cover 3 to the three-receiver side, and cover 2 to the two-receiver side (Figures 12-7 and 12-8).

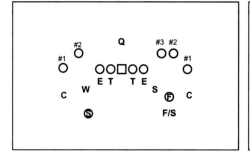 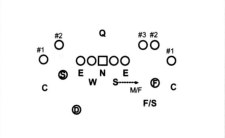

Figure 12-7. Eagle cover zero versus empty Figure 12-8. 50 cover zero versus empty

Eagle Cover Zero (Figure 12-9)

Figure 12-9. Eagle cover zero

Strong Corner: Inside-third player, and reads the #2/#3 box

Free Safety: Plays the #3/#2 receiver box as one receiver; if one of them does not go deep, plays the other as a deep threat.

Falcon: Curl/flat player, and drops over the #2 receiver.

Sam: Plays the #3/#2 box, and drops over #3 strong.

Will: Drops over #2 weak (two-receiver side); can banjo with the corner.

Stud and Weak Corner: Both should read #2. If #2 goes to the flat, the corner settles and the Stud goes over the top of #1; if #2 goes vertical, both play over the top of #1 and #2.

50 Cover Zero

One adjustment is made in cover zero from the 50 front, with cover 3 to the three-receiver side, and cover 2 to the two-receiver side (Figure 12-10). A skate principle is played to the three-receiver side of the empty; the same combo coverage to the two-man side, but the Stud plays over the #2 receiver instead of Will.

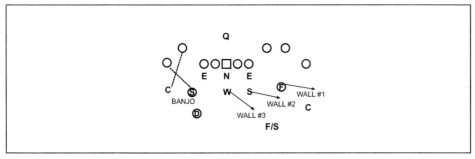

Figure 12-10. 50 cover zero adjustment

Free Safety: Same as with the Eagle front.

Strong Corner: Divider player; reads the #2/#3 box.

Falcon: Buzzes #1 to take away the three-step drop, hitch slants, and runs with (carries) the wheel by the #2 receiver.

Sam: Drops over #2 and pattern reads #2 to #1.

Will: Drops over #3 and pattern reads #3 to #2.

Stud: Drops over #2 weak and pattern reads #2 to #1.

Dime and Weak Corner: Play combo and read off #2.

Tampa Coverage From the 50 Front (Figure 12-11)

Tampa is a five-across coverage look. Tampa provides combo coverage to both sides with a deep-hole (deep middle-third) player similar to "key" coverage versus trips.

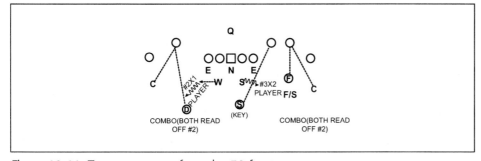

Figure 12-11. Tampa coverage from the 50 front

Pressure Scheme

The pressure scheme is primarily a zone-blitz package. The secondary must make a Utah (state) call that alerts the defense that pressure will be applied with a five- or six-man blitz.

The scouting report on the opponent's offensive protections and what has been successful against them in previous games is important to make decisions as to the best pressure package to implement. Similar types of five-

or six-man zone blitzes are best from both Eagle and 50 fronts. However, if these blitzes are ineffective in the game, try to get pressure from the four-man and three-man fronts. Zone blitzes and four- and three-man front blitzes are covered in detail in other chapters of this book.

Five-Man Pressure (Figures 12-12 and 12-13)

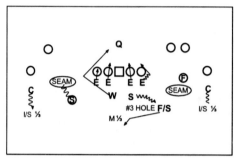

Figure 12-12. Crash weak or strong from the Eagle front

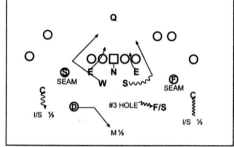

Figure 12-13. Crash weak and strong from the 50 front

Six-Man Pressure

Stinger blitz from the Eagle front (Figure 12-14): The Falcon and the Stud make a "you" call to the Sam and Will that alerts them that they are the blitzers. This call allows the Falcon and the Stud to remain in pass coverage.

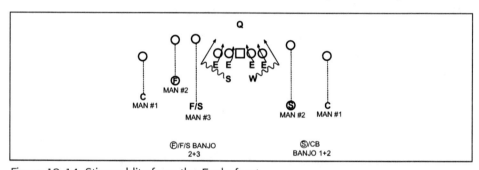

Figure 12-14. Stinger blitz from the Eagle front

Sic 'em blitz from the 50 front (Figure 12-15): The Falcon makes a "you" call to the Sam that tells Sam that he will replace the Falcon in the blitz, taking responsibility for outside force on the quarterback. The Falcon is involved in the coverage and has the #2 receiver to the three-receiver side. The Stud can change up the blitz with a "you/me" call to the Will that tells both of them that they blitz to the weakside.

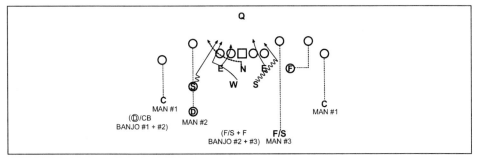

Figure 12-15. Sic 'em blitz from the 50 front

Sic 'em with Falcon blitz from the 50 front (Figure 12-16): Another change-up to the Sic 'em blitz is to blitz the Falcon from the strongside if protection indicates better success on rushes from the three-receiver side. Blitzing the Falcon from the strongside is good from the Tampa (five-across) secondary look.

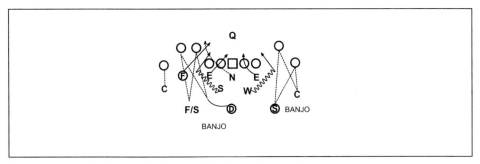

Figure 12-16. Sick 'em with Falcon blitz from the 50 front

Cluster (Bunch) Adjustments

Cover-6 Adjustments Versus Cluster (Figures 12-17 and 12-18)

When the secondary recognizes the cluster formation, he should make a "cluster" call to alert all defensive personnel. The cluster formation is played just like any other trips formation.

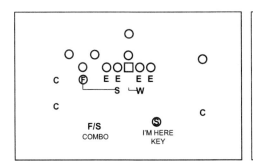 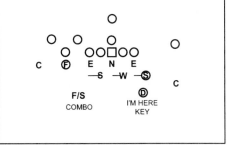

Figure 12-17. Eagle cover 6 versus cluster   Figure 12-18. 50 cover 6 versus cluster

Free Safety: Makes a combo call to the strong corner and the Falcon.

Falcon: Aligns over the #2 receiver, attacks him on the run (two-gaps him), and plays the curl on pass.

Strong Corner and Free Safety: Read all three receivers as one; adjust combo coverage to the route being run from the cluster. Typically, the route to the three receivers is one outside, one inside, and one deep. The corner should get depth, settle on a flat threat, and be ready to break on the shoulders and eyes of the quarterback. If the corner and free safety are threatened by two verticals, they should stay over the top of #1 and #2.

Stud: Makes a "key" call, and reads all three receivers in the cluster as the #3 receiver.

Sam: Plays #3/#2 players from the inside-out.

Will: Has the back (screen) and the first crosser, and is late help on inside cuts by the #1 receiver weak.

Weak Corner: Plays man on the #1 receiver with heavy inside leverage.

Cover-3 Adjustments Versus Cluster (Figures 12-19 and 12-20)

With cover 3 versus the cluster, the secondary checks to skate or sling.

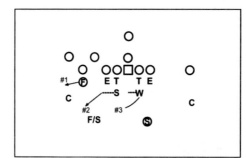 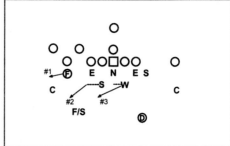

Figure 12-19. Eagle cover 3 versus cluster   Figure 12-20. 50 cover 3 versus cluster

Check Skate

Strong Corner: Plays outside third with outside leverage on #1 (key for crack); looks for the corner route.

Falcon: Presses over #2; forces player versus the run and flat defender versus the pass.

Sam: Walls #2 (slides to five-man surface).

Will: Walls #3 (slides to five-man surface).

Free Safety: Middle-third player; must be aware of #3 to #2 receivers.

Stud: Has the back (screen) and the first crosser.

Weak Corner: Plays man from an inside alignment on #1 weak (will play cloud, bracket, or true cover two to take away the weakside throwing game).

Check Sling (Figure 12-21)

This adjustment is the same as combo/key from cover 6.

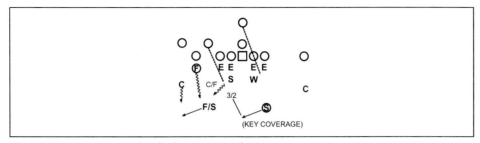

Figure 12-21. Cover-3 check sling versus cluster

Strong Corner: Sinks and reads the cluster triangle; if flat threat exists, settles under the post corner; jumps the flat receiver on the quarterback's shoulders or the thrown ball.

Free Safety: Plays the outside third to the cluster side; triangles the #1 and #2 receivers.

Falcon: Plays the curl/flat.

Sam: Plays #3/#2.

Will: Plays man on the back and first crosser; becomes short inside help on #1.

Stud: Keys and reads to #3; if no vertical threat out of the cluster, gets depth and fast breaks on the quarterback's shoulders or the thrown ball.

Weak Corner: Plays man with inside leverage on the #1 receiver weak (will play cloud, bracket, or true cover to take pressure off the backside corner).

Man Coverage Versus Cluster (Figures 12-22 and 12-23)

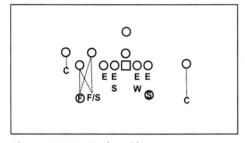

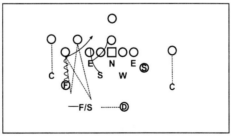

Figure 12-22. Eagle with man coverage   Figure 12-23. 50 with man coverage

Strong Corner: Plays press man on the #1 receiver.

Free Safety and Falcon or Dime: Banjo the #2 and #3 receivers.

Sam and Will: Blitz the remaining back. If neither linebacker is involved in the blitz, the linebacker to flow will read blitz, and the other linebacker will be the low-hole (short middle-field) player.

Weak Corner: Plays man on #1.

Leopard Check Adjustment Versus Cluster (Figures 12-24 and 12-25)

The Leopard check slants the defensive line toward the cluster with the Stud blitzing from the weakside from both the Eagle and 50 fronts. The linebackers also need to make a call to slant the front toward the cluster. The "check leopard" trumps all other defensive calls. The defense plays cover 3 with the Eagle front, and cover 6 with the 50 front.

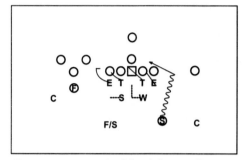 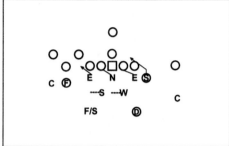

Figure 12-24. Eagle "check leopard"   Figure 12-25. 50 "check leopard"

Leopard Aztec Check Adjustment From a 50 Front (Figure 12-26)

The Leopard Aztec check moves the noseguard in the 50 front to a 3 technique. Aztec call enables us to moe from our 50 to our 4-2 (Eagle) front.

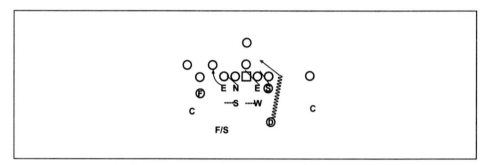

Figure 12-26. 50 check leopard Aztec

Adjustment to Bootleg Pass

Most offenses use the bootleg pass as an integral part of their play-action passing game. In zone coverages, it is important to play a match-up zone to the routes being run both to and away from formation strength. The defense should have sound match-ups on the "chipper" (the tight end or wide receiver who releases into the flat toward the bootleg), short or deep drags, and the throw back to the back. The rules regarding defense of the bootleg need to be consistent in all coverages.

Match-Up Cover 6 Versus Bootleg (Figure 12-27)

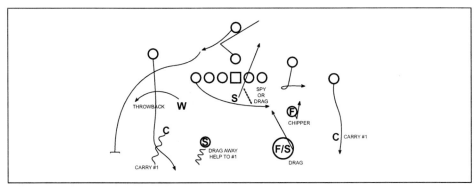

Figure 12-27. Match-up cover 6 versus doubles (2x2) bootleg away from tight end

Sam: Spies or plays drag route.

Whip (Will): Plays throw back to the back versus bootleg away.

Falcon: Plays the chipper versus bootleg toward.

Corner to the Bootleg: Carries the #1 receiver.

Corner Away From the Bootleg: Keep leverage on #1 receiver.

Free Safety and Stud: Play deep drag versus bootleg toward; double #1 versus bootleg away. The exception is a trips (3x1) formation, in which the free safety must check the #3/#2 box for deep threat before playing the drag.

Match-Up Cover 6 Versus Bootleg Toward Trips (3x1) (Figure 12-28)

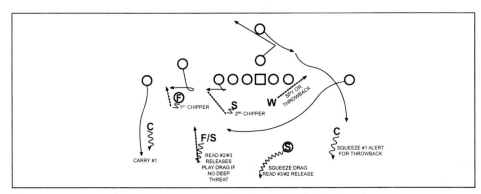

Figure 12-28. Match-up cover 6 versus bootleg toward trips (3x1)

Sam: Plays the #2 chipper.

Falcon: Plays the #1 chipper.

Bootleg Corner: Carries the #1 receiver.

Will: Plays the throw back to the back.

Free Safety: Plays the deep drag if no deep threat comes from the #2 and #3 receivers. As an adjustment with the Stud, the free safety helps the corner on post routes by the #1 receiver strong, and the Stud plays the drag.

Stud: Reads #3; if no deep threat, squeezes the drag to the free safety.

Corner: If the back goes away, the corner squeezes inside with the drag route; if the back goes toward, the corner should be aware of the wheel to the back.

Match-Up Cover 6 Versus Bootleg Away From Trips (3x1)
(Figure 12-29)

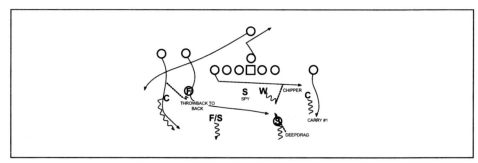

Figure 12-29. Match-up cover 6 versus bootleg away from trips (3x1)

Sam: Spies or wheels to find the drag.

Will: Plays the chipper (the shallow drag becomes the chipper).

Falcon: Gets depth, and must be aware of the throw back to the back.

Corner Toward the Bootleg: Carries the #1 receiver.

Corner Away From the Bootleg: Leverages #1, and must be aware of the throw back to the back.

Free Safety: If #2 and #3 drag, doubles to the #1 receiver (may squeeze the deep drag of the #2 receiver).

Stud: Plays the deep drag.

Match-Up Cover 6 Versus Bootleg Away From Cluster (Figure 12-30)

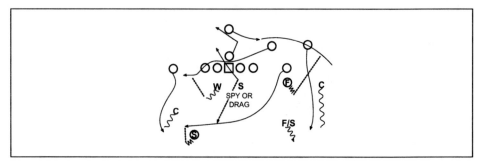

Figure 12-30. Match-up cover 6 versus bootleg away from cluster

Adjustment: Stud plays the chipper, and the free safety plays the drag.

Match-Up Cover 6 Versus Bootleg Weak From 11 Trey (3x1)
(Figure 12-31)

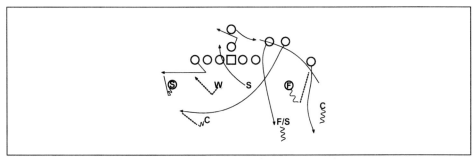

Figure 12-31. Match-up cover 6 versus bootleg weak from 11 trey (3x1)

Free Safety: Reads the #3/#2 box; clears the deep threat before driving on the drag.

Will: Spies; or to be consistent with the bootleg rules, maintains coverage on the chipper because the Stud may be in a "socks" call from the nub tight-end side.

Match-Up From Eagle Cover 3 Versus Doubles Bootleg (Figures 12-32 and 12-33)

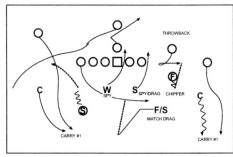
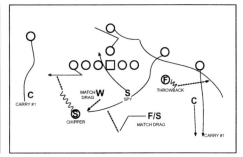

Figure 12-32. Match-up from Eagle cover 3 versus doubles (2x2) bootleg away from the tight end

Figure 12-33. Match-up from Eagle cover 3 versus doubles (2x2) bootleg toward the tight end

Sam: Spies (reads blitz); or plays (matches) the drag.

Corners: Carries the deep routes of the #1 receiver.

Stud/Falcon: Responsible for the chipper on bootleg toward, and the wheel of the back on bootleg away.

Free Safety: Plays middle third, and matches up with the drag.

Match-Up From 50 Cover 3 Versus Doubles Bootleg

(Figures 12-34 and 12-35)

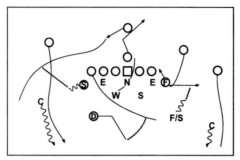 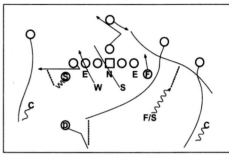

Figure 12-34. Match-up from 50 cover 3 versus doubles (2x2) bootleg away from the tight end

Figure 12-35. Match-up from 50 cover 3 versus doubles (2x2) bootleg toward the tight end

Will: Spies (reads blitz)

Sam: Plays (matches) the drag.

Corners: Carries the #1 receivers.

Stud/Falcon: Falcon rushes; Stud drops and plays the chipper if bootleg toward, and carries the back on the throwback if the bootleg is away.

Free Safety: Rocks down, and must be aware of chipper on bootleg toward; plays the back on the throw back if the bootleg is away.

Dime: Plays the middle third, and must be ready to match the drag.

Match-Up From 50 Cover 3 Versus Trips (3x1) Bootleg

Adjustment to Trips Bootleg Toward Trips (Figure 12-36): Sam linebacker must play the second chipper instead of wheeling and matching the drag.

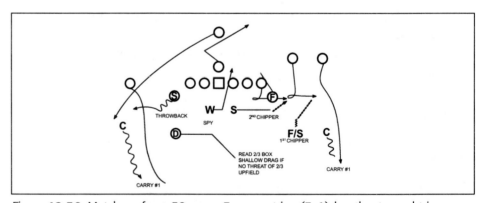

Figure 12-36. Match-up from 50 cover 3 versus trips (3x1) bootleg toward trips

Adjustment to Trips Bootleg Away From Trips (Figure 12-37): Stud plays the shallow drag, which is the equivalent of the chipper versus a 2x2 formation.

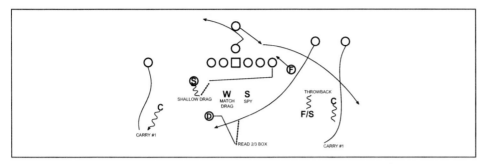

Figure 12-37. Match-up from 50 cover 3 versus trips (3x1) bootleg away from trips

Match-Up From Eagle Cover 2 Versus Trips (3x1) Bootleg
(Figures 12-38 and 12-39)

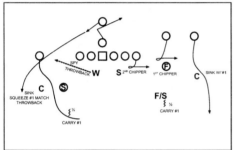

Figure 12-38. Match-up from Eagle cover 2 versus bootleg toward trips (3x1)

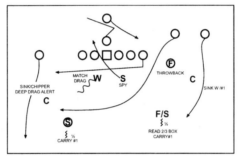

Figure 12-39. Match-up from Eagle cover 2 versus bootleg away from trips (3x1)

Match-Up From Eagle Cover 2 Versus Doubles (2x2) Bootleg
(Figures 12-40 and 12-41)

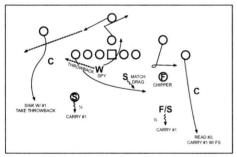

Figure 12-40. Match-up from Eagle cover 2 versus doubles (2x2) bootleg away from the tight end

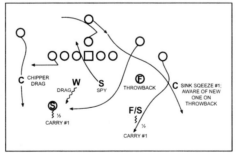

Figure 12-41. Match-up from Eagle cover 2 versus doubles (2x2) bootleg toward the tight end

Note: With two coverage, the corner to the bootleg can sink, with #1 reading #2 for the chip (flat) route. The free safety can work over the top of #1, enabling the Ⓕ to initially get depth and width with the chipper, with awareness of the drag.

Match-Up From 50 Cover 2 Versus Doubles (2x2)
(Figures 12-42 and 12-43)

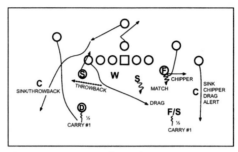 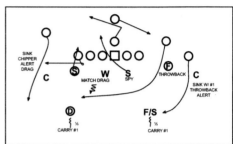

Figure 12-42. Match-up from 50 cover 2 versus doubles (2x2) bootleg away from the tight end

Figure 12-43. Match-up from 50 cover 2 versus doubles (2x2) bootleg toward the tight end

Formation to Boundary Adjustments

It is important for the defense to have a solid adjustment for teams that put their formation into the boundary. Through film study of the opponent's offense, a good understanding of what they are trying to do with this maneuver will become evident. From an offensive standpoint, several different approaches exist, and generally they fall into the following categories:

- Can the offense outnumber the defense in both the running and passing games?
- Is the offense doing this maneuver more for adjustment reasons to determine how the defense adapts to motion, Y trade, and so forth?
- Some spread/shotgun offenses always set the tight end or formation to the offense's right side. Thus, the strength of the formation would at all times be to the defense's left. In this situation, the defense should play like no hash marks exist on the field. Every call is made like it is a middle-of-the-field call with the strength call to the defense's left.

Being prepared for formations into the boundary should enable the defense to be sound in defending the run and pass objectives of the opponent, and minimize the number of times the defense will see this strategy in a game.

Eagle Cover 6 Versus 21 Formation to the Boundary (Figure 12-44)

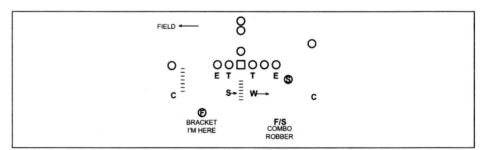

Figure 12-44. Eagle cover 6 versus 21 formation to the boundary

Free Safety: Aligns in the guard/tackle gap; makes a robber or combo call to corner and the Stud.

Falcon: Makes the "I'm here" call to the linebackers so they can slide away from him; makes the "bracket" call to the corner.

Eagle Cover 6 Versus 21 Twins Formation to the Boundary
(Figure 12-45)

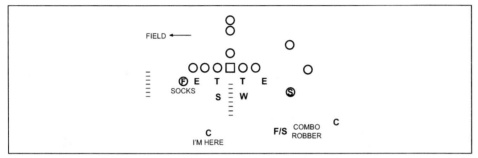

Figure 12-45. Eagle cover 6 versus 21 twins formation to the boundary

Free Safety: Makes a combo or robber call to the Stud and the corner.

Field Corner: Makes the "I'm here" call to the linebackers for run support.

Falcon With Nub Tight End: Can give a "socks" (rush) call with the backs in the I or in a strong set.

Eagle Cover 6 Versus Trips (3x1) to the Boundary (Figure 12-46)

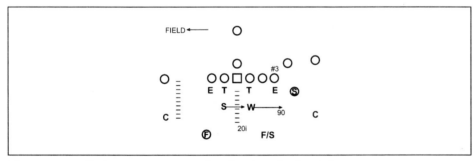

Figure 12-46. Eagle cover 6 versus trips (3x1) to the boundary

Falcon: Reads the #3 receiver, and makes the "I'm here" call to the linebackers; plays late bracket with the corner.

Sam and Will: Slides to the formation; Will is in a 70 or 90 technique, and the Sam is in a 20i technique.

Field Corner: Man on the #1 receiver.

Free Safety: Makes a combo or robber call.

Stud: Aligns in an 8 technique on the #2 receiver in the wing position. Is an outside force on a run; has curl/flat responsibilities on a pass.

Eagle Cover 6 Versus 21 With Motion to the Field (Figure 12-47)

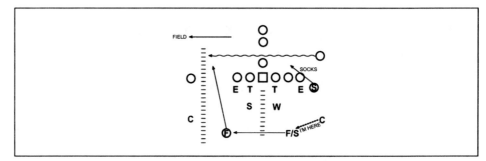

Figure 12-47. Eagle cover 6 versus 21 with motion to the field

Field Corner: Goes from man coverage to combo/robber on the call by the free safety.

Falcon: Makes the "I'm gone" call to the linebackers; slides down to play over the #2 receiver; plays a combo or robber based on the call of the free safety.

Free Safety: Slides toward and aligns over the #2 receiver; makes a combo/robber call to the Falcon and field corner.

Boundary Corner: Reduces down toward the tight end; makes the "I'm here" call to alert linebackers where to slide and run support from secondary.

Stud: Can give a "socks" (rush) call to the nub tight-end side with the backs in an I or strong set.

Eagle Cover 6 Versus 21 Twins With Motion to the Field
(Figure 12-48)

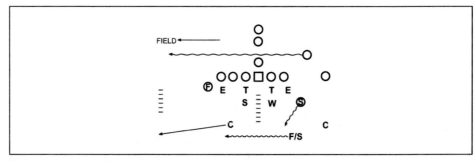

Figure 12-48. Eagle cover 6 versus 21 twins with motion to the field

Field Corner: Makes the "I'm gone" call to the linebackers; slides to the field with motion; plays combo or robber based on the call of the free safety.

Free Safety: Slides with the motion, and aligns over the tight end (one yard outside and 8 to 10 yards deep); makes a combo or robber call to the field corner and the Falcon.

Stud: Gets depth, and makes the "I'm here" call to the linebackers, and a bracket call to boundary corner.

Boundary Corner: Goes from a combo or robber call to a bracket call on the weakside of the formation.

Falcon: Gets out of the socks (rush) call and plays a combo or robber on the call of the free safety.

Eagle Cover 6 Versus Motion From Trips (3x1) to Doubles (2x2)
(Figure 12-49)

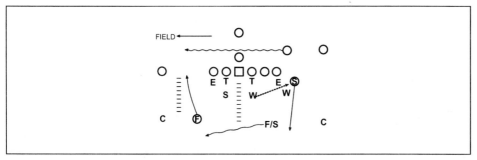

Figure 12-49. Eagle cover 6 versus motion from trips (3x1) to doubles (2x2)

Field Corner: Goes from bracket to combo or robber, depending on the call of the free safety.

Falcon: Rocks down over the #2 receiver; makes an "I'm gone" call to the linebackers; goes from a bracket to a combo or robber on the call of the free safety.

Free Safety: Slides with the motion; makes a combo or robber call to the Falcon and the field corner.

Stud: Gets depth and aligns over the tight end; makes the "I'm here" call for run support; makes a robber or combo call to the Will and the boundary corner.

Will: Lines up in a whip alignment and plays combo or robber coverage on the call of the Stud.

Boundary Corner: Plays combo or robber with the Stud and Will, depending on the call of the Stud.

50 Cover 6 Versus 21 Formation to the Boundary (Figure 12-50)

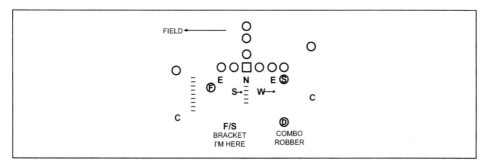

Figure 12-50. 50 cover 6 versus 21 formation to the boundary

Field Corner: Brackets the #1 receiver.

Free Safety: Makes a "bracket" call to the secondary, and an "I'm here" to the front.

Sam: Slides away from the "I'm here" of the free safety to a 10 field technique.

Will: Slides to a 40 technique.

Dime: Aligns over the tight end one yard outside and 8 to 10 yards deep; makes a combo or robber call to the Stud and the corner.

Boundary Corner: Plays combo or robber on the call of the dime.

Adjustment: When the offense motions or Y-trades to the field, the defense must adjust: if the 4 and 6 techniques are to the boundary, checks to cover 6; if the 5 and 9 technique are to the boundary, checks to cover 3.

50 Cover 6 Versus 21 Twins to the Boundary (Figure 12-51)

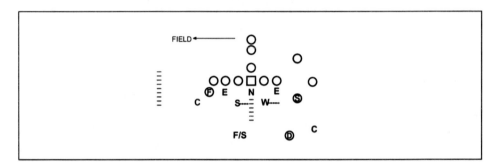

Figure 12-51. 50 cover 6 versus 21 twins to the boundary

Stud: Aligns over the #2 receiver, and plays combo or robber on the call by the dime.

Boundary Corner: Plays combo or robber.

Sam and Will: Slides away from the "I'm here" call by the free safety.

Dime: Aligns over #2 and makes a combo or robber call to the Stud and cornerback.

Field Corner: Makes a "socks" call versus nub tight end and backs in an I or strong set.

Free Safety: Makes the "I'm here" call to the front for run support.

50 Field Cover 6—Check to Cover 3 Versus Formation to the Boundary—Larry Call (Figure 12-52)

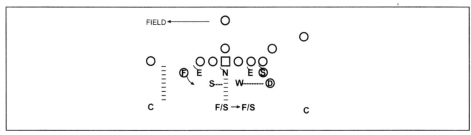

Figure 12-52. 50 field cover 6—check to cover 3 versus formation to the boundary (Larry call)

Field Corner: Plays the inside third on the wide receiver.

Dime: Walks up outside the wing, and aligns in a light 8 technique on the wing.

Free Safety: Aligns over the guard to the boundary.

Sam and Will: Slide to the four-man surface.

Falcon: Aligns in fold position off the hip of the defensive end.

Weak Corner: Plays inside third on the #1 receiver.

50 Field Cover 6—Check Cover 3 Versus Formation to the Boundary, Check Cover 6 Versus Motion to the Field (Figure 12-53)

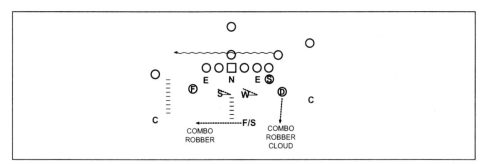

Figure 12-53. 50 field cover 6—check cover 3 versus formation to the boundary, check back to cover 6 versus motion to the field

Strong Corner: Goes from the inside third to combo or robber on call by the free safety.

Falcon: Aligns on the #2 receiver, and plays the call by the free safety.

Sam and Will: Slide back to a 30 technique over the guards versus a balanced 2x2 formation.

Dime: Gets depth to align over the tight end; makes a robber or combo call to the corner and Will. Gives an "I'm here" call to the linebackers for run support.

Boundary Corner: Moves from the inside third to a combo or robber call by the dime.

13

Eagle, Under, and Hammer Fronts

Multiplicity

Modern offenses—with a multiplicity of formations and personnel groups as well as the ability to stretch defenses both horizontally and vertically—put tremendous pressure on the defense to defend all of these strategies. The solution to successfully defend these offensive strategies is to utilize multiple fronts that do not require multiple techniques. Multiple fronts also create four- and five-man anchor points with defensive linemen, linebackers, and defensive backs fitting into gaps or blitzing. With defensive backs fitting into gaps or blitzing, the defense puts an extra man at the point of attack or in the cutback lane. Thus, the defense is able to create eight-man fronts that are needed in gap control versus the run. In addition, covering and uncovering the center with the 50 and under/over look, plus aligning in or sliding into the four-man front, complicates the blocking schemes of the offense and creates hesitancy on the part of the offensive linemen. The defenses that fit these concepts best are the Eagle (4-2-5) and 50 fronts.

Eagle Front With Cover 6 and Cover 2
(Figure 13-1)

When the Eagle is called, it is tagged with a call to indicate the technique of the two defensive tackles. With a base call, the defensive tackles align in a zero technique. The emphasis for them is to attack the guard in a vertical move. They should not worry about getting reached, as their first responsibility is to knock the guard back. They should play under the reach block and force the guard to flatten by turning his shoulders perpendicular to the line of scrimmage. The linebackers should also attack on the initial run key with emphasis on fast key, fast press, and fast attack. Linebackers must constantly be aware that the offense will try to attack the bubbles (gaps for which linebackers are responsible) in the defense. They should press to the butt of the defensive tackles and adjust to the angle of the back and the ball while keeping the arm free to the side of the initial flow. Both linebackers must be ready to pitchfork (inside or outside the defensive tackles) to the back's commitment and daylight.

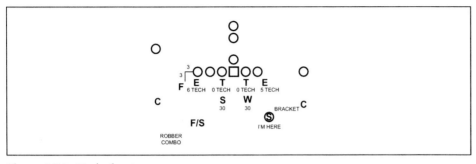

Figure 13-1. Eagle front

Larry and Roger Calls (Figures 13-2 through 13-7)

The defensive tackles can also slant from zero techniques to 3 and 1 techniques if it is deemed beneficial. They should start in zero to eliminate any pre-snap read. Larry or Roger calls are made to move the defensive tackles, depending on the following pre-snap calls:

- Field
- Boundary
- Formations (toward strength of formation)
- Weak (away from formation strength)
- Tight (to the tight end)
- Split (away from the tight end)
- Tilt (to the tilt back)
- Numbers (away from tilt back)

Points to remember about Larry and Roger calls include:
- *Tight:* Makes the call to the formation when no tight end or two tight ends.
- *Split:* Makes the call away from the formation when no tight end or two tight ends.
- *Tilt:* Makes the call to the formation if no tilt back.
- *Numbers:* Makes the call away from the formation if no tilt back.

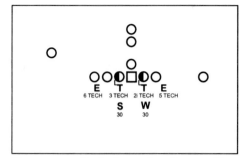

Figure 13-2. Eagle formation (Larry call)

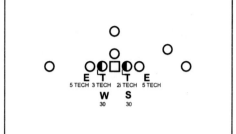

Figure 13-3. Eagle weak (Larry call)

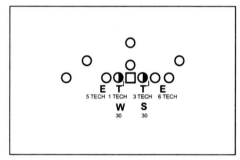

Figure 13-4. Eagle tight (Roger call)

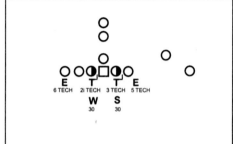

Figure 13-5. Eagle split (Roger call)

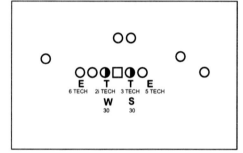

Figure 13-6. Eagle tilt (Roger call)

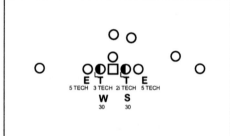

Figure 13-7. Eagle numbers (Larry call)

Eagle Bat (Figures 13-8 and 13-9)

On a "bat" call, the defensive tackles step and penetrate their gap responsibility. They align in a 3 technique and 2i technique opposite their gaps. On the snap, they cross-face the guards and penetrate their gap responsibility. The emphasis is: quick move/quick attack/quick gap switch. The "bat" call is preceded by a directional call ("field/boundary," "formation/weak," "tight/split," or "tilt/numbers") to indicate the direction for them to go. All defensive-line movement is intended to break the chain on zone blocking schemes or beat the down block, create quick decisions for the backs, and make cutback lanes fuzzy for the backs.

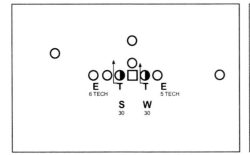 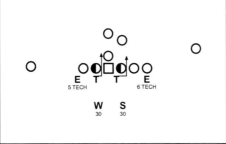

Figure 13-8. Eagle tight bat (Larry call)   Figure 13-9. Eagle tilt bat (Roger call)

Gaps (Figures 13-10 through 13-12)

Like the "bat" call, the "gaps" call is preceded by a directional call ("field/boundary," "formation/weak," "tight/split," or "tilt/numbers") along with a Larry or Roger call. The defensive line aligns in their original position and moves late to the gaps.

The defensive end on the open side will slide late from the 5 technique to a wide alignment and angle-charge through the near hip of the offensive tackle. If the offensive tackle blocks down, the defensive end flattens to his heels and mentally checks for reverse and bootleg. If the tackle blocks out, the defensive end squeezes the hole from the outside-in and reduces the hole.

Figure 13-10. Formation gap (Larry call)   Figure 13-11. Eagle tight gaps (Roger call)

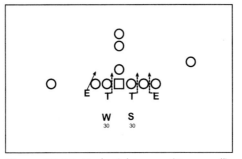

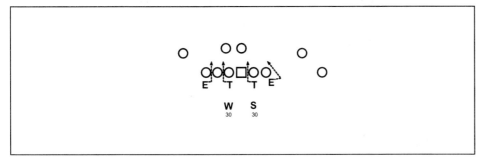

Figure 13-12. Eagle tilt gaps (Larry call with a defensive end flatten technique)

Eagle AC (Figures 13-13 through 13-16)

AC is an inside stunt for the defensive end and the defensive tackle. They lead step, read on the run, and react off the block of the offensive tackle and offensive guard. Their aiming point is the facemask of the offensive linemen. Versus a down block, they flatten and look to spill (wrong-arm) the first blocking threat. Versus a turnout block, they go under the turnout with a strong rip of the backside arm and explosion of their feet. The defensive tackle away from the AC plays a base 3 technique.

The linebackers know that the A and B gaps are taken so they become second-level players on inside plays and first-level players on outside plays. The bubble they should take away is the C gap or wider. They should press the ball from the inside-out and prevent any cutback. Versus option, they play the quarterback. AC is called like bat and gaps. The double AC takes away the inside cutback lanes and is a good change-up versus the gun option and strong inside running game.

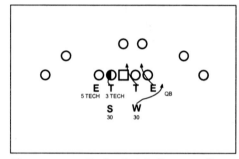

Figure 13-13. Eagle tilt AC (Roger call)

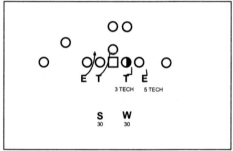

Figure 13-14. Eagle numbers AC (Larry call)

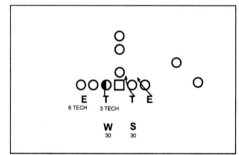

Figure 13-15. Eagle formation AC (Roger call)

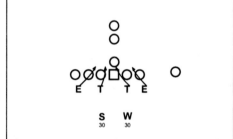

Figure 13-16. Eagle double AC (Larry call —make calls to formation on double calls)

Star (Figures 13-17 through 13-19)

Star is a two-back call versus the 20, 21, and 22 sets. The only one-back formation it should be used against is a 12 set. It is a combination of Lake/River and AC stunts. An Eagle Formation Star Base call has the defensive tackles attacking inside with the Falcon and defensive end blitzing from outside- in. It is an excellent first-and-10 and second-down call against opponents that have a 50/50 balance on run and pass. Cover 6 can be played with two or three linebackers behind the Star call. Cover 6 is the preferred coverage because it creates the equivalent of a double rock down from the Stud and the free safety for run support. The linebackers slide away from the "I'm here" call by the Stud. Versus pass, the Sam expands to the curl and replaces the Falcon. The Will drops over the #3 receiver.

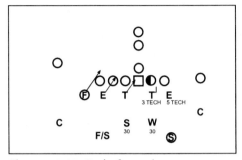

Figure 13-17. Eagle formation star

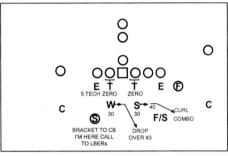

Figure 13-18. Eagle formation star base

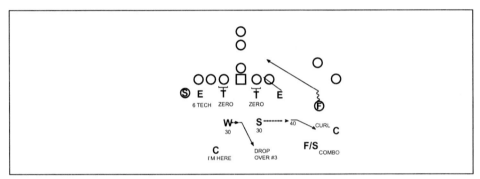

Figure 13-19. Eagle formation star base versus 21 twins

Star Echo (Figure 13-20)

Star echo is a change-up with the Falcon and defensive end. The defensive end goes first, moves up field to squeeze the run from the outside, is outside force versus pass, has pitch versus the option, and checks for reverse or bootleg on flow away. The Falcon plays off the heels of the defensive end and reads the block of the tackle on the run. If the tackle blocks down, the Falcon chases the tackle's hip; if the tackle turns out, the Falcon cross-faces to the B gap. The echo call is discussed in more detail in Chapter 16.

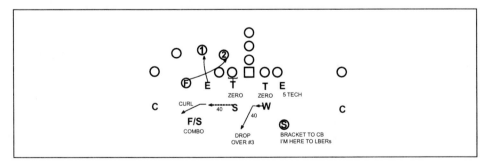

Figure 13-20. Eagle star echo base cover 6

Socks (Figures 13-21 through 13-25)

Socks is a call made by the Stud versus a nub tight end (tight end with no wide receiver to his side) to the backside of the formation (21 twins, 22 pro, 12 trips, or 11 trey). The Stud alerts the defense that he is blitzing: he spills all blocks, has the quarterback versus the option, forces the pass, and mentally checks for reverse or bootleg on flow away. The socks is run when the offense is in an I or tilt strong set. The socks will not be run when the offense is in a weak tilt or split backs because of the threat of the back running a flat or wheel route.

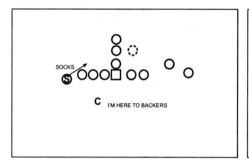

Figure 13-21. Socks versus 21 twins

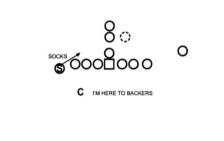

Figure 13-22. Socks versus 22 pro

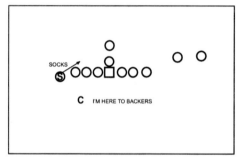

Figure 13-23. Socks versus 12 trips

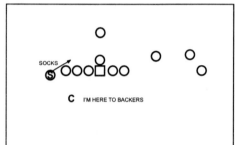

Figure 13-24. Socks versus 11 trey

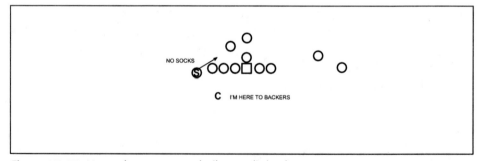

Figure 13-25. No socks versus weak tilt or split backs

Socks Adjustment Versus Motion (Figure 13-26)

The weak corner is typically the "I'm here" player and is man on the tight end. For the Stud versus any back motion creating a 2x2 formation, the Socks is "off." Stud backs up into four across and makes a robber or combo call to the corner to alert him how to play the two receivers. He becomes the "I'm here" player.

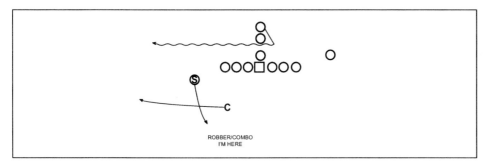

Figure 13-26. Socks adjustment versus motion

Pirate Adjustment (Figure 13-27)

The Stud can make a "pirate" call with socks. The pirate is game-planned, depending on the offense's threat to the tight-end side.

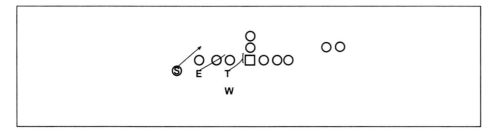

Figure 13-27. Pirate adjustment

Wide Defensive End Adjustment (Figure 13-28)

A wide call puts the defensive end in a heavy 9 technique on the tight end. This alignment provides a strong anchor point on the tight end from the outside-in. The Stud makes the "I'm here" call and also makes a robber or combo call to the corner. With a wide call, the linebacker will not make a whip adjustment.

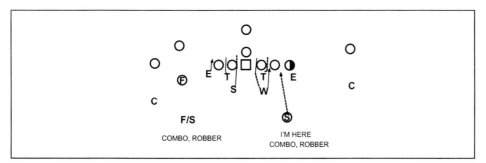

Figure 13-28. Wide defensive end adjustment

Whip Technique

(Figures 13-29 through 13-31)

The whip technique aligns the Will versus a 2x2 (11 and 12 doubles) formation outside the tight end, and to a midpoint alignment versus a 10 doubles formation. The whip technique/alignment is only used versus a one-back formation, and is never used versus any two-back or one-back with a nub tight end (11 trey and 12 trips). The mid-point for the whip is in the triangle between the tackle and the #2 receiver, and slightly closer to the tackle.

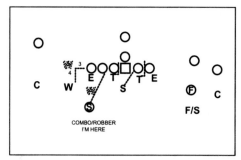

Figure 13-29. Whip versus 11 doubles

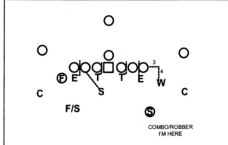

Figure 13-30. Whip versus 12 doubles

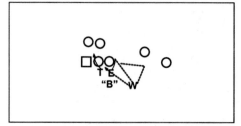

Figure 13-31. Whip versus 10 doubles

Spike and Pirate Calls (Figures 13-32 and 13-33)

The whip can make one of two calls to the defensive end if he is unable to cover his A- or B-gap responsibility. If he has an A-gap fill, he can make a "spike" call to the defensive tackle; the tackle takes the A gap, and the linebacker will be responsible for the B gap. If he has B-gap fill, he can make a "pirate" call to both the defensive tackle and end; the tackle takes the A gap, the end takes the B gap, and the Whip takes the C gap. The pirate call is the same as an AC stunt.

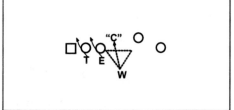

Figure 13-32. Spike call

Figure 13-33. Pirate call

Motion and Y-Trade Adjustments (Figures 13-34 through 13-36)

The whip moves inside to a 30 technique versus any motion or Y trade that creates one receiver to his side. The whip must give an "off" call to the tackle and the end to take them out of spike or pirate and back to their original assignment.

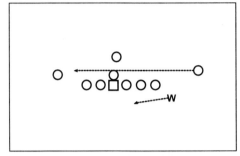

Figure 13-34. Versus motion away from whip

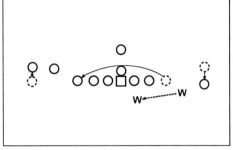

Figure 13-35. Versus Y trade away from whip

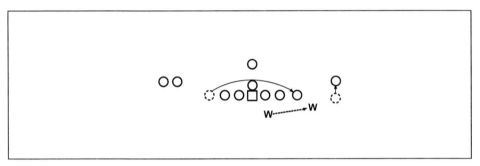

Figure 13-36. Versus Y trade to whip

Whip in a 6-Stack Alignment (Figure 13-37)

The whip can also play in a 6-stack alignment to create a different look for the offense to address.

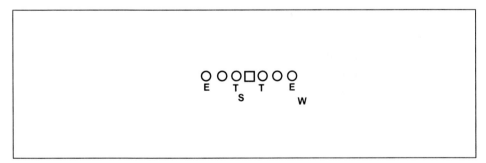

Figure 13-37. Whip in a 6-stack alignment

Move From Base to Whip Alignment (Figure 13-38)

It is important for the whip to move late and bluff to keep the offense off-balance and have to guess when the linebacker is going to be in a whip alignment or not. If the linebacker is outflanked by two receivers in a one-back formation, whether by initial alignment, motion, or Y trade, he should assume a whip position.

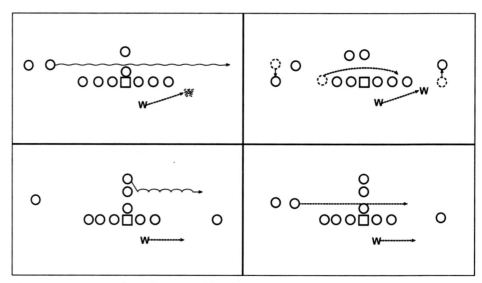

Figure 13-38. Move from base to whip alignment

Whip Technique

- When to Play
  - ✓ Versus a 2x2 set away from the formation
  - ✓ Versus 10 doubles, 11 doubles, and 12 doubles
- When Not to Play
  - ✓ Versus a two-back set
  - ✓ To the backside of 3x1 (trips)
- Alignment
  - ✓ *Versus tight end:* Aligns cocked inside at a 45-degree angle, three yards outside the tight end at linebacker depth (four yards).
  - ✓ *Versus split end (10 doubles):* Aligns in mid-point between the tackle and the #2 receiver at five to seven yards deep (the stance is squared, not cocked).
- Versus Run
  - ✓ Becomes the D-gap player.
  - ✓ Spills the tight end versus a turnout block.
  - ✓ Spills any blocks coming from the inside.
  - ✓ Plays the quarterback versus the option.

✓ Responsible for reverse on flow away.

✓ Folds versus flow away (must remember the fence over the outside hip of the tight end).

- Versus Pass (Combo)

✓ Spot-drops and splits the distance between the #1 and #2 receivers.

✓ Sees the quarterback, feels the release of the #2 receiver, and drops to a depth of 12 yards.

✓ *If #2 goes vertical:* Takes a peek at the #1 receiver, and must be ready to break on his smash or under route.

✓ *If #2 goes to the flat or flare:* Widens with #2's release, maintains depth, breaks to #2 on the quarterback's shoulders or the release of the ball.

✓ If #2 is not a threat (blocks or goes away): Finds and feels #1.

✓ Plays the chipper versus bootleg.

✓ Must be aware of the screen.

✓ Fast-breaks on the quarterback's eyes and shoulders.

✓ If quarterback's eyes look away, looks for a crosser.

- Versus Pass (Robber)

✓ Drives to the inside number of the #1 receiver.

✓ Takes away the hitch/slant by #1.

✓ Must be ready to run with #2 on the wheel.

✓ Plays the chipper versus bootleg.

✓ If #2 goes to the flat or flare, maintains depth, breaks on #2 on the quarterback's shoulders or the release of the ball.

✓ If #2 is not a threat, plays under #1.

Whip Stunts

- *Whip Crash Z Spin* (Figure 13-39): Whip linebacker can run the stunt from depth or on the line of scrimmage. He should spill the tight end versus the turnout block, spill any blocks from the inside of the down block of the tight end, play the quarterback versus the option, and be responsible for the reverse and bootleg on flow away.

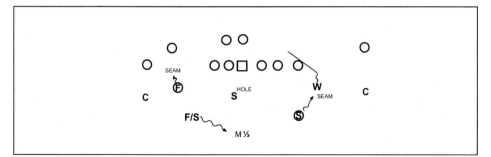

Figure 13-39. Whip crash Z spin

- *Whip Crash Echo* (Figure 13-40): The defensive end and the whip backer exchange assignments. The whip is the C-gap player and reads the offensive tackle. If the tackle turns out, the whip plays under the turnout block and spills; if the tackle blocks down, the whip closes tight off his heels and spills the first threat from the inside. The defensive end squeezes all blocks from the outside-in, checks reverse and bootleg on flow away, pressures the quarterback from the outside-in versus pass, and plays the quarterback versus the option.
- *Whip Crash Echo With Man Coverage* (Figure 13-41): The Stud and corner to the stunt side can play man, while the frontside continues to play cover 6.
- *Whip AC Cover 6* (Figure 13-42): With the Will linebacker involved in a stunt, it is difficult to play robber from cover 6. Combo and cloud can be played to the backside with Sam replacing Will as the weak hook-to-curl player. Combo or cloud, or man coverage to the weakside, enables the defense to play cover 6 with robber or combo to the strongside.

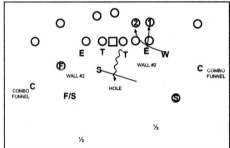

Figure 13-40. Whip crash echo

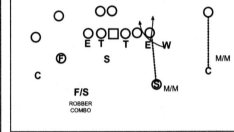

Figure 13-41. Whip crash echo with man coverage

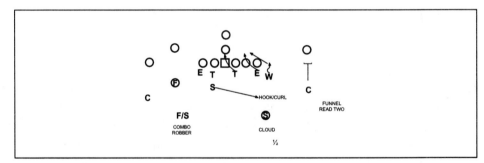

Figure 13-42. Whip AC cover 6

Eagle Pass Rushes

- *Jet* (Figure 13-43): Plays the pass first and the run second; stops the run on the way to the passer; if any doubt, rushes the passer.
- *Net* (Figure 13-44): Net is a gap-control pass rush. Stays in rush lanes and doesn't get even with or behind the quarterback; stays in front of him. Uses the bull rush technique; looks for deflections.
- *Twist—You/Me* (Figure 13-45): Reads the center on twist; the defensive tackle opposite the center's movement is the penetrator and goes first.

Figure 13-43. Jet

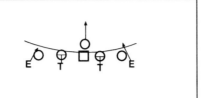

Figure 13-44. Net

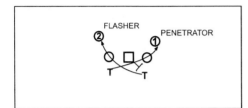

Figure 13-45. Twist—you/me

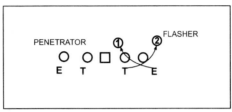

Figure 13-46. Wrap

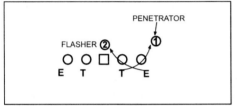

Figure 13-47. Swap

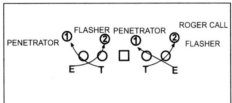

Figure 13-48. Weave—wrap strong/swap weak

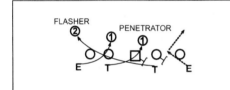

Figure 13-49. Trio

Figure 13-50. Knife

- *Wrap* (Figure 13-46): Can be fast or delayed, depending on the set=up of the offensive linemen, down-and-distance, and so forth.
- *Swap* (Figure 13-47): Can be fast or delayed, depending on the set-up of the offensive linemen, down-and-distance, and so forth.
- *Weave—Wrap Strong/Swap Weak* (Figure 13-48): A combination of the two stunts.
- *Trio* (Figure 13-49): The defensive tackles can read the center similar to twist. The defensive tackle opposite the center's movement is the penetrator and goes first. Both defensive ends go inside and read through the guard to the center; if they read guard and the center turns out to them, they try to get back outside to regain outside force on the ball.
- *Knife* (Figure 13-50): Defensive ends can't be wrong; they go inside or outside on a speed rush; they make something happen. Defensive tackles knock the guards back and fill where needed; if the ends stay outside, the tackles stay inside; if the ends go under the offensive tackles, the tackles play to the outside; they make the defensive end right.

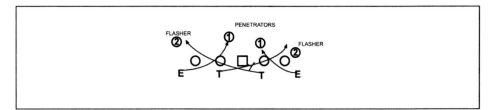

Figure 13-51. Scissors

- *Scissors* (Figure 13-51): Scissors is a combination of wrap and twist. Both defensive tackles read the center; the defensive tackle opposite the center's movement goes first. The defensive tackles are wrapping to the opposite side that they lined up on.

The Under Front

Under possesses some of the same characteristics as hammer and flex that are discussed later in this chapter. It is used primarily versus two-back formations with a tight end, but it has enough flexibility to use it versus no-tight-end formations as well. A tight call is made to align the defense to the tight end. However, by calling "under" with a field or formation declaration, the defense can be aligned without any regard to where the tight end lines up and the Falcon and Stud don't have to switch positions; therefore, the defense will be able to execute fire zones from the under front versus any formation.

Formation Under Declaration (Larry Call) (Figures 13-52 through 13-55)

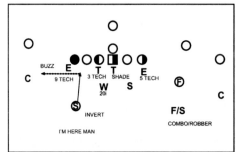

Figure 13-52. Formation under versus 21 pro

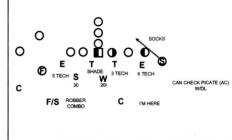

Figure 13-53. Formation under versus 21 twins

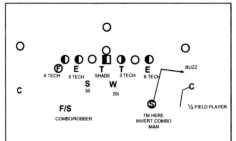

Figure 13-54. Formation under versus 12 doubles

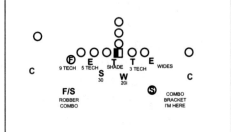

Figure 13-55. Formation under versus 11 doubles

The defensive end can play a wide technique on the tight end ("Check wide" is called by the linebacker); Stud makes the "I'm here" call and an invert, man, or combo call.

Under Alignment and Techniques (Figure 13-56)

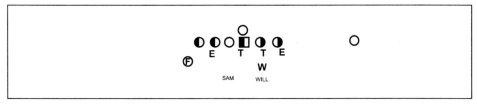

Figure 13-56. Under front alignment

Tackles: Three-point stance. The nose tackle shades on the center, and the other tackle is in a 3 technique on the guard. The nose tackle (shade) technique is the same as the nose angle technique explained in Chapter 5; the 3 technique is also explained in detail in Chapter 5.

Ends: Three-point stance in a 5 technique on the tackles. The 5 techniques are explained in detail in Chapter 5.

Falcon: Two-point stance in 9 technique on the tight end. Puts the inside foot forward in toe instep alignment, cocked inside at 45-degree angle with outside foot up. The 9 techniques for the Falcon are explained in detail in Chapter 7.

Sam: Two-point stance in 30 technique. Keeps the feet parallel with the toes at five yards. The Sam inside linebacker techniques is explained in detail in Chapter 6.

Will: Two-point stance in 20i technique. Keeps the feet parallel with toes at five yards. The Will inside linebacker techniques is explained in detail in Chapter 6.

Under Stunts

- *Split AC (pirate)* (Figure 13-57): AC is a stunt with the 3 technique and the 5 technique to the weak side. Both will cross the face of the guard and tackle to take away the A and B gap to force the ball to bounce outside. The will linebacker can make a Pirate call which is an automatic AC when he feels the offense is oversplitting the A and B gap.

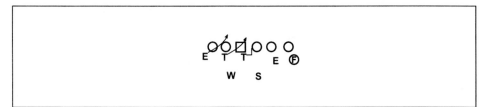

Figure 13-57. Split AC (pirate)

- *Stick* (Figures 13-58): Defensive end reads on the run; if the guard turns out, cross-faces on the turnout; if the guard blocks down, spills the first threat. The nose tackle scrapes hard over the heels of the defensive end; if the tackle down blocks, the nose goes over the top of his block, reads on the run, and searches for an open window and the angle of the back and the ball.
- *Spike* (Figure 13-59): Spike is an angle stunt by the 3 technique.
- *Hike* (Figure 13-60): Hike is a stunt by the 3 technique and the nose tackle. They should read the split of the guards. If a tight split, the nose tackle and the 3 technique flatten their charge and get ready to cross-face the down block; if wide splits, they should move upfield and get penetration.
- *Ed* (Figure 13-61): Ed is an angle stunt by the 5 technique through the B gap.

Figure 13-58. Stick

Figure 13-59. Spike

Figure 13-60. Hike

Figure 13-61. Ed

Hammer and Flex

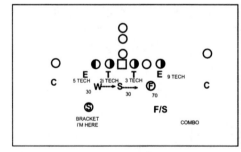

Figure 13-62. Hammer alignment versus 21 pro

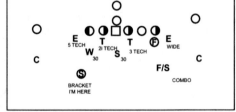

Figure 13-63. Flex alignment versus 21 pro

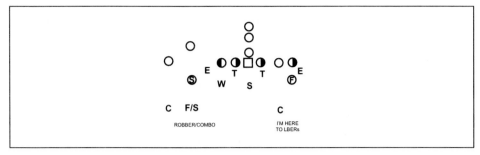

Figure 13-64. Hammer versus 21 twins

Both the hammer and flex are primarily called versus two backs with a tight end. These calls are also used on the goal line versus one-back formations with man coverage. Common hammer and flex alignments are shown in Figures 13-62 through 13-64. The Falcon always aligns to the tight-end side, regardless of whether he is to or away from the formation. The Stud aligns opposite the Falcon. The Falcon, defensive end, and the two linebackers stem to the hammer or flex from the Eagle front.

Hammer and Flex Alignment

Falcon: Hammer—aligns in light 70 technique (outside foot on the inside foot of tight end) at linebacker depth. Has C-gap responsibility versus run; leverages all runs from the outside-in. Has normal cover-6 pass-drop responsibilities versus the pass. *Flex*—aligns in a light 70 technique with the toes at the defensive end's heel depth. Same run and pass responsibilities as hammer.

Defensive Tackles: Align in base or tight (toward the tight end). The base, 2i, and 3 techniques are explained in detail in Chapter 5.

Defensive End to Tight End: Hammer—aligns in heavy 9 technique. *Flex*—aligns in wide. The 9 and wide techniques are explained in detail in Chapter 5.

Defensive End Away From the Tight End: Aligns in a 5 technique. The 5 techniques are explained in detail in Chapter 5.

Hammer Versus 21 Pro Formation to the Boundary (Figure 13-65)

With the formation into the boundary (tight end to the boundary), the Falcon aligns to the tight end and the Stud goes to the field.

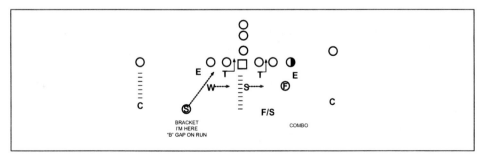

Figure 13-65. Hammer versus 21 pro formation to the boundary

Hammer or Flex Versus Back Motion From 22 or 21 Twins to a 2x2 Formation

The Falcon will call "off/off" to alert the linebackers to get out of hammer or flex. The Falcon gets depth over his position and makes the "I'm here" call to the linebackers, and a "combo" call to the corner that widens with the motion. The linebackers do not adjust their alignment because they have already aligned away from the original "I'm here" call by the corner. Figure 13-66 depicts hammer versus 21 twins with back motion to twins (2x2).

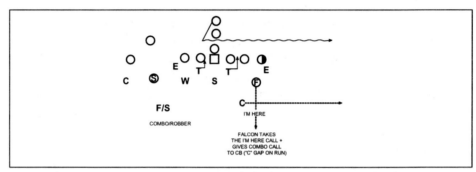

Figure 13-66. Hammer versus 21 twins with back motion to twins (2x2)

Hammer or Flex to a Nub Tight End on the Backside of a 22 Formation

The defense can still get a socks and pirate with the hammer and flex (depends on the set of backs and the game plan). Figure 13-67 depicts hammer versus 22 with a nub tight end.

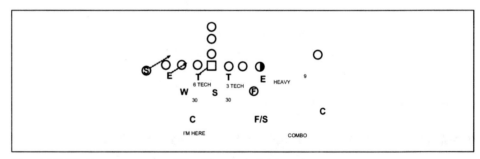

Figure 13-67. Hammer versus 22 with a nub tight end

Hammer Stunts

The primary stunt with hammer is the AC stunt (Figure 13-68). AC can be called to both sides (double AC) or where designated with directional calls ("field/boundary," "formation/weak," "tight/split," or "tilt/numbers"). Additional stunts used with hammer in short-yardage and goal-line situations are explained in detail in Chapter 18.

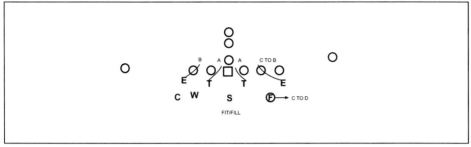

Figure 13-68. Hammer double AC

Flex Stunts

The number-one stunt with flex is the flex Falcon stunt (Figure 13-69). This stunt puts the Falcon on a penetrating charge through the hip of the tackle. The Falcon squeezes the turnout of the tackle; spills the first threat from inside when the tackle blocks down; if the tight end blocks down, flatten and go under the block. The Sam widens his initial alignment (mentally if not physically) to replace the Falcon in coverage.

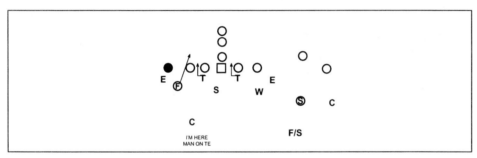

Figure 13-69. Flex Falcon

Falcon and Inside Linebacker Run Techniques With Hammer

Falcon Light 70 Technique When the Tight End Blocks

- *Versus a tight-end turnout* (Figure 13-70): Attacks the line of scrimmage, and searches the C gap. Plays all blocks with the inside arm and shoulder. Keeps the shoulder pads square. Presses the blocker (tackle or guard) back into the hole, reduces the hole with the man.

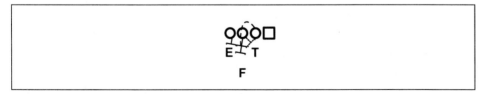

Figure 13-70. Versus a tight-end turnout

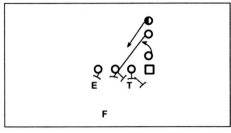

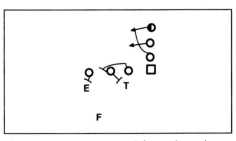

Figure 13-71. Versus a tight-end turnout with two backs in the hole

Figure 13-72. Versus a tight-end reach block

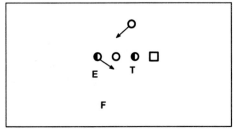

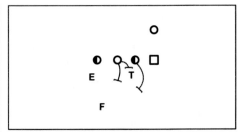

Figure 13-73. Versus a tight-end down block on flow to

Figure 13-74. Versus a tight-end down block on flow away

- *Versus a tight-end turnout with two backs in the hole* (Figure 13-71): Attacks the line of scrimmage, and searches the C gap. Plays all blocks with the inside arm and shoulder. Keeps the shoulder pads square. Presses the blocker (back) back into the hole; reduces the hole with the man.

- *Versus a tight-end reach block* (Figure 13-72): Presses the hip of the defensive end. Sees and feels the defensive end and must be ready to fill where needed (the defensive end can't be wrong). Presses inside or outside the defensive end. Plays all blocks with the inside arm and shoulder. Keeps the shoulder pads square. Hits and sheds the blocker on the run.

- *Versus a tight-end down block on flow to* (Figure 13-73): Keys the tight end, and visualizes the near back as the down block looks the same whether flow to or away. Presses the butt of the defensive end, and must be ready to fill inside or outside where needed. Anticipates that the defensive end will spill the ball outside.

- *Versus a tight-end down block on flow away* (Figure 13-74): Clears the tackle (doesn't run from tackle, but makes him sit down). Presses the tackle or guard hard and crosses the upfield shoulder. Gets to the A gap (gets the arm free to side of flow). Once clear, the cutback turns into "hit man" from the backside.

- *Versus option with a tight end reach or veer release* (Figure 13-75): Searches the C gap from depth. Responsible for the dive outside and the quarterback inside.

- *Versus option with a tight-end down block* (Figure 13-76): Presses the hip of the defensive end and scrapes outside. Alley player (responsible for the quarterback outside and the pitch inside).

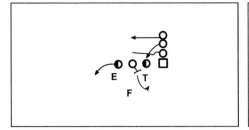

Figure 13-75. Versus option with a tight-end reach or veer release

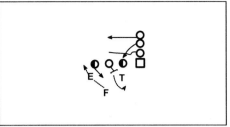

Figure 13-76. Versus option with a tight-end down block

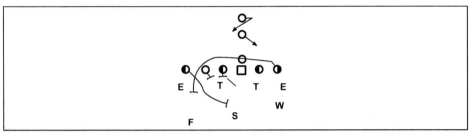

Figure 13-77. Versus counter

- *Versus counter* (Figure 13-77): Redirects (punches back and retraces steps). Yells "counter." Presses the butt of the defensive end. Plays all blocks as a base block. Anticipates the defensive end spilling the play, but must be ready to fill where needed.

Sam Linebacker 10 Technique (Shade to the Tight-End Side)

- *Versus Base Block by the Center* (Figure 13-78): Keys the backs and visualizes blocking schemes and the ball. Attacks and reduces the angle on the center. Presses the center back while keeping leverage on the ball (keeps the arm free to the side of flow).
- *Versus Scoop Block* (Figure 13-79): Shuffles and presses the butt of the 3-technique defensive tackle. Attacks and reduces the angle on the guard. Presses the guard back and crosses his upfield shoulder (shocks and sheds on the run).

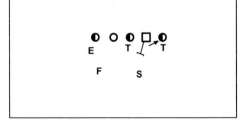

Figure 13-78. Versus base block by the center

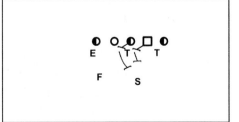

Figure 13-79. Versus scoop block

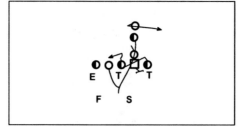

Figure 13-80. Versus trap

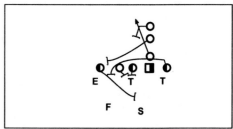

Figure 13-81. Versus sprint draw

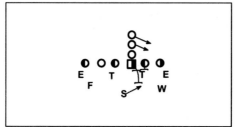

Figure 13-82. Versus weakside action

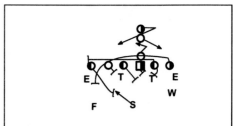

Figure 13-83. Versus counter

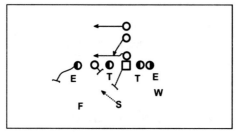

Figure 13-84. Versus option strong

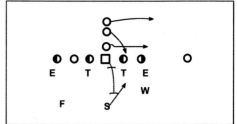

Figure 13-85. Versus option weak

- *Versus Trap* (Figure 13-80): Gets downhill as he mirrors the fullback's angle. Fills where needed, and gets big in the hole. If the guard influences, plays inside the trapper. If the guard down-blocks, plays outside the down block. Linebackers are trap stoppers; tackles are trap squeezers.

- *Versus Sprint Draw* (Figure 13-81): Presses the butt of the 3 technique. Squeezes the down block of the tight end from the inside-out. If the offensive tackle goes to the second level, the 3-technique defensive tackle must make the play. Adjusts fit to the angle of the back and the ball.

- *Versus Weakside Action* (Figure 13-82): Reduces the angle on the weakside guard. Presses the guard back into the hole as he crosses the guard's outside shoulder. Help from the inside-out.

- *Versus Counter* (Figure 13-83): Redirects (retraces steps). Yells "counter" to alert the other defenders. Gives ground to get around the down blocks. Knocks the blocker back into line of scrimmage as he squeezes from the inside-out.

- *Versus Option Strong* (Figure 13-84): Mirrors the fullback. Whips the center, and presses the butt of the 3 technique (helps on the dive from the inside-out). If the tackle goes to the second level, the 3 technique must make play.

- *Versus Option Weak* (Figure 13-85): Mirrors the fullback. Presses the heel line and makes the play on the fullback from the inside-out.

Will 50 Technique

- *Versus Flow to With One Back in the B Gap* (Figure 13-86): Searches the B gap, attacks with the inside arm and shoulder.

- *Versus Flow to With Two Backs in the B Gap* (Figure 13-87): Gets downhill on the lead blocker with number-on-number. Attacks with the inside arm and shoulder, and presses the blocker back into the hole. Keeps the shoulders square.

- *Versus Bounce Play* (Figure 13-88): Presses the butt of the defensive end, and reduces the angle on the blocking back. Plays all blocks as a base block with the inside arm and shoulder, keeping the shoulders square. Hits and sheds the blocker on the run; doesn't hang on to the block.

- *Versus Option To* (Figure 13-89): Presses the butt of the defensive end. Reads the tackle box (veer read). If the tackle blocks down, scrapes tight to the quarterback; if the tackle base blocks or hooks the end, plays the dive from the outside-in.

- *Versus Flow Away With the Ball Outside* (Figure 13-90): Fast-reads, and clears the tackle (gets the arm free to the side of flow). Clears the A gap, and gets over the top immediately.

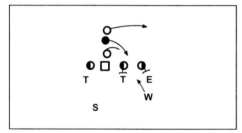

Figure 13-86. Versus flow to with one back in the B gap

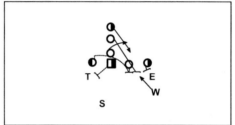

Figure 13-87. Versus flow to with two backs in the B gap

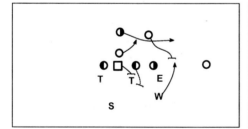

Figure 13-88. Versus bounce play

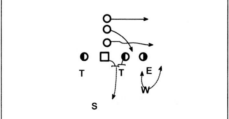

Figure 13-89. Versus option to

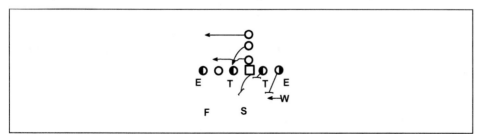

Figure 13-90. Versus flow away with the ball outside

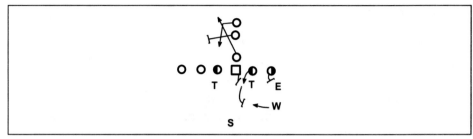

Figure 13-91. Versus flow away with the ball inside

- *Versus Flow Away With the Ball Inside* (Figure 13-91): Slow-reads, and clears the center. Presses the line of scrimmage, and must be aware of the cutback. Keeps the arm free to the side of flow.

Hammer Gap Fills Versus Various Run Plays

☐ Versus Power G Strong (Figure 13-92)

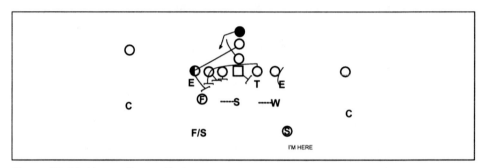

Figure 13-92. Versus Power G strong

Defensive End: Force player. Attacks through the tight end from the outside-in. Versus the tight-end turnout, knocks the tight end back and doesn't worry about where the head is. Versus the tight end down, forces him to take a flat release, and spills the first threat. Doesn't want a one-for-one swap. Keeps the shoulders square, and gets upfield to knock off the pulling guard. Creates a wreck in the C gap, and forces the ballcarrier to bounce outside.

Falcon: Plug player. Steps and stacks on the defensive end; presses to the line of scrimmage; must be outside the pulling guard; pushes the ball outside to the free safety (plug player).

Sam: Spill player. Must be inside the kick-out by the fullback and inside the puller.

Will: Spill player. Must be inside the puller; adjusts press and fit to the angle of the back.

3 Technique: Attacks the guard with good hands and hat fit. If double-team, beats the guard, and squeezes to the outside to force the tackle to block him or be late getting to the linebackers.

Free Safety and Will: Plug players from the inside-out.

❑ Versus Sweep Strong (Figure 13-93)

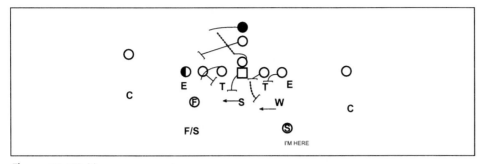

Figure 13-93. Versus sweep strong

Defensive End: Force player. Gets upfield quickly; turns the shoulders of the tight end perpendicular to the line of scrimmage, and sets the wall tight to reduce the cutback lane.

Falcon: Plug player. Attacks the C gap; plays all blocks with the inside arm and shoulder. Fits off the defensive end, and makes him right.

Sam: Spill player. Presses to stack on the defensive tackle; keeps the shoulders square; must be ready to shock and shed. Plays to daylight; if he encounters darkness, adjusts the press to daylight and the angle of the back; keeps inside leverage to prevent the cutback.

Will: Flattens, and keeps the shoulders square; must beat the scoop by the center or the guard. Plays inside-out off the Sam linebacker. Pursuit must eliminate the cutback lane.

❑ Versus Isolation Strong (Figure 13-94)

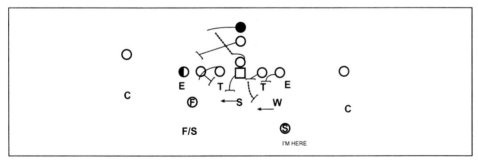

Figure 13-94. Versus isolation strong

Falcon: Force player. Must be outside the lead blocker.

Sam: Spill player. Must be inside the lead blocker.

Will: Presses the center, and creates darkness in the A gap; eliminates the cutback threat. Must be a fast, physical plugger.

Free Safety and Stud: Must be fast, physical pluggers.

❑ Versus Isolation Weak (Figure 13-95)

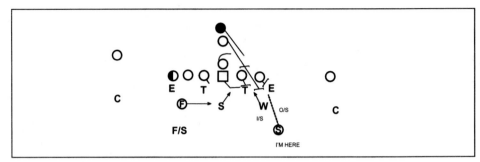

Figure 13-95. Versus isolation weak

Will: Spill player. Attacks the inside portion of lead blocker, and spills the ball to the Stud.

Stud: Force player. Rocks down from the secondary, and must be outside-in on the fullback.

Sam: Presses the center to his A-gap responsibility; eliminates the cutback; must be ready to fit inside or outside to the ball.

Falcon: Presses to a stack on the defensive tackle, must have a slow-to-go mentality and be ready to pitchfork to the angle of the back.

Sam, Falcon, Free Safety, and the Defensive Line: Plug players from the inside-out.

❑ Versus Counter Strong (Figure 13-96)

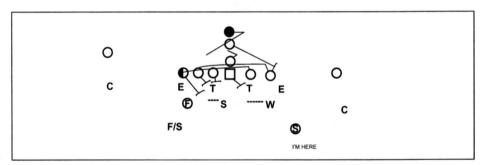

Figure 13-96. Versus counter strong

Defensive End: Spill player. Steps down with the tight end, and forces him to take a flat release (protects the Sam and Will); closes and wrong arms the first blocker to spill the ball outside. If the ball stays inside, makes the tackle. Plays upfield to eliminate the second blocker so the ball will bounce outside naked.

Falcon: Force player. Presses the inside hip of the defensive end to create a gap swap with the defensive end in the C gap and the Falcon in the D gap. Spills the ball outside to the unblocked secondary and pursuit (pluggers).

Sam and Will: Step with the original move of the back; upon recognition of the back and pulling linemen, they redirect and yell "counter." Give ground to get around the blocks if necessary, and work inside-out to the ball. Spill the ball outside. Must be ready to cut the cutter and create a wreck.

❑ Versus Counter Weak (Figure 13-97)

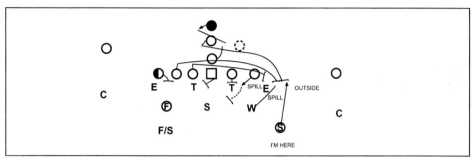

Figure 13-97. Versus counter weak

Defensive End: Spill player. Forces a flat release by the tackle to protect the linebackers. Spills the first threat.

Will: Spill player. Redirects, and spills the second puller.

Stud: Force player. Squeezes the block of the fullback, and keeps the cutback lane tight.

Sam: Plug player. Redirects, gives ground to get around the blocks if necessary, and plays from the inside-out.

14

50 Front (3-4)

The 50 package (3-4) and its variations is a tremendous defensive package against a variety of offenses because of its simplicity and sound schemes. Furthermore, it allows the defenders to play fast with a high degree of effectiveness. The strengths that make this possible include the following:

- Head-up alignments on the line of scrimmage and a four-across look in the secondary eliminates pre-snap reads by the offense, thus a majority of reads must be made after the snap.

- The head-up technique causes hesitation on the offensive line because they don't know whether the defender is going to slant inside, loop outside, or play base.

- The defense has the ability to play multiple fronts (under, over, Eagle) by slanting or stemming the defensive front.

- The linebackers can hide their rush or drop intentions.

- It is difficult to predict the defense's 5- and 9-technique or 4- and 6-technique sides.

- The defense can use the outside linebackers' speed and power on backs, or pass rush on offensive tackles.

- Fire-zone package can be concealed, and it is easy to adjust to movement (motion, shifts, tight-end trade).

- The four-across look makes all route adjustments happen after the snap.

- An aggressive powerful nose can put pressure on the center and change the complexion of the game.

Aligning the 50 Front

The linebackers make a Larry or Roger call to set the direction of the 5 and 9 techniques. The 4 and 6 techniques are always played away from the call. For the 50 front, stunts or blitzes are called the same as the other fronts that have previously been discussed:

- Field/boundary (ball on hash)
- Formation/weak (middle of field)
- Tight/split (tight end)
- Tilt/numbers (backs)

The Sam linebacker aligns to the field or formation. The Will aligns to the boundary or away from the formation. They are not aligned strictly to the 59 side or the 46 side so as not to show a tendency. The tight/split and tilt/numbers require a double call for the secondary. The coverages played with the 50 front consist of the following:

- Cover 6 (quarter, quarter, half)
- Cover 3 (4 under, 3 deep)
- Cover 2 (5 under, 2 deep)
- Two backer (similar to cover 2 except the two inside linebackers, two outside linebackers, or a combination of the two wall the #2 receiver)
- Purple (man coverage)

Examples of 50 Front Calls

- *50 Field Cover 6* (Figure 14-1): Reduction to the boundary. The 6 technique spills on flow to, slow-plays the quarterback on the option, checks for reverse and bootleg on flow away, and rushes the passer from the outside-in. The 9 technique squeezes on flow to, becomes the pitch player on the lead option, and becomes the quarterback player on the load option, folds on flow away, and drops into coverage on the pass.

- *50 Boundary Cover 3* (Figure 14-2): Reduction to the field. Falcon/Stud plays the 6 technique in a heavy 9 alignment, and becomes the C-gap player from the outside-in instead of inside-out.

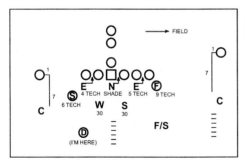

Figure 14-1. 50 field cover 6 (Roger call)

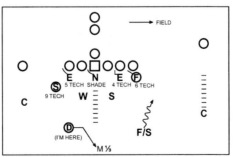

Figure 14-2. 50 boundary cover 3 (Larry call)

- *50 Field Cover 6* (Figure 14-3): Reduction to the tight end.
- *50 Boundary Cover 3* (Figure 14-4): Reduction to the two stand-up wide receivers.
- *50 Formation Cover 6* (Figure 14-5): Reduction to the weakside.
- *50 Weak Cover 3* (Figure 14-6): Reduction to the formation. Falcon plays a 6 technique from heavy 9 alignment.
- *50 Tight Check Cover 6 or 3* (Figures 14-7 and 14-8)
- *50 Tilt Check* (Figures 14-9 and 14-10): Cover 6 if tilt to the formation; cover 3 if the tilt is weak.
- *50 Numbers Check Cover 6 or 3* (Figures 14-11 and 14-12)

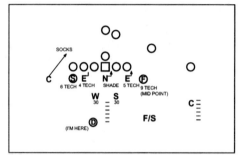

Figure 14-3. 50 field cover 6 (Roger call)

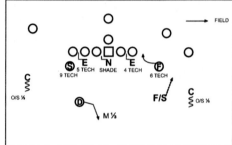

Figure 14-4. Boundary cover 3 (Larry call)

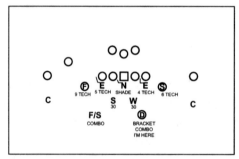

Figure 14-5. 50 formation cover 6 (Larry call)

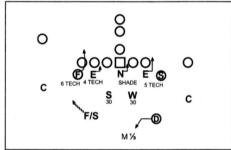

Figure 14-6. 50 weak cover 3 (Roger call)

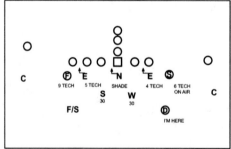

Figure 14-7. 50 tight cover 6 (Larry call)

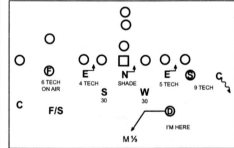

Figure 14-8. 50 tight cover 3 (Roger call)

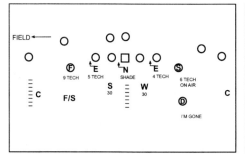

Figure 14-9. 50 tilt check cover 6 (Larry call)

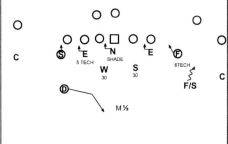

Figure 14-10. 50 tilt check cover 3 (Larry call)

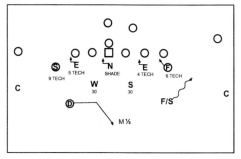

Figure 14-11. 50 numbers check cover 3 (Larry call)

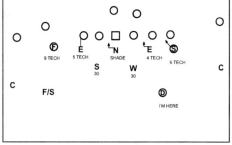

Figure 14-12. 50 numbers check cover 6 (Larry call)

Aztec (50 to Eagle) and Aztec Under

It is common practice for defenses to substitute when adjusting from an Eagle to a 50 front, or the reverse from a 50 to an Eagle front. When this method is used, the usual defensive adjustment is to substitute a defensive back for a defensive lineman when going from an Eagle to a 50; and substitute a defensive lineman for a defensive back when going from a 50 to an Eagle.

Although this substitution is easily done, the preferred way is to disguise the movement from 50 to Eagle or under, so that the opponent does not have a read on what front they are going to see prior to lining up on the ball. It is important to look at each opponent's pre-snap procedure to determine when is the best time for the Sam linebacker to make a "move" call. On the "move" call, the entire front slides toward the formation. All Eagle and under stunts, fire zones, blitzes, and adjustments can be used with Aztec (Eagle) and Aztec under (Figures 14-13 and 14-14).

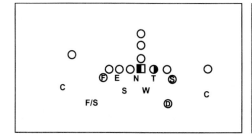

Figure 14-13. Aztec under

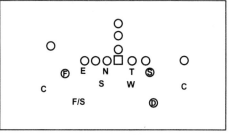

Figure 14-14. Aztec (Eagle)

50 Front Stunts

The 50 front stunts are either on the 59 side (5 and 9 techniques), or the 46 side (4 and 6 techniques). The 59 stunts are blast, base, and fold. The 46 stunts are attack, angle, A, and exchange. The exchange stunt is only used versus an option team, so the explanation of this stunt is covered in Chapter 20. Even though it is not considered a stunt, the nose tackle can execute a directional zero technique, which sends him to an A gap on the huddle call "50 formation zero." He should get penetration in the A gap to the call. This variation can work in conjunction with base or stunt calls.

59 Side Stunts

50 Tight Blast (Figure 14-15)

The 50 tight blast is a stunt by the Sam or Will to the 59 side through the B gap. Blast can be run from depth or from a bluff look. Sam or Will should emphasize first-step quickness, accelerate downhill, attack the window, dominate the gap, get big on the run and small on the pass, and expect the ball to attack the assigned gap. The blitzing linebacker needs to remember that the gap moves but never changes; he must be ready to flatten in or flatten out to the angle of the back and the ball.

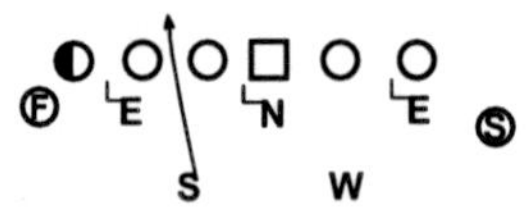

Figure 14-15. 50 tight blast

50 Tight Base (Figure 14-16)

For 50 tight base, the defensive end wants to beat the offensive lineman on his get-off. He should attack and create a new line of scrimmage. He doesn't worry about being reached, gets the knock back and two-gaps the tackle; versus double-team, presses into the tight end's block and anchors the area. The linebacker presses to daylight and makes the defensive end right as he finds light or darkness during penetration.

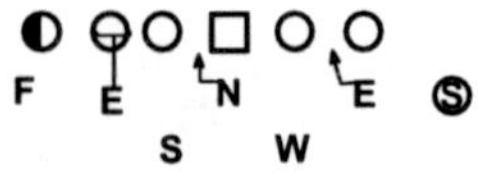

Figure 14-16. 50 tight base

50 Fold (Figure 14-17)

50 fold is used primarily as an open-end stunt. It is a gap swap for the defensive end with the Falcon or Stud. The defensive end makes a quick upfield move. He squeezes on flow to, checks reverse, bootleg on flow away, his assignment is outside force on the pass, and the quarterback on the option. Falcon goes tight off the hip of the defensive end and tries to get quick penetration. He spills the hole on flow to, flattens in pursuit on flow away, inside rushes on the pass, and takes the dive on the option.

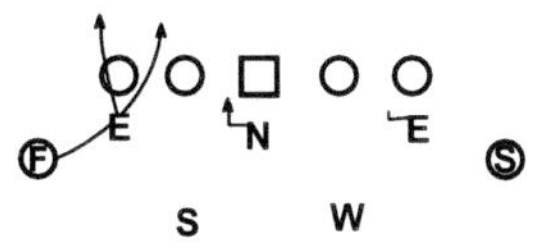

Figure 14-17. 50 fold

46 Side Stunts

50 Attack (Figure 14-18)

50 attack is a stunt by Will or Sam backer through the A gap to the 46 side. Same principles apply to the attack stunt as used on the blast. The linebacker feels the gap and visualizes the angle of the back. If he encounters darkness, presses and fits to daylight; if the ball is outside (sweep, stretch), he reads out of the stunt and flattens down the line of scrimmage; becomes the hit man from the inside-out on the ball.

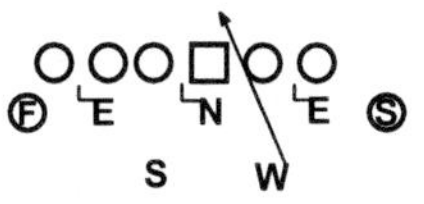

Figure 14-18. 50 attack

50 Angle (Figure 14-19)

For 50 angle, the defensive end and Stud lead step with the inside foot at a 45-degree angle through the V of the neck of the guard (defensive end) and the tackle (Stud). If a turnout block, squeezes the hole with the man; reduces the hole with the guard and tackle; keeps the outside arm and leg free; doesn't run around the block. If a down block by the guard, the defensive end spills all blocks on flow to; chases down the ball on flow away; plays inside rush on the pass and takes the dive on the option. If the tackle down-blocks, the Stud spills all blocks on flow to; chases on flow away and checks for reverse or bootleg.

He has outside force on the pass and the quarterback on the option. Will and Sam are fast outside on flow to; they stack on the nose and find the fit on flow away; hook/curl on the pass; alley players on option (taking the quarterback outside the Stud and having the pitch inside the safety and cornerback).

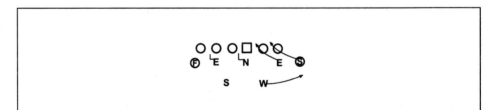

Figure 14-19. 50 angle

50 A (Figure 14-20)

With 50 A, the defensive end and Stud can align slightly deeper on the A stunt, but not too deep so as not to give away the stunt. Their aiming point is the facemask of the guard and tackle. Their responsibility on the down block is similar to the angle stunt. The exception is the Stud: he is responsible for the dive on the option and doesn't have any reverse or bootleg responsibilities on flow away. He spills all blocks on flow to; chases down the ball on flow away; has inside rush on the pass and dive on the option. Versus the turnout block, they both cross the face of the guard and the tackle, with the defensive end responsible for the A gap and the Stud responsible for the B gap. Both are dive players on the option, spill all blocks on flow to, chase the ball on flow away, and have inside force on the pass. Will and Sam are the second-level players on inside plays and the first-level players on outside plays. They shuffle to the stunt on snap and squeeze all runs from the outside-in on flow to; they check for counter, reverse, and bootleg on flow away; they have late force on the pass, and the quarterback on the option with inside-out position on the quarterback.

Figure 14-20. 50 A

50 Pinch (Figures 14-21 through 14-24)

- *50 Pinch:* This stunt is a 46 to both sides. The direction call (Larry or Roger) is to the formation. It is good against the inside run game and in run-down situations especially in short-yardage and goal-line situations. The nose tackle plays a zero technique and back-doors all run plays, which makes the backside linebacker responsible for the frontside A gap. Both linebackers are fast flow players. Sally is a secondary call that is the same as cover 3. Sally alerts secondary that a 46 is to both sides. Because pinch is used primarily versus option teams, the safeties need to be aware of front movement.

- *50 Pinch Attack* (Figure 14-24): This stunt is a double A-gap stunt by both linebackers. Can also be either a formation attack with Sam, or weakside with Will.

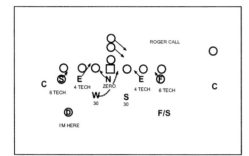

Figure 14-21. 50 pinch Sally (Roger call)

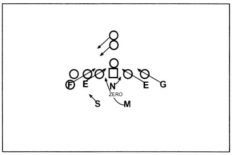

Figure 14-22. 50 pinch angle

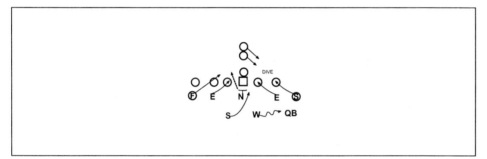

Figure 14-23. 50 pinch A

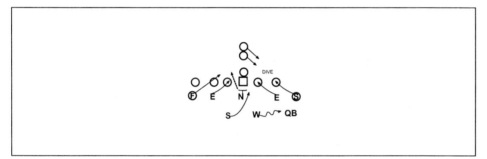

Figure 14-24. 50 pinch attack

How 50 Stunts Are Called

The stunts are tagged in the same manner listed earlier in this chapter:
- Field/boundary (ball on the hash)
- Formation/weak (middle of field)
- Tight/split (tight end)
- Tilt/numbers (backs)

Following are examples of fronts and stunt calls from the 50 defense (Figures 14-25 through 14-27). The 59 side is always to the callside, and the 46 side is always away from the callside.

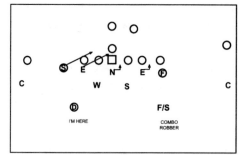

Figure 14-25. 50 formation angle cover 6 (Roger call)

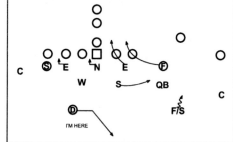

Figure 14-26. 50 tight A cover 6 or 3 (Larry call)—cover 3

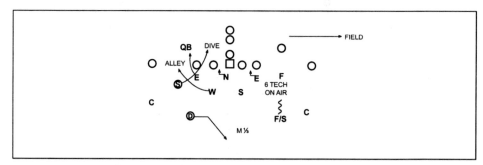

Figure 14-27. 50 boundary fold cover 3 (Larry call)

50 Split Fold A Z-Spin Backer, or Two Backer (Figure 14-28)

This stunt is a double stunt with spin coverage to the formation side.

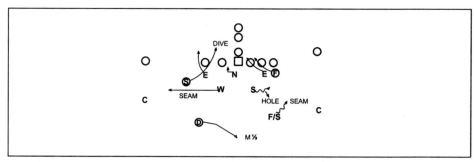

Figure 14-28. 50 split fold A Z-spin backer, or two backer (Larry call)

55 Front

55 Base Cover 6 (Figure 14-29)

The 55 front is only used versus the option. The defensive ends play a two-gap technique on the tackles; the nose tackle plays a zero technique on the center; the Sam and Will are fast flow players responsible for the A and B gaps to flow.

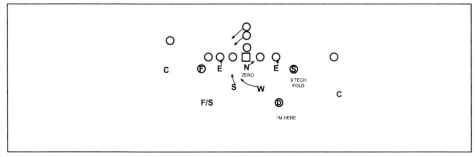

Figure 14-29. 55 base cover 6

55 Double Fold (Figure 14-30)

55 double fold is a 55 front change-up from the base call. The defensive ends go first and the Stud and Falcon go second off the end's heels.

Defensive End: Spills all blocks on flow to; checks for reverse and bootleg on flow away; has the quarterback on the option and outside force on the pass.

Falcon and Stud: Spill all blocks on flow to; pursue flat on flow away; have inside rush on the pass and dive on the option.

Playside Linebacker: Plays like the A stunt; presses the C or D gap; must be ready to squeeze all blocks on flow to; pursues on flow away; drops into coverage on the pass; takes the quarterback outside on the option (the defensive end has the quarterback inside).

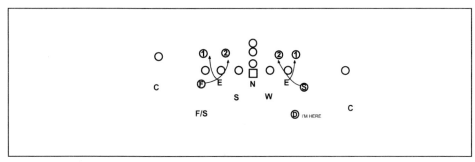

Figure 14-30. 55 double fold

50 Front Four-Man Rushes

A linebacker can be put into the rush to get a four-man rush with the same calls as used for setting the fronts and stunts (e.g., field/boundary, formation/weak, etc.). A wrap call indicates the outside rusher goes first and the nose tackle second; a swap call indicates the nose tackle goes first and the outside rusher second.

- *50 Tilt Backer Wrap or Swap* (Figure 14-31): The linebacker has two-gap responsibility on the tackle; if the tackle blocks down or out, the linebacker is outside force player on the quarterback.

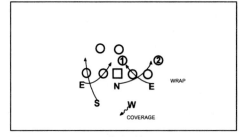

Figure 14-31. 50 tilt backer wrap or swap (Larry call)

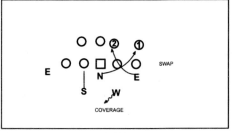

Figure 14-32. 50 tilt blast wrap or swap (Larry call)

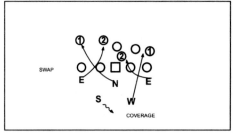

Figure 14-33. 50 tilt blast pick wrap or swap (Roger call)

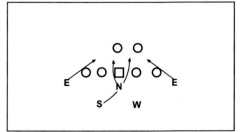

Figure 14-34. 50 tilt attack X double jet

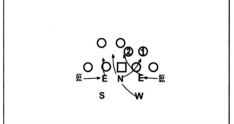

Figure 14-35. Bear tilt attack swap

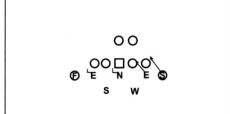

Figure 14-36. 50 numbers angle (Larry call)

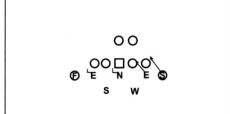

Figure 14-37. 50 numbers angle echo (Larry call)

- *50 Tilt Blast Wrap or Swap* (Figure 14-32): The linebacker has the option to beat the guard either inside or outside.
- *50 Tilt Blast Pick Wrap or Swap* (Figure 14-33): The linebacker can stunt from his base or bluff alignment.
- *50 Tilt Attack X Double Jet* (Figure 14-34)
- *Bear Tilt Attack Swap* (Figure 14-35): Bear alerts the defensive ends to slide late into 3 techniques.
- *50 Numbers Angle* (Figure 14-36)
- *50 Numbers Angle Echo* (Figure 14-37)

50 Fire Zones (50 Front Five-Man Rushes With Zone Coverage)

Fire-zone concepts and responsibilities from different fronts are covered in detail in Chapter 16. Figures 14-38 through 14-55 provide examples of fire zones from the 50 front versus a variety of formations.

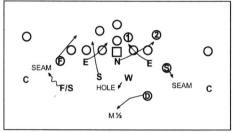

Figure 14-38. 50 tilt thunder wrap Z-spin (Larry call)

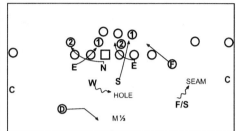

Figure 14-39. 50 formation thunder pick wrap Z-spin (Roger call)

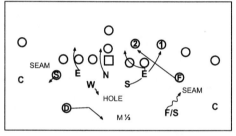

Figure 14-40. 50 split thunder switch Z-spin (Roger call)

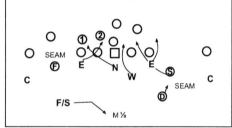

Figure 14-41. 50 split lightning swap Z-spin (Roger call)

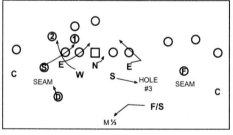

Figure 14-42. 50 tilt tornado Z-spin (Larry call)

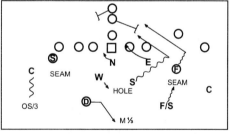

Figure 14-43. 50 left river (echo) Z-spin (Larry call)

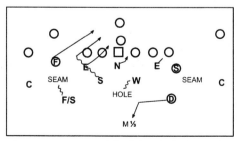

Figure 14-44. 50 right lake (echo) Z-spin (Roger call)

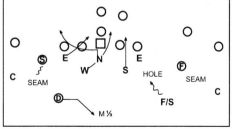

Figure 14-45. 50 formation blaze wrap Y, Z-sky (Roger call)

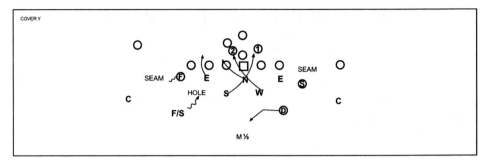

Figure 14-46. 50 tilt smoke Z, Y (Larry call)

Make the Larry or Roger call to the formation.

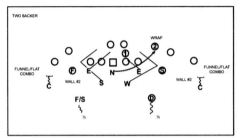

Figure 14-47. 50 crash wrap or swap Z-spin backer or two backer

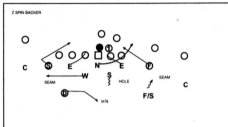

Figure 14-48. 50 smack wrap or swap Z-spin backer or two backer

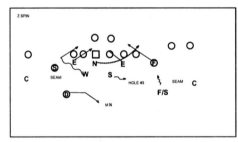

Figure 14-49. 50 storm wrap or swap Z-spin or two backer (Roger call)

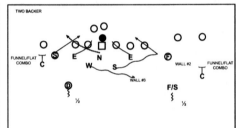

Figure 14-50. 50 wind wrap or swap Z-spin or two backer (Larry call)

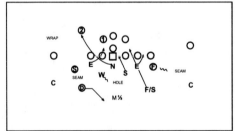

Figure 14-51. 50 tight fire wrap or swap Z (Roger call)

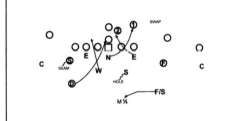

Figure 14-52. 50 tight flame wrap or swap Z (Larry call)

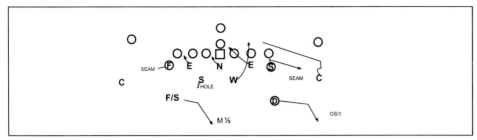

Figure 14-53. 50 Rambo change-up—Rambo is a change-up to the base stunt that brings the Stud and the corner, and covers the flat with the Will.

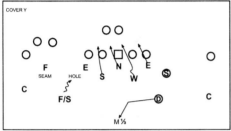
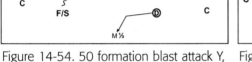

Figure 14-54. 50 formation blast attack Y, Z, two backer (Larry call)

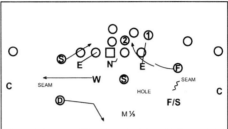

Figure 14-55. 50 formation fold angle Z-spin (Roger call)

50 Front Four-Man Rushes With Cover 1

Cover 1 can be played with a four-man rush from the 50 front. One of the inside linebackers becomes the fourth rusher. Wrap or swap calls can be used for the linebackers. Some slight adjustments in coverage are made with cover 1 from the 50 front, but not a significant difference from cover 1 with the Eagle front. The call for the blitzing linebacker is like all other calls: field/boundary, formation/weak, tilt/numbers, tight/split. The Sam is responsible for getting the front set with a Larry or Roger call. The following are examples of 50 front four-man rushes with cover 1.

Cover-1 Assignments Versus Two-Back Formations

(Figures 14-56 through 14-59)

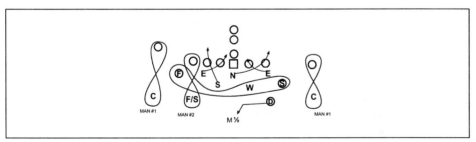

Figure 14-56. Versus 21 pro (funnel coverage by Falcon, Will, and Stud on two backers)

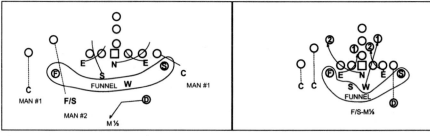

Figure 14-57. Versus 21 twins

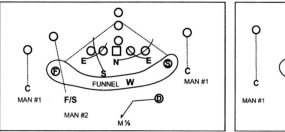

Figure 14-58. Versus 20 pro

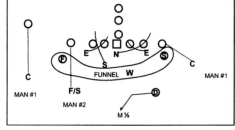

Figure 14-59. Versus 22 pro

Cover-1 Assignments Versus Doubles Formations
(Figures 14-60 through 14-62)

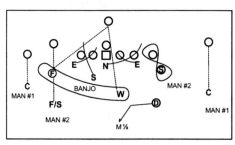

Figure 14-60. Versus 11 doubles

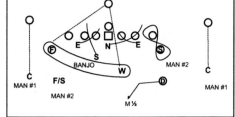

Figure 14-61. Versus 12 doubles

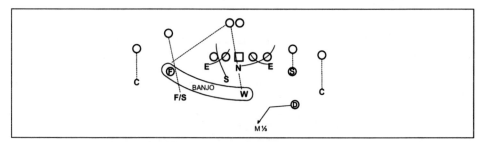

Figure 14-62. Versus 10 doubles

Cover-1 Assignments Versus Trips Formations
(Figures 14-63 through 14-66)

Banjo is normally played to the #2 and #3 receiver, but can also be played to the #1 and #2 receiver with the corner and the free safety if the scouting report indicates this is the best match up. Banjo with the corner and free safety is preferable, but the Falcon can be used if he is good enough to execute with the corner.

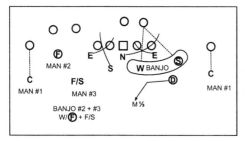

Figure 14-63. Versus 11 trips

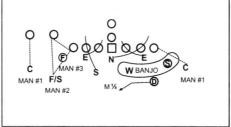

Figure 14-64. Versus 12 rips

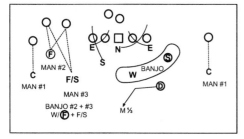

Figure 14-65. Versus 10 trips

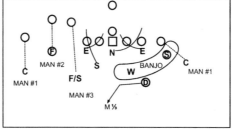

Figure 14-66. Versus 11 trey

50 Cover-1 Adjustments Versus Motion and Y Trade

Versus 21 Pro With Motion to Twins (Figures 14-67 through 14-69)

The Falcon, Stud, and non-blitzing linebacker play funnel.

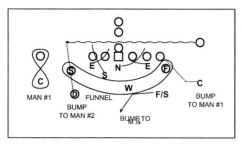

Figure 14-67. Versus 21 pro with motion to twins

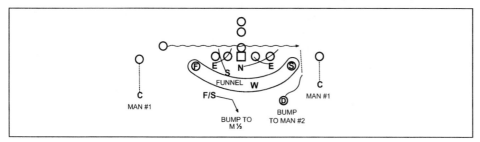

Figure 14-68. Versus 21 twins with motion to pro

Figure 14-69. Versus 20 pro with motion

Versus 22 With Motion (Figures 14-70 and 14-71)

Two ways exist to adjust coverage to motion from the 22 formation. With a bump call, the four secondary players bump man coverage toward the motion. With a stay call, the corner runs through with the motion man, thus only one defender has to adjust.

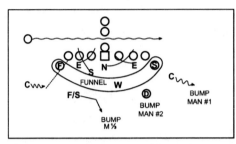

Figure 14-70. Versus 22 with motion–bump adjustment

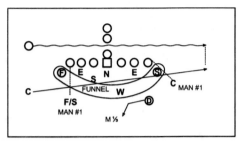

Figure 14-71. Versus 22 with motion–stay adjustment

Versus 11 Doubles With Motion to Trips (Figures 14-72 through 14-80)

The non-blitzing linebacker and Stud banjo the tight end.

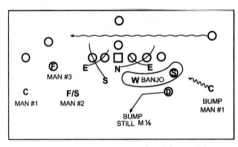

Figure 14-72. Versus 11 doubles with motion to trips

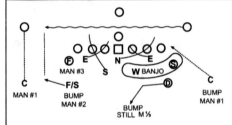

Figure 14-73. Versus 12 doubles with motion to trips

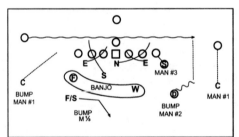

Figure 14-74. Versus 10 doubles with motion to trips

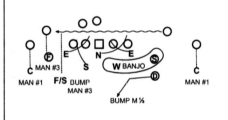

Figure 14-75. Versus 10 doubles with motion to trips

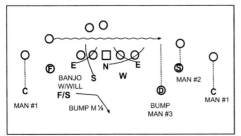

Figure 14-76. Versus 10 doubles with motion to trips

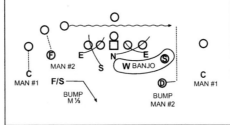

Figure 14-77. Versus 11 trips with motion to doubles

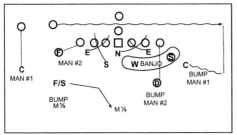

Figure 14-78. Versus 12 trips with motion to doubles

Figure 14-79. Versus 10 trips with motion to doubles

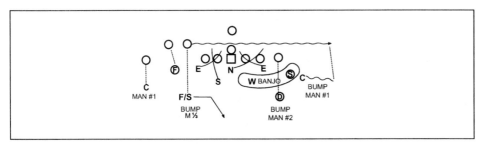

Figure 14-80. Versus 11 trey with motion to doubles

Versus Y Trade (Figures 14-81)

The Falcon and Stud swap assignments versus tight-end trade. The front call can be adjusted with an "opposite" call. On an "opposite" call, the linebackers exchange responsibilities relating to blitz and coverage.

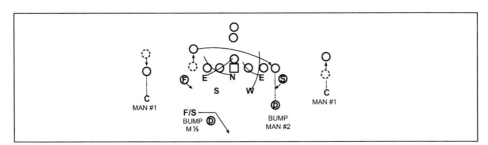

Figure 14-81. Versus Y trade

50 Cover-1 Four-Man Rushes

(Figures 14-82 through 14-91)

With 50 cover-1 four-man rushes, the non-blitzing linebacker should bluff. All blitz rules and techniques apply, and the defensive ends align in a jet technique.

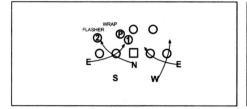

Figure 14-82. Tilt backer wrap

Figure 14-83. Tilt backer swap

Tilt Backer Trio (Figures 14-84)

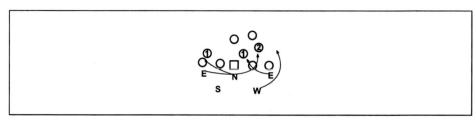

Figure 14-84. Tilt backer trio

Nose Tackle (Penetrator): Crosses the face of the guard, and then look for the open window inside or outside the offensive tackle; has outside force on the quarterback; plays across the face of the tackle if any question about the open space.

Defensive End (Penetrator): Reads the guard on the move; if the guard goes inside, gets immediate depth upfield to collapse the pocket; if the guard turns out, cross-faces and gets penetration.

Defensive End (Flasher): Steps to the offensive tackle, and then goes behind the nose and finds daylight; shouldn't be in a hurry, and must be ready to scrape off the second penetrator (defensive end).

Tilt Backer Blast (Figure 14-85)

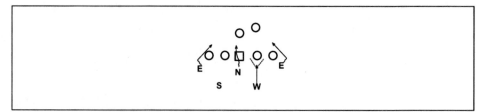

Figure 14-85. Tilt backer blast

Linebacker: Maintains outside force on the quarterback.

Nose Tackle: Can wrap or swap. If the nose doesn't wrap or swap, he can angle away from the blitzing linebacker. He stays active as a rusher, but can also grab the center if the game dictates it.

Blitzing Linebacker: Has a two-way go on the guard; attacks the window; slip-blocks with a rip or swim move.

Tilt Backer Blast Pick (Figure 14-86)

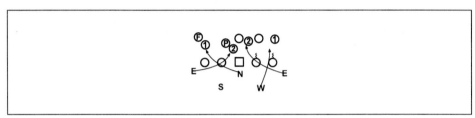

Figure 14-86. Tilt backer blast pick

Blitzing Linebacker: Attacks the B gap. If he beats the guard and the tackle, has force on the quarterback from the outside-in.

Defensive End: Steps to occupy the tackle, and then scrapes off the linebacker; searches for the open window off the guard.

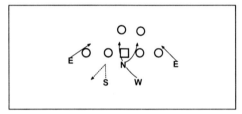

Figure 14-87. Tilt backer X

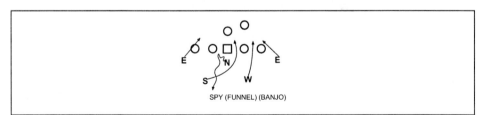

Figure 14-88. Tilt backer attack (linebacker in A gap)

Figure 14-89. Tilt blaze spy (nose replaces the linebacker and plays either funnel or banjo with the Falcon and Stud)

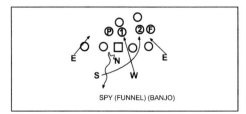

Figure 14-90. Tilt blaze cross spy

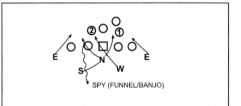

Figure 14-91. Tilt smoke spy

15

Six-Man Pressure From Eagle and 50 Fronts

The six-man pressure package complements the zone-blitz (fire-zone) package because it creates problems for the offensive pass-protection schemes. Even though several blitzes can be run from six-man pressure, it is best to limit them to only one blitz each from the Eagle and 50 fronts for each game in order to have perfect execution. However, variations can be built into each blitz. Regardless of whether using a five-man pressure or six-man pressure, it is important to utilize the bluff package to create the illusion that the defense is blitzing on every down. By bluffing, the defense forces the offense to make all reads after the ball has been snapped. Furthermore, bluffing in combination with actual blitzes creates a sense of urgency to release the ball quickly, takes away the quick answers, and breaks the rhythm and timing of pass routes for the offense. The blitzers must beat blocks and pressure the quarterback, and the secondary must successfully cover receivers man-for-man for any blitzing scheme to be effective.

Eagle Front Six-Man Blitzes

Eagle Stinger (Figure 15-1)

The linebacker covering the back needs to hug-up on the back; when he does so, the outside rusher to the side the back blocks can beat the block either inside or outside; the cover linebacker makes the rush linebacker right.

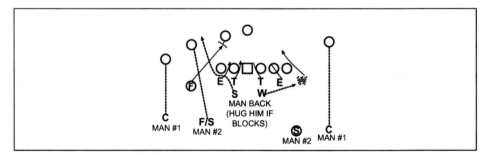

Figure 15-1. Eagle stinger

Eagle Stinger Variations: Tilt Wrap or Swap, Double Wrap or Swap
(Figures 15-2 through 15-7)

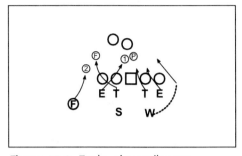

Figure 15-2. Eagle stinger tilt wrap (2 technique to the side of the back wraps to contain to allow the Falcon to rush inside or outside the back)

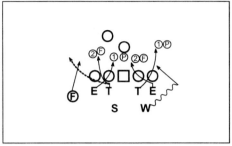

Figure 15-3. Eagle stinger weave (wrap strong, swap weak)

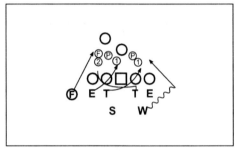

Figure 15-4. Eagle stinger trio

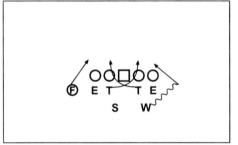

Figure 15-5. Eagle stinger twist

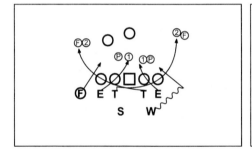

Figure 15-6. Eagle stinger scissors

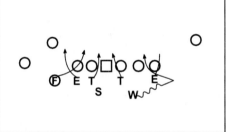

Figure 15-7. Eagle stinger echo (can twist inside)

Purple Coverage Versus Two-Back, 2x2, and 3x1 Formations

Purple Versus Two-Back Formations (Figures 15-8 through 15-11)

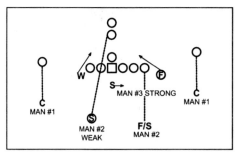

Figure 15-8. Versus 21 pro

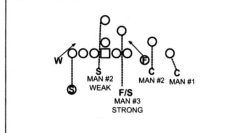

Figure 15-9. Versus 21 twins (corners over to twins)

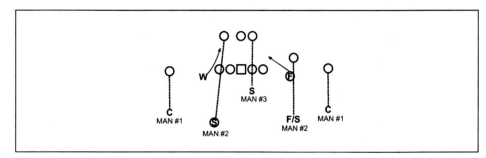

Figure 15-10. Versus 20 splitbacks

Versus 22 (Figure 15-11): On the nub tight-end side, the Stud makes a "me" call that alerts the linebacker that the Stud is blitzing and the linebacker covers #2 weak. If both backs move either strong or weak, the linebacker to flow takes the first back outside and the backside linebacker takes the first back inside.

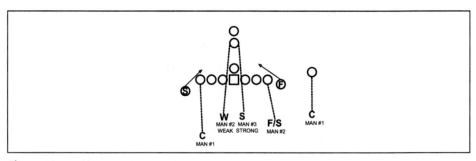

Figure 15-11. Versus 22

Purple Versus 2x2 Formations (Figures 15-12 through 15-14)

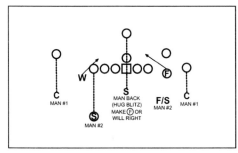

Figure 15-12. Versus 11 doubles

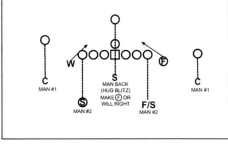

Figure 15-13. Versus 12 doubles

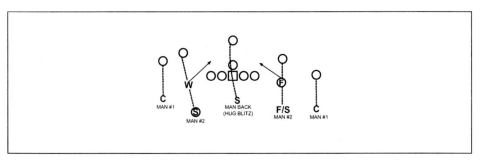

Figure 15-14. Versus 10 doubles

Purple Versus 3x1 Formations (Figures 15-15 through 15-18)

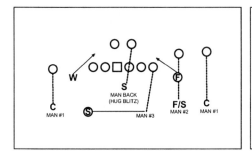

Figure 15-15. Versus 11 trips

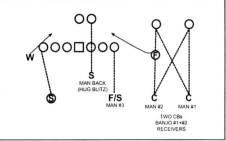

Figure 15-16. Versus 12 trips

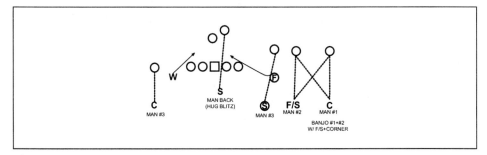

Figure 15-17. Versus 10 trips

Versus 11 Trey (Figure 15-18): If motion is a big part of the opponent's trey formation strategy, play the corners to the Trey side. Switch the corner and the free safety so that the corner mans #3 and the free safety mans #2.

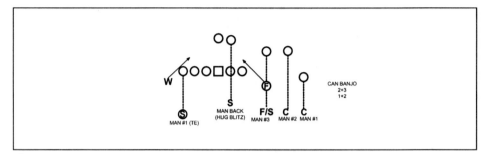

Figure 15-18. Versus 11 trey

Purple Coverage Motion Adjustments Versus Two-Back, 2x2, and 3x1 Formations

Purple Versus Motion From Two-Back Formations
(Figures 15-19 through 15-23)

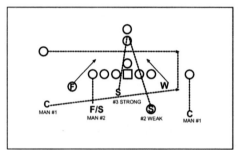

Figure 15-19. Versus 21 pro with motion to twins

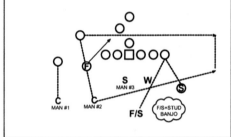

Figure 15-20. Versus 21 twins with motion to pro

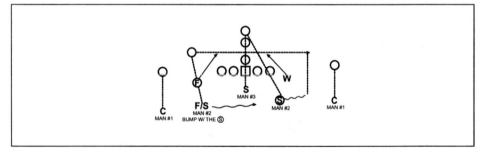

Figure 15-21. Versus 20 with inside-receiver motion

Versus 22 With Back Motion (Figure 15-22): The Falcon or Stud to the back motion side makes a "you" call to the linebacker. The linebacker becomes the blitzer, and the Stud or Falcon covers the back motion.

Versus 22 With Wide Receiver Motion (Figure 15-23): On the nub tight-end side, the Stud makes a "me" call to the Will; Stud is the blitzer, and Will has coverage. The corner to the motion side widens and covers the motion man.

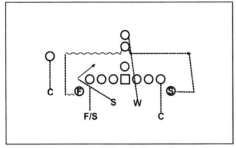

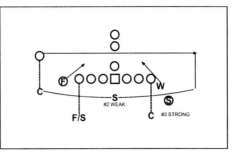

Figure 15-22. Versus 22 with back motion

Figure 15-23. Versus 22 with wide receiver motion

Purple Versus Motion From 2x2 Formations

(Figures 15-24 through 15-27)

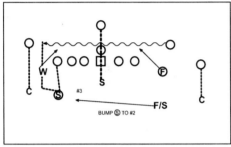

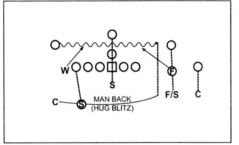

Figure 15-24. Versus 11 doubles with motion to trips (FS and Ⓢ can stay locked)

Figure 15-25. Versus 11 doubles with motion to trey

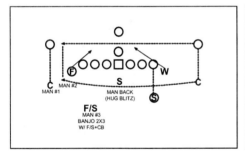

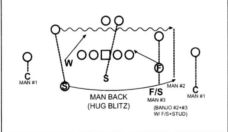

Figure 15-26. Versus 12 doubles with motion to trips

Figure 15-27. Versus 10 doubles with motion to trips

Purple Versus Motion From 3x1 Formations

(Figures 15-28 through 15-31)

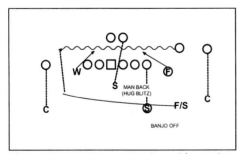

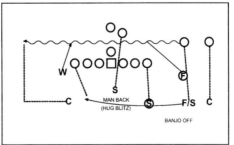

Figure 15-28. Versus 11 trips with motion to doubles

Figure 15-29. Versus 12 trips with motion to doubles

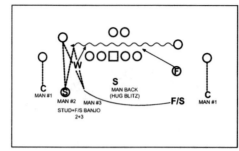

Figure 15-30. Versus 10 trips with motion to trips

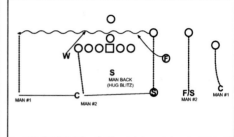

Figure 15-31. Versus 11 trey with motion to doubles

Purple Coverage Versus Y Trade

(Figures 15-32 and 15-33)

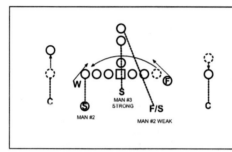

Figure 15-32. Versus 21 pro

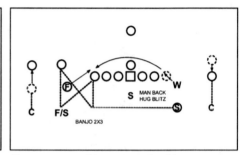

Figure 15-33. Versus 11 doubles

50 Front Six-Man Pressure (Blitzes)

The blitzing linebacker is called the same as with all other blitzes, (e.g., field/boundary, formation/weak, tight/split, tilt/numbers). Wrap or swap can also be called with these blitzes.

50 Formation Sic 'Em (Figure 15-34): If the back blocks the Sam, Sam goes inside the back, and the Falcon goes outside the back.

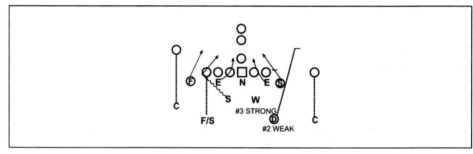

Figure 15-34. 50 Formation Sic 'em

Variations of 50 Sic 'Em (Figures 15-35 through 15-38)

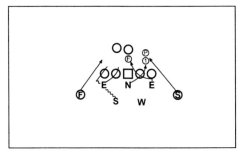

Figure 15-35. 50 sic 'em swap

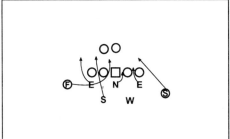

Figure 15-36. 50 tilt sic 'em echo

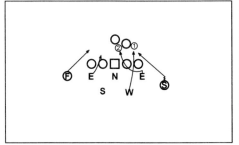

Figure 15-37. 50 tilt sic 'em pick

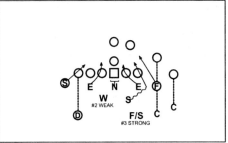

Figure 15-38. 50 tilt sic 'em lightning

Purple Coverage With 50 Sic 'Em (Figures 15-39 through 15-42)

Purple coverage is the same with both Eagle and 50 blitzes. The dime back replaces the Stud and applies the same coverage rules versus the two-back, 2x2, and 3x1 formations. The corners are over on the 21 twins (Figure 15-40), 12 trips, and 11 trey (Figure 15-42), and are ready to run with motion.

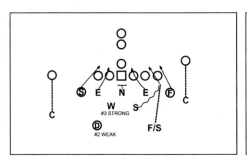

Figure 15-39. Versus 21

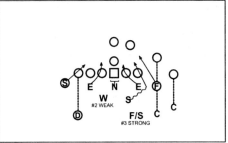

Figure 15-40. Versus 21 twins

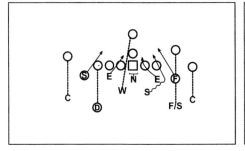

Figure 15-41. Versus 11 doubles

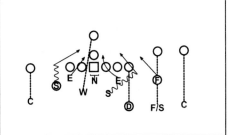

Figure 15-42. Versus 11 trey

16

Zone Blitzes

Zone Blitz Concepts

Traditional six- or seven-man blitzes with cover 1 (man/free) or straight man coverage are effective defensive schemes. However, they have a tendency to allow the offense to make big plays, resulting in key first downs or touchdowns. On the other hand, zone blitzes (fire zones), with a variety of five-man rushes and zone coverage, are very successful in preventing big plays, but still provide for pressure on the offense.

When teaching zone blitzes it is essential to make each defense, each stunt, and each blitz as sound and simple as possible, and to make sure the players know the strengths and weaknesses of each defense.

The following criteria that should be met when developing each zone blitz:
- Stop the run.
- Stop the pass.
- Keep gap integrity.
- Emphasize the defense's strengths against the offense's weaknesses.

In addition, each zone blitz should try to achieve the following results:
- Create a sense of urgency in the minds of the quarterback, receivers, and offensive line.
- Speed up all decisions by the offense.
- Reduce routes being run by the offense to keep the secondary from having to defend the entire route tree.
- Dictate the offensive play calls.
- Create mismatches and confusion in protection.
- Disrupt rhythm and timing.
- Create "hot" routes and throws.

- Penetrate point of attack in running game.
- Get sacks, hurries, and hits on the quarterback.

Opponents know that defenses include zone blitzes in their arsenal; thus, it is to the defense's advantage to keep them guessing as to when, where, or how the zone blitzes will be executed. Other advantages of zone blitzes include the ability to rush every position except the strong corner, to strike at any point on the line of scrimmage, and to employ all types of combinations whether from an Eagle or 50 fronts. In fact, seven different combinations are possible, including the following:

- Both inside linebackers (Sam/Will)
- Falcon and Stud together
- Falcon with Sam or Will
- Stud with Sam or Will
- Free safety with Sam or Will
- Dime with Sam or Will (50 front only)
- Weak corner with Sam or Will

The possibilities of seven different combinations create protection problems and force a sense of urgency in the minds of the quarterback, backs, and offensive line. Decisions on which zone blitzes to use and where to attack a particular opponent should be based on the following criteria:

- Field/boundary
- Formation/weak
- Tight (to tight end)/split
- Tilt (to off-set back)/numbers (away from off-set back)
- To a particular back (attack a poor blocker, keep a strong blocker out of the route)
- To the weakest offensive lineman (attack personnel, attack protection)
- To the wide receiver
- To a particular protection (attack protection, attack personnel)
- To the tight end to stop the run or pass

Zone-Blitz Strategy

The strategic approach of the zone-blitz package is a key ingredient in determining its success. Consider down-and-distance, field zones, behind the 50, offense having crossed the 50, the tolerance of the coach to a certain amount of gambles, and the ability of the defense to execute the blitz when developing strategy. The following tips can help shape zone-blitz strategy:

- The best time to blitz is immediately following a blitz.
- Chart where they are throwing the three-step pass or screen (rocket, bubble), and blitz to the favorite receiver.
- Chart successful blitzes other teams have shown against them in previous games according to down-and-distance, field position, and such.

- Show blitz to them in a way they haven't seen before (make it look different).
- Blitz when they don't expect it.
- Know how they block a particular blitz. If you don't get an answer the first time you call blitz, call it again until you get an answer.
- Use the same blitz from the opposite side.
- Call a blitz, but use a different coverage from the two-shell look.
- Blitz from a bluff position. Show bluff, but don't blitz, and then run the same blitz.
- Bluff inside, and blitz outside; bluff outside, and blitz inside.
- Show blitz on one side, and then blitz from the opposite side.

Principles of Success for Zone Blitzes

Certain principles of blitzing should be emphasized to give the defense the best chance for consistent efficiency. The defensive players need a sound knowledge of what they are trying to accomplish so they can execute the blitzes with intelligence, quickness, and power. The following principles are the foundation for success in the zone-blitz package:

- Disguise: Fire zones are great out of two-deep shell.
- The front and secondary should eliminate all pre-snap reads: force all reads to be post-snap.
- Collapse the pocket.
- Blitzes: Outathlete the offensive linemen and outphysical the back.
- Contain the quarterback: Contain players must know their responsibility.
- Take away the inside routes in coverage.
- Make the quarterback throw the longest throw.
- Disguise with bluff. Blitz, then bluff; bluff, then blitz.
- Give the impression of coming every series (perceived pressure). This approach enables a three-man rush and four-man rush to apply effective pressure because of urgency that has been created
- Confuse the gaps.
- Predicate the blitz on where the back will block.
- Zone blitz against four wide receivers.
- Maintain proper alignment of hole and seam players.
- Take away the quick decisions: press the corners, show zone late; press the corners, play cover 2 or two-man.
- Take the game out of the offensive coordinator's hands and put it on the quarterback.

Zone Blitz Coverages

Z Coverage (Figures 16-1 and 16-2)

Z coverage is used with five-man pressure and utilizes three underneath droppers and three deep-third droppers. The underneath droppers will consist of two seam players and a #3 dropper. The underneath droppers play a match-up zone with each of the seam players dropping to a depth of 12 yards outside the #2 receiver with vision on #3. The seam players carry any inside release of #2 until there becomes a new #2 receiver, then he "delivers" the new #3 to the #3 dropper. The #3 player drops over the #3 receiver and carries the receiver until he is delivered a new #3 receiver from the seam player. Vision and communication is a must in playing good Z coverage by the underneath droppers. The seam players should always be conscious of a four vertical route. The seam players do not carry vertical routes by #2, but reroute all verticals inside and sink to create a difficult throw. In Z coverage, the free safety is the middle-third defender, and each of the corners will be outside-third players.

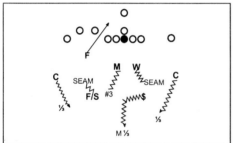

Figure 16-1. Z coverage versus 10 trips

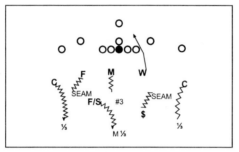

Figure 16-2. Z coverage versus 10 doubles

Z Spin (Backer) (Figures 16-3 through 16-6)

Z spin alerts the secondary that when the blitz is to or away from the formation, the free safety or the dime is the seam player, and the Stud (Eagle) or dime (50) is the middle-third player. If the blitz is to the weakside, the Stud or Will (Eagle) or the dime (50) is the seam player and the free safety is the middle-third player. The "backer" tag to a blitz alerts the Will that he is the seam player (the Sam is never a seam player to the strength of the formation).

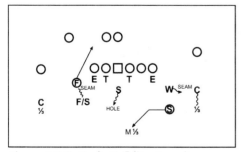

Figure 16-3. Eagle Z (blitz strong)

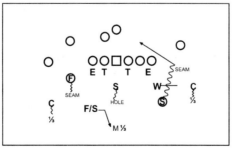

Figure 16-4. Eagle Z (blitz weak)

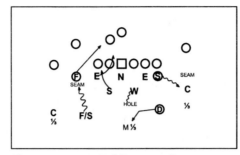 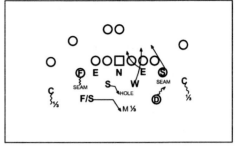

Figure 16-5. 50 Z (blitz strong)   Figure 16-6. 50 Z (blitz weak)

Z Match

Z match puts the corners and the seam player to their side in man coverage on the #1 and #2 receivers. The seam player matches the flat route by the #2 receiver and carries the wheel. The corner matches the post by #1 and carries the dig. The hole player cuts all shallow crossers and carries them (he has no one to deliver them to). Match is never played with the linebackers as a seam player.

Y Coverage (Figure 16-7)

Y is called with inside zone blitzes that allow the free safety or the dime to rock down as the hole player. It is a good change-up to get better leverage from depth on inside routes and gives a different look to the quarterback in the hole position.

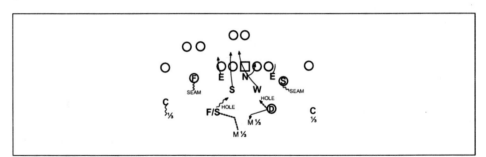

Figure 16-7. Y coverage

Two Backer

Two backer is a cover-2 coverage: the two inside linebackers, two outside linebackers, or a combination of the two wall the #2 receiver from inside-out, cut the slant, wheel with the dig, carry the crosser, and run with the vertical; they seek a peek at #1 and must be ready to come off on the under route. Versus a 3x1 formation, the linebackers push to the #2 and #3 receivers, and wall them from the inside-out. Two backer can be run from both the Eagle and 50 fronts (Figure 16-8).

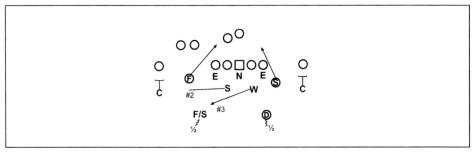

Figure 16-8. Two backer from a 50 front

Two Man (Macho)

Two man (macho) is a blitz coverage from the 50 front with five-under/two-deep man coverage (Figure 16-9). The two defensive ends play blitz peel rules (flare control).

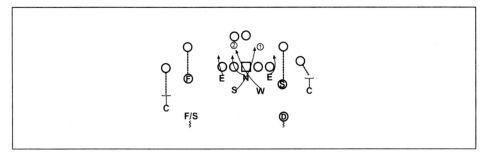

Figure 16-9. Two man (macho) from the 50 front

Coverage Definitions

Hole: Designates the player who drops over the #3 receiver. When executing the hole technique versus any 20 formation (20, 21, 22) or a 2x2 set, the hole player opens to the back on the back's movement, gets depth with vision, and is alert for the #2 receiver becoming #3 so he can match up on any threat created by the route. Versus 3x1 formations, the #3 is identified by alignment. The hole player pushes out to #3, and reads to match on #3 or any new #3 that appears in the route.

Seam: Curl/flat player aligns initially at seven yards depth over the #2 receiver, drops to a 12-yard depth outside #2, reading the #2 and #3 receivers as one. He carries the inside release of #2 with vision on #3 until a new #2 receiver appears; if a new #2 appears, he delivers the new #3 to the hole player.

Sky: The Falcon (Eagle front) and the Falcon/Stud (50 front) always become the seam player until they hear "sky" call. The "sky" call by the free safety or the dime alerts the Falcon or Stud that he will become the hole player, and the call man (free safety or dime) will become the seam player.

You/Me: A call made by the Falcon, Stud, or the two inside linebackers that communicates a change of assignment regarding who blitzes and who covers.

Carry/Match/Deliver: Terms that describe the play of the two seam players and the hole player. Alerts them to their responsibilities and is important to communicate the match-ups that may occur on the routes.

Y Coverage: Coverage that makes the free safety or dime the hole player regardless of the formations. No "sky" call is made.

Triangle: Refers to the alignment of linebackers when there are two or three wide receivers to their side. The backer lines up at the apex of the triangle, and splits the difference between the receiver and the tackle. He plays at a five-yard depth, keys the tackle, and visualizes the near back and the ball. He should react quickly to the low-hat (run), or high-hat (pass) of the tackle.

Seam Coverage Responsibilities

Seam (strong): Defender should know the formation to his side: single-width, twins single-width, twins (double-width), or three receivers (3x1 with a tight end, or 3x1 with three stand-up wide receivers).

- Single-width: If pass, plays under the #1 receiver. If wide split and the quarterback sets quick, thinks slant by the #1 receiver. If tight split and the quarterback sets quickly, thinks out route by #1. While playing under #1 and the quarterback looks hard outside, reacts to his eyes and shoulders.

- Double-width: Plays off the #2 receiver; gets depth, and mirrors the quarterback's eyes and shoulders with vision of the route. If a slant by #2, cuts and carries. If #2 goes to flat, zones and holds the curl area. If #2 goes vertical and breaks off on the option route 8 to10 yards deep, plays any cut within his area as man. If #2 is vertical and makes no attempt to break off the route, collisions and reroutes all verticals from the outside-in, sinks to force the quarterback to put air under the ball, and buys time for the corner and middle-third defender. As reroutes #2, seeks a peek at #1; if reads a smash route or the quarterback looks outside, drives on the #1 receiver.

- 3x1: Zones the curl area versus any bubble or flat route by #3 or #2. Drives on bubble when the quarterback shows his intentions (Figure 16-10). Breaks to the flat on the quarterback's shoulders or a thrown ball (Figure 16-11).

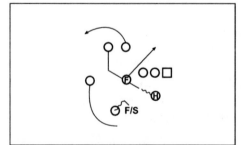

Figure 16-10. Drive on bubble receiver (drive on bubble when QB shows his intentions)

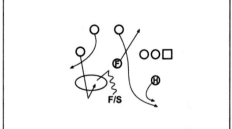

Figure 16-11. Break to flat receiver (break up to flat receiver on QB shoulders or thrown ball)

If #2 and #3 align tight, alert linebackers of a likely stack route. Versus Stack routes, whether inside or outside (Figures 16-12 and 16-13), the hole player always takes the low player, and the seam player always takes the high player. Versus three slants, the seam player drives on #2, and the hole player drives on #3 (Figure 16-14).

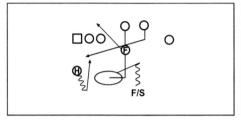

Figure 16-12. Versus inside stack route

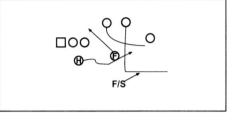

Figure 16-13. Versus outside stack route

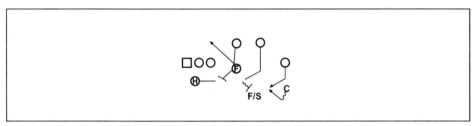

Figure 16-14. Versus three slants

Seam (weak): On single-receiver side, leverages the #1 receiver with body position; reacts off the split of the receiver and the quarterback's eyes. Must be ready to cut the slant by #1, or get underneath the out or dig based on the quarterback's eyes and shoulders. If no threat, gets depth, looks for work, checks screen, and alerts for the first crosser.

Seam versus the tight end: Gets width and depth. Carries the wheel; shouldn't be outflanked by the flat route receiver; if no threat, gets depth and fast-breaks on the quarterback's shoulders or the thrown ball.

Hole Coverage Responsibilities

The hole player should always know who is the #3 receiver. Must always be alert that #3 can change with motion or a tight-end trade.

Versus a 20 formation (20, 21, and 22) or a 2x2 formation (Figures 16-15 and 16-16): Drops over #3; get to a 12-yard depth and reads the routes to the quarterback. Plays from deep to short, squeezes, and always anticipates that the release of #3 will create a new #3 for the match-up. Communicates a banjo call to the seam players versus 2x2 formations (Figure 16-15). If a quick flare by the back, he will banjo the flare to the seam player and match up on the new #3 that comes inside; if #3 (back) blocks, pushes to new #3. If no threat, gets depth and fast-breaks on the quarterback's eyes or thrown ball. Delivers the under routes to the seam players, and anticipates dig routes. If two crossers (Figure 16-16), delivers the first crosser to the seam player, and matches up on the second crosser.

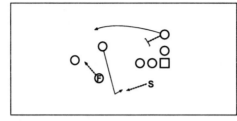

Figure 16-15. Versus 2x2 with back flare or blocks

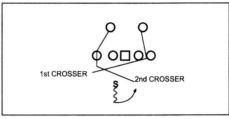

Figure 16-16. Versus two crossers

Versus trips (3x1) (Figures 16-17 and 16-18): It is important for the hole player to slide out to #3. Trips with a tight end (11 or 12 trips) will not require as much adjustment as a three stand-up trips. Tries to conceal his alignment as much as possible, but three stand-ups may require the proper ability alignment to successfully carry out coverage responsibilities. Expands to #3; keeps inside leverage; sees the #2 and #3 receivers as one so he can deliver and match up as quickly as possible. Cuts and carries the slant; wheels with the dig; and carries the vertical. If drag by the #3 receiver, passes the tight-end drag (11 trips, 12 trips) and cuts the #3 wide receiver drag (10 trips, 11 trey)—this can be a scouting-report decision. Listens to the seam communicating the possibility of a high/low stack route by the #2 and #3 receivers. Whether the route is inside or outside, always takes the low player in the stack, and the seam will always take the high player in the stack.

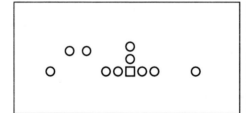

Figure 16-17. Versus trips (no tight end)

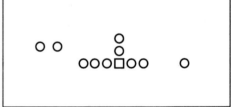

Figure 16-18. Versus trips (with a tight end)

Seam and Hole Players Sky Call Adjustments

Tough adjustment to motion from 2x2 formations (Figures 16-19 through 16-22): Initially, the free safety makes a sky call to alert the Falcon to take the hole. With motion, sky is called off by the free safety. The dime makes a sky call to the Stud to alert him to take the hole; the dime takes the seam.

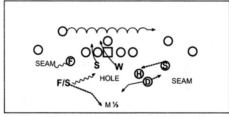

Figure 16-19. Versus motion from 10 doubles (sky is called off by the free safety)

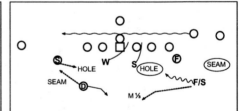

Figure 16-20. Versus motion from 11 trips (sky is called off by the free safety)

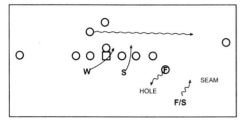

Figure 16-21. Versus motion
(free safety calls "sky")

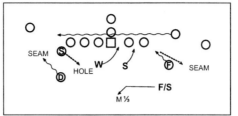

Figure 16-22. Tough adjustment to
motion from a 2x2 formation

Corner Coverage Responsibilities

Corners use a controlled shuffle because they should anticipate that the ball
will be thrown fast. They should verbalize the words "three-step drop" to
mentally remind themselves of the quick throw and speed up the drop. They
play inside third to single-width, and a divider technique to two stand-ups. Must
be aware of the #2 receiver, but concentrate more on #1 in the Z coverage.
Points of emphasis for corners include the following:

- The deeper the single receiver gets, the more of a man player he becomes.
- The corner can chase the dig versus single-width receiver.
- If non-threatening route by the #1 receiver to twins (two stand-ups), the
  corner drops and pushes to the next upfield threat.
- If a quick crosser by either wide receiver in the divider technique, begins to
  squeeze the remaining vertical threat.
- If the #2 receiver cancels out (blocks or inside move) in the divider
  technique, anticipates an inside cut by #1
- When in divider technique, the deeper the receivers go, the more inside
  the corner should play.
- Versus the curl/wheel route: Once the corner sees #1 break on the curl,
  he pushes back out and gets ready to run with the wheel route.

Eagle Zone Blitzes

Basic Fronts

The Eagle front provides a true four-man front (Figure 16-23). A four-man front
can also be achieved by sliding the 50 front into an Eagle alignment, which is
called Aztec (Figure 16-24).

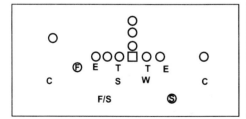

Figure 16-23. Eagle front

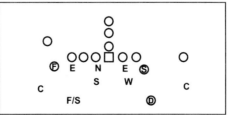

Figure 16-24. Aztec front

A variation of these is the under front, which fits well into the zone-blitz schemes (Figures 16-25 and 16-26).

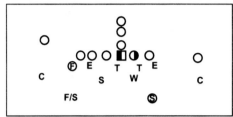

Figure 16-25. Eagle under front   Figure 16-26. Aztec under front

Eagle River or Lake

Left River or Right Lake With Z Spin Backer, Z Backer, or Two-Backer Coverage Calls (Figures 16-27 and 16-28): These calls are always hash calls that come from the field or boundary. The Larry or Roger call is made for the defensive line.

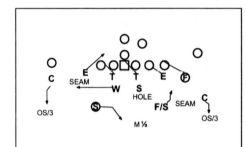
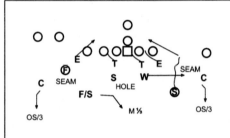

Figure 16-27. Left river Z spin backer versus 21 pro (Larry call)   Figure 16-28. Left river Z backer versus 11 trips (Larry call)

Eagle River or Lake Variations

Left River Echo or Right Lake Echo (Figures 16-29 and 16-30): This call is a good change-up for the Falcon or Stud and defensive end. The Falcon or Stud goes inside, and plays off the block of the offensive tackle or back, either to the inside or outside because the defensive end will make him right.

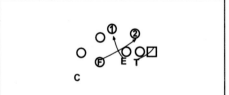
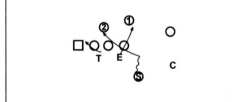

Figure 16-29. Left river echo   Figure 16-30. Right lake echo

Left River Gaps or Right Lake Gaps (Figures 16-31 and 16-32): This call is best when the Stud blitzes from the boundary. The four defensive linemen move late into the gaps and get penetration upfield to create a new line of scrimmage or get the jump on the pass rush.

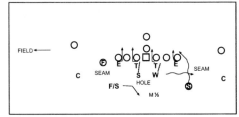

Figure 16-31. Left river gaps from the boundary (tight-end side) (Larry call)

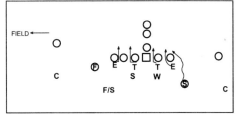

Figure 16-32. Left river gaps from the boundary (split-end side) (Larry call)

Aztec Left River or Aztec Right Lake (Figures 16-33 and 16-34): This call is the same as Lake and River off the Eagle with 50 personnel sliding to the Eagle front.

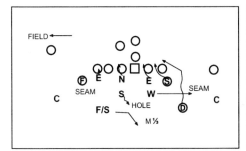

Figure 16-33. Aztec left river from the boundary (weakside)

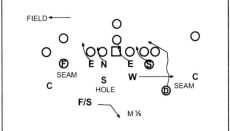

Figure 16-34. Aztec left river from the boundary (tight-end side)

Eagle Tilt Crash Z (Figures 16-35 through 16-38)

Wrap or swap can be called to or away from the blitz side. The linebacker can slide late to the line of scrimmage or execute the blitz from his original alignment for concealment.

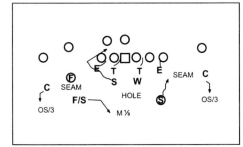

Figure 16-35. Eagle tilt crash versus 11 doubles (Larry call)

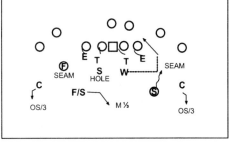

Figure 16-36. Eagle tilt crash versus 10 doubles (Roger call)

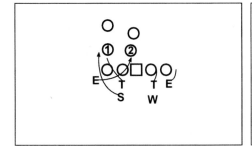

Figure 16-37. Eagle tilt crash swap

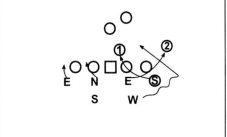

Figure 16-38. Aztec tilt crash wrap

Eagle Field Hurricane Z Spin or Eagle Boundary Hurricane Z Backer
(Figures 16-39 and 16-40)

This blitz brings four from either the field or the boundary. It can be called from the Aztec front, which has the advantage of sliding the front late from the 50 front.

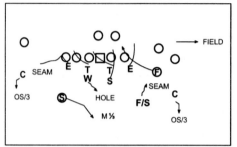 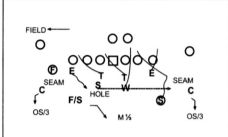

Figure 16-39. Eagle field hurricane Z spin versus 11 doubles (Roger call)

Figure 16-40. Eagle boundary hurricane Z backer versus 11 doubles (Roger call)

Aztec Field Hurricane Z Spin or Aztec Boundary Hurricane Z Backer
(Figures 16-41 and 16-42)

With the boundary call versus a tight end, the Will executes the blitz and Sam plays the seam. Versus two stand-up receivers, makes a "you" or "me" call to have the Sam execute the blitz and Will play the seam.

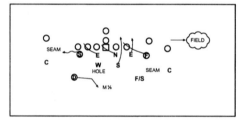

Figure 16-41. Aztec field hurricane Z spin versus 10 doubles

Figure 16-42. Aztec boundary hurricane Z backer versus 11 doubles

Eagle Left or Right Rambo Z Cloud Backer
(Figures 16-43 through 16-46)

This call is a hash blitz from the boundary. Can be called from both Eagle and Aztec fronts. Wrap or swap can be called away from the callside.

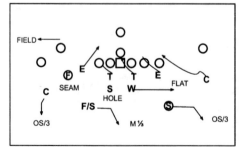 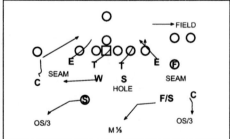

Figure 16-43. Eagle left Rambo Z cloud backer versus 11 doubles (Larry call)

Figure 16-44. Eagle right Rambo Z cloud backer versus 11 trips (Roger call)

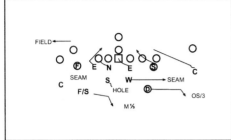

Figure 16-45. Aztec left Rambo Z cloud backer versus 11 doubles (Larry call)

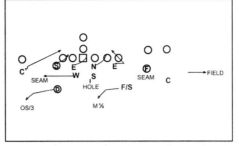

Figure 16-46. Aztec right Rambo Z cloud backer versus 11 trips (Roger call)

Under Blaze Z (Figures 16-47 through 16-53)

Under blaze Z can be called from both Eagle under and Aztec under fronts. Blaze cross and blaze switch are change-ups.

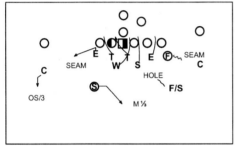

Figure 16-47. Under blaze Z" versus 21 tilt (Roger call)

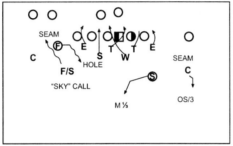

Figure 16-48. Under blaze Z" versus 11 trips (Larry call)

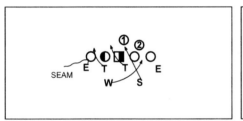

Figure 16-49. Under blaze cross change-up

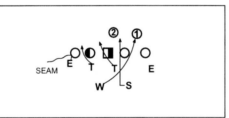

Figure 16-50. Under blaze switch change-up

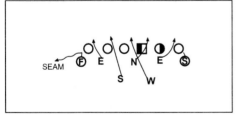

Figure 16-51. Aztec under blaze

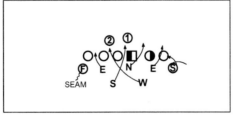

Figure 16-52. Aztec under blaze cross change-up

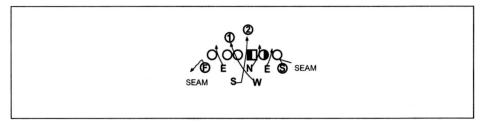

Figure 16-53. Aztec Under blaze switch change-up

Under Smoke Z or Y (Figures 16-54 through 16-59)

Under smoke Y or Z can be called from both Eagle under and Aztec under fronts. A "switch" call changes which linebacker blitzes first. Typically, Sam goes first, but the switch call sends Will first. Y coverage keeps the free safety as the hole player regardless of the formation, which gives him good leverage on high-/low-level patterns and intermediate routes.

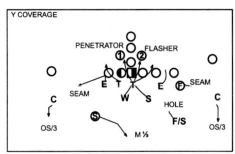

Figure 16-54. Under smoke Z or Y versus 21 pro (Roger call)

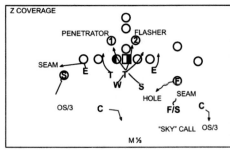

Figure 16-55. Under smoke Z or Y versus 21 twins (Roger call)

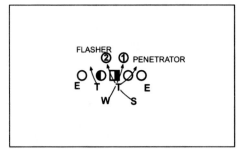

Figure 16-56. Under smoke switch change-up

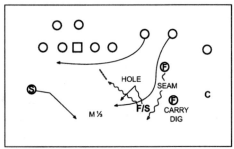

Figure 16-57. Under smoke Y coverage call (low and high hole stack)

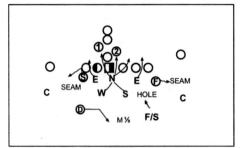

Figure 16-58. Aztec under smoke versus 21 pro

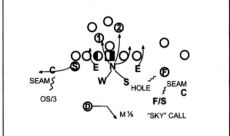

Figure 16-59. Aztec under smoke versus 21 twins

Under Thunder Z or Y (Figures 16-60 through 16-64)

Under thunder Y or Z can be called from both Eagle under and Aztec under fronts. Wrap and swap are a change-up to the backside, and pick and switch are change-ups to thunder.

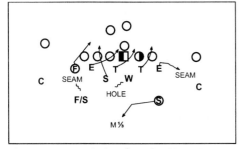

Figure 16-60. Under thunder Z or Y versus 21 tilt (Larry call)

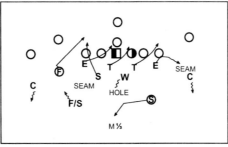

Figure 16-61. Under thunder Z or Y versus 11 doubles (Larry call)

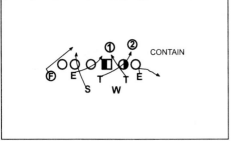

Figure 16-62. Under thunder wrap change-up

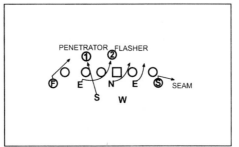

Figure 16-63. Aztec under thunder pick

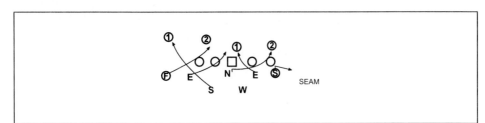

Figure 16-64. Aztec under thunder switch/wrap

Aztec Buck (or Cross) (Figures 16-65 and 16-66) **With Y or Two Backer, and Aztec Ant (or Ant Twist) With Y or Two Backer**

The buck and buck cross calls tell the linebackers whether or not to cross on their blitz of the A gaps; the 2 technique tackles penetrate the B gaps (Figure 16-65). The ant and ant twist calls tell the 2-technique tackles to either penetrate the A gaps or to twist; the linebackers blitz the B gaps (Figure 16-66). Buck and buck cross: versus tilt back, the linebacker toward the tilt goes first; if no tilt back, the linebacker toward the formation goes first.

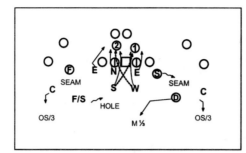 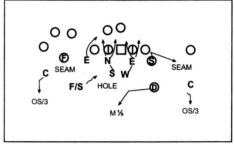

Figure 16-65. Aztec buck (or cross) versus 10 doubles

Figure 16-66. Aztec ant (or twist) versus 10 trips

Several Scheme Adjustments to Enhance the Efficiency of the Zone-Blitz Package

Dropping Defensive Linemen

Dropping defensive linemen can make a significant contribution to the success of the zone-blitz package. Some defensive linemen have the ability to be more versatile than just players at the line of scrimmage. When linemen display this ability, it is advantageous to utilize the player(s) to drop into a hole or seam on pass coverage. The advantage of dropping a defensive lineman into coverage eliminates pre-snap reads, and his sudden appearance in coverage may confuse the quarterback. When dropping as a seam player, he becomes a real benefit on the rocket (jailbreak) screen and the back screen, because the offensive linemen release downfield, which enables the dropper to come under them as an unblocked defender. When dropping into a hole position, the quarterback may be completely unaware of him, and the dropper can mirror the passer's eyes for timely deflections and prevent scrambles for positive yardage. Similar to the seam player, the hole player can pursue down the line of scrimmage to make key tackles on screens and prevent runs.

Thunder Blitz

Thunder blitz is the foundation of the zone blitz package (Figure 16-67). As explained earlier in this chapter, three calls exist away from the primary stunt: push, wrap, and swap.

Thunder trio is an additional call to enhance the effectiveness of the thunder zone blitz. Thunder trio can be called from Eagle, 50, and Aztec fronts (Figures 16-68 through 16-70). However, it is most effective from the under front in Eagle or Aztec (Figures 16-71 and 16-72).

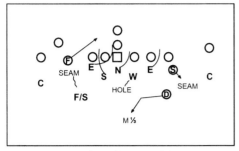

Figure 16-67. Thunder zone blitz

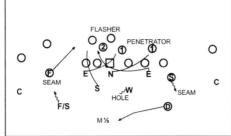

Figure 16-68. 50 thunder trio

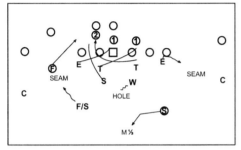

Figure 16-69. Eagle thunder trio

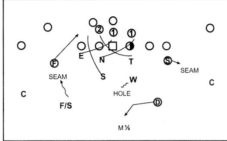

Figure 16-70. Aztec thunder trio

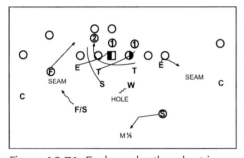

Figure 16-71. Eagle under thunder trio

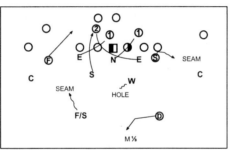

Figure 16-72. Aztec under thunder trio

Y Coverage With the Free Safety or Dime as the Hole Player
(Figures 16-73 and 16-74)

This coverage uses leverage to defend level routes and intermediate routes inside. Either the free safety or dime player drops down from depth (10 to12 yards) to the hole to become the second-level linebacker for pass coverage or run support.

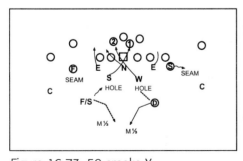

Figure 16-73. 50 smoke Y

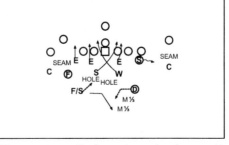

Figure 16-74. Eagle or Aztec buck cross Y

50 Orange Coverage

This coverage is traditionally used versus option teams when they get into their unbalanced formation to provide strong run support to the unbalanced side (Figures 16-75 through 16-81). However, it can also be used effectively with the zone-blitz concepts versus two-back, 2x2, and 3x1 formations by blitzing the free safety or Falcon, or the free safety and Falcon from the same side.

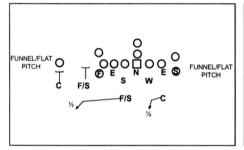

Figure 16-75. 50 orange versus unbalanced formation

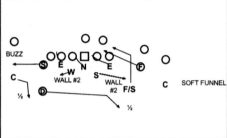

Figure 16-76. 50 orange with free-safety and Falcon blitz

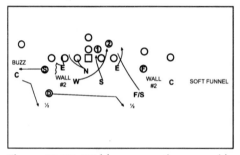

Figure 16-77. 50 blaze cross (orange with free safety or Falcon blitz)

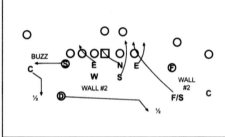

Figure 16-78. Aztec blitz (orange with free-safety blitz)

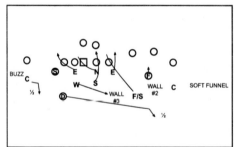

Figure 16-79. Aztec blitz versus trips (orange with free-safety blitz)

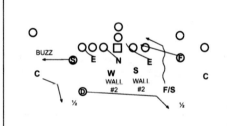

Figure 16-80. Aztec lake/river (orange with free-safety blitz)

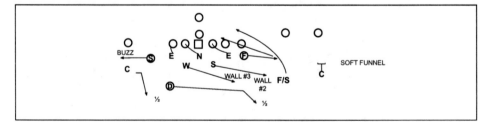

Figure 16-81. Aztec lake/river versus trips (orange with free-safety blitz)

50 Orange Coverage Change-Up With the Free Safety and the Stud
(Figure 16-82)

The Stud can drop to be the half-field player, and the weak corner is the soft-funnel player. The Stud plays the half-field safety position in the Eagle defense when a cloud call is made, so this call is not new to him. The Stud only drops as a half-field player in the 50 front.

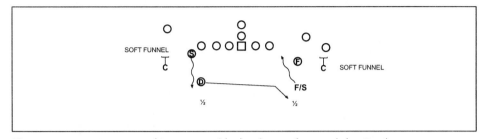

Figure 16-82. 50 orange change-up with the free safety and the Stud

Two-Man (Macho) Coverage (Figures 16-83 through 16-86)

The ability to play five-under man coverage with the zone-blitz package is a good complement to the two-backer coverage call.

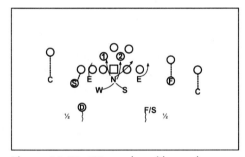

Figure 16-83. 50 smoke with macho coverage

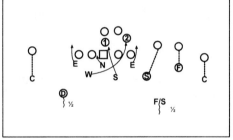

Figure 16-84. 50 blaze with macho coverage

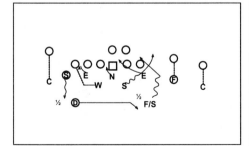

Figure 16-85. Macho coverage with free-safety blitz

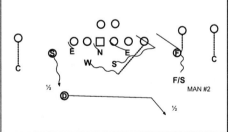

Figure 16-86. Macho coverage with free-safety blitz versus trips

Macho Versus Trips: Several adjustments to macho versus trips can benefit the zone-blitz package.

• Align the Will in a success alignment so he can cover #3.
• Check from river to smoke zone blitz.

- Check from left river to a thunder or thunder pick call: The Sam makes a "you" call, Will becomes the blitzer, and Sam plays man on the #3 receiver.
- Check to a Z-spin versus trips (3x1) formations: The free safety rocks down as a seam player to the strength of the formation; the dime becomes the middle-third defender; and the Stud drops to the seam on the backside.

50 Zone Blitzes With Z Spin Coverage

Tilt Thunder Wrap (Figures 16-87 and 16-88)

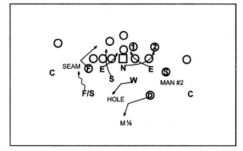
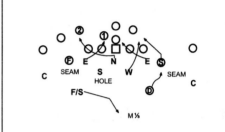

Figure 16-87. Tilt thunder wrap versus 21 pro (Larry call)

Figure 16-88. Tilt thunder wrap versus 20 weak tilt (Roger call)

Formation Thunder Pick Wrap (Figures 16-89 through 16-91)

The blitzing linebacker goes first through his assigned gap, and the defensive end steps upfield and then scrapes behind the linebacker. Sam and Will can make a "you" or "me" call to the trips side (Figure 16-91) if the hole player is too far removed to effectively cover the #3 receiver.

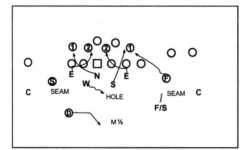
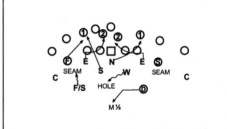

Figure 16-89. Formation thunder pick wrap versus 11 trips (Roger call)

Figure 16-90. Formation thunder pick wrap versus 10 doubles (Larry call)

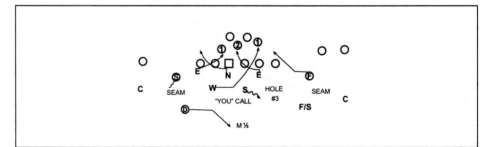

Figure 16-91. "You" call by Sam to Will

Split Thunder Switch (Figures 16-92 and 16-93)

The inside linebacker goes first off the heels of the defensive end, and the outside linebacker goes behind and adjusts his rush to the offensive tackles block. If the offensive tackle blocks down, the linebacker stays outside; if the offensive tackle turns out, the linebacker plays across his face and gets penetration.

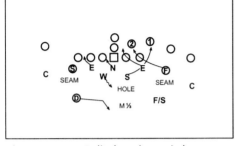

Figure 16-92. Split thunder switch versus 11 doubles (Roger call)

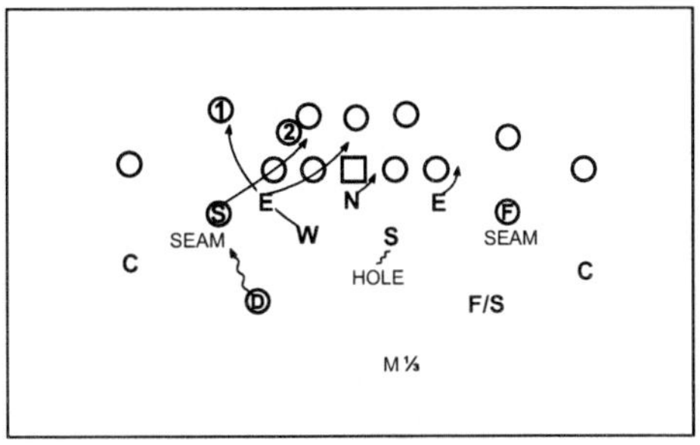

Figure 16-93. Split thunder switch versus 20 split (Larry call)

Tight Lightning Swap or Switch (Figures 16-94 through 16-96)

A lightning switch call involves the inside linebacker and the outside linebacker exchanging gaps (Figure 16-96).

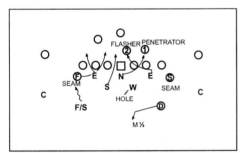

Figure 16-94. Tight lightning swap versus 12 doubles (Larry call)

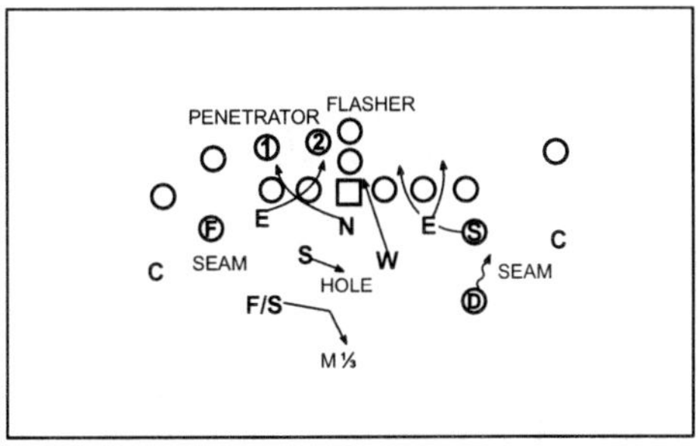

Figure 16-95. Tight lightning swap versus 11 doubles (Roger call)

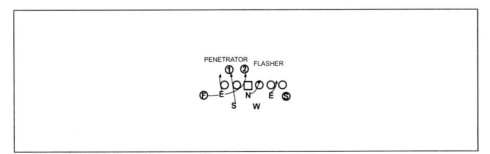

Figure 16-96. Lightning switch gap exchange call

Tilt Tornado (Figures 16-97 and 16-98)

The outside linebacker goes first on the blitz, and the inside linebacker scrapes outside to assume the outside force position. As a rule, check the tornado to a thunder versus a tight end.

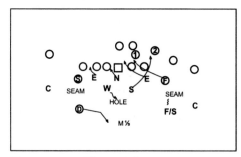

Figure 16-97. Tilt tornado versus 11 doubles (Roger call)

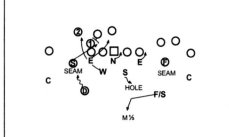

Figure 16-98. Tilt tornado versus 10 trips (Larry call)

Left River and Right Lake (Figures 16-99 and 16-100)

Lake and River blitzes are primarily called from the boundary. The inside linebacker calls Larry or Roger to indicate the direction of movement by the defensive line.

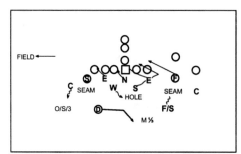

Figure 16-99. Left river versus 21 twins (Larry call)

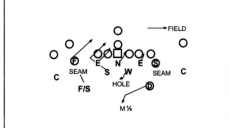

Figure 16-100. Right lake versus 11 doubles (Roger call)

Lake and River Variations

Lake Check Z Spin: With the ball in the middle of the field or on the hash, lake check is preceded with where the fire zone should come from (e.g., tilt lake check). This call enables the defense to put the blitz at the point of attack, where it is most beneficial (from the field or boundary, formation or weak, tight or split, tilt or numbers). The inside linebacker calls Larry or Roger to indicate the direction of movement by the defensive line. Figure 16-101 depicts a tilt lake check.

Lake or River Echo: Echo is an assignment swap between the blitzing linebacker and the Falcon or Stud. Figure 16-102 depicts a left river echo Larry call.

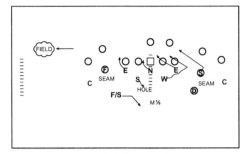

Figure 16-101. Tilt lake check

Figure 16-102. Left river echo (Larry call)

50 Zone Blitzes With Z, Z-Backer, Two-Backer, or Y Coverages

Formation Blaze Wrap (Figures 16-103 and 16-104)

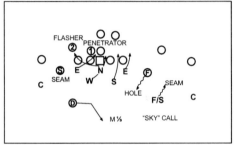
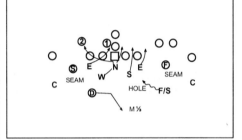

Figure 16-103. Formation blaze wrap Z versus 21 tilt (Roger call)

Figure 16-104. Formation blaze wrap Y versus 10 trips (Roger call)

Blaze Variations

The nose tackle and the away defensive end execute one of three techniques: push, wrap or swap. The wrap and swap are made with a call, but push is automatically built into the zone blitz if the other two (wrap/swap) are not called. The backside linebacker can read out of the blitz versus obvious flow away. The gaps for the two linebackers can be changed with a cross or switch call (Figures 16-105 and 16-106).

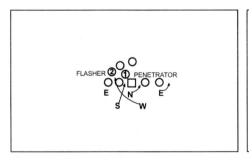

Figure 16-105. Tilt blaze cross

Figure 16-106. Tilt blaze switch

Tilt Smoke (Figures 16-107 and 16-108)

The second linebacker can read out of the blitz if flow is to his original side or no ball threat is inside to the blitz.

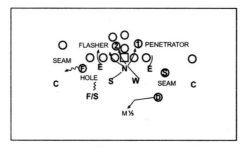

Figure 16-107. Tilt smoke Z versus 21 (Larry call)

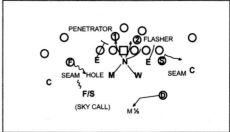

Figure 16-108. Tilt smoke Z versus 11 doubles (Roger call).

Smoke Variations

Tilt Smoke Switch (Figure 16-109): The "switch" call changes the order of the blitzing linebackers.

Numbers Smoke Pick (Figure 16-110): This variation is a good change-up to counter man protection and the tight set of an offensive line.

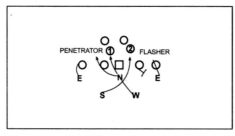

Figure 16-109. Tilt smoke switch

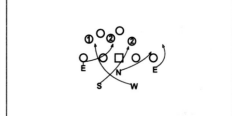

Figure 16-110. Numbers smoke pick

Crash Wrap or Swap With Z, Y, or Two-Backer Coverage
(Figures 16-111 and 16-112)

The linebacker makes a Larry or Roger call toward a tilt back. If no tilt, the call is toward the formation; if the tilt back moves, check the Larry or Roger call toward movement. The nose tackle drops into coverage with a "spy" call.

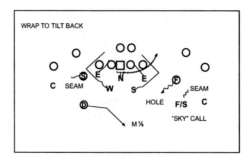

Figure 16-111. Crash wrap or swap Z versus 10 doubles (Roger call)

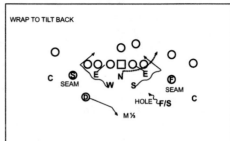

Figure 16-112. Crash wrap or swap Y versus 11 doubles (Roger call)

Smack With Z-Backer and Two-Backer Coverages
(Figures 16-113 and 16-114)

Wrap or swap can be called with the smack blitz. Apply the same rules as crash. The nose tackle drops into coverage with a "spy" call from two-backer coverage.

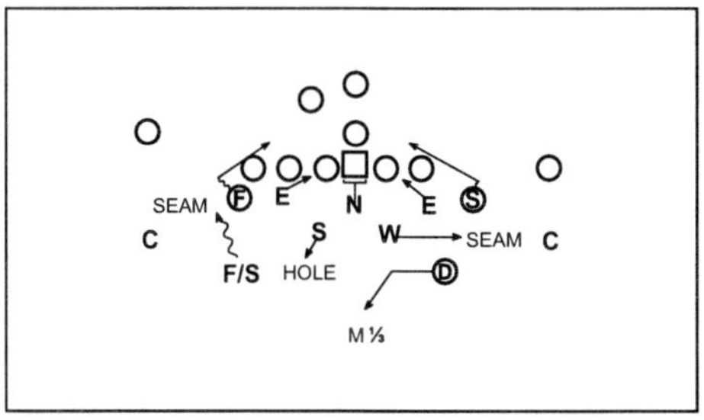

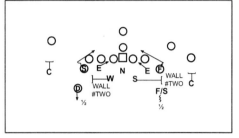

Figure 16-113. Smack Z backer versus 21 pro (Larry call)

Figure 16-114. Smack two backer versus 11 doubles (Roger call)

Cyclone With Z Spin and Two-Backer Coverage
(Figures 16-115 and 16-116)

Cyclone is a formation or field call with the Larry or Roger call. The Falcon and the Will linebacker are the blitzers. Wrap or swap can be called with the cyclone blitz: use a Liz or Riz call by the linebackers for the wrap or swap because the Larry or Roger call is used to indicate the field or formation regardless of the set of the tilt.

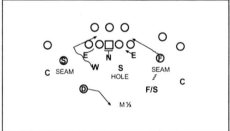
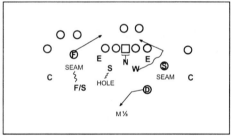

Figure 16-115. Cyclone versus 20 split (Roger call)

Figure 16-116. Cyclone versus 10 trips (Larry call)

Wind With Z Spin or Two-Backer Coverage (Figures 16-117 and 16-118)

Wind is a boundary or weakside blitz. The Stud and the Sam backer are the blitzers. Wrap or swap can be called with Wind. The nose tackle drops into coverage with a "spy" call from two-backer coverage.

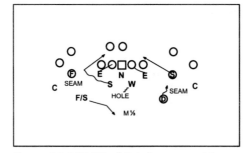

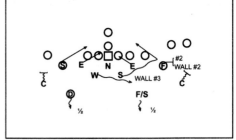

Figure 16-117. Wind Z spin versus 10 doubles (Roger call)

Figure 16-118. Wind two backer versus 11 trips (Larry call)

Tight Fire or Flame with Z Coverage (Figures 16-119 and 16-120)

The nose tackle and defensive end away from the call execute push, wrap, or swap.

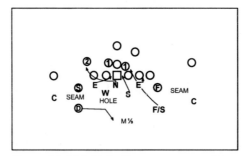

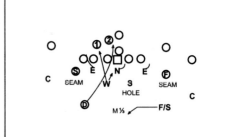

Figure 16-119. Tight fire wrap versus 21 tilt (Roger call)

Figure 16-120. Tight flame versus 11 doubles (Larry call)

Left or Right Rambo With Z Cloud Backer Coverage
(Figures 16-121 through 16-123)

This blitz is best called with ball on the hash. It can be run in the middle of field, but the split of the wide receiver may affect its success because the distance may eliminate the blitzing corner's disguise. Will linebacker can pick to the blitz side (Figure 16-123). The nose guard and defensive end can wrap or swap away from the blitz.

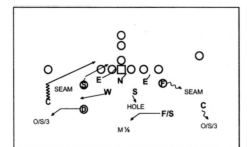

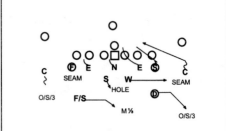

Figure 16-121. Left Rambo versus 21 pro (Roger call)

Figure 16-122. Right Rambo versus 12 doubles (Larry call)

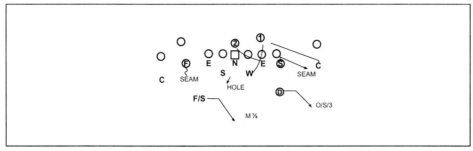

Figure 16-123. Will linebacker wrap

Additional 50 Zone Blitz Ideas

Double Plug (Figure 16-124)

Inside linebackers have a two-way go on the guards, and the defensive ends spy. The nose tackle can spy (hole player) or wrap to the tilt back.

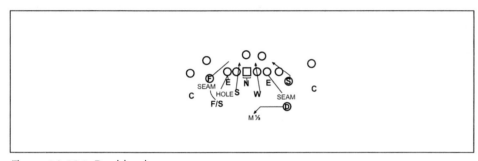

Figure 16-124. Double plug

Double Lightning G-Pick (Figure 16-125)

The nose tackle can either wrap or spy (hole player).

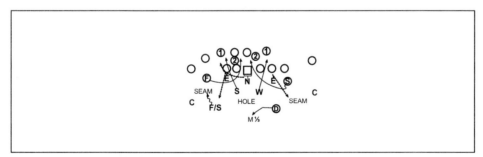

Figure 16-125. Double lightning G-pick

Double Pick With Nose Tackle Wrap (Figure 16-126)

Play Y or two-backer coverage with this blitz.

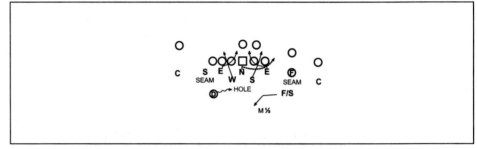

Figure 16-126. Double pick with nose tackle wrap

Bear Front Zone Blitzes (Figure 16-127)

The two defensive ends will slide from 5 techniques to 3 techniques. The two linebackers can execute a cross in the A gaps. The nose guard can wrap to the tilt back or the formation.

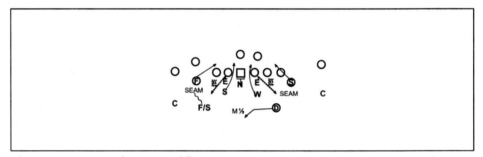

Figure 16-127. Bear front zone blitzes

17

Nickel and Dime Packages

Nickel Package

Nickel is typically a long-yardage situation defense played with four defensive linemen, six defensive backs, and one linebacker (Figure 17-1). The four defensive linemen should be the best pass rushers available, regardless of what position they play. Whether it is defensive linemen, linebackers, Falcon, or Stud, the ultimate goal is to put players on the field who have excellent pass-rush techniques. The coverages used with the nickel package include: cover 6, cover 2, cover-2 man, two backer, and purple man. The dime secondary player usually replaces an inside linebacker.

For nickel versus 2x2 formations with a tight end (11 doubles and 12 doubles), the Stud assumes the whip alignment, and the dime assumes the Stud's deep-quarter position and makes the "I'm here" call to the single inside linebacker. Figure 17-2 depicts nickel versus 11 doubles.

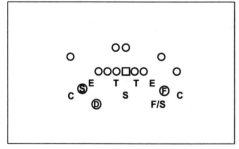

Figure 17-1. Nickel alignment and personnel

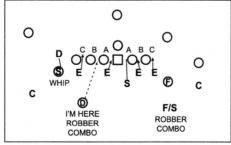

Figure 17-2. Nickel versus 11 doubles

Nickel Four-Man Rushes

The four defensive linemen should always rush with the mindset of playing the pass first and run second. If they have any doubt, they should rush the passer.

- *Jet* (Figure 17-3)
- *Net* (Figure 17-4): The net is a gap-control pass rush. Defensive tackles use bull rush technique and stay in front of the quarterback.
- *Twist With "You" or "Me" Call* (Figure 17-5): The defensive tackles read the center on the twist. The defensive tackle opposite the center's move goes first as the penetrator.
- *Wrap or Swap* (Figures 17-6 and 17-7): The wrap or swap can be fast or delayed, depending on factors such as the set of the linemen, down-and-distance, and the like.
- Weave Wrap Strong, Swap Weak (Figure 17-8)
- *Trio* (Figure 17-9): The defensive tackles can read the center's movement similar to twist (the tackle opposite the center's move goes first). Both defensive ends go inside and read through the guards to the center; if either guard or center turns out, the end should get back outside and be a force player.
- *Knife* (Figure 17-10): The defensive ends can't be wrong—they should go inside or outside on a speed rush and make something happen. Defensive tackles should knock the guards back and fill where needed. If the defensive end stays outside, the tackles stay inside; if the defensive end goes inside, the tackles play to the outside and make the defensive end right.
- *Scissors* (Figure 17-11): Scissors is a combination of wrap and twist stunts by the defensive linemen.

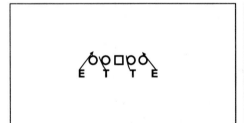

Figure 17-3. Jet

Figure 17-4. Net

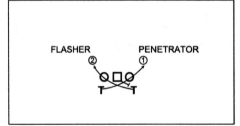

Figure 17-5. Twist with "you" or "me" call

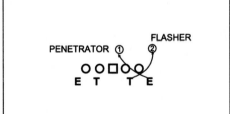

Figure 17-6. Wrap

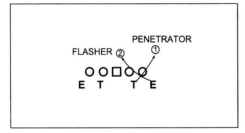

Figure 17-7. Swap

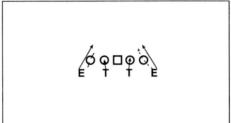

Figure 17-8. Weave wrap strong, swap weak (Roger call)

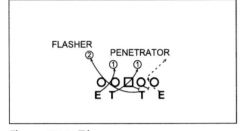

Figure 17-9. Trio

Figure 17-10. Knife

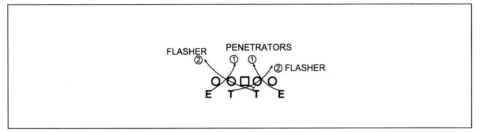

Figure 17-11. Scissors

Nickel Coverages

All the coverages played from Eagle and 50 fronts can be played in the nickel package.

Cover 6 (Figure 17-12)

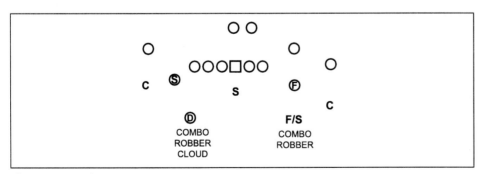

Figure 17-12. Cover 6

Cover 2—Two, Two Backer, Two Man (Macho) (Figure 17-13)

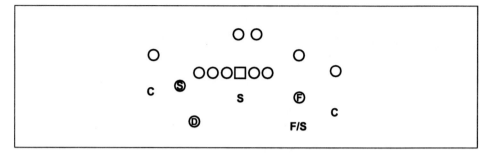

Figure 17-13. Cover 2 (Two, two backer, two man (Macho))

Tampa—Five-Across Secondary (Figure 17-14)

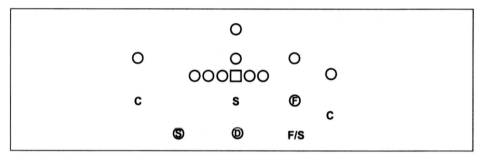

Figure 17-14. Tampa (five-across secondary)

Z Spin, Y (Figures 17-15 and 17-16)

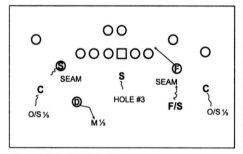 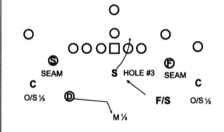

Figure 17-15. Z Spin   Figure 17-16. Y

Purple—Man Coverage (Figure 17-17)

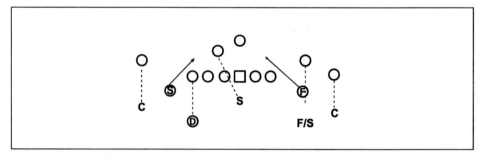

Figure 17-17. Purple (man)

Cover 2 Man—Macho (Figures 17-18 through 17-22)

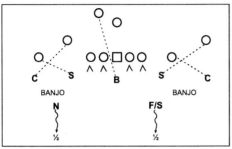

Figure 17-18. Macho versus 2x2 formation

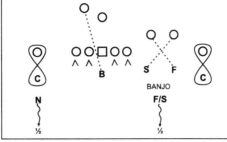

Figure 17-19. Macho versus 3x1 formation

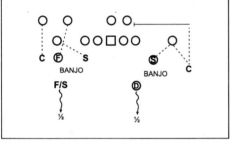

Figure 17-20. Macho versus back motion to the single wide receiver

Figure 17-21. Macho versus back motion to the tight end

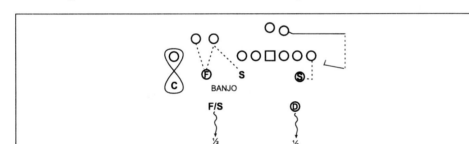

Figure 17-22. Macho versus an empty formation

Nickel Blitzes

Having one six-man blitz from each front with variations simplifies the learning process for the players because no new calls or techniques are necessary. The same four-man pass-rush stunts and zone blitzes can be applied to the nickel package.

Stinger With Purple (Man) Coverage (Figure 17-23)

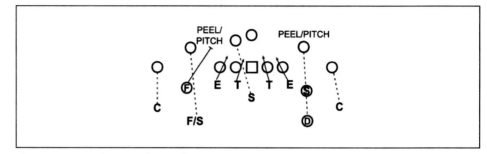

Figure 17-23. Stinger with purple (man) coverage

Stinger Variations (Figures 17-24 through 17-28)

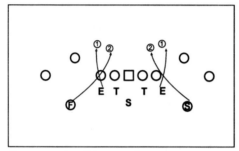

Figure 17-24. Stinger echo

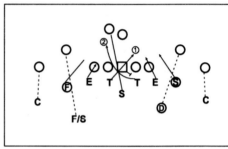

Figure 17-25. Stinger twist

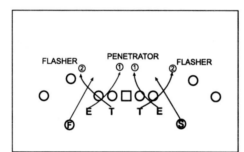

Figure 17-26. Stinger double wrap

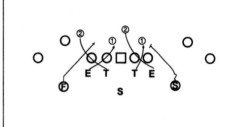

Figure 17-27. Stinger weave (wrap strong, swap weak)

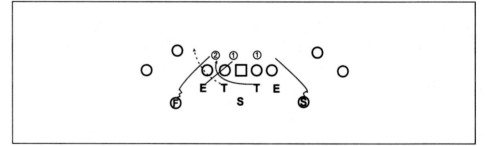

Figure 17-28. Stinger trio

Nickel Zone Blitzes With Z, Y, or Two-Backer Coverages
(Figures 17-29 through 17-31)

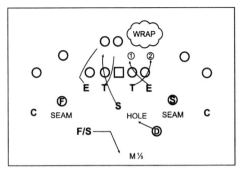

Figure 17-29. Tilt blast wrap or swap Z (Larry call)

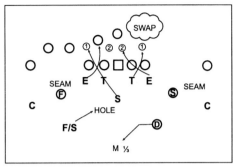

Figure 17-30. Tilt blast pick wrap or swap Y

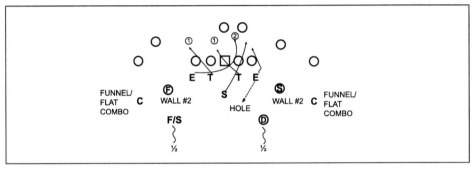

Figure 17-31. Tilt blast trio two backer (defensive end can drop and be hole player)

The Dime Package

The dime package is a maximum coverage scheme with seven defensive backs (including a dime and a nickel), two defensive linemen, and two inside linebackers (Figure 17-32). The defensive secondary is aligned in five across to disguise the various coverages used from the 2-4-5 alignment. Two-, three-, four-, five-, or six-man rushes can be utilized from the dime alignment. The continuous bluffing of the inside and outside linebackers is a key ingredient for success. The dime package can be used versus every formation (two backs, 2x2, 3x1, empty) so that it can be called on any down-and-distance situation.

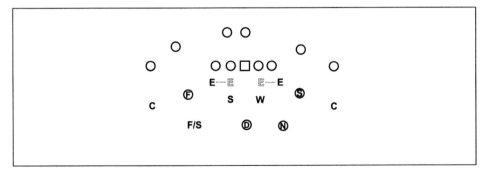

Figure 17-32. Dime alignment and personnel

The drop players should put a tremendous emphasis on collision and rerouting the receivers to break the rhythm and the timing of the passing game. The linebacker's spot drop to 10- to 12-yard depth, pattern read off the quarterback's eyes, and expand their vision with good awareness of the release of the #2 and #3 receivers.

Although the dime package is primarily a defend defense, a limited pressure package should be included to keep the urgency factor in the mind of the offense. Cover-6, cover-3, cover-2, two-backer, and Tampa-2 coverages can be played from the five-across alignment. In reality, the dime package should be used about six to eight times in a game.

Two-Man Rushes

Bluffing and stemming by the defensive line and inside and outside linebackers is important to disguise the defense's intentions.

Knife (Figure 17-33)

The defensive ends have the freedom to go inside or outside the blocks by the offensive tackles or backs. The inside linebackers stack and are low-hole and high-hole players.

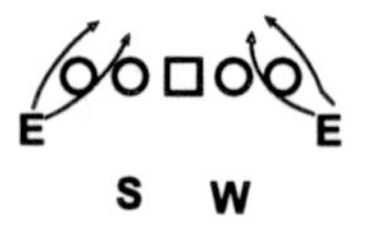

Figure 17-33. Knife

Twist (Figure 17-34)

The defensive ends line-up in the jet position and slide late to execute the twist. The defensive end away from the center's move goes first.

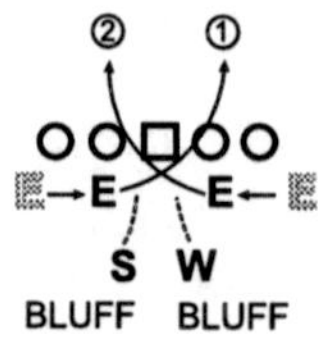

Figure 17-34. Twist

Three-Man Rushes

(Figures 17-35 and 17-36)

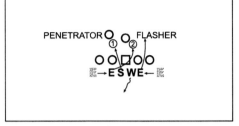

Figure 17-35. Tilt backer swap

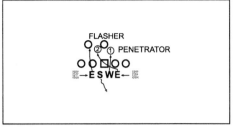

Figure 17-36. Numbers backer swap

Four-Man Rushes

- *Double Wipe* (Figure 17-37): The defensive ends rush inside or outside the tackles or backs. The two linebackers bull-rush the guards, and fit off the defensive ends to make them right, regardless of whether they go inside or outside.
- *Double Swap* (Figure 17-38): Linebackers can execute both swap and wrap from bluff position or normal linebacker depth. Double swap is similar to a double pick so the teaching is minimal.
- *Double Wrap* (Figure 17-39): The defensive ends can stem their alignment from outside to inside, or inside to outside.

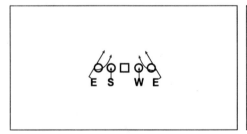

Figure 17-37. Double wipe

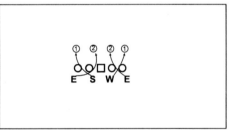

Figure 17-38. Double swap

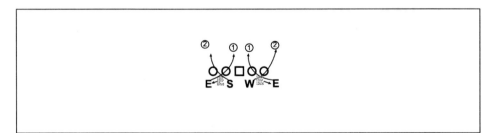

Figure 17-39. Double wrap

Buck Cross (Figure 17-40)

Linebacker to the tilt back goes first.

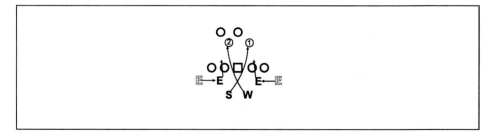

Figure 17-40. Buck cross

Tilt Thunder Check Two Backer (Figure 17-41)

The defensive end away from the blitz side slides to a shade on the center with a "shade" call.

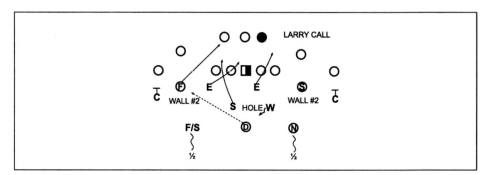

Figure 17-41. Tilt thunder check two backer

Tilt Flood Check Z Spin or Two Backer (Figures 17-42 through 17-44)

Z spin puts the remaining linebacker and the dime back in a low-hole/high-hole coverage. Versus a trips formation, the dime back makes a "key" call, and the linebacker plays the #3 to #2 receiver. The free safety or nickel to the blitz side rocks down to wall the #2 receiver.

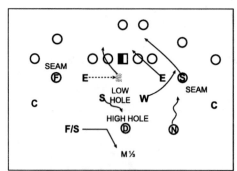

Figure 17-42. Tilt flood check Z spin versus 10 doubles (Roger call)

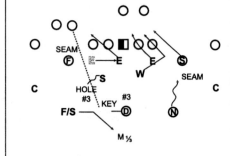

Figure 17-43. Tilt flood check Z spin versus 10 trips (Roger call)

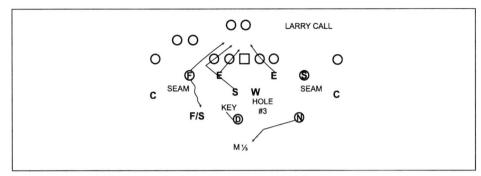

Figure 17-44. Tilt flood check versus 10 trips (Larry call)

Five-Man Rushes

Formation Thunder Plus Two Backer (Figures 17-45 and 17-46)

The "plus" alerts the Stud or the Falcon away from the Larry/Roger call that they are also blitzers. This blitz can be played with or without a spy player (the defensive end not involved in the zone blitz). The peel rule for the two inside linebackers is in effect.

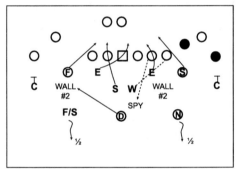

Figure 17-45. Formation thunder plus two backer versus 11 doubles (Larry call)

Figure 17-46. Formation thunder plus two backer versus 10 trips (Larry call)

Formation Flood Plus Z Spin (Figures 17-47 and 17-48)

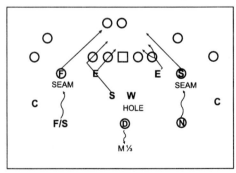

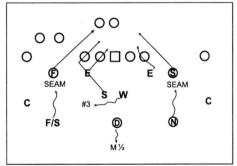

Figure 17-47. Formation flood plus Z spin versus 10 doubles (Larry call)

Figure 17-48. Formation flood plus Z spin versus 10 trips (Larry call)

Six-Man Rushes With Purple Coverage

Vegas Double Thunder Purple (Figures 17-49 and 17-50)

Man coverage versus Y trade and any motion. It is possible to banjo the 2x2 and 3x1 formations: the nickel moves over to man the #3 or be alert to the banjo with the free safety.

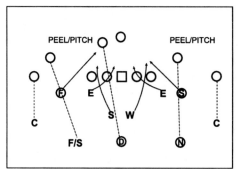

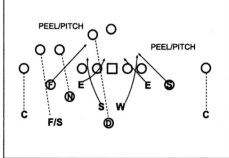

Figure 17-49. Vegas double thunder purple versus 10 doubles

Figure 17-50. Vegas double thunder purple banjo versus 10 trips

Vegas Double Flood (or Echo) Purple (Figures 17-51 through 17-53)

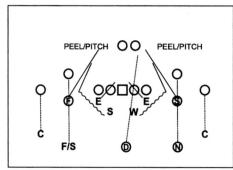

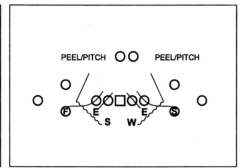

Figure 17-51. Vegas double flood purple versus 10 doubles

Figure 17-52. Vegas double echo versus 10 doubles

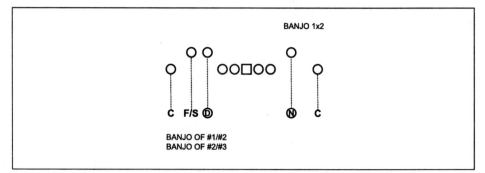

Figure 17-53. Vegas double flood/echo versus empty

Examples of Alignment and Coverages by Formation

Versus 21 and 12 Formations

Check all coverages to cover 6 (Figure 17-54). The free safety becomes the Falcon, and the dime becomes the free safety by alignment and assignment.

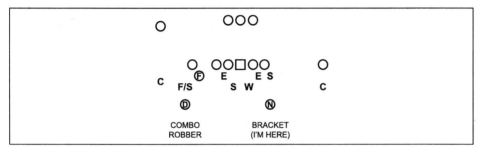

Figure 17-54. Check to cover 6 versus 21 split

Alignment to 11 Doubles (Figure 17-55)

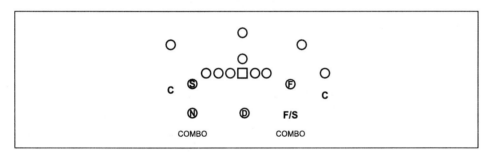

Figure 17-55. Alignment to 11 doubles (dime deep middle help)

Check to Cover 2 Versus 10 Trips (Figure 17-56)

The dime can make a "key" call to the Sam. Dime plays #3 deep, and Sam plays #3 short. If #3 motions to doubles, they check out of cover 2 to cover 3 or 6 (Figure 17-57).

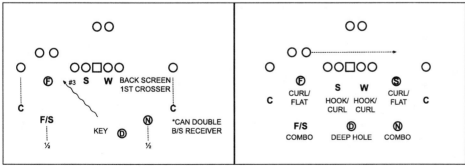

Figure 17-56. Check to cover 2 versus 10 trips—check to the cover 6 on motion from 10 trips to 10 doubles

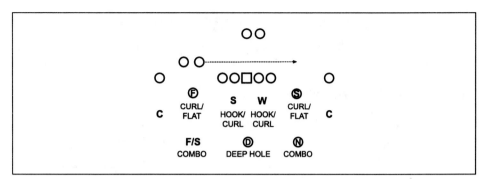

Figure 17-57. Check to cover 3 or 6 versus motion to doubles

Cover 3 Versus 10 Doubles (Figure 17-58)

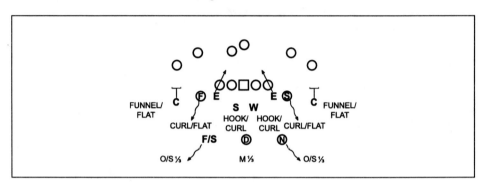

Figure 17-58. Cover 3 versus 10 doubles

Check to Cover 6 Versus 12 Doubles and 12 Trips
(Figures 17-59 and 17-60)

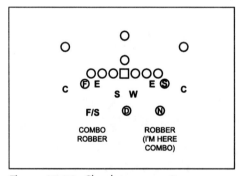

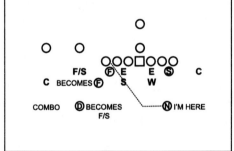

Figure 17-59. Check to cover 6 versus 12 doubles

Figure 17-60. Check to cover 6 versus 12 trips

Check to Cover 6 Versus 22 Pro (Figure 17-61)

The dime makes a robber call to the Falcon and corner. The corner on the nub tight-end side can play socks (blitzes), and the Stud plays the nub tight-end man. Low hat reads (run key) will get nine men in the box quickly.

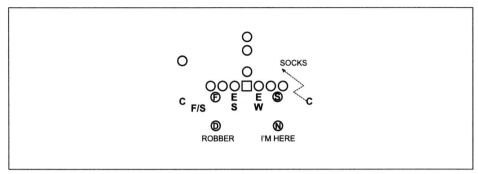

Figure 17-61. Check to cover 6 versus 22 pro

Combo Both Sides Versus 20 Formation (Figure 17-62)

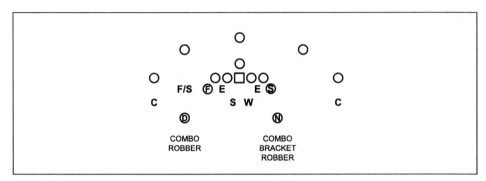

Figure 17-62. Combo both sides versus 20 formation

Alignment and Coverages Versus Empty Formations
(Figures 17-63 and 17-64)

Versus an empty formation, the defense should check to cover zero (cover 3 to three receivers, cover 2 to two receivers) (Figure 17-63). The defense can banjo the corner and Stud on the #1 and #2 receivers to the weakside. To blitz the empty formation, call weak thunder pick plus Z or two backer (Figure 17-64).

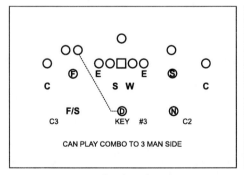

Figure 17-63. Defend with cover zero (cover 3 to three receivers, cover 2 to two receivers)

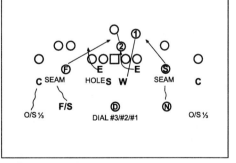

Figure 17-64. Blitz with weak thunder pick plus Z

Tampa 2 (Figure 17-65)

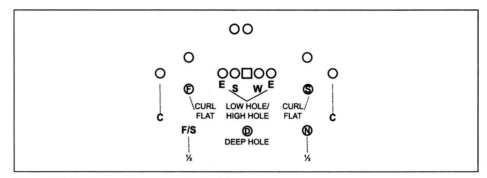

Figure 17-65. Tampa 2 versus 10 doubles

Cover-3 Man Versus 2x2 Formations Checking to Cover-2 Man Versus 3x1 Formations (Figures 17-66 through 17-68)

- Versus motion to Trips, the Falcon becomes peel blitzer.
- Versus motion to doubles, the Stud goes from peel blitzer to man on new #2; dime goes from man on #2 to the middle-third player.

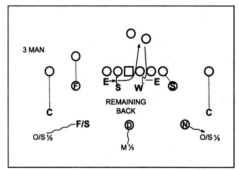

Figure 17-66. Cover-3 man versus 11 doubles

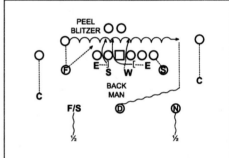

Figure 17-67. Check to cover-2 man versus motion to trips

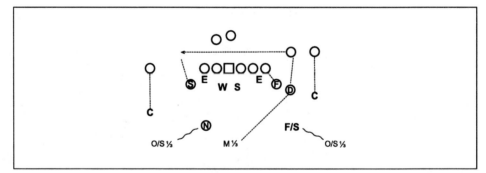

Figure 17-68. Check to cover-3 man versus motion to doubles

Victory Defense (Figure 17-69)

Victory is a five-deep coverage with the Falcon, Stud, and two inside linebackers collisioning and rerouting the vertical routes.

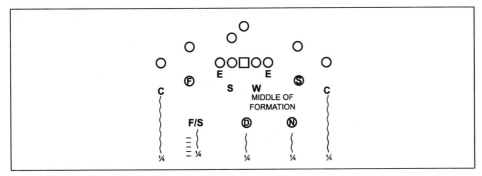

Figure 17-69. Victory versus 10 doubles

Jet 3 With a Four-Man Rush (Figure 17-70)

Versus trips, the Falcon makes a "you" call to the Sam. Sam takes the blitz; Falcon remains in coverage. The Falcon and free safety work together. If the Falcon walls #3, the free safety plays #2 to #1; if the free safety walls #3, the Falcon plays #2 to #1. The dime makes a "key" call to the #3 and carries him on a vertical or post route. The Will is the low-hole player, and is alert for the quarterback draw.

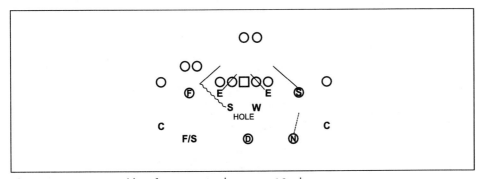

Figure 17-70. Jet 3 with a four-man rush versus 10 trips

18

Goal-Line and Short-Yardage Defense

The ability to play well in goal-line and short-yardage situations (GL/SY) is a key factor in winning football games. The philosophy in these situations should be to aggressively attack what an offensive team does well and make sure they are not successful with their standard GL/SY runs or passes. In typical field situations, the defense is trying to limit the offense to three yards or less per down, and create a punting situation on fourth-and-one. Goal-line defenses are usually deployed from the 8-yard line to the goal line. If the offense gets three yards per play on three downs from the 8-yard line, they will not be lining up to punt, unfortunately, but to kick an extra point after they have scored a touchdown. It is helpful to use a number of fronts in GL/SY with emphasis on inside and outside pressure. This plan fits into a defensive approach of using multiple fronts but not multiple techniques, and this approach provides good carryover from game to game. It is beneficial for the secondary to use a combination of man and zone coverages with emphasis on bluffing, doubling receivers, and banjo (in/out, short/deep) to eliminate pre-snap reads. Not all the fronts discussed in this chapter should be used each week. The important issue is to choose the fronts and coverages that can best accomplish the goal of stopping a particular opponent's offense in GL/SY situations.

Hammer Front

The hammer front is very effective versus one-, two-, and three-back formations: 21, 21 twins, 22, 32 (three backs, two tight ends), 23 (two backs, three tight ends), 11, and 12. It is easy to adjust and matches up well with man coverage.

Hammer Tight, Base Cover 6 (Zone) or Purple (Man)
(Figures 18-1 and 18-2)

On the nub tight end to the backside of the 22 formation, the Stud can call a socks or a pirate (AC) stunt. The free safety and backside corner make the "I'm here" call to alert the linebackers to spill the ball regardless of flow to force the ball to bounce east and west into unblocked support. The secondary plays cover 6 (zone) or purple (man) coverage. The Stud always goes away from the Falcon in the hammer defense, which definitely rules out a socks call against a 21 twins formation (Figure 18-2).

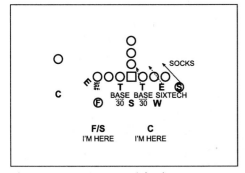

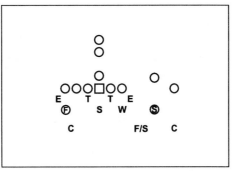

Figure 18-1. Hammer tight, base cover 6 or purple versus 22 pro

Figure 18-2. Hammer versus 21 twins

Hammer Stunts

- *Hammer AC* (Figure 18-3): The AC stunt can be run from both sides (double AC) or from one side (formation or weak). Falcon and Will are second-level players on inside plays and first-level players on outside plays. They spill all blocks on flow to. The Sam and the Will or Falcon away from flow press the line of scrimmage, and find their fit according to daylight and the angle of the back. It is important for defensive ends versus the turnout block to cross the face of the tackles.

- *Hammer Crash* (Figure 18-4): If a split end is to the backside or two receivers (2x2), the Will replaces the Stud on the crash stunt. The outside rusher (Falcon and/or the Stud/Will) spills all blocks on flow to and chases on flow away. Must be alert for the reverse or bootleg; has outside rush on the pass.

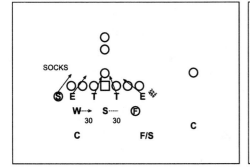

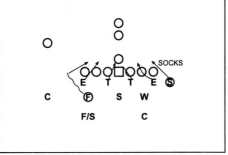

Figure 18-3. Hammer double AC with socks call versus 22 pro

Figure 18-4. Hammer crash versus 22 pro

- *Hammer Crash Echo* (Figure 18-5): This stunt is a gap switch for the defensive ends and the Falcon and Will. Falcon and Will show outside and then penetrate the C gap; it is important to stunt from the outside-in, and to never go inside the down block of the tight end.
- *Hammer Nose (Kill)* (Figure 18-6): Used in third-and-one and fourth-and-one (one yard or less) situations. The Falcon, Sam, and Will slide late to their alignments: Sam to the nose in a four-point stance; the Falcon and Will to a 30 technique. They fill and fit to the angle of the ball and are the second hitters on the ball (up-and-over plugger). Sam knocks the center back; the defensive tackles take out the outside leg of the guards. The "kill" call alerts the free safety and Stud to blitz from the outside.
- *Hammer Nose Gap Kill* (Figure 18-7): With a "gap" call, the defensive ends slide late to C-gap alignment and penetrate to create a new line of scrimmage. The "kill" call alerts the Stud and corner to blitz from the outside.
- *Hammer Tight Blitz* (Figure 18-8)
- *Hammer Gaps Blitz (Kill)* (Figure 18-9)

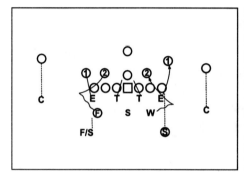

Figure 18-5. Hammer crash echo versus 12

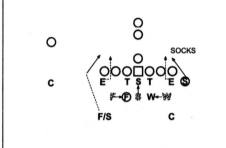

Figure 18-6. Hammer nose (kill)

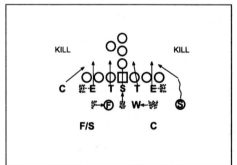

Figure 18-7. Hammer nose gap kill versus 32

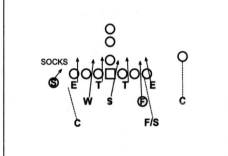

Figure 18-8. Hammer tight blitz purple versus 22

Figure 18-9. Hammer gaps blitz (kill) versus 22

65 Front

The defense slides late to the 65 front from the hammer front alignment (Figures 18-10 and 18-11). The late slide may draw the offense to illegally move prior to the snap of the ball. Stunts from the 65 include: a Bear call, in which the Sam and Will run through the B gap on flow, and a formation or weak Bear, in which the linebacker to the callside runs through the B gap. The defensive line can slant to strength or tendency.

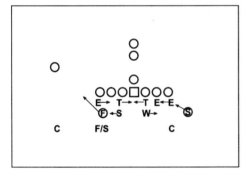

Figure 18-10. Slide from hammer to 65 front versus 22

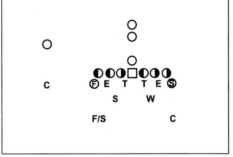

Figure 18-11. 65 front alignment versus 22

53 Front With White or Two-Backer Coverage

The 53 front includes five defensive linemen, three linebackers, and three defensive backs. A defensive lineman usually replaces a corner. Several combinations of backs in the secondary exist, based on the strengths of personnel and what is best to accomplish the GL/SY goals for a particular opponent. The 53 can be played versus 21, 22, 12, and 11 formations. Two corners must be on the field instead of the Stud versus 2x2 formations. White, a man-coverage call with three defensive backs, is discussed later in this chapter. Kill blitz can be called with white coverage. Two-backer coverage can also be played versus 22, 32, and 23 formations with a nub tight end to the backside. Figure 18-12 depicts 53 white or two-backer versus 22.

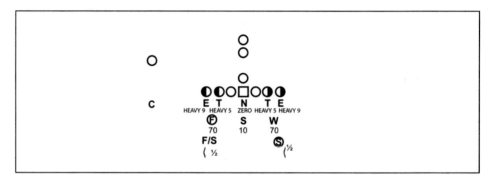

Figure 18-12. 53 white or two-backer versus 22

53 Base Two Backer (Figure 18-13)

Figure 18-13. 53 base two backer versus 22

53 Stunts

- *53 Pinch (Kill)* (Figure 18-14)
- *53 Pinch A (Kill)* (Figure 18-15): The Falcon and Will are second-level players inside and fill where needed. Sam presses and fits to seams inside and must be alert for cutback.
- *53 Pinch Echo (X)* (Figure 18-16): The Falcon and Will slide outside late, and then penetrate the C gap off the butt of the defensive ends. An "X" call alerts the nose and Sam to stunt the A gaps (Sam makes a verbal call or taps the nose on the butt for the nose's direction).
- *53 Loop X* (Figure 18-17): The Falcon and Will step inside to fill the B gaps; they are second-level players outside, and first-level players inside. On flow to play all they block with the inside arm.
- *53 Nose (Kill)* (Figure 18-18)
- *53 Nose Gap (Kill)* (Figure 18-19): The defensive ends and tackles slide late to the C and B gaps.
- *53 Crash* (Figure 18-20)
- *53 Crash Gap* (Figure 18-21): The defensive ends and tackles slide late to the C and B gaps.

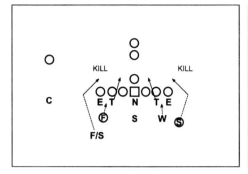

Figure 18-14. 53 pinch (kill) versus 22

Figure 18-15. 53 pinch A (kill) versus 22

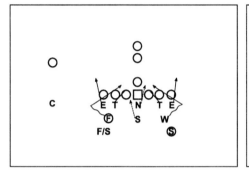

Figure 18-16. 53 pinch echo versus 22

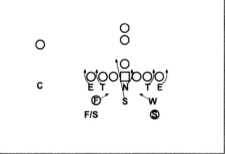

Figure 18-17. 53 loop X versus 22

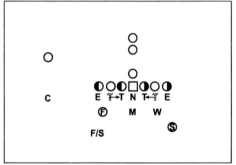

Figure 18-18. 53 nose (kill) versus 22

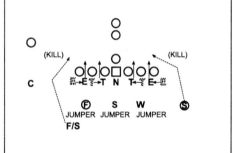

Figure 18-19. 53 nose gap (kill) versus 22

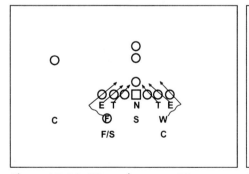

Figure 18-20. 53 crash versus 22

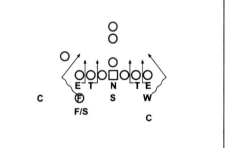

Figure 18-21. 53 crash gap versus 23

55 Front With Cover 6, Purple, or Two-Backer Coverages

The 55 front includes five defensive linemen, two linebackers, and four defensive backs. The four defensive backs provide more flexibility to defend multiple formations. The hammer and 53 stunts carry over to the 55 front. With repetition of techniques and stunts from week to week, these fronts have great carryover value each week for different opponents. The defensive ends play heavy 9 techniques versus 21, 22, 23, and 32 formations (two tight ends). Figure 18-22 depicts the 55 front base versus the 12 formation.

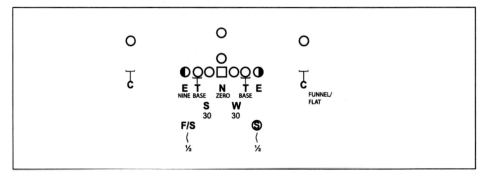

Figure 18-22. 55 base versus 12

55 Stunts

- *55 Pinch (Kill)* (Figure 18-23): The free safety and weakside corner make the "I'm here" calls, unless the free safety is involved in the kill blitz.
- *55 Pinch A (Kill)* (Figure 18-24)

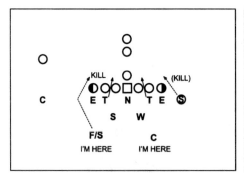 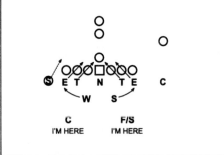

Figure 18-23. 55 pinch (kill) versus 22   Figure 18-24. 55 pinch A versus 22

- *55 Nose Gaps (Kill)* (Figure 18-25)
- *55 Tilt Slant* (Figure 18-26): Sam linebacker makes an "opposite" call versus back motion to get the slant toward the direction of the new formation strength.

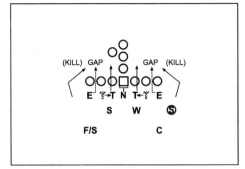

Figure 18-25. 55 nose gaps (kill) versus 32

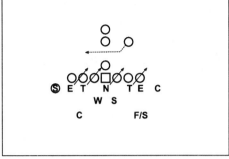

Figure 18-26. 55 tilt slant versus 32 (linebackers make opposite/opposite call to get slant to motion)

Slide From Hammer to the 55 Front

The advantage of sliding the front from hammer to 55 eliminates the need to make substitutes that allow the offense to know what front the defense will be in. Furthermore, the late movement can create confusion for the offense. Figure 18-27 shows the slide from hammer to the 55 front versus 22.

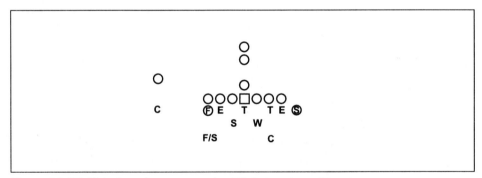

Figure 18-27. Slide from hammer to the 55 front versus 22

Purple Coverage

Purple Coverage With the Hammer Front (Figure 18-28)

For purple coverage with the hammer front, the Stud always goes to the opposite side of the Falcon. The Falcon always aligns to the tight-end side. If there is no tight end (or two tight ends), the Falcon aligns to the formation side. The free safety, Stud, and corners banjo with excellent communication so that all players know their assignment.

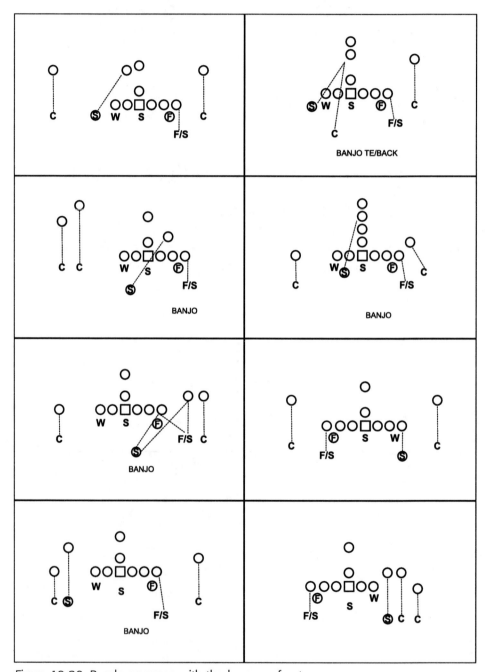

Figure 18-28. Purple coverage with the hammer front

Purple Coverage With the 55 Front (Figure 18-29)

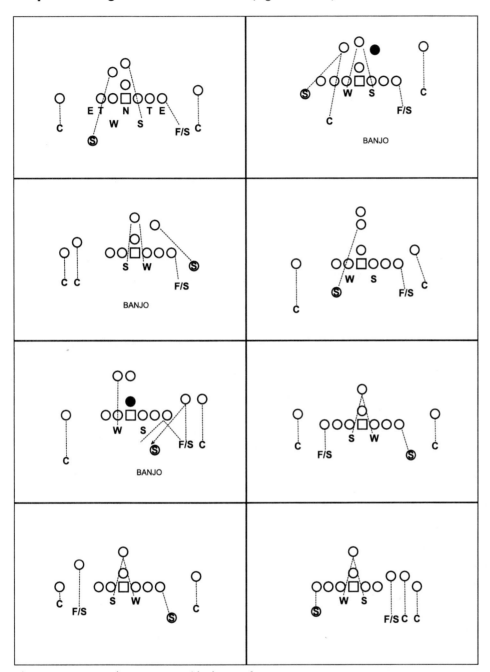

Figure 18-29. Purple coverage with the 55 front

White Coverage With the 53 Front (Figure 18-30)

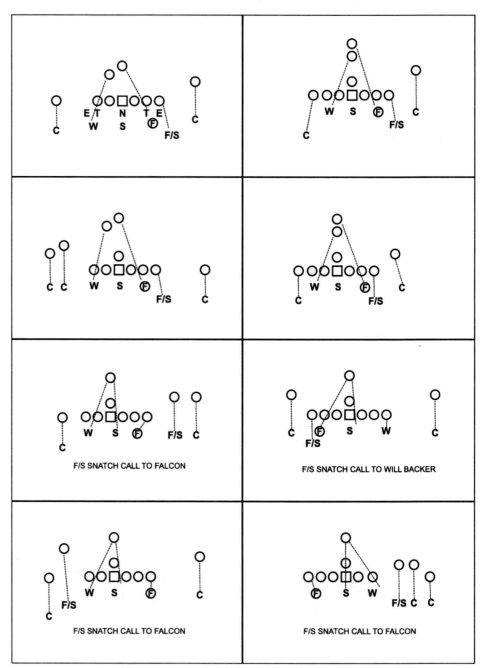

Figure 18-30. White coverage with 53 front

Gold Coverage With 50 Zone Blitzes

Gold is a goal-line (8-yard line to goal line) coverage. It is a match-up zone concept played with zone blitzes. The concept behind gold is to overplay the defenders either inside or outside the receivers to be in the most advantageous position to cover the combination of routes seen in this situation.

Formation Thunder Wrap Gold (Figures 18-31 through 18-33)

The hole player goes away from the dime except versus a 3x1 formation. The corners align outside the #1 receiver. The free safety and Stud align outside #2. The dime and the hole line up inside the #2 receivers. The corners show press, and then bail to take away the fade, out, or post-corner routes. The free safety and Stud take away the slant or dig of #1, and the flat route of #2. The dime and the hole are responsible for the slant or curl of #2; if #2 releases outside, they find a new #2 on an inside route. Once the #1 or #2 receiver comes inside, they play the inside receiver whether he continues inside or works back outside.

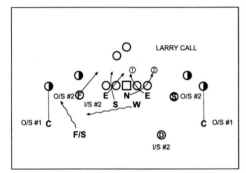

Figure 18-31. Formation thunder wrap gold versus 10 doubles

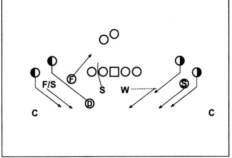

Figure 18-32. Will (hole player) covers inside receiver

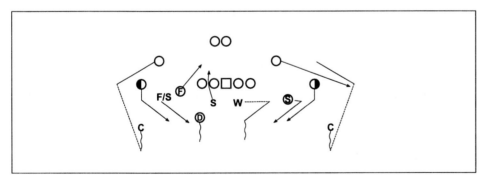

Figure 18-33. Dime (hole player) covers new inside receiver

Versus a Trips Formation (Figures 18-34 and 18-35)

Versus a trips formation (3x1), the dime and the hole player align to the three-receiver side. The dime lines up outside the #3 receiver, and the hole aligns inside #3. The free safety will cut and carry #1 inside, the dime will cut and carry #2 inside, and the hole will cut and carry #3 inside.

If motion to trips, the hole or the dime travel with the motion and assume the responsibility of inside cuts by #3. If no inside threat, they get eyes back to the quarterback, feel the routes, and fast break on the quarterback's eyes and shoulders.

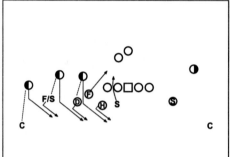 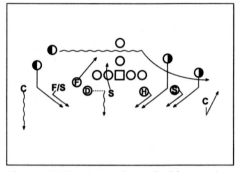

Figure 18-34. Versus a trips formation   Figure 18-35. Motion from doubles to trips

Zone Coverage

Several different zone concepts can be used on the goal line. Each differ from the others, but certain fundamentals carry over to all zone coverages:
- Play aggressive zone.
- Play underneath the receivers.
- Collision and reroute the receivers.
- Play no deeper than midway in the end zone (prefer to be too shallow rather than too deep).
- Drop with speed, and set down quick.
- Clamp onto the receivers in the responsible zone.
- Tighten the cushion on the receiver when the quarterback reads toward; loosen the cushion when the quarterback reads away.

Picket Fence (Figures 18-36 through 18-38)

The droppers spot drop to an assigned position on the field, while adjusting the landmarks to splits and formations. The free safety, Falcon, and the dime can exchange drop points if formation, position of the ball on the field, or scouting report dictates.

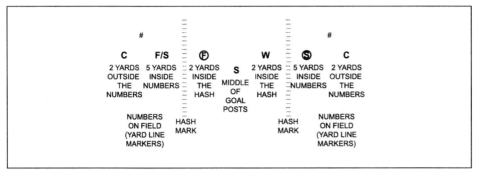

Figure 18-36. Picket fence landmarks

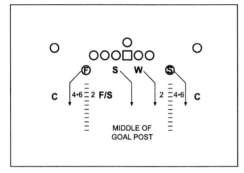

Figure 18-37. Eagle front drops with four-man rush

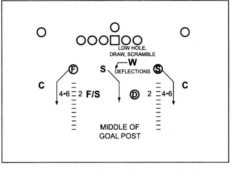

Figure 18-38. 50 front drops with three-man rush

Cover 6 (Figures 18-39 through 18-42)

Cover 6 allows the defense to play quarters inside the 10-yard line regardless of formations.

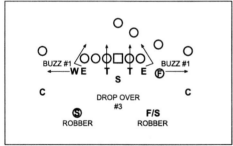

Figure 18-39. Eagle (four-man rush) cover 6 versus 11 doubles

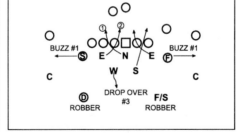

Figure 18-40. 50 (four-man rush) cover 6 versus 11 doubles

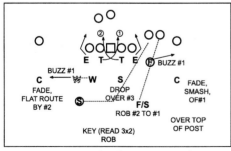

Figure 18-41. Eagle (four-man rush) cover 6 versus 10 trips

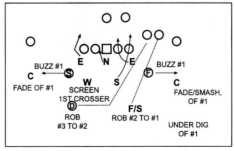

Figure 18-42. 50 (four-man rush) cover 6 versus 10 trips

White Coverage

Flow Call (Figures 18-43 and 18-44)

Versus 32 and 23 formations, white (man) must be checked to flow coverage to handle multiple releases of the receivers to either side of the formation.

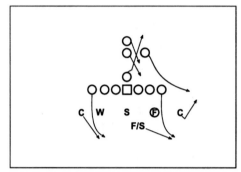 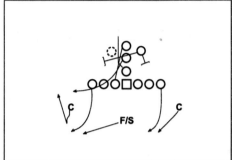

Figure 18-43. Check to flow versus 32 (CB has short; free safety has deep to flow of ball)—Flow to formation

Figure 18-44. Check to flow versus 32 (CB has short; free safety has deep to flow of ball)—Flow away from formation

Banjo

Versus 23 formations with a wing, the corner and the free safety must banjo the wing, back, and tight end. Also, they must be alert to switch the banjo if motion occurs (Figure 18-45).

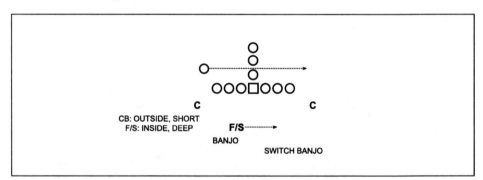

Figure 18-45. Switch the banjo versus motion

Snatch Call (Figures 18-46 through 18-50)

Versus 22 formations with back motion, the Falcon or Will must get a "snatch" call to put the correct player on the motion back. The free safety or corner can make a snatch call to the Falcon or Will in conjunction with kill blitz whether in white or purple coverage.

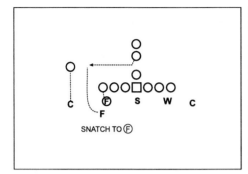

Figure 18-46. Snatch call versus back motion to formation

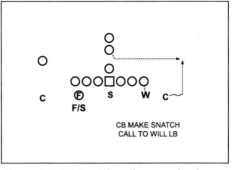

Figure 18-47. Snatch call versus back motion weak

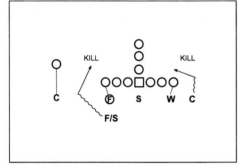

Figure 18-48. Snatch call to Falcon or Will from 53 white

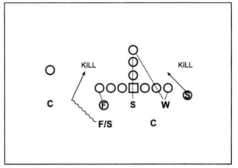

Figure 18-49. Snatch call to Falcon or Will from hammer purple

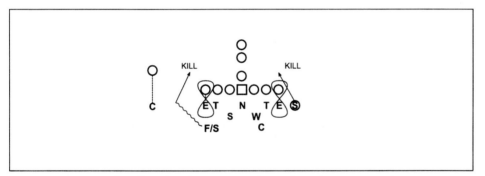

Figure 18-50. Snatch call to the defensive end or Falcon from 55 purple

Versus Two-Back Formations

On flow, the linebackers do not have any pass responsibilities, so they can play the run all the way. If they read pass, they play a read-blitz technique (an exception would be man coverage versus a one-back formation or splitbacks).

Empty Adjustment With Purple Coverage (Figures 18-51 and 18-52)

The linebackers (Sam and Will) read-blitz or play a double low hole; must be alert for the draw, quarterback scramble, or crossers.

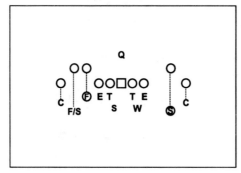

Figure 18-51. Empty adjustment with purple (Eagle front)

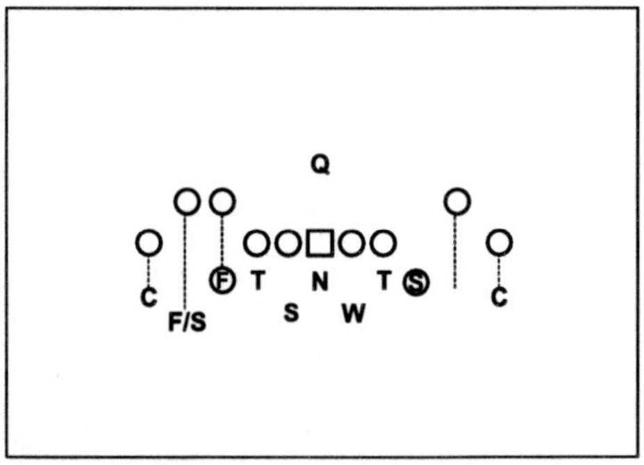

Figure 18-52. Empty adjustment with purple (55 front)

Empty Adjustment With White Coverage (Figure 18-53)

The linebacker (Sam) read-blitzes or plays a low hole; must be alert for the draw, quarterback scramble, or crossers.

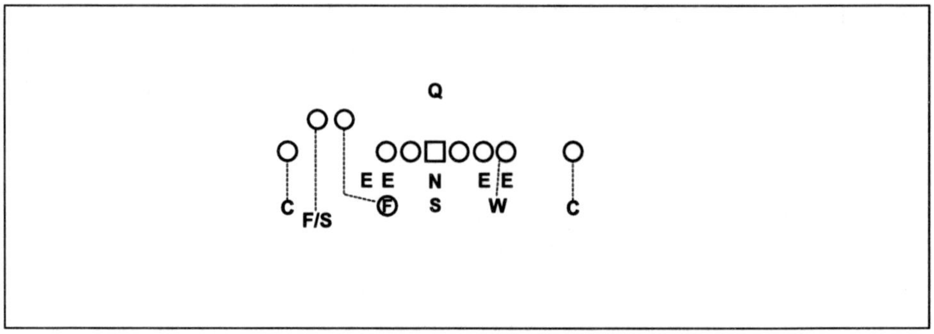

Figure 18-53. Empty adjustment with white (55 front)

19

Defending the Shotgun Spread Offense

The shotgun spread offense forces the defense to defend the width and depth of the field with an efficient horizontal and vertical throwing game. It can also combine elements of the option offense, utilize four or five wide receiver formations, and use dropback, play-action, sprint-out, bootlegs, and screens to complement the running game. The quarterback aligns at least five yards deep and with multiple set-up and throwing spots for him, which makes it difficult to effectively blitz on a consistent basis. The running back(s) align at six yards deep, which enables them to get the ball with their shoulders square to the line of scrimmage and get upfield quickly on runs or passes. Furthermore, many teams who are predominantly in the shotgun spread can walk the quarterback up under the center and create a good running and throwing game from this position. Motion by the receivers and back(s) can produce a one-back, two-back, or no-back formation (empty), and change from doubles (2x2) to trips (3x1) receiver alignments. All this being said, it is challenging and exciting for defensive coaches to produce schemes to defend the multiplicity of the shotgun spread offense.

Strengths of the Shotgun Spread Offense

- The quarterback is ready to throw earlier from the shotgun.
- The split of receivers forces the defense to defend the complete width of the field.
- A defense that utilizes a zone coverage concept is forced to defend a larger area of the field.
- A man-to-man coverage defense finds defenders more isolated with less assistance from teammates.
- With the quarterback in the shotgun, it is more difficult for second-level blitzers (linebackers) to pressure or sack him.

- The use of motion enables the offense to go from a balanced formation (2x2) to a trips formation (3x1), and conversely from a trips formation (3x1) to a balanced doubles formation (2x2).
- The motion can also be used by the offense to determine whether the defense is playing a zone or man scheme.
- The splits by the offensive line force rushers to come from a greater distance.

Weaknesses of the Shotgun Spread Offense

- The quarterback momentarily takes his eyes off the secondary to get the snap.
- Regardless of how the quarterback signals for ball to be snapped (knee pump, open hands, etc.), he momentarily loses concentration on how many defenders are rushing.
- The spread formation without a tight end creates a short corner for the outside rush.
- The remaining back(s) must be a part of pass protection, thus the defense can achieve a mismatch on the back in the rush scheme.
- Covering the center with an aggressive nose tackle may prove uncomfortable for the center and create bad snaps and/or force the guards to help him on pass protection.
- Wide splits by the offensive line isolate blockers. This isolation helps the defense create 1-on-1 situations without any help for the offensive linemen; the defense may be able to outquick the linemen and outphysical the backs.

Tendencies of the Shotgun Spread Offense

- Watch wide receivers, because they may give away their routes by their splits:
  ✓ Wide splits = inside routes (e.g., slant)
  ✓ Tight splits = outside routes (e.g., out)
- Option, quick slants, and screens are common adjustments to blitzes.
- A heavy dose of vertical routes is used versus three-deep zone coverage.
- Post-corner, level routes (shallow/deep), and double crossers are used versus cover 2 and 6.
- Always read how many defenders are in the box: no less than five, generally six, and no more than seven.
- Option routes are used by the inside receivers (e.g., #3 receiver from trips), and the backs out of the backfield on linebackers.
- Bubble or rocket (jailbreak) screens are used versus outside blitzes.
- Trips (3x1) is used to outnumber the defense: 3-on-2 or 4-on-3 (must be alert for the bubble screen).

- Will attack the walked off defender (not the walked up defender) versus a balanced defense.
- Can handle blitzes with hot receivers.
- Two backs created by motion is a heavy run tendency (Figure 19-1).
- Trips (3x1) with the back set to the weakside is a heavy pass tendency.
- In trips (3x1) with the back tilted to the trips, the speed option is often run to the trips side because the defense can be outnumbered and the overhang player is eliminated.
- With the tight end in the game, the offense likes to run inside toward the tight, and option toward the open side.
- On 10 trips, the offense likes to reverse to the backside. (Figure 19-2).
- With a doubles (2x2) formation, the routes the #2 receiver runs when aligned on the line of scrimmage and routes he runs when off the line of scrimmage may show some tendencies.
- The shovel option can be run many different ways with different personnel, thus the defense should know how to defend it according to what defender has each element of the option (quarterback, pitch, and shovel) (Figure 19-3).
- With jet motion and a tilt back, whether the quarterback is in the shotgun or under the center, the defense must be alert for the speed sweep (Figure 19-4).

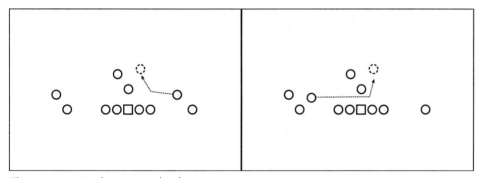

Figure 19-1. Motion to two backs

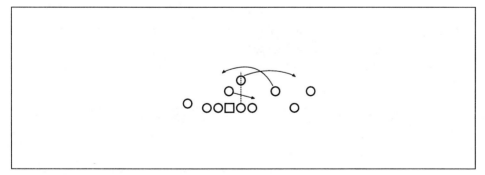

Figure 19-2. Reverse away from the trips side

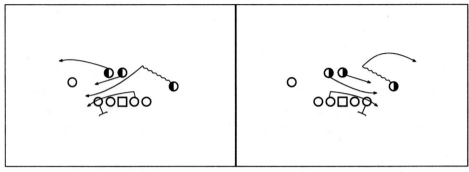

Figure 19-3. Shovel option

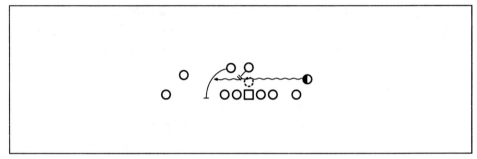

Figure 19-4. Speed sweep

Thoughts When Defending the Shotgun Spread Offense

- Press technique can cause problems, particularly the bubble and rocket screens.
- A defensive end chasing from the backside causes problems. However, the offense can combat the chasing defensive end by slowing him down with zone/option with the quarterback keeping, and with reverse and bootleg plays.
- Disguised defenders after the snap of ball can be used to confuse the quarterback (e.g., the defensive end dropping into coverage, or a secondary player dropping down as a hole defender).
- Defensive linemen should align head-up so no pre-snap read for the reduction side of the defense exists.
- Blitz the A and B gaps with linebackers from standard and bluff alignments.

Eagle Versus the Shotgun Spread

The defensive front is set the same way as other fronts, although as was suggested previously, it is beneficial to align the tackles in a head-up position:

- Formation/weak
- Field/boundary
- Tight/split
- Tilt/numbers

Versus Doubles (Figure 19-5): If the #2 receiver motions toward the ball, the Will slides inside to a 30 technique. The Stud moves toward the ball and makes the "I'm here" call to the inside linebackers so they can slide strong.

Versus Trips (Figure 19-6): The linebackers slide toward the trips.

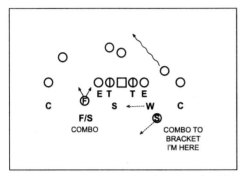 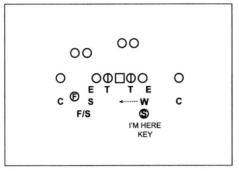

Figure 19-5. Eagle versus shotgun doubles Figure 19-6. Eagle versus shotgun trips

Eagle Tilt

It is preferable to align the 3-technique tackle to the tilt back and the 2i technique away from the Tilt back. If the offense shifts the back to the opposite side, the linebackers should make an "Opposite" call with a Roger or Larry call. The defensive end to the Tilt back goes hard to the face mask of the back and adjusts his angle to the back while reading on the run. (change-up is the Exchange stunt that puts the end on the quarterback),

Eagle Tilt Change-Ups for the Defensive Tackles

- *Eagle Tilt Shade* (Figure 19-7): The shade is a change-up for the defensive tackles. The tackle away from the tilt slides to a shade on the center. The defensive end flattens down once he clears the line of scrimmage.
- *Eagle Base* (Figure 19-8): The tackles play head-up on the guards. They attack the guards aggressively and get upfield. The tackles do not worry about being reached; they play backdoor on the reach, and two-gap the base block.

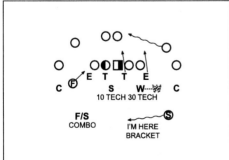 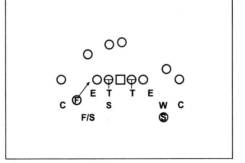

Figure 19-7. Eagle tilt shade   Figure 19-8. Eagle base

- *Eagle Tilt Bat* (Figure 19-9): The tackles align head-up, and then as the quarterback and offensive line get into their calls, the tackles slide opposite the called (tilt) alignment. On the snap, they slant across faces of the guards, and penetrate upfield in the B gap to the tilt and the A gap away from the tilt.

Figure 19-9. Eagle tilt bat

Combination Stunts With the Defensive Ends and Tackles

- *Eagle Tilt Wrap From Shade* (Figure 19-10): Wrap can be run two ways, one as a pass stunt, and the other as a run stunt. If a run stunt, the defensive end goes first through the V of the guard's neck and is the penetrator; the defensive tackle scrapes tight off the butt of the end and is the flasher. The Sam is the dive player and late alley player.

- *Eagle Tilt Weave* (Figure 19-11): This wrap is to the tilt side, and the swap to the backside. To the swap, the tackle is the penetrator, and the end is the flasher. Swap is not run to a tilt back, so if the back motions, the tackle can check to wrap (double wrap) or check back to base with an "Omaha" call.

- *Eagle Tilt Exchange From Shade* (Figure 19-12): The end to the tilt side attacks the facemask of the back, but instead of adjusting to the back's angle, he continues on his path to attack the quarterback.

- *Eagle Tilt AC From Shade* (Figure 19-13): The end and tackle angle through the facemask of the guard and tackle; both have dive responsibility. The Sam has the quarterback from the inside-out. Falcon has quarterback outside, or pitch inside. The free safety and corner rally to the pitch.

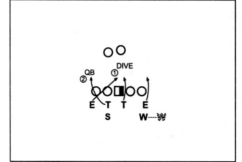

Figure 19-10. Eagle tilt wrap from shade

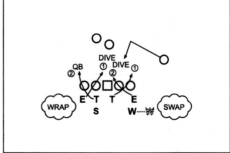

Figure 19-11. Eagle tilt weave

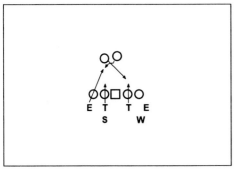

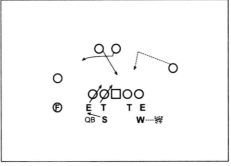

Figure 19-12. Eagle tilt exchange from shade

Figure 19-13. Eagle tilt AC from shade

Linebacker Stunts

- *Eagle Tilt Crash* (Shade/Swap Away) With Z, Y, or Two-Backer Coverage (Figure 9-14): Sam slides late and blitzes from the outside. The end and tackle slant inside (AC) on the callside. The Sam is a quarterback player on the option with the end and tackle responsible for the dive.

- *Eagle Tilt Crash Echo* (Figure 9-15): Crash echo is a change-up for the end and Sam.

- *Eagle Tilt Attack (Shade, Swap) With Z, Y, or Two-Backer Coverage* (Figure 9-16): With the #2 receiver removed, the free safety makes a "sky" call to the Falcon. Sky alerts the Falcon to be the hole player, and the free safety is the seam player. The end takes the dive outside and the quarterback inside with Sam blitzing through the A gap for the dive.

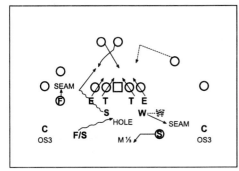

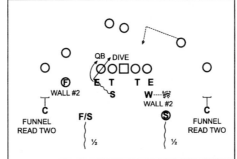

Figure 19-14. Eagle tilt crash Y

Figure 19-15. Eagle tilt crash echo two backer

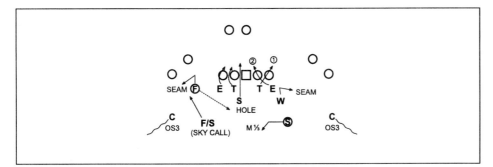

Figure 19-16. Eagle tilt attack swap 2

Falcon and Stud Stunts

- *Eagle Tilt Lake (Echo) With Z-Spin or Z-Backer Coverage* (Figure 19-17): The defense can call a swap or wrap to the backside. The end and tackle slant (AC) to the callside.

- *Eagle Tilt Lake Echo Z-Spin* (Figure 19-18): The Stud makes a "you" call to the Will linebacker; Will becomes the blitzer, and Stud rocks down to the seam. It is best to keep Stud in coverage with two stand-ups.

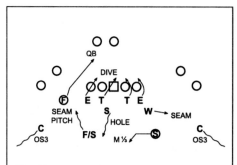

Figure 19-17. Eagle tilt lake Z-spin

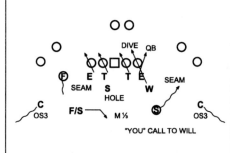

Figure 19-18. Eagle tilt lake echo Z-spin

50 Versus the Shotgun Spread

The 50 (3-4) is an excellent shotgun spread defense because of the variety of options available to create problems for the offense (Figure 19-19). The available options include the following:

- Align the defense line in head-up positions to eliminate pre-snap reads on the reduction and 5-technique sides.

- The cover-2 secondary shell makes all coverage reads by the offense occur after the snap of the ball.

- Two overhang players (Falcon and Stud) are in position to bounce and bluff and make it difficult to determine who are the rusher and/or dropper prior to the snap.

- The center is covered by the nose tackle to produce uncertainty about the snap and blocking responsibilities.

- Three-, four-, five-, and six-man rush potential exists with excellent concealment until the snap.

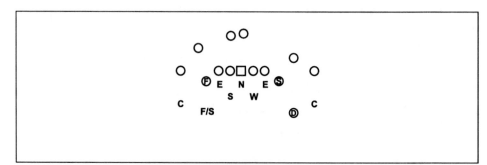

Figure 19-19. 50 versus the shotgun spread

46 and 59 Line Stunts (Figures 19-20 through 19-26)

Multiple line stunts are available to both the 46 side (A, angle, exchange, and attack) and the 59 side (fold, blast, and directional zero by the nose).

Figure 19-20. Attack from 46

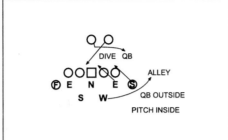

Figure 19-21. Angle from 46

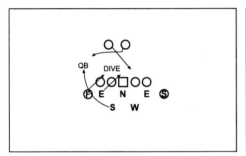

Figure 19-22. A from 46

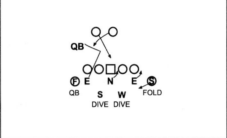

Figure 19-23. Exchange from 46

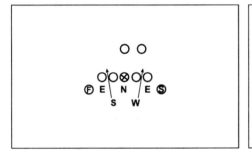

Figure 19-24. Blast from 59

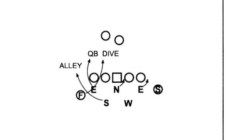

Figure 19-25. Fold (exchange) from 59

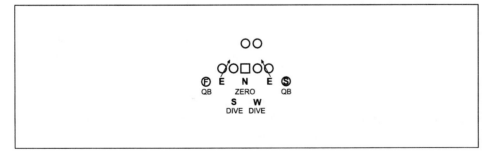

Figure 19-26. Pinch from double 46. (This can be called 50 pinch or 44.) When stunts are called off pinch (A, angle, exchange, attack) they will be executed from both sides.

50 Stunts With Coverage Calls

50 Tilt (59 side to tilt back, 46 side away) With a Roger or Larry Call (Figure 19-27): The Sam and end play a tacklebox read with option responsibility depending on the blocking scheme of the offense. If the tackle base or reach blocks, the end has the quarterback and the Sam has dive; if the tackle down-blocks, the end has dive, and Sam has the quarterback. The dime aligns over the backside guard, keys #3 strong for vertical, and makes the "I'm here" call to the linebackers to alert them he is the weakside A- or B-gap filler. Linebackers slide to the trips; Sam aligns in a 40 technique, and the Will in a weak 10 on the center. With no back aligned to the weakside, the Stud can automatically execute an angle charge. Following are the double secondary calls when setting the 59 side to or away from the tilt back with the tilt or numbers call:

- Tilt
  - ✓ Back to the free safety: cover 6
  - ✓ Back away from the free safety: cover 3
- Numbers
  - ✓ Back to the free safety: cover 3
  - ✓ Back away from the free safety: cover 6

With tilt, the coverage call is 63 or 6 check (Figure 19-28). With numbers, the coverage call is 36 or 3 check. If the back shifts from the strongside to the weakside, the defense should make an "opposite" call with a Roger or Larry call. The secondary checks from cover 6 to cover 3.

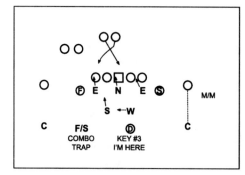

Figure 19-27. 50 tilt (Larry call)

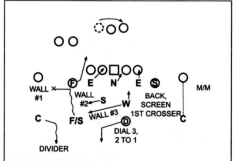

Figure 19-28. Check from cover 6 to 3 versus back shift from strongside to weakside (skate check versus trips)

50 Numbers (59 side away from tilt, 46 side to tilt) With a Roger or Larry Call (Figure 19-29): If the back shifts, the defense makes an "opposite" call with a Roger or Larry call, and checks to cover 6.

50 Tilt Lake (Echo) Z Check With a Roger or Larry Call (Figures 19-30 through 19-32): If the back shifts, the defense makes an "opposite" call with a Roger or Larry call.

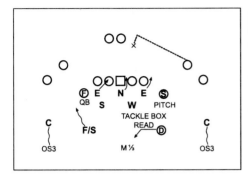

Figure 19-29. 50 numbers versus doubles (Roger call)

Figure 19-30. 50 numbers versus back shift

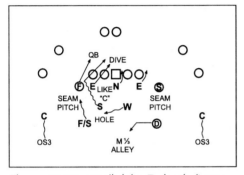

Figure 19-31. 50 tilt lake Z check (Larry call) versus doubles

Figure 19-32. 50 tilt versus back shift versus doubles ("opposite" with Roger calls)

50 Tilt Lake Echo (Figure 19-33): The Stud or Falcon and inside linebacker switch gaps. The Falcon or Stud blitz from the outside-in off the butt of the linebacker and read the offensive tackle. If the tackle blocks down, they stay tight to his hip for dive; if the tackle blocks out, they go under him for dive.

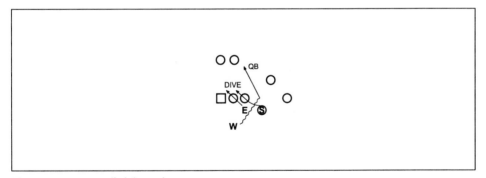

Figure 19-33. 50 tilt lake echo

50 Tilt Blaze (Switch) with Y or Two-Backer Coverage With a Roger or Larry Call (Figures 19-34 and 19-35): Blaze switch is a good change-up because it allows the linebacker away from the tilt to adjust his blitz to mirror the angle of the back and the ball. If the back shifts, make an "opposite" call, but make no change to the Y or two-backer coverage call.

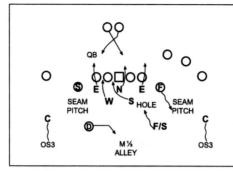

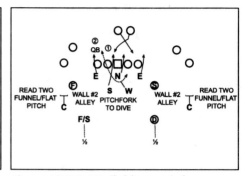

Figure 19-34. 50 tilt blaze versus trips (Larry call)

Figure 19-35. 50 tilt blaze switch two backer versus doubles (Larry call)

50 Pinch Angle With Purple (Man) or Two-Backer Coverage With a Roger or Larry Call (Figure 19-36): Z-spin backer can also be called to the field or formation. The Will can take the seam, or the Stud can make a "you" call for the Will to blitz, and the Stud takes the seam.

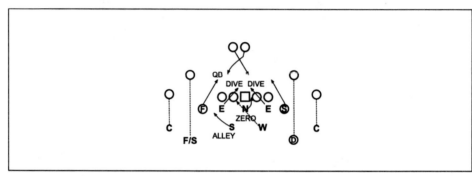

Figure 19-36. 50 pinch angle purple versus doubles (Larry call)

50 Double Pinch A Two Backer Versus Trips (Figure 19-37)

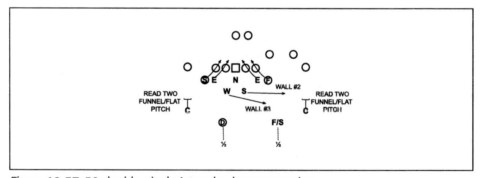

Figure 19-37. 50 double pinch A two backer versus trips

50 Indian Wind With Z-Spin or Two-Backer Coverage With a Roger or Larry Call (Figure 19-38)

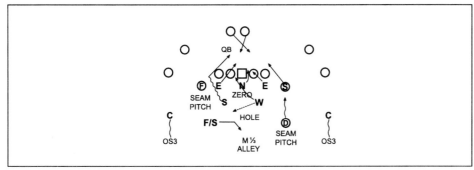

Figure 19-38. 50 Indian wind Z-spin versus doubles

50 Indian Storm With Z-Spin or Two-Backer Coverage With a Roger or Larry Call (Figure 19-39)

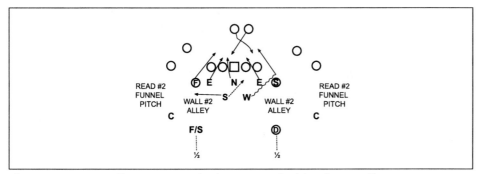

Figure 19-39. 50 Indian storm two backer versus doubles (Larry call)

50 Tilt Flame or Fire With Z coverage With a Roger or Larry Call (Figures 19-40 and 19-41): Versus trips, the Sam can make a "you" call, the Will becomes the blitzer, and Sam is the hole player.

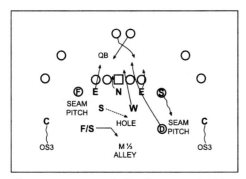
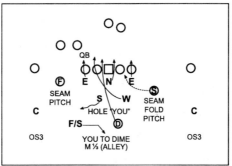

Figure 19-40. 50 tilt fire Z versus doubles (Roger call)

Figure 19-41. 50 tilt flame Z versus trips (Larry call)

50 Tilt Lightning With Z-Spin or Two-Backer Coverage With a Roger or Larry Call (Figures 19-42 and 19-43): Versus back shift, several adjustments/calls must be made. "Opposite" changes the blitz to the other side with the inside and outside linebackers exchanging assignments. The inside linebackers need to make a "you/me" call.

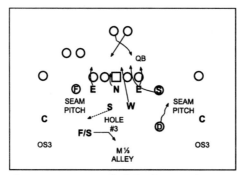

Figure 19-42. 50 Tilt lightning Z-spin versus trips (Roger call)

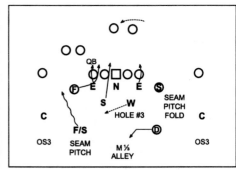

Figure 19-43. 50 tilt lightning Z-spin versus back shift from trips (calls: opposite, Larry, you/me)

Eagle Front Coverages Versus the Shotgun Spread

Eagle Tilt Cover 6 Versus Doubles (2x2) (Figure 19-44)

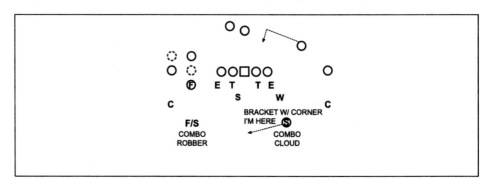

Figure 19-44. Eagle tilt cover 6 versus doubles

Play Combo or Robber: Robber with #2 receiver on the line of scrimmage (vertical threat). Combo with the #2 receiver off the line of scrimmage (flat, wheel)

Robber: Falcon buzzes the flat for #1 on a three-step drop by the quarterback; picks up #2 in the flat and carries the wheel of #2. Free safety reads #2 for UPS (up, post, and seam); #2 blocks, goes inside or outside rob the inside routes of #1. Strong corner keys through the #2 receiver to the ball. Plays an inside 1/3 protecting the post (gets big on the post). If #2 receiver pushes vertical squeezes back to the #1 receiver; if the #2 receiver is flat, keeps the inside position on #1 playing big on the fade and the post.

Combo: Falcon is a curl player. The corner and the free safety key the #2 receiver; if #2 goes to the flat, the corner squeezes down, and the safety plays over #1; if #2 goes vertical, the safety has #2 on UPS (up, post, seam), and the corner carries #1 on the vertical.

To the Backside: Stud gives the corner and Will a combo or cloud call. Combo is the same as strongside with the corner and Stud reading #2. Cloud is cover 2 to the backside to help on #1 and for run support. Generally, when playing cover 2, the corner plays a funnel technique. Will drops over #2 as the curl player. Stud checks out of combo or cloud if the slotback motions into the backfield; he makes a "bracket" call to a single receiver with the Stud doubling #1 with the corner. With bracket, the Will mans #2. If the linebacker has trouble covering a back, a combo or cloud call gives him relief. With bracket, the Stud moves inside and makes the "I'm here" call to alert the linebackers that he has the A or B gap backside.

Eagle Cover 6 Versus Trips (3x1) (Figure 19-45)

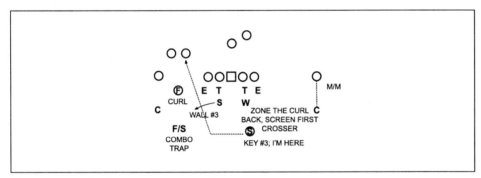

Figure 19-45. Eagle cover 6 versus trips

The safety gives a "combo" or "trap" call to the corner and Falcon.

Combo: The safety and the corner key #2 and play the same as versus doubles. Safety is aware of #2 or #3; if #1 or #2 is non-threatening, he pushes to next deepest threat. The Falcon on both combo and trap is a curl player and reroutes #2 by alignment or collision. Stud will key #3 ready to carry #3 on the vertical. If #3 is non-threatening, the Stud works backside for a late racket with the corner.

Trap: The corner is a true cover-2 player. Once #1 clears, the corner reads #2 and #3 as one. If #2 is non-threatening, the safety reads the release of #1. If outside release, the safety alerts to fade; if inside release, he keeps inside position on post and must be ready to break over the top of the post corner. Stud aligns to the middle of the formation and reads #3; if #3 goes deep, Stud stays with him; if #3 goes short, the Sam has him. If #3 is non-threatening, the Stud goes to the backside for a late bracket with the corner. The Stud makes the "I'm here" call. Will spot-drops and is alert for the back, screen, and first crosser; Will gives late help to the corner on inside intermediate routes. The Sam drops over #3 to play the slant, wheel with the dig, and carry #3 on vertical to the Stud.

Eagle Zero Versus Empty

Defend the empty formation with either a zero call (zone), or a Utah call (blitz). It is advisable to change up from zero to Utah each series or by quarters. It is important to have a specific call for defending or blitzing, and all fronts and coverages do not need to be matched up versus the empty. Both the Eagle and 50 fronts are good versus an empty formation.

Zero (Figure 19-46): A three-man rush with the two defensive ends aligned over the tackles and rushing inside or outside. The two technique to the formation works over the center and mirrors the quarterback. The two technique to the weakside slants outside working to an outside force on the quarterback. The defensive end to the two-man side drops/spies over the ball (low hole), and mirrors the quarterback with his head on a swivel.

Utah (Figure 19-47): The jet defensive end and Will blitz from outside the tackles. If they get caught inside, the defensive tackles will cover for them.

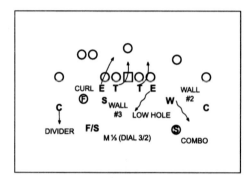

Figure 19-46. Eagle zero versus empty

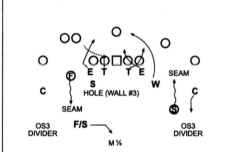

Figure 19-47. Eagle Utah (Will crash/wrap) Z spin versus empty

Lock

To stay in a particular defense against all sets, including the empty, give a lock call/signal (turn the key) from the sideline.

50 Front Coverages Versus the Shotgun Spread

Versus Doubles (2x2) (Figure 19-48)

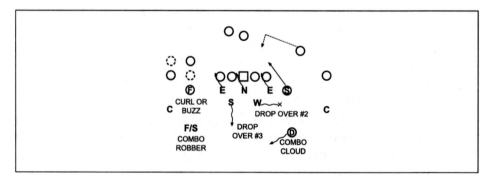

Figure 19-48. 50 formation cover 6 versus doubles (Larry call)

If the slotback goes in motion from either side to create a two-back set, the safety or the dime make a "bracket" call to the corner and the Will or Falcon. The dime checks out of the combo/cloud, makes a "bracket" call to double the #1 receiver with the corner. Will is man on the back, and as the dime moves inside, he makes the "I'm here" call.

Cover 6 Versus Trips (3x1) (Figure 19-49)

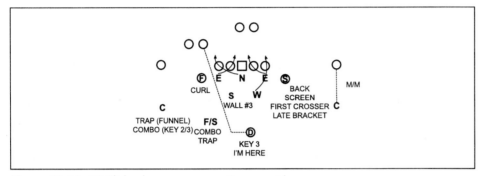

Figure 19-49. 50 tilt backer wrap cover 6 versus trips

Cover 3 Versus Trips (3x1) (Figure 19-50)

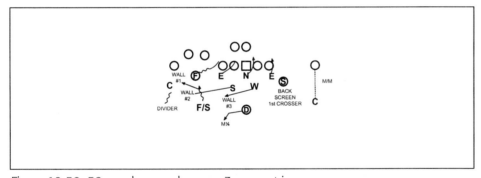

Figure 19-50. 50 numbers angle cover 3 versus trips

When in cover 3 versus trips, check skate to allow the defense to wall the trips side receivers with the safety, Sam, and Will. The safety walls #1 for the three-step drop slant, and carries #2 in the flat and the wheel. Sam walls #2, and Will walls #3 with both players responsible for cutting the slant, wheeling with the dig, and carrying the verticals by #2 and #3. If #2 or #3 go outside, Sam and Will expand outside and look for a new #2 or #3 on inside cuts. The corner plays an inside divider technique and reads #2 and #3 as one. The dime is a middle-third player, and keeps inside leverage on #3 to #2. Stud spot-drops and checks back, screen, first crosser, and late bracket on #1 with the corner.

50 Zero Versus Empty (Figure 19-51)

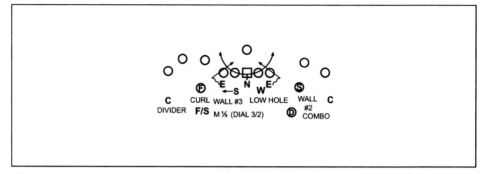

Figure 19-51. 50 zero nose wipe versus empty

Zero is cover 3 to the three-receiver side and two combo to the two-receiver side. The most productive three-man rush is nose wipe. Both ends move out into jet position and rush inside or outside. The nose starts upfield to collapse the pocket and mirrors the quarterback to prevent the scramble or get a deflection.

50 Utah Versus Empty (Figures 19-52 and 19-53)

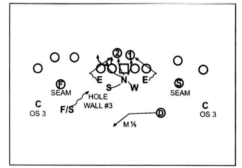

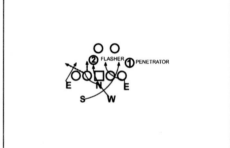

Figure 19-52. 50 formation smoke Y versus empty (Larry call)

Figure 19-53. 50 formation smoke pick (smoke change-up)

50 Front Four-Man Rushes
(Figures 19-54 through 19-60)

The linebacker is called into the rush with the same calls used to align the front:
- Field/boundary
- Formation/weak
- Tilt/numbers
- Tight/split

When there is no "wrap" or "swap" call, the defensive end away from the call moves out to a jet alignment.

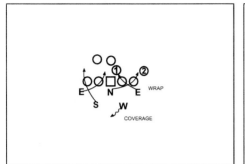

Figure 19-54. 50 tilt backer wrap
(Larry call)

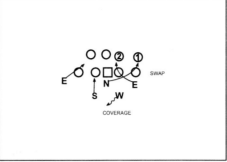

Figure 19-55. 50 tilt blast swap
(Larry call)

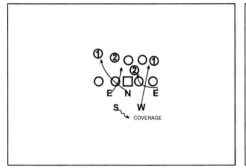

Figure 19-56. Tilt blast pick swap
(Roger call)

Figure 19-57. 50 tilt attack-X (double jet)

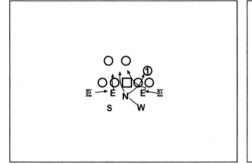

Figure 19-58. Bear numbers attack swap

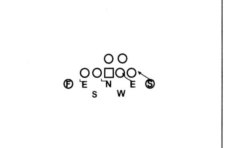

Figure 19-59. 50 numbers angle
(Larry call)

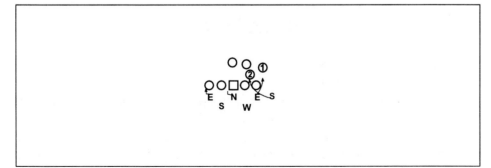

Figure 19-60. 50 numbers angle echo (Roger call)

Defending the Shovel Option

Defending From the 50 Front (Figure 19-61)

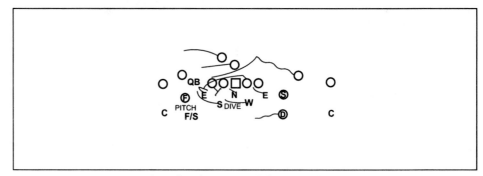

Figure 19-61. 50 versus shovel option toward the 59 side

The 5-technique defensive end squeezes the down block of the tackle, and forces him to take a flat release to prevent him from getting to the linebacker. He has first threat outside the tackle, two-gaps the pull guard, and gets upfield to the quarterback. The frontside linebacker plays outside the pull guard and is the alley player (quarterback outside/pitch onside); the backside linebacker plays inside the pull guard. The nose squeezes the dive. The outside linebacker (Falcon or Stud) has pitch.

Defending From the Eagle Front (Figure 19-62)

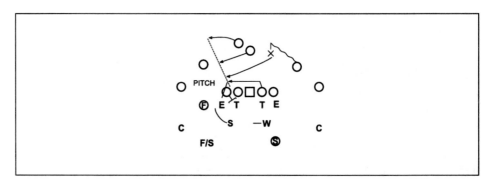

Figure 19-62. Eagle versus the shovel option

Aztec Front

As discussed previously, the Aztec front gives the defense the ability to play an Eagle front without making substitutions. This ability is an advantage because the defense does not have to show its alignment prior to the offense lining up on the ball. Only the Stud has to learn new techniques, but he has the experience of lining up over a tight end, which has good carryover value to the overhang player to the open-end side. The front can change from the 50 to Aztec (Eagle), and from Aztec (Eagle) to the 50. This stemming provides the ability to move from a three-man front to a four-man front and vice versa, and creates blocking and protection problems for the offense. The Stud always aligns weak, and the defensive line moves strong to keep it as simple and sound as possible. When the Stud moves to the line of scrimmage, he makes a Liz or Rip call to the defensive line to tell them which way to move/stem. The linebackers make a Roger or Larry call to tell the tackles which way to move or on what side a stunt may occur on the defensive line.

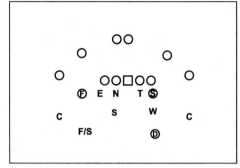

Figure 19-63. Aztec versus the shotgun spread

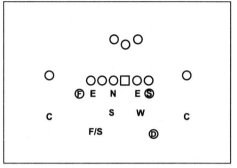

Figure 19-64. Aztec versus 21 pro

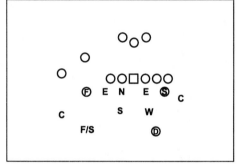

Figure 19-65. Aztec versus 21 twins

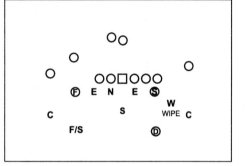

Figure 19-66. Aztec versus 11 doubles

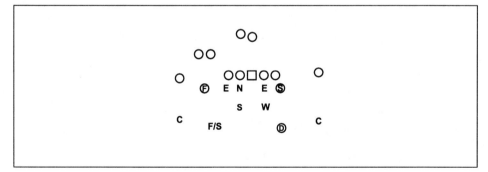

Figure 19-67. Aztec versus 10 trips

Purple (Man) Coverage With Six-Man Blitzes
(Figures 19-68 and 19-69)

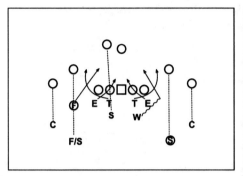 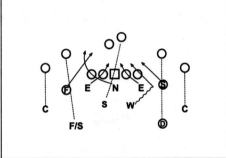

Figure 19-68. Eagle stinger purple versus doubles

Figure 19-69. 50 sick 'em purple versus doubles

20

Defending the Flex Bone Option Offense

The flex bone option offense takes the emphasis off ability and talent and stresses the importance of execution. Regardless of talent, the defense must be disciplined and have at least one defender on the dive, quarterback, and pitch on every play or the option offense will quickly find and exploit defensive weaknesses. Because the option offense is unique and only used by a few teams, defenses face limited practice time to prepare. Plus, the ability of the scout team to execute the speed of the option offense makes it extremely difficult to adequately prepare. This chapter evaluates the advantages of the option attack and presents a sound and simple defensive scheme to be successful versus the option offense.

Strengths of the Flex Bone Option Offense

- Mirrored offense (equally effective to both sides)
- Goal-line to goal-line offense
- Adjustments after the snap depending on defensive reactions
- Forces the defense to play a balanced defensive scheme (four defenders committed to option on both sides)
- Consistent game plan from week to week
- Forces the defense to defend a maximum area with wide splits
- Mesh with the fullback to both sides
- Pressure on the defense to defend both the run and the pass
- Simplified blocking schemes
- Quick pressure on the defense in three areas along the line of scrimmage
- Difficult for the defense to get a good scout look in practice
- Forces the defense to play assignment defense, rather than reaction defense
- Removes the advantage of ability, and replaces it with execution

Key Characteristics of the Option Offense

- Wide splits of receivers make it a 9-on-9 game.
- 90 percent of formations are tight wing, double slot, trips, unbalanced, and/or split unbalanced.
- Offensive calls are made quickly in an attempt to create a panic mode for the defense.
- Defenders need to understand the angle of the fullback and how it relates to plays being run.
- Option teams will run plays into the boundary.
- Good plays are repeated on the same down-and-distance in the next series.
- If the defense has trouble stopping a play, the offense will repeat it over and over until the defense finds the answer to stopping it.
- The offense likes to throw on the first play after getting the ball on a turnover across the 50-yard line.
- The sweep is run to the reduction side of the defense.
- The freeze (long count) will be used on third-and-short and fourth-down situations. The defense should react on the ball, not on sound; they shouldn't jump.
- Trips, tackle over, and split unbalanced are primarily hash-mark formations.
- Slot doubles is primarily a middle-of-the-field and hash-mark formation.
- All formations should be able to be run with the same personnel (no substitution tendencies exist).

Ideas on Defending the Option

- Front personnel play run on every down.
- Defending the option is a game of angles.
- Expect repeat calls.
- Make the same call to the opposite side.
- It is important to get the defense lined up by making the defensive call quickly.
- The defense should make things happen quickly for the quarterback (make offense speed up everything they do).
- Hit the fullback as deep as possible to force the quarterback to bubble back from the line of scrimmage (penetration hurts the option offense).
- Create a guessing game as to what the defense is doing to put pressure back on the offense.
- Hits on the quarterback and the fullback are the key to defensive success (create turnovers).
- Use defensive movement before the snap.
- Less is better.
- The secondary should be hungry to be involved in stopping the run.

- Take a four- or five-day section in spring practice and pre-season to work versus the option.
- During the season, take each Monday prior to playing the option team to use a 15- to 20-minute period to practice against the option, regardless of that week's opponent.
- Tackle the fullback low and on every play.
- Keep calls on until the offense actually runs an option at the call.
- Run down the quarterback from the backside (tackle him low).
- Make all reads by the offense post-snap, not pre-snap.

Flex Bone Formations

The defense should be ready to successfully defend against five formations. Certain plays are usually run from each formation. Although these plays can vary according to a particular opponent, a number of these plays fit each formation regardless of the opponent. Figures 20-1 through 20-7 depict the formations and the major plays used with each formation.

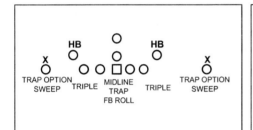

Figure 20-1. Slot doubles

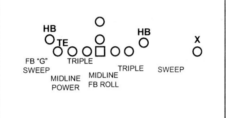

Figure 20-2. Tight wing

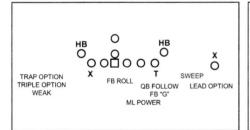

Figure 20-3. Unbalanced tackle over

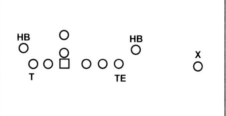

Figure 20-4. Unbalanced tight end over (plays are same as unbalanced tackle over)

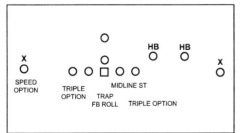

Figure 20-5. Trips

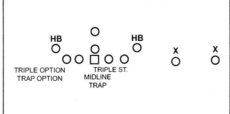

Figure 20-6. Split unbalanced

Figure 20-7. Split unbalanced (shift to create trips)

Use of Motion in the Flex Bone Option Offense

The motion of the halfbacks is an integral part of the option offense. It is important that linebackers and defensive backs expand their vision on motion to get a pre-snap read on the type of plays that may be executed from the particular motion being used. Motion generally falls into one of three categories, with certain plays run with each type of motion.

Two-Step Motion

The plays generally run with two-step motion include the triple option, trap option, midline, and counter (Figures 20-8 through 20-11).

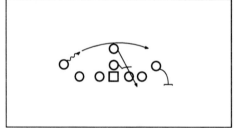

Figure 20-8. Triple option

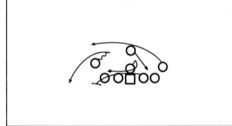

Figure 20-9. Trap option

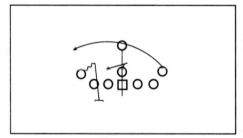

Figure 20-10. Midline

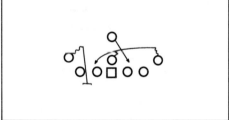

Figure 20-11. Counter

Toss Motion (Figure 20-12)

The plays generally run with toss motion include toss, trail pass, belly, and fullback dive. The snap is usually when the motion man reaches the fullback.

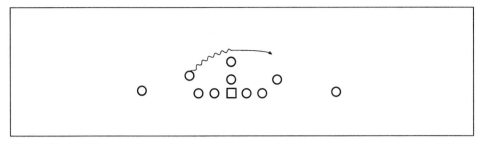

Figure 20-12. Toss motion

Lead Motion (Figure 20-13)

The plays generally run with lead motion include midline power and power pass. The snap is usually when the motion man gets beyond the fullback. The key to lead motion is the motion man begins to gather and chop his feed when he gets behind the fullback.

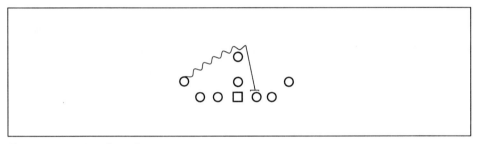

Figure 20-13. Lead motion

50 Front Position Alignments and Responsibilities Versus the Option

Inside Linebackers

The inside linebackers align in 30 techniques on the offensive guards at a five-yard depth. Their primary key is the fullback while visualizing the guards. The Sam linebacker always aligns to the formation, and the Will linebacker to the backside of the formation. It is important that they know whether they are aligned to the 59 side or the 46 side of the defense. The linebacker to the 59 side has B-gap responsibility on flow to him; he plays the B gap from the outside-in. The angle of the fullback triggers whether he has a mental or physical fill in the B gap. If the triple option is run to the 59 side, he will have a tackle-box read with the defensive end. If daylight shows inside the defensive end, he has dive responsibility (Figure 20-14). If the 59 linebacker encounters darkness as he presses the B gap, he will immediately scrape over the top of the defensive end for the quarterback (Figure 20-15). If flow is away, the 59 linebacker is responsible for the playside A gap, and the angle of the fullback determines whether he has a physical or mental fill in the A gap.

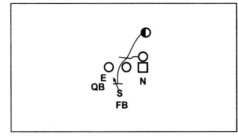

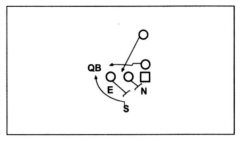

Figure 20-14. Linebacker fills B gap for dive

Figure 20-15. Linebacker scrapes for quarterback

The 46 linebacker is the C-gap player on flow to, and the backside A-gap player on flow away. He plays the C gap from the inside-out, pressing at an angle to beat the zone scoop of the tackle. If flow to, he runs with the quarterback and is the alley player (quarterback outside, pitch inside). On flow away, the 46 linebacker presses the backside A gap for the fullback; he is ready to pitchfork to the angle of the fullback and the ball.

The biggest key for linebacker success is to use pre-snap and post-snap reads. Pre-snap reads that give an advantage prior to the ball being snapped include the following:
- Offensive line splits
- Heavy or light stances
- Depth of the fullback
- Alignment of the slotbacks
- Motion of the slotback

Post-snap reads that immediately come into play on snap include the following:
- Angle of the fullback
- Low-hat or high-hat movement of offensive linemen
- Pull of the guards

The linebackers' approach to the passing game should be similar to how they play the run. Since so much of the passing game is off play-action it is important that the linebackers press the run and blitz to the pass. Thus, there should not be any hesitation versus the run, and by attacking can hit daylight versus the pass for pressure and sacks on the quarterback. Dropping into pass coverage is a secondary reaction for the linebackers; however, the following rules can apply to certain formations/motions:
- *Double slot with no motion of the halfbacks:* Sam and Will drop over the #2 receiver.
- *Double slot with motion:* Sam and Will read blitz (find daylight on the run and mirror blitz the quarterback).
- *Tight wing:* Sam and Will read blitz regardless of flow.

- *Unbalanced:* Sam and Will read blitz to the angle of the fullback and the set of the quarterback. They should not come inside the turnback protection of the offensive line.
- *Split unbalanced:* Sam and Will read blitz to the angle of the fullback and the set of the quarterback.
- *Trips:* Sam and Will play two ways, depending on the call of the safety (skate or combo) (Figures 20-16 and 20-17).

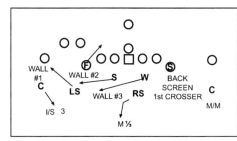

Figure 20-16. Skate call to linebackers versus trips

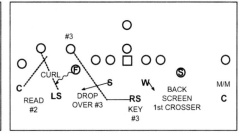

Figure 20-17. Combo call to linebackers versus trips

Defensive Linemen

The three defensive linemen line up on the nose of the center and two offensive tackles in a four-point stance to eliminate all pre-snap reads. This alignment prevents the offense from determining the 59 and 46 sides until the snap. When called, the defensive linemen can bluff by stepping opposite the direction they are going. This disguise gives the offense the illusion of a 5 technique instead of a 4, or a 4 technique instead of a 5. This disguise not only causes hesitation for the offensive line, but creates indecision on the part of the quarterback as to whether his read is a give or keep after the snap. Defensive line option techniques include the following:

Nose Tackle: Uses a directional zero to the 59 side when called in the framework of the defense. He attacks with the knowledge that he is not a back-door player, but is responsible for securing the A gap to the 59 side.

4 Technique: If a big split in the B gap exists, he can penetrate the gap without a call, but can't get cut off. If a tight split and light read, plays a normal 4 technique. If a big split, penetrates inside unless he reads light stance by the guard, then plays a normal 4 technique. Chases the hip of the guard, and creates a train wreck. Cannot be hooked by the guards.

5 Technique: If a big split, plays a heavy 5 technique, and mirrors the reach block; if a normal split, plays the quarterback outside the tackle; if a big split, stretches the tackle and comes under for the quarterback. If the tackle down-blocks, squeezes and closes the space.

Falcon and Stud (Outside Linebackers)

The Falcon and Stud align on the line of scrimmage and have both a run technique and a pass technique on every snap. The Larry or Roger call identifies who is on the 59 side and who is on the 46 side (reduction side). The 59 side is always to the Larry or Roger call, and the 46 is always away from the call. Pinch is a 50 front change-up with a 46 to both sides. The outside linebacker to the 59 side plays a 9 technique, and a 6 technique to the 46 side. The Falcon aligns to the formation, and the Stud away from the formation. They can align according to the three-man surface (tight end or unbalanced tackle) also.

6 technique to the split end: Aligns in a hip position with his toes on the heels of the defensive end, and one yard outside the defensive end. Uses a chip technique on the tackle's outside release; punches the tackle with the near hand to keep him from a clean release to the linebacker or free safety. Responsible for the first threat outside the tackle; a majority of times, it is the quarterback, but he must also be ready to play the fullback on the crease play that hits outside the tackle. Uses a layer technique unless an attack stunt (A, angle) is called; sinks and stays inside and in front of the quarterback; keeps the shoulders square; maintains a one- to two-yard outside position; must be ready to drop-step and sprint (great exit angle) if the ball is pitched; delays the quarterback's decision to allow pursuit and secondary support to get to the ball. If the tackle releases outside, punches him to keep him from getting a quick release to either the safety or the linebacker. If the defensive end slides and penetrates the B gap versus a wide split, must be alert for the fullback bouncing outside the tackle's block on the defensive end. If flow away, checks the reverse and runs down the quarterback from the backside. If dropback or play-action pass to, rushes. If play-action pass away, drops for drag and second-level help on the quarterback scramble.

6 technique to the tight end/tackle over: Align in heavy 9 technique over the tight end (or tackle over) with inside foot splitting the crotch of the tight end; he is always the quarterback player. If the tight end blocks down, spills the first threat. If flow away, checks the reverse and bootleg. Rushes the passer on dropback or play-action pass to. If play-action pass away, must be aware of wheel on turnaround motion. If unbalanced, always rushes on the pass with peel rule; must be alert to take the motion back on the trail pass.

9 technique to the split end: Aligns on the heels of the defensive end, whether 46 or 59 to the split end (disguise). Mirrors the slot; if outside release (arc), widens and takes a good exit angle, must be aware of quarterback outside and pitch inside. If load or fold inside, plays the quarterback. If flow away, folds inside with second-level help on the reverse. If pass, buzzes or curl dropper; it will be late buzz or late curl versus play-action passes.

9 technique to the tight end or tackle over: Aligns on the line of scrimmage with the inside foot splitting the crotch of the tight end; keys through tight end to the fullback. Quarterback player versus all options. If the tight end blocks down, spills the first threat. If dropback or play-action pass to or away, drops into pass coverage; must be aware of wheel on turnaround motion versus play-action away. If unbalanced, must be alert to peel with the trail pass by the motion back.

Stud to backside of unbalanced: If cover 3, makes a pigeon call to the corner; this call alerts the corner that the Stud plays a 9 technique and has pitch on the option. If cover 6, makes a "quail" call to the corner; this call alerts the corner that the Stud has the quarterback on option.

Versus a back on the line of scrimmage: Plays position as if he is invisible because he will hardly ever block the Falcon or Stud from that alignment.

"I'm here" and "I'm gone" calls: Alerts the linebackers as to whether they will need to replace the Stud or Falcon in pass coverage. Stud or Falcon drop into coverage on the "I'm here" call. Stud or Falcon blitz on the "I'm gone" call, and the linebacker must replace him in coverage.

Secondary

A number of different ways exist to provide secondary run support versus the option. In whatever way is planned, whether zone or man, the secondary should be coached to support the run aggressively, but still be able to defend the play-action pass.

The corners align outside the wide receiver until the receiver goes outside the numbers. All four defensive backs key through the uncovered linemen and are always aware of the release of the #2 receiver. Must know which way the front is aligned: the linebackers can raise an arm to indicate which is the 59 or 46 side. If the option is run to the 59 side, the quarterback will probably give the ball to the fullback; if to the 46 side, the quarterback will probably keep the ball.

Three kinds of keys can trigger the defensive backs reactions:
• Sure run (low hat of linemen).
• Sure pass (high hat of linemen).
    ✓ Playside tackle and guard turn back protection block.
    ✓ Backside tackle hinges off the line of scrimmage.
• Unsure key: keep shuffling (never trigger on an unsure key).

Secondary Responsibilities Versus Run Strong and Weak
(Figures 20-18 and 20-19)

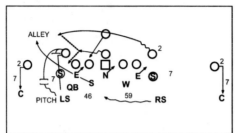 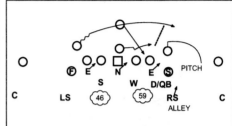

Figure 20-18. 50 cover 3 run support to 46 side versus double slot

Figure 20-19. 50 cover 3 run support to 59 side versus double slot

Strong Corner: Outside third; plays the pass first, the run second. Reads the release of #1; must be alert for a crack block by the outside receiver. If crack back, makes a "crack" call; the release angle of the receiver and height of numbers determine the threat of the crack pass, and how quickly the corner should run support. If slot outside releases, squeezes from the outside-in. If the wide receiver releases flat with low numbers, indicates run; if upfield release with high number, indicates the crack pass.

Left Safety: Attacks the outside shoulder of arc block; has pitch responsibility, and keeps outside leverage.

Right Safety: Must know which way the front is moving. The raised arm of the linebacker indicates the 59 or 46 side. Clears the dive on the run, and plays inside-out to the alley (quarterback to pitch). Remember, if the front is to flow, thinks fullback; if the front is away from flow, thinks alley.

Both Safeties: Initial move on flow away is a shuffle to help get a run-pass read from the offensive line and motion (two-step motion, turnaround motion, etc.). The goal is to shuffle to the A gap with a better angle as an alley player, and be able to react back quicker to turnaround motion on the trap option.

Weak Corner: Plays an inside-third position, man coverage on the wide receiver with motion away, and deep pursuit on the run after checking for the reverse.

Safety and Stud (to the 59 side): Two ways exist to play run toward:
- If the slot arc blocks, the Stud has the pitch, and the safety is the alley player and has the quarterback outside and pitch inside. If the slot loads inside or folds inside, the Stud mirrors the slot from the outside-in and has the quarterback; the safety has the pitch (true rollover player). On the 59 side, the linebacker and end play a tackle-box read with one of them on the quarterback and the other the fullback, determined by the blocking pattern of the guard and tackle.
- The other way is for the Stud to widen and become the alley player from the line of scrimmage; he plays the quarterback outside and the pitch inside. The safety is the pitch player; he plays through the arc block. If the slot loads or folds, the Stud mirrors him and plays the quarterback from the outside-in; the safety has the pitch.

Cover 3 Coverage Versus the Play-Action Pass Strong and Weak
(Figures 20-20 and 20-21)

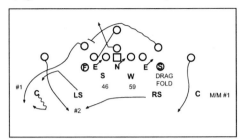

Figure 20-20. 50 cover 3 versus play-action pass to the 46 side

Figure 20-21. 50 cover 3 versus play-action pass to the 59 side

Strong Corner: Plays the fade/wheel route; uses a divider technique so he can squeeze the post.

Left Safety: Plays the wheel by the slotback (wheel becomes #1). Runs with the wheel to force the elevated throw by the quarterback, and must be in position to make the quarterback throw the ball through him or over him on the stop-wheel route.

Right Safety: If he gets a high hat read, reads to the #2 receiver strongside. Must be ready to carry #2 on the vertical. If #2 is outside, expands with depth to the post route by the #1 receiver.

Weak Corner: Plays inside position on #1 (man).

Secondary: Reacts to the play-action pass weak the same way as versus the play-action pass strong.

50 Cover 3 Secondary Run Support Versus Tight End and Wing
(Figure 20-22)

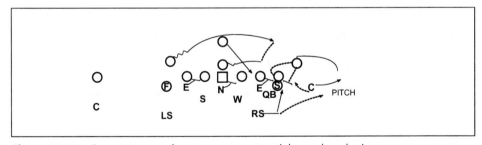

Figure 20-22. Cover 3 secondary run support to tight end and wing

Regardless of the coverage called (cover 3, cover 6, Sally with pinch), they are all played the same way versus the tight end/wing formation (cloud call).

Tight Corner: Aligns two yards outside the Stud at a depth of two yards. With the "cloud" call, he mirrors the slotback. If the slot arc blocks, plays pitch; if the slot load blocks, plays outside-in on the quarterback; if the slot fold blocks, mirrors the slot, and plays the quarterback inside the Stud.

Right Safety: Aligns in the B gap at seven yards deep. Shuffles for width, and reads the uncovered linemen for run-pass recognition. If run, fits opposite the corner with a rollover technique. If the slot loads or folds, plays pitch; if the slot arc blocks, plays the quarterback from the inside-out. If the slot blocks the safety, fights outside the block and forces the ball back to the unblocked defender (backside safety).

Left Safety: Reads the uncovered linemen for run-pass recognition. Must be aware of the direction of the defensive line with respect to the quarterback's reads (59 side, fullback give; 46 side, quarterback keep) and brings the ball outside (alley player from the inside-out).

Strong Corner: Man-to-man coverage on the #1 receiver backside. Checks the reverse and takes a deep pursuit angle.

Stud/Falcon: Versus any tight end or tackle over (three-man surface), the Stud or Falcon plays the quarterback on option. If the tight end blocks down, spills the first threat; if flow away, checks the reverse and bootleg. Makes a "quail" call to the corner to alert him that the Stud has the quarterback on option.

Cover 3 Secondary Run Support Away From the Tight End and the Wing (Figure 20-23)

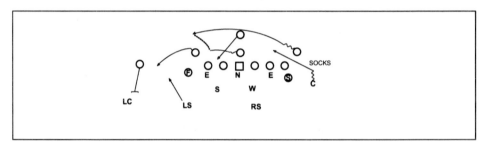

Figure 20-23. Cover 3 secondary run support away from the tight end and the wing

Run support away from the tight end and wing is the same as versus double slot, except the tight corner can socks (automatic blitz) from the backside or man the tight end.

Cover 3 Coverage Versus Play-Action Pass to the Tight End and the Wing (Figure 20-24)

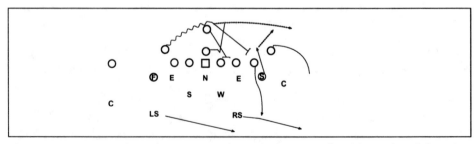

Figure 20-24. Cover 3 coverage versus play-action pass to the tight end and the wing

Tight Corner: Rolls with the wing's wheel route.

Right Safety: Plays over top of the corner and expands with the wheel.

Left Safety: Reads on the run. If he gets a pass read, must be ready to carry the tight end on the vertical.

Strong Corner: Man-to-man on the wide receiver from the inside-out.

Stud: Rushes the passer, and applies the "peel rule" if the motion man flares.

Cover 3 Versus Play-Action Pass Away From the Tight End and the Wing—Tight End Vertical and Wing Wheel (Figure 20-25)

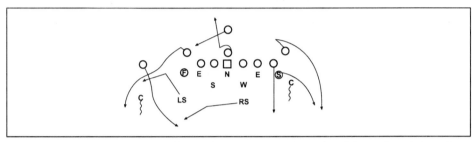

Figure 20-25. Cover 3 versus play-action pass away from the tight end and the wing (tight end vertical and wing wheel)

Strong Corner: Same as post/wheel versus double slot.

Stud: Loosens the alignment with wing motion; mans the wing if he wheels.

Left Safety: Same as post/wheel versus double slot.

Right Safety: Same as post/wheel versus double slot; keys #2 for vertical or outside routes.

Tight Corner: Gets depth with motion, and must be alert to carry the tight end on the vertical.

Cover 6 Versus Play-Action Pass to the Strongside (Figure 20-26)

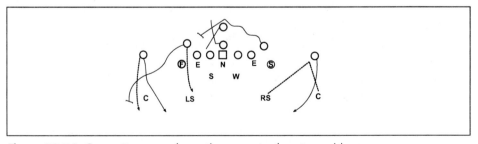

Figure 20-26. Cover 6 versus play-action pass to the strongside

Strong Corner and Left Safety: Plays combo; reads the release of the #2 receiver. If #1 and #2 go vertical, the corner carries #1, and the safety carries #2 and runs with the up route. If #2 goes to the flat (becomes #1), the corner sinks for the flat or wheel route, and the safety carries the #1 receiver on the post.

Falcon: Late buzzes to force the quarterback to elevate the ball on the wheel route, and forces the ball to be thrown over or through the Falcon on the wheel stop.

Right Safety: If he gets a turnback look from the offensive tackle and #2 (slotback) motions past the #1 (fullback), brackets #1 with the weak corner.

Cover 6 Run Support Versus Option Strong (Figure 20-27)

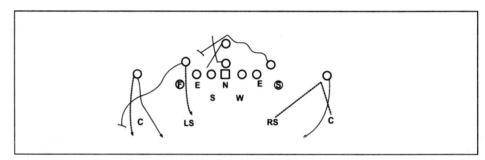

Figure 20-27. Cover 6 run support versus option strong

Strong Corner: Plays inside the stalk block of the wide receiver, then cross-faces back outside to reduce the running lane. If he gets a crack-back block by the wide receiver, calls "crack" and squeezes the arc block of the slot from the outside-in, forcing the pitch back inside. Attacks the arc block and squeezes the running lane aggressively as he crack replaces the safety.

Left Safety and Falcon: The Falcon is a 9 technique; he can play the pitch and the quarterback with the safety one of two ways. Both the Falcon and the safety read the slotback's release; they play a rollover principle with the Falcon mirroring the release of the slot, and the safety does the opposite.

- Option #1: If the slot arcs, the Falcon plays the pitch; the safety rocks down as the alley player, and plays the quarterback outside and the pitch inside. Must remember that, to the 59 side, either the linebacker or the defensive end has the quarterback inside based on the blocking scheme of the offense. If the slot loads inside or folds inside, the Falcon mirrors the slot from the outside-in and has the quarterback; the safety rocks down and has the pitch (true rollover).
- Option #2: If the slot arcs (Figure 20-28), the Falcon widens with the arc block and becomes the alley player from the line of scrimmage; he plays the quarterback outside and the pitch inside. The safety plays the pitch. If the slot loads or folds (Figure 20-29), the Falcon still mirrors the slot and plays the quarterback from outside in; the safety rolls over for the pitch.

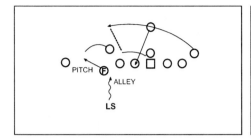

Figure 20-28. Falcon and safety versus slot arc

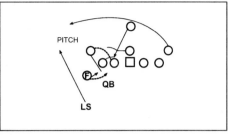

Figure 20-29. Falcon and safety versus slot load or fold

Right Safety: Gets depth initially, and must be aware of which way the defensive front moves with the flow of the ball; thinks give to the fullback into the 59 side clearing the dive and then works inside-out to the alley.

Weak Corner: Gets depth, checks for reverse and then deep pursuit angle.

Cover 6 Secondary Run Support Versus Option Weak (Figure 20-30)

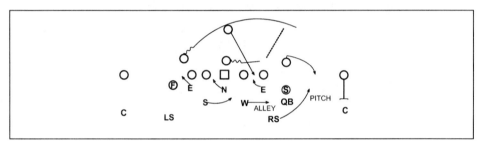

Figure 20-30. Cover 6 secondary run support versus option weak

The secondary plays option weak the same as cover 3 when the option is run to the strongside.

Cover 6 Coverage Versus Play-Action Pass Weak (Figure 20-31)

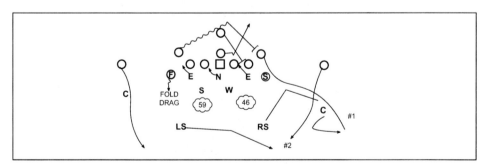

Figure 20-31. Cover 6 coverage versus play-action pass weak

Weak Corner: Must be alert for the post/wheel route to the 46 side; weak corner plays a divider technique and is responsible for the wheel and squeezes the post.

Right Safety: Plays under the wheel by the #1 receiver (slotback); the wheel becomes #1, and the post becomes #2 as the routes unfold. Safety runs with the wheel so he can force the elevated throw by the quarterback and be in position to make the quarterback throw the ball through him or over him on the stop-wheel route.

Left Safety: Reads the #2 receiver to the weakside; must be ready to carry #2 on the vertical. If #2 is outside, expands with depth to the post of the new #2 receiver.

Falcon: Drops and looks for the drag route, or folds to the draw.

Cover-6 Adjustments

Cover 6 Versus Wide Slot (Figure 20-32): If the slot is removed wide, the Falcon plays the quarterback, and the safety plays the pitch.

Cover 6 Cloud Versus Tight End Wing (Figure 20-23): The secondary plays cloud coverage to the tight end and wing side on both cover 3 and 6.

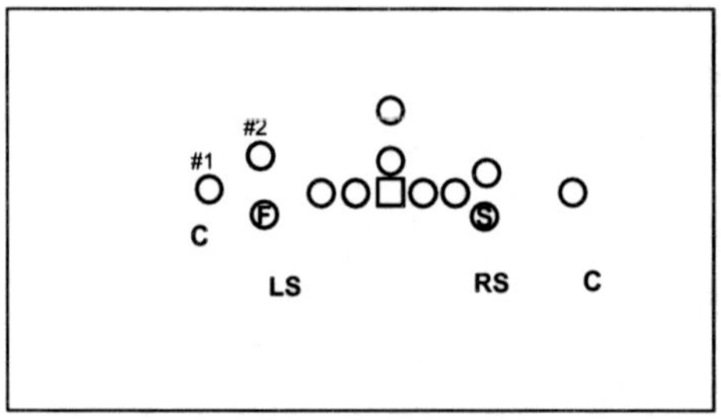

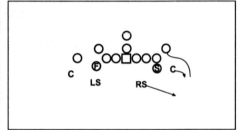

Figure 20-32. Cover 6 versus wide slot   Figure 20-33. Cover 6 cloud versus tight end wing

Cover 6 Double Combo Versus Double Slot With No Motion (Figure 20-34): The secondary plays combo to both sides versus double slot with no motion. The corners and safeties pattern read off #2. If #2 goes vertical, the corner and the safety match up on #1 and #2. If #2 goes to the flat, the corner settles and sinks; the safety reads release of #1 for fade, post, or post-corner.

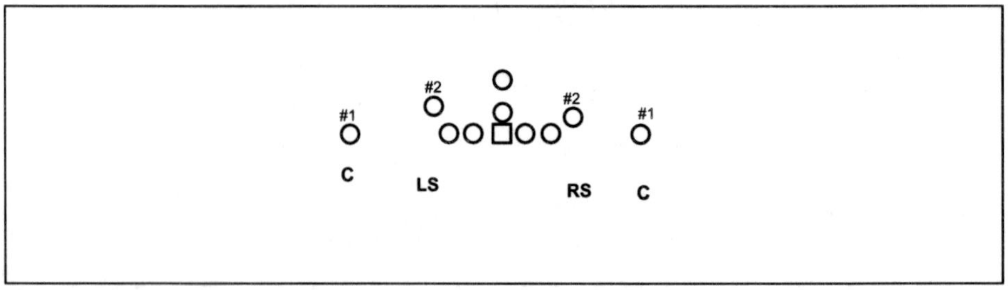

Figure 20-34. Cover 6 double combo versus double slot with no motion

Match-Up Zone

Match-Up Zone Secondary Coverage Responsibilities
(Figures 20-35 through 20-38)

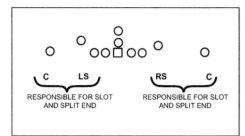

Figure 20-35. Versus double slot

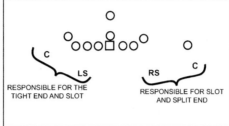

Figure 20-36. Versus tight end and wing

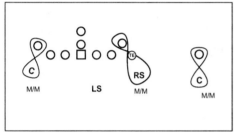

Figure 20-37. Versus tight end unbalanced with one receiver backside

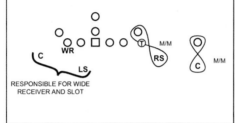

Figure 20-38. Versus tackle over unbalanced with two receivers backside

Match-Up Run Support Reads (Figures 20-39 and 20-40)

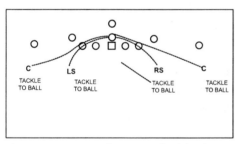

Figure 20-39. Reads versus double slot

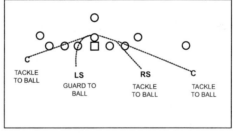

Figure 20-40. Reads versus tight end and wing

Match-Up Zone Run Support to the Split End (Figure 20-41)

The corner and safety fight through or outside the stalk/arc, or switch blocks and force the ball back to the unblocked defenders. The left safety (backside safety) should be aware of the direction the defensive front is moving. If the front moving to flow, thinks fullback; if the front moving away from flow, thinks alley (quarterback to pitch). The backside corner checks for the reverse and counter, and then takes a deep pursuit angle.

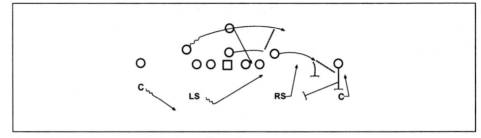

Figure 20-41. Run support to the split end

Match-Up Zone Run Support to Tight End and Wing (or to Nub Side of an Unbalanced Formation) (Figure 20-42)

The Stud makes a "quail" call ("I'm taking the quarterback") to the corner; the corner moves to the line of scrimmage, and keeps leverage on the quarterback and pitch. The left safety fights outside the slot's block and turns the ball back to the unblocked defender (backside safety). Backside corner checks the reverse and counter, and then takes a deep pursuit angle.

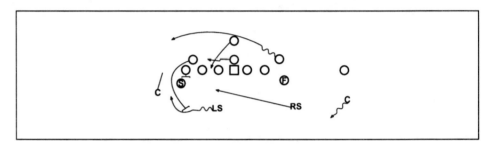

Figure 20-42. Run support to the tight end and wing

Match-Up Zone Run Support to Unbalanced Formation (Figure 20-43)

The corner and the right safety should always be outside the block of the arc or switch block; they force the ball back to the unblocked defender (left safety). Left safety fights across the block of the tackle or tight end. The Falcon (9 technique) punches the tackle to prevent a free release on the safety; he plays the quarterback to a three-man surface.

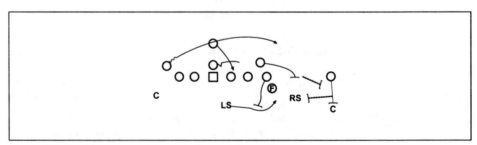

Figure 20-43. Run support to unbalanced formation

Match-Up Coverage (Figures 20-44 through 20-49)

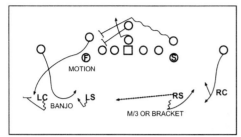

Figure 20-44. Versus play-action pass with motion from double slot

Figure 20-45. Versus play-action pass with no motion from double slot

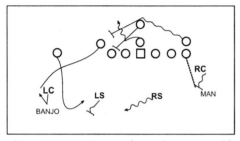
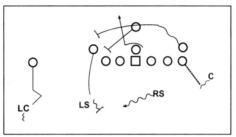

Figure 20-46. Versus play-action pass with motion from the tight end and wing

Figure 20-47. Versus play-action pass with motion from the tight end and wing

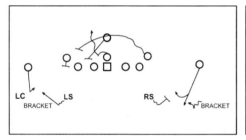
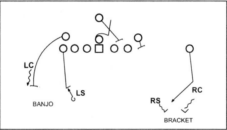

Figure 20-48. Versus play-action pass (two receivers) from double slot

Figure 20-49. Versus play-action pass away from the tight end and wing

50 Front Versus the Option

- The 50 front has been covered in detail in earlier chapters, but it is important to review some basic concepts before moving forward with a discussion of the 50 front versus the option.

- The nose tackle and defensive ends align head-up so no pre-snap reads exist with regard to where the 59 and 46 (reduction) side will be.

- The 59 side is always to the Roger or Larry call (the exception is 50 pinch, which is a 46 to both sides).

- Roger or Larry call can be switched to the 46 side if the offense is picking up the call and making adjustments.

- The front is set with the following three calls (50 tilt/50 numbers is not used versus the flex bone option teams):

  ✓ 50 field/50 boundary (ball on hash)

✓ 50 formation/50 weak (middle of field)

✓ 50 tight/50 split

- Change-ups from the 59 side include base, blast, and fold.
- Change-up from the 46 side include attack, angle, A, and exchange.
- The 50 is not used in the huddle call. The call is simply field/boundary, formation/weak, or tight/split.
- The Falcon and Sam go to the formation or field; the Stud and Will go away from the formation or into the boundary.
- Corners and safeties go left and right. However, it is possible to flip them to play to the strengths of the secondary.
- When pinch (reduction to both sides) is called with attack, angle, A, or exchange, it is understood that they are stunts from both sides (double).
- A directional zero call for the nose is made to have him get a knock back on the center and not an angle charge. The nose squeezes toward flow rather than back door like he does on pinch.

50 Stunts

(Figures 20-50 through 20-59)

The 50 stunts are called: field/boundary, formation/weak, or tight/split. The 59 side is always to the side of the call; the 46 side is always away.

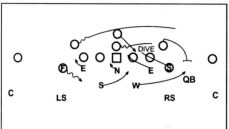

Figure 20-50. Formation A cover 3 (Larry call)

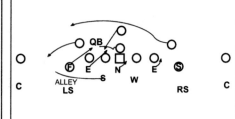

Figure 20-51. Weak angle cover 6 (Roger call)

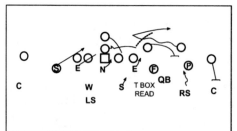

Figure 20-52. Field A cover 6 (Roger call)

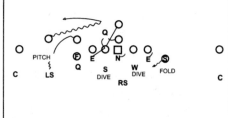

Figure 20-53. Boundary exchange cover 3 (Roger call)

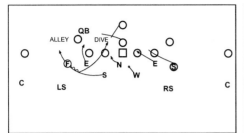

Figure 20-54. Formation fold A cover 6 (Larry call)

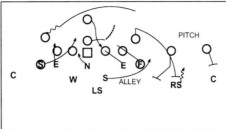

Figure 20-55. Weak fold angle cover 3 (Larry call)

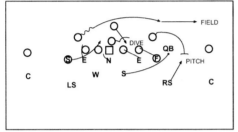

Figure 20-56. Boundary fold A cover 3 (Larry call)

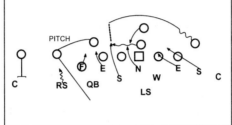

Figure 20-57. Formation blast angle cover 6 (Larry call)

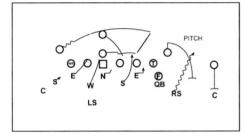

Figure 20-58. Tight blast attack cover 6 (Roger call)

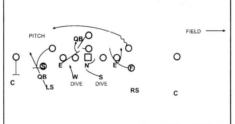

Figure 20-59. Field fold exchange cover 6 (Roger call)

33 Front

The 33 front is a 50 defense change-up that becomes a 43 alignment by moving the front seven defenders (Figure 20-60). The 33 is only called on the hash mark to keep the front sound and simple with very little adjustment of personnel. Coverages played with the 33 include Sally, two, and two backer (similar to the pinch). Stunts are mirrored to both sides of the defense. The front can stem from the 50 to the 33, and vice versa to create confusion for the offense. A "stem" call can facilitate the stem of the front players. The three defensive linemen slide to the boundary, and the linebackers and Stud slide to the field on a "move" call by the Sam.

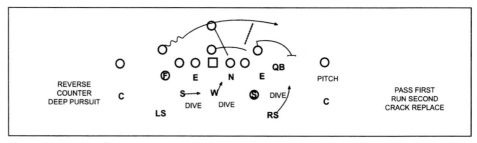

Figure 20-60. 33 front

The defensive end and nose align head-up on the guards to eliminate pre-snap reads. The Sam and Stud align in a heavy 50 over the tackles. The Falcon and defensive end align in a heavy 9 on the slotbacks.

Base 33 Sally (Figure 20-61): Falcon and defensive end over the slotbacks have the quarterback/crease (first threat outside the tackle) on flow to; they check the reverse and bootleg as they chase the hip of tackle on flow away; they rush the pass on dropback and play-action pass to, drop on play-action away, and check for slot drag or draw. Sam and Stud are responsible for dive on flow to, backside A or B gap (fit off the defensive end and the nose) on flow away, and drop over #2 on dropback (with no motion). Will (middle linebacker) fits into the A or B gap to flow; he reads blitz on all pass (dropback and play-action). The defensive linemen over the guards play a base technique; they attack vertical and try to get upfield on the guards.

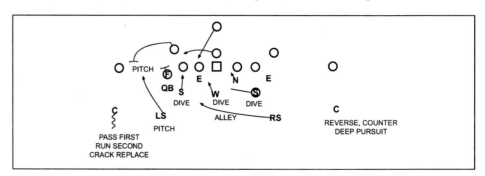

Figure 20-61. Base 33 Sally

33 Stunts (Figures 20-62 through 20-66)

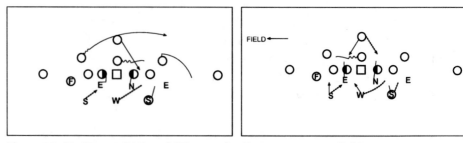

Figure 20-62. 33 ant (NG and DE control the A gaps)

Figure 20-63. 33 field

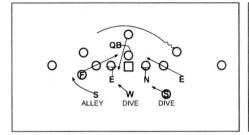

Figure 20-64. 33 base angle

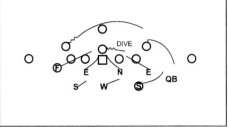

Figure 20-65. 33 A

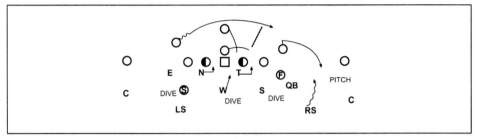

Figure 20-66. 33 formation bat (Roger call)

33 Front Adjustments

Versus the Midline (Figure 20-67): It is important for the Sam to stay outside the fold block, and Will to stay inside.

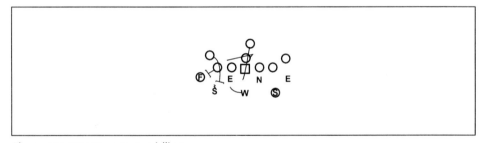

Figure 20-67. 33 versus midline

Versus the Nose (Figure 20-68): 33 nose is a good short-yardage and goal-line call. The Will should stem late to the nose alignment.

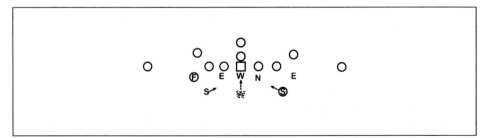

Figure 20-68. 33 versus nose (Sam/Stud move to 30 technique)

Versus Two Backer (Figure 20-69): 33 two backer is a good third-and-medium to -long situation call. The Sam and Stud wall the #2 receiver from the inside-out; they cut and carry the drag, and run with the vertical; if #2 goes outside, they expand to a new #2. The Will read blitzes versus pass. The corners and safeties read #2; if #2 goes vertical, the corner carries #1 on fade, and the safety carries #2. If #2 goes to the flat, the corner plays the flat and wheel, and the safety pushes outside for post, fade, and post corner.

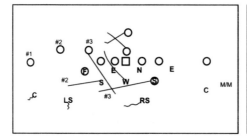

Figure 20-69. 33 versus two backer

Versus Trips (Figure 20-70 and 20-71): Will and Stud can make "you/me" call; Will drops over #3; Stud is responsible for screen, first crosser, and second-level help on the draw. The corner and the left safety read #2 and #3 as one, with the right safety in "key" coverage on #3. The right safety carries #3 on vertical; if #3 drags weak, the right safety is the late bracket on the #1 receiver with the backside corner.

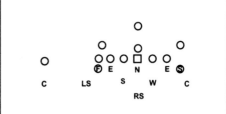

Figure 20-70. 33 versus trips

Figure 20-71. Check out of 33 to a 50 pinch or 50 formation versus a three-man surface (unbalanced or tight end and wing)

Defending Formations and Specific Plays

Trips Run (Midline) (Figures 20-72 and 20-73)

The preferred defense versus trips is a 50 with the 59 side to the trips. 59 on the midline side provides a good squeeze on the tackle's turnout block by the defensive end, and a mirror/match by the Falcon. The Sam plays inside the fold, and the Falcon plays outside. A good change-up is to place the 46 side to trips with an "exchange" or "A" call to successfully defend the midline. By being in a 4 technique to the trips, the defense loses its ability to mirror/match the fold with the outside backer. The exchange brings the unblocked defensive end to the quarterback and eliminates him as a ballcarrier. The A stunt takes away the inside seams in the A and B gaps as the defensive end and Falcon cross the face of all turnout blocks, which forces the quarterback to bounce outside into a scrape linebacker and secondary run support. The linebackers can stem late to try to nullify the fold, but mix up the call between a 59 backside and a 46 backside (Figure 20-73).

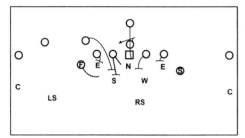 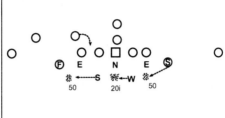

Figure 20-72. Trips midline

Figure 20-73. Linebackers stem to nullify the fold block on the midline

The offensive answer to these defensive adjustments is to give to the fullback on the triple option, and speed option to the split-end side. With the 59 side to the split-end side, the defense can eliminate the success of the speed option, yet may not be able to hold up the fullback on the triple option if the quarterback gets a read into the 59 side. A 46 base and A or angle provide a chance for success with the linebacker running to the alley. Also, a cloud to the backside is a change-up to get quick run support to the pitch from the corner.

Trips Pass (Figure 20-74)

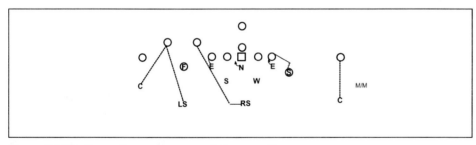

Figure 20-74. Formation angle cover 6 (Larry call)

Strong Corner and Left Safety: Combo coverage; they read #2 receiver. If #2 goes vertical, both carry #1 and #2 on up route. If #2 goes to the flat, the corner levels and sinks, the safety plays #1 on the post, fade, and post-corner. If the corner gets a bubble read, he immediately drives on #3 in bubble.

Falcon: Makes the "I'm here" call to the Sam; drops over #2 as curl/yogi/late flat player; takes away the inside part of the curl.

Right Safety: Reads the #3 receiver; takes him on the vertical. If #3 drags weak; the right safety goes backside to bracket with the corner on inside cuts by #1. If #3 releases outside, the right safety maintains depth and pushes outside to #2. If #3 blocks, the safety goes weak to help on #1.

Weak Corner: Mans on #1.

Stud: Makes the "I'm gone" call to Will, which alerts him to an angle stunt to the weakside.

Sam: Drops over #3 and gets ready to cut the slant and wheel (with the dig) routes. If #3 goes outside, Sam pushes outside, and looks for a new #3.

Will: Back, screen, first crosser, late help on intermediate cuts by #1.

Cover 3 Skate Check Versus Trips (Figure 20-75)

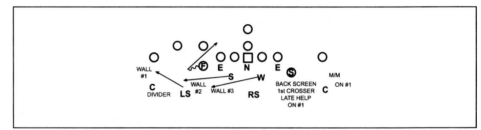

Figure 20-75. Cover 3 skate check

Strong Corner: Runs a divider technique and if #2 goes to the flat, drives on the inside cut of #1.

Left Safety: Buzzes the flat; carries the wheel by #2. Identifies the flat receiver (#1) on the smash route.

Right Safety: Middle third, and reads from #3, #2, to #1. Gives post help to the weak corner.

Falcon: Makes a "heads" call to Sam and rushes the quarterback.

Sam and Will: Pushes to #2 and #3; walls them from the inside-out; must be alert to cut the slant, wheel with the dig, and carry the vertical. If the receivers go out, looks for a new #2 and #3 receiver.

Stud: Back, screen, first crosser, late help on #1. Makes the "I'm here" call to the Will.

Zero (Man Coverage) Versus Various Formations and Motion

Zero Versus Double Slot (Figure 20-76): The left and right safeties can banjo.

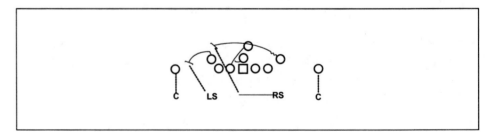

Figure 20-76. Zero versus double slot

Zero Versus Trips (Figure 20-77)

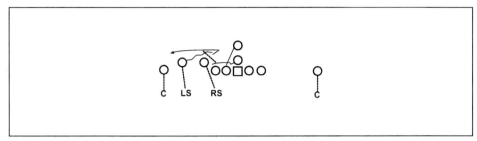

Figure 20-77. Zero versus trips

Zero Versus Unbalanced Split With Motion Toward Split (Figures 20-78 and 20-79): The #2 receiver is ineligible. The Left safety should move to a head up alignment and keep him from crack blocking the right safety; can blitz on pass or peel with the trail pass to help the backside corner.

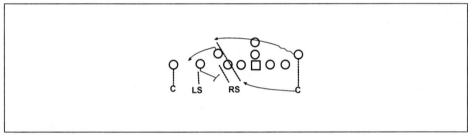

Figure 20-78. Zero versus unbalanced split with motion toward split

Zero Versus Unbalanced Split With Motion Away From Split (Figure 20-79): The right safety and the weak corner can banjo.

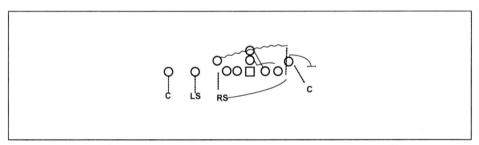

Figure 20-79. Zero versus unbalanced split with motion away from split

Zero Versus Tackle Over Unbalanced (Figure 20-80): The right safety and weak corner initially banjo before motion. After motion, the right and left safeties can banjo.

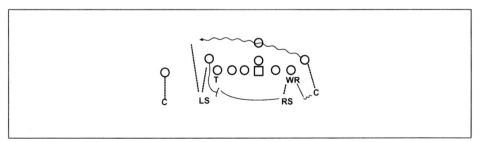

Figure 20-80. Zero versus tackle over unbalanced

Zero Versus Tackle Blocking the Alley (Figure 20-81): When the defense plays a lot of zero, the offense will try to release the tackle or guard upfield to block the alley safety coming from the backside.

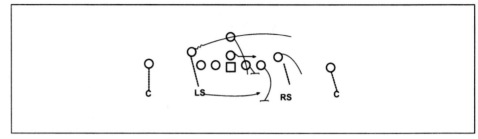

Figure 20-81. Zero versus tackle blocking the alley

Defending the Unbalanced Tackle Over

The Front Defenders (Figures 20-82 and 20-83)

The defense can play 46 (reduction) or 59 to the three-man surface, depending on the type of plays the opponent likes to run from the unbalanced formation. The 59 is preferred if the offense runs a heavy dose of the lead option or sweep. Offenses also like to run more of the fullback on outside veer G with the quarterback follow, and the midline power, which makes the reduction (46) to the three-man side the better alignment. It is important regardless of whether 59 or 46 to the unbalanced surface that the linebackers slide and stack.

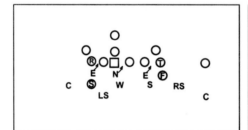

Figure 20-82. 50 formation with linebackers stacked

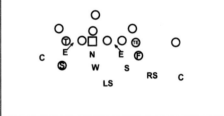

Figure 20-83. 50 pinch with linebackers stacked

Falcon Heavy 9 Technique: Plays the quarterback.

Sam: Makes a tackle-box read with the 5 technique, but must be heavy on the fullback (Falcon has the quarterback).

Will: Mirrors the fullback on flow.

Stud: Quarterback (46) or pitch (59) player on flow toward. If flow away, the Stud is already in the fold position (59); if to the reduction side (46), checks for the reverse or bootleg.

Nose: The nose should try to not move away from the three-man surface, so the primary calls should be formation/tight, and pinch. If a reduction (46) is called to the unbalanced side, the nose should get a directional zero so he is in better shape to help to the three-man side (50 weak zero).

The defense can still align in the stack with an "angle" or "A" call on the backside, which involves the Stud. The Stud starts in the stack alignment, and stems late to run the angle or A stunt.

If the offense motions to the backside (two-man surface), the linebackers all slide back to their original position and play the defense called. A "lock" call keeps the linebackers in their non-stack alignment (50 lock formation), or they can start in the stack and stem to the non-stack alignment before the snap.

Depending on whether the defense is in a 46 or 59 to the two-man surface, the Stud makes a call to alert the corner how the option will be played. If 46 (reduction), the Stud makes a "quail" call, which tells the corner that the Stud has the quarterback. If 59, the Stud makes a "pigeon" call, which tells the corner that the Stud is the pitch player. The Stud has the quarterback (quail) or pitch (pigeon), regardless of the slotback release. With a "quail" call, the corner mirrors/matches the slot (arc, pitch, load or fold, quarterback). With a "pigeon" call, the corner has the quarterback outside; the defensive end or linebacker has the quarterback inside, depending on the blocking scheme of the offense (tackle-box read).

Secondary Run Support (Figures 20-84 through 20-91)

The secondary can play either man or zone versus the unbalanced formation. The run support is the same in both coverages. Both provide rollover support, plus the slotback fold can be handled to the two-man and strongside (safety). The backside safety adjusts his alignment versus either one or two receivers backside to improve run support.

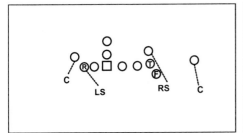

Figure 20-84. Safety alignment to two receivers backside

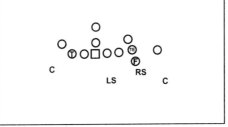

Figure 20-85. Safety alignment to one receiver backside

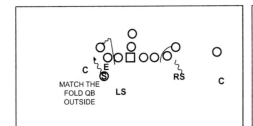

Figure 20-86. Versus slot fold

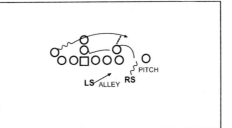

Figure 20-87. Versus slot arc

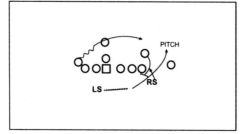

Figure 20-88. Versus slot load

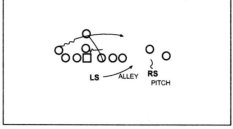

Figure 20-89. Versus wide slot (rollover is off)

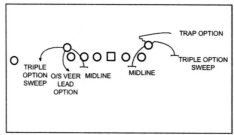

Figure 20-90. Understanding the slots releases (play tendencies)

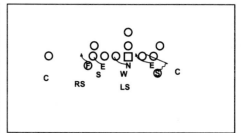

Figure 20-91. 50 formation loop (base, A, or angle to backside)

Zone Coverage Versus an Unbalanced Formation (Figure 20-92)

It is critically important to know all the eligible receivers versus unbalance formations. The secondary can play combo coverage to both sides, and read the #2 receiver. The Falcon should be in peel alert so that he is in position to take the trail flare by the motion back.

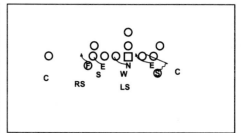

Figure 20-92. Zone coverage versus an unbalanced formation

Orange Coverage (Figure 20-93)

Orange coverage gives the defense the opportunity to attack the unbalanced from the strongside. The Falcon reads the block of the tight end or tackle over. The Falcon cross-faces a turnout block; has the quarterback on the option; chases the hip of the tight end or tackle down block, and spills the first threat in the C gap. The defensive end cross-faces the turnout block, chases the hip of the guard on the down block, and spills first threat. The nose can angle or play a directional zero. The Will and defensive end tackle-box read on the backside. The left safety slides up late and blitzes from the edge. The strong corner has pitch support; if the wide receiver has widened the run lane with his split, the strong corner makes a "slice" call to the safety, which alerts the safety that corner will play the pitch flat and quick. The right safety aligns over the strong-side guard; on snap, he gets width and depth and reads the #1 receiver. The backside corner reads to the #2 receiver strong, and must be alert for #2 vertical. The Stud is man on the backside receiver.

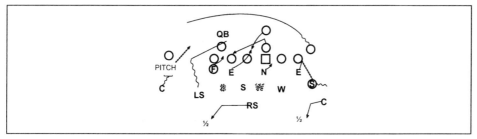

Figure 20-93. Formation flood orange coverage

Match Coverage Versus Tackle Over (Figure 20-94)

This front is primarily used against tackle over if the Falcon is having a hard time holding up versus the tackle. Two calls can be made to help if this situation occurs: match 50 formation and match 50 pinch. These calls align the backside defensive end over the tackle to the three-man surface. The Falcon aligns over the receiver on the backside in a stand-up 6 technique. The Falcon cannot be placed in a 5 technique because it requires a tackle-box read.

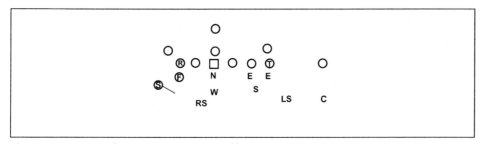

Figure 20-94. Match coverage versus tackle over

Blitzes Versus Unbalanced (Figures 20-95 through 20-97)

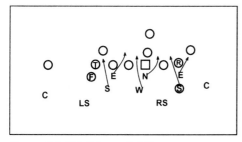
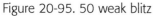

Figure 20-95. 50 weak blitz

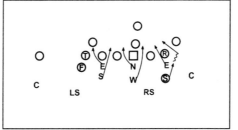

Figure 20-96. 50 formation blitz

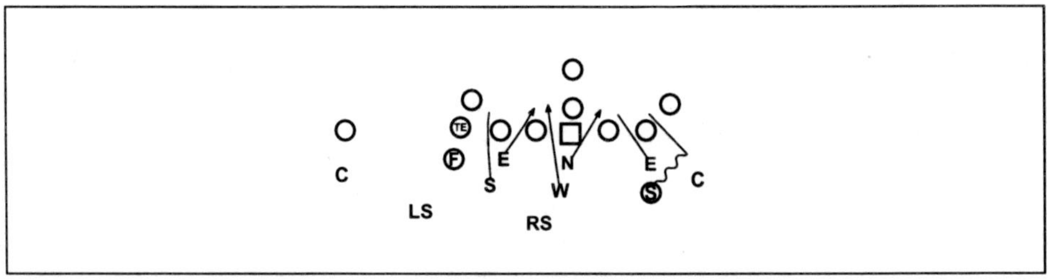

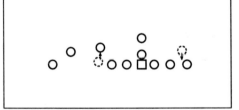

Figure 20-97. 50 pinch blitz

Versus Split Unbalanced With No Three-Man Surface

- *Split unbalanced formation (#2 not eligible)* (Figure 20-98): Defensive coverage personnel must know who the eligible receivers are. The #2 receiver to the strongside is not eligible. If he releases downfield, it is not pass, because he is not eligible; if he flares behind the line of scrimmage, be alert for the pass. The linebackers do not slide. With long motion from the backside slot, the backside corner blitzes; he does not blitz with short motion.

- *Slotbacks move up and back to trips* (Figure 20-99): The offense changes formations when they walk the two slotbacks up and back. The defense must be able to recognize the new formation and identify the eligible receivers quickly.

- *Split unbalanced with switch block to the split side* (Figure 20-100): The two safeties check out of rollover strong. They should expect the switch block to the split side.

- *Safety in press alignment on #2* (Figure 20-101): The safety walks up to press alignment over #2; the defense does not let #2 off inside to block the safety. The safety will also blitz from this press alignment so he is in position to disrupt the offense with penetration.

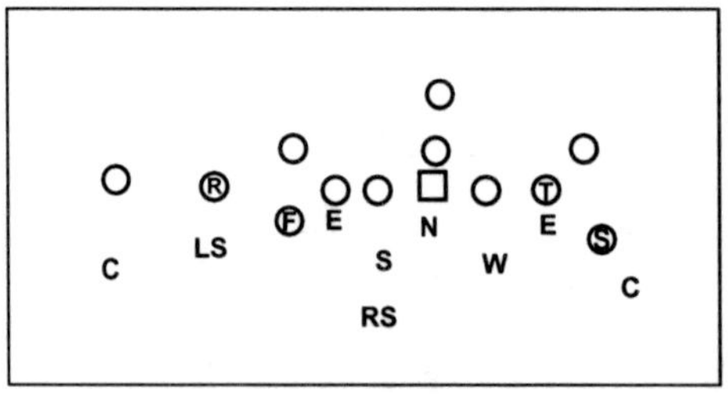

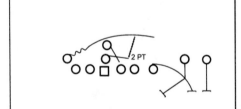

Figure 20-98. Split unbalanced formation (#2 not eligible)

Figure 20-99. Slotbacks move up and back to trips

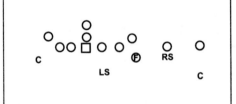

Figure 20-100. Split unbalanced with switch block to the split side

Figure 20-101. Safety in press alignment on #2

Know What the Offense Is Trying to Do With the Alignment of the Backs

- *Slotback Is Not Eligible, and No Pitchman Exists to the Backside* (Figure 20-102): Strongside plays emphasis—triple option and midline option with the switch block.
- *Slotback Is Eligible, and No Pitchman Exists to the Frontside* (Figure 20-103): Backside plays emphasis—triple option, and midline power.
- *Unbalanced Split* (Figure 20-104): Unbalanced split plays emphasis—triple option strong with the switch block; trap, and trap option weak with turnback motion.
- *Play-Action Pass Backside* (Figure 20-105)

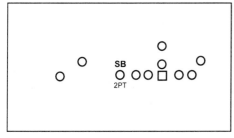

Figure 20-102. Slotback is not eligible, and no pitchman exists to the backside

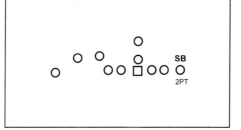

Figure 20-103. No pitchman exists to the frontside.

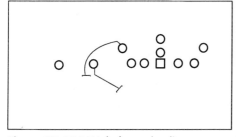

Figure 20-104. Unbalanced split

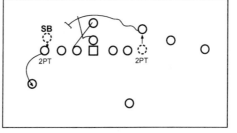

Figure 20-105. Play-action pass backside

Super Unbalanced

The right safety makes a "super/super" call (Figure 20-106). Two coverage options exist with the "super" call: skate or Z spin.

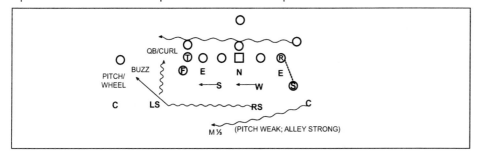

Figure 20-106. 50 super versus super unbalanced

- *Skate:* The left safety rocks down and aligns 3x3 outside the Falcon; he has the quarterback outside and the pitch inside versus the run; walls #2 versus the pass. The right safety drops down over the motion man (seven yards deep) and has pitch responsibility on the run, and flat wheel versus the pass. The weak corner rotates to middle third to help the strong corner on the post, and the Stud on the receiver to the backside; the weak corner is the alley player strong versus run. The strong corner plays an inside third because the weak corner may be limited in playing the middle third. The Stud is man on the backside receiver; quarterback outside, and pitch inside regardless of whether he is a 6 or 9 technique. The Sam drops over #3 versus the pass. The Will can read blitz or take the back, screen, and first crosser.

- *Z-Spin Formation or Orange Flood Check* (Figures 20-107 and 20-108)

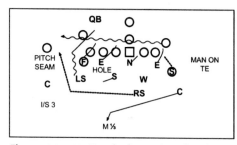

Figure 20-107. Z-spin formation flood check

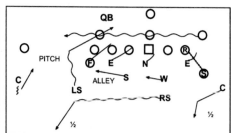

Figure 20-108. Orange flood check

Pass Situation Blitzes

(Figures 20-109 through 20-112)

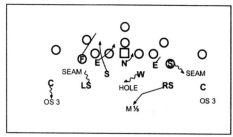

Figure 20-109. Formation/field thunder Z

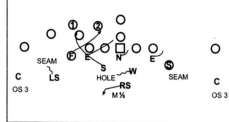

Figure 20-110. Formation/field thunder switch Z

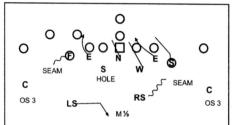

Figure 20-111. Boundary/weak thunder attack

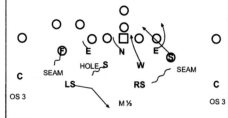

Figure 20-112. Boundary/weak thunder attack echo

Formation Thunder or Flood Check

The defense should check to formation check thunder when the offense lines up in double slot, trips, tight wing, or split unbalanced (Figure 20-113). The coverage played with thunder is Z spin.

The defense should check to formation check flood when the offense lines up in tight end or tackle over unbalanced (Figure 20-114). The coverage played with flood is orange.

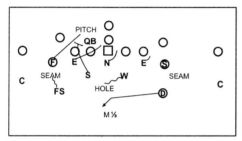

Figure 20-113. Formation thunder check (Larry call)

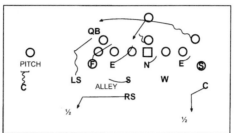

Figure 20-114. Formation check flood (Larry call)

21

Game Planning

Game planning begins on Sunday for that week's opponent. Through game footage/DVD review of the opponent's offense, general plans are developed at this time. The defensive staff can meet and discuss their ideas Sunday evening. On Monday morning, a computer printout of the opponent's offensive tendencies is available for all coaches. The coaches continue their individual preparation Monday morning and are ready to meet as a staff in the early afternoon. At this time, the entire defensive staff reviews the opponent's protections and passing philosophy, and potential coverages, stunts, and blitzes. Each coach will also offer his thoughts on the opponents overall strengths and weaknesses, keys to success, philosophical approach, and how best to prepare for practice and meetings during the week. The in-depth game-plan preparation begins on Tuesday morning. The defensive coordinator has all formations drawn up on a board or overhead visual with a run and pass breakdown for each formation. The following checklist is used to make sure that all areas are covered during the week of preparation:

- Huddle/no-huddle (alignment in huddle)
- Fast/slow no-huddle
- How plays are called:
   ✓Hand signals
   ✓Run players on/off the field
- Who is the call man on the sideline?
- Personnel groupings (Can signals be picked up on groupings?)
- Snap count
- Formations (run-pass breakdown)
- Formation tendencies
- Field-position tendencies (run/pass)
- Down-and-distance (overall run-pass for each down-and-distance situation)

- Coverages
  - ✓ By formation
  - ✓ By down-and-distance
  - ✓ Double calls on checks needed to be made
- Protections
- Zone blitzes
- Man blitzes (run/pass blitzes)
- Bootlegs
  - ✓ Down-and-distance
  - ✓ Formations
  - ✓ Predominantly run to defensive left or defensive right
  - ✓ Field position
- Screens
  - ✓ Back screen
  - ✓ Hitch screen
  - ✓ Rocket screen
  - ✓ Formation
  - ✓ Down-and-distance
  - ✓ Field position
- Red zone, short yardage, and goal line
- Fourth down
- Two-point plays
- Sudden-change attitude (e.g., when the offense gets the ball on the plus side of 50, are they going for the big play on first-and-10?)
- Offense feature any option
- Trick plays (when, where, who, how), reverses, throwback to quarterback, tailback pass
- First-and-10
  - ✓ Second-and-short (three or less)
  - ✓ Second-and-medium (four to six)
  - ✓ Second-and-long (seven or more)
  - ✓ Third-and-short (one to two)
  - ✓ Third-and-medium (three to six)
  - ✓ Third-and-long (seven or more)
  - ✓ Fourth down
- Down-and-distance situations
  - ✓ P-10 (First-and-10 to begin each series by run/pass)
  - ✓ First-and-10 run second-and-seven + (run/pass breakdown)
  - ✓ First-and-10 pass second-and-seven + (run/pass breakdown)
  - ✓ By field zones

- Formation to boundary (run/pass breakdown)
  - ✓ What are the opponents trying to accomplish?
  - ✓ Primarily motion out, or Y trade out
  - ✓ Y trade to
- Use of movement (motion; Y trade): What are the opponents trying to accomplish with motion?
- Runs
  - ✓ Favorite by down-and-distance
  - ✓ Blocking schemes
  - ✓ Draw (lead, quarterback)
  - ✓ How to play runs (base defense/stunts)
- Passing game
  - ✓ Vertical/horizontal philosophy
  - ✓ By formation
  - ✓ By down-and-distance
  - ✓ Dropback
  - ✓ Play-action pass
- Empty formation
- Cluster (bunch)
- Unbalanced
- Shotgun
  - ✓ How to snap (hands or raised leg of quarterback)
  - ✓ One running back
  - ✓ Two running backs
  - ✓ Motion back to tilt position
- Audibles, checks
- Disguises (when, where, who, how)
- Two-minute calls before the half/end of game (fronts and coverages to use)

Suggested defensive staff responsibilities for developing the game plan include the following:
- Defensive line coach
  - ✓ Runs (blocking schemes)
  - ✓ Stunts to stop runs
  - ✓ Goal line and short yardage
  - ✓ Red zone
  - ✓ Fourth down
  - ✓ Running game audibles
  - ✓ Disguises
- Falcon/Stud coach
  - ✓ Bootlegs
  - ✓ Screens
  - ✓ Pass protections
  - ✓ Trick plays
  - ✓ Unbalanced
  - ✓ Cluster
  - ✓ Zone blitzes (fire zones)
  - ✓ Man blitzes
- Secondary coach
  - ✓ Formation to boundary
  - ✓ Personnel groups
  - ✓ Huddle
  - ✓ Passing game

✓ Coverages by formation
  and down-and-distance

✓ Passing game audibles

✓ Last play of the half or the game

• Defensive coordinator

✓ Formations (run-pass breakdown)

✓ Field position tendencies
  (run-pass)

✓ Defensive calls by down-and-
  distance

✓ Two-point calls

✓ Empty

✓ Use of movement

✓ Formation tendencies

✓ Down-and-distance
  (P-10, field position)

Ideas should be shared and valued by all staff members with a spirit of cooperation. One adage should rule supreme: "We're not interested in who's right. Our goal is to do what's right." The staff is an extension of the team, and the definition of team also applies to the staff: TEAM = Together Everyone Accomplishes More

The scouting report for players is given to the players at the Monday individual position meetings. The report consists of a personnel sheet with a two-deep depth chart consisting of height, weight, and class of each offensive player. A separate page or pages includes individual photos the offensive players that contain a short bio from their media guide. This page is followed by a run-pass, down-and-distance breakdown (Figure 21-1), a field zone chart, and a personnel/formation down-and-distance breakdown (Figure 21-2). A computer picture of each formation with pertinent run-pass information is attached to provide a visual of the opponent's formations (Figure 21-3). Then, top runs, passes by formation, bootlegs and screens, protections, and finally runs/passes in goal-line and short-yardage situations are included.

Down-and-Distance	Run	Pass
First-and-one-plus	95 (62%)	58 (38%)
Second-and-short	12 (75%)	4 (25%)
Second-and-medium (4-6)	19 (73%)	7 (27%)
Second-and-long (7+)	39 (53%)	34 (47%)
Third-and-short	7 (87%)	1 (12%)
Third-and-medium (4-6)	6 (19%)	27 (81%)
Third-and-long (7+)	4 (11%)	32 (89%)
Fourth-and-one	9 (75%)	3 (25%)

Figure 21-1. Run/pass by down-and-distance chart

Formation	1st and 1+	2nd and 1-3	2nd and 4-6	2nd and 7+	3rd and 1-2	3rd and 3-6	3rd and 7+	4th and 1+	Total
21 Flanker	Plays 67 Runs 51 76.1% Passes 13 19.4%	Plays 2 Runs 2 100.0% Passes 0 0.0%	Plays 14 Runs 12 85.7% Passes 2 14.3%	Plays 25 Runs 13 52.0% Passes 12 48.0%	Plays 3 Runs 3 100.0% Passes 0 0.0%	Plays 6 Runs 4 66.7% Passes 1 16.7%	Plays 4 Runs 0 0.0% Passes 4 100.0%	Plays 2 Runs 2 100.0% Passes 0 0.0%	Plays 123 Runs 87 70.7 Passes 32 26.0%
11 Trips	Plays 16 Runs 4 25.0% Passes 12 75.0%	Plays 2 Runs 2 100.0% Passes 0 0.0%	Plays 1 Runs 0 0.0% Passes 0 0.0%	Plays 10 Runs 5 50.0% Passes 5 50.0%	Plays 1 Runs 1 100.0% Passes 0 0.0%	Plays 13 Runs 2 15.4% Passes 11 84.6%	Plays 8 Runs 0 0.0% Passes 7 87.5%	Plays 2 Runs 1 50.0% Passes 1 50.0%	Plays 54 Runs 15 27.8% Passes 37 68.5%

Figure 21-2. Personnel/formation by down-and-distance chart

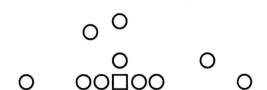

[Insert photo of formation]

20 Tilt Weak Twins

Personnel	Formation	R/P	Play	Count	Percent	Gain	Average
		Run		8	21.1%	50	6.3
			Draw WK	3	37.5%	20	6.7
			Draw ST	2	25.0%	15	7.5
			Stretch WK	2	25.0%	6	3.0
			Cut WK	1	12.5%	9	9.0
		Pass		30	78.9%	148	4.9
			5 Step	18	60.0%	82	4.6
			3 Step	10	33.3%	58	5.8
			5 Step PA	1	3.3%	8	8.0
			5 Step PA Screen	1	3.3%	0	0.0

Figure 21-3. Sheet showing formation with run/pass information

WINNING DEFENSIVE FOOTBALL

Eagle
1. Eagle check (to #46)
   (opposite/opposite)
2. Tilt Eagle (10 personnel)
3. Field/form
   Boundary/weak
   Tilt/numbers
   Tight/split
4. Base
5. Check
   Tilt AC
   Form
6. Check
   Tilt gaps
   Form

Eagle Stunts
1. Whip crash
   Whip crash echo (6/Z)
2. Right lake (echo) Z spin (BOH)
   Left river (echo) Z backer
3. Form flood (echo) Z spin (MOF)
   Weak flood (echo) Z backer

Eagle Versus Option
1. Tilt
2. Tilt AC (swap B/S)
3. Tilt wrap
4. Tilt weave

50
3 Man
1. 50 nose wipe (spy)
2. 50 form (A/angle) (spy)
3. 50
   Left/right
   Form/weak
   Tilt/numbers (Wrap/swap)
   Field/boundary
4 Man
1. Tilt backer (Wrap/swap)
2. Tilt blast (Wrap/swap)
3. Form angle 6
4. Tilt leopard
5 Man
1. Crash (spy)
   Crash (echo) spy (Two/backer)
2. Thunder
   Thunder switch

3. (BOH)
   Right lake (echo) Z spin
   Left river (echo) Z
4. (MOF)
   Form flood (echo) Z spin
   Weak flood (echo)
6 Man (Purple)
1. Eagle stinger (echo)
2. 50 double thunder spy
3. 50 double thunder pick spy
4. 50 double flood (echo)
50 Versus Option
1. Formation (A/angle 6)
53 (GL/SY) (Two, Purple)
1. 53
2. 53 tilt
3. 53 pinch
4. 53 gaps (kill)
5. 53 nose gaps (kill) (Rus/Russell)
6. 53 Loop (X)
Coverages
6
1. 6 combo
2. 6 cloud
3. Robber
4. Bracket
5. Trap
2
1. 2
2. 2 double cloud (spy)
3. 2 backer
Purple
Two-Point Defense
1. Right lake/left river
2. Form/weak flood (echo) purple
3. 50 double thunder (pick) purple
Hurry/Hurry
1. 50 (dime)
2. Eagle (base)
Last Play of Half/Game
1. Victory
Empty
1. Check zero
Mayday
1. Formation Eagle 6
2. (50) formation 6

Figure 21-4. Game plan call sheet

Two days prior to the game, each defensive coach gives his position players a tip sheet, emphasizing key points to make them aware of what they must accomplish to have a chance to win. Each player also receives a test relative to his position that he must complete and turn in to his coach the day preceding the game. At the day before the game meeting, a game plan call sheet (Figure 21-4) and opponent formation sheet (Figure 21-5) are given to the defensive players to provide them with a quick review. The players have these sheets available up until game time for their personal review. Another good idea at this meeting is to separate by position, and each coach take 5 to 10 minutes to orally test their players to gauge how knowledgeable they are about runs, passes, formations, and situations they will face during the game.

	Run	Pass
1-10	59 (45%)	55 (41%)
2-S	10 (90%)	1 (9%)
2-M	14 (63%)	8 (34%)
2-L	24 (44%)	30 (56%)
3-S	9 (81%)	2 (19%)
3-M	4 (22%)	14 (78%) (43-5 pass)
3-L	1 (3%)	29 (97%) (43-5 pass)
4-	6 (75%)	2 (25%)

Figure 21-5. Opponent formation chart

The continual emphasis during the week's preparation is that the players will play faster if they are prepared to react to, not think through, conditions they will confront once the game begins. When the game starts it is time to: play, have fun, make something positive happen, and finish.

22

Practice Organization

The proper use of practice time is critical to the defense's success on game day. It is essential to be well organized in each area of emphasis during each practice session. Daily practice areas of emphasis should include:

- Agilities
- Tackling (individual, tackling circuit)
- Fundamentals (key drills, catch drills, 1-on-1 strip drills, shed drills)
- Kicking game
- Group work (inside drill, half line, pass skeleton, 7-on-7)
- Pursuit
- Team (down-and-distance emphasis, formation emphasis, field position emphasis, screen/draw emphasis, blitz emphasis, goal-line and short-yardage emphasis)
- Best on best: 10- to 15-minute segment, best against the best, 11-on-11, to get the speed of the game and competitive blocking situations. Constantly emphasize that this is a double-win situation for both the offense and the defense.

The week-to-week preparation and approach depends on a number of factors relating not only to physical preparation, but also to the mental and emotional needs of the team that particular week. The issues that need to be addressed include:

- The personality of the opponent's team (For example, a team that throws 40 to 50 times a game may require the pass defenders spending additional time in pass skeleton and the defensive line, working on pass-rush techniques and blitzes versus the offense line.)
- The physical condition of the team coming out of the previous game relating to injuries, fatigue, mental disposition, etc.
- The time in the season (early, middle, or late), which determines the length of practice and the ability to achieve goals in the time allotted

- The ability of the team to achieve the required results in full gear, or helmets and shoulder pads
- Unique problems the opponent may cause (flex bone option, run and shoot, etc.)
- Whether the team is a heavy favorite, underdog, or the game is a toss-up (Each of these scenarios presents different points of emphasis physically, mentally, and emotionally as the team prepares during the week.)

Following is a suggested practice format for a week of preparation with game day on Saturday.

Monday Practice

- 2:30–2:45: Head coach comments (If Sunday is a day off, this is the first time to review the previous game.)
- 2:45–3:00: Kicking game review of the previous game (Responsible coach presents his area of the kicking game and makes appropriate positive and corrective remarks.)
- 3:05–4:15: Position coaches show previous game footage
- 4:20–5:10: Practice

  ✓ Stretch (10 minutes)

  ✓ Correct mistakes (15 minutes)

  ✓ Scouting report on upcoming opponent (15 minutes)

  ✓ Pass skeleton (linemen to the weight room) (10 minutes)

- 5:15–6:15: Everyone in the weight room (The emphasis is not on maintaining strength but increasing strength throughout the season.)

Tuesday Practice (Two-Hour Practice)

- 2:30: Kicking meeting (emphasis on punt protection and punt block)
- 2:45–3:30: Individual position meeting
- 3:35: Practice (Stress rapid-fire, high-energy, intense concentration and all-out pursuit to the ball. Coach and correct on the run. During group or team periods, each position coach has his players around him and instructs them on each play. The players are expected to know the defense and be able to comment on the play of their peers. If they are not in on a play physically, they should be mentally playing the technique, and visualizing their execution of assignments. The emphasis on Tuesday is on the base defense so that players get the proper fits and fills against the opponents various blocking schemes.)
- Practice periods (five minutes per period)

1. Stretch/agilities
2. Stretch/agilities
3. Tackle/strip circuit (two minutes at each station with 30 seconds for change)

WINNING DEFENSIVE FOOTBALL

4. Rapid-fire drills

5. Fundamentals

6. Fundamentals

7. Kicking

8. Kicking

9. Kicking

10. Inside drill (two offensive teams rapid fire; goal to get 25 to 30 snaps)

11. Inside drill (two offensive teams rapid fire; goal to get 25 to 30 snaps)

12. Inside drill (two offensive teams rapid fire; goal to get 25 to 30 snaps)

13. Pass skeleton (two offenses run routes; goal is 40 snaps)

14. Pass skeleton (two offenses run routes; goal is 40 snaps)

15. Pass skeleton (defensive line pass rush versus the offensive line)

16. Pass skeleton (defensive line pass rush versus the offensive line)

17. Team (40 minutes with emphasis on formation recognition/plays): versus 20 sets (two back)

18. Versus 20 (continued from 17)

19. Versus doubles (2x2) formations (11, 12, 10)

20. Versus doubles (2x2) formations (11, 12, 10)

21. Versus trips (3x1) formations (11, 12, 10)

22. Versus trips (3x1) formations (11, 12, 10)

23. Zone blitzes (fire zones)

24. Zone blitzes (fire zones)

The 40-minute team period consists of ten minute segments with a goal to get 20 plays run in each 10-minute time period; and 150 snaps of the opponent's offense within the framework of the entire practice time.

Wednesday Practice

The time of the season will determine whether the team is in full gear or helmets and shoulder pads with shorts/sweats for Wednesday's practice. This plan may change due to the offense played that particular week. For example, if you are playing an option team, you will see more blocks on knees and ankles, so it is advantageous to be in full gear to better prepare for the game. Following is the schedule for a one hour and 45 minute Wednesday practice:

- 2:30: Kicking meeting (emphasis kickoff coverage/kickoff return/field goal/PAT block and protection)
- 2:45–3:30: Individual position meeting
- 3:35: Practice (Stunts are included to get a good gauge on their effectiveness versus particular runs and passes.)
- Practice periods (5 minutes per period)

1. Stretch/agilities
2. Stretch/agilities
3. Fundamentals
4. Fundamentals
5. Goal line and short yardage
6. Goal line and short yardage
7. Kicking
8. Kicking
9. Kicking
10. Inside drill
11. Inside drill
12. Pass skeleton
13. Pass skeleton (defensive line pass rush versus offensive line)
14. Pass skeleton (defensive line pass rush versus offensive line)
15. First-and-10, second-and-medium situations (emphasis on down-and-distance)
16. First-and-10, second-and-medium situations (emphasis on down-and-distance)
17. Second-and-long situation
18. Second-and-long situation
19 Third-and-medium, third-and-long situations
20. Third-and-medium, third-and-long situations
21. Field goal versus PAT block

The goal is to 100 snaps on Wednesday in the one hour and 45 minute practice time. As the season progresses, it is advisable to consider shortening the Wednesday practice to one hour and 30 minutes. The goal is to put a rested, prepared football team on the field on game day. A good football team will practice hard regardless of the allotted practice time. Following is the schedule for a one hour and 30 minute Wednesday practice:

- 2:30–2:45 Special teams meeting
- 2:45–3:30 Position meeting
- 3:35 Practice periods (5 minutes per period)

1. Stretch/agilities
2. Stretch/agilities
3. Fundamentals (tackling)
4. First-and-10 emphasis
5. First-and-10 emphasis
6. Kicking
7. Kicking
8. Inside drill
9. Inside drill
10. Pass skeleton

11. Pass skeleton (defensive line pass rush versus offensive line)
12. Pass skeleton (defensive line pass rush versus offensive line)
13. Second-and-long situation
14. Second-and-long situation
15. Third-and-medium, third-and-long situations
16. Third-and-medium, third-and-long situations
17. Goal line and short yardage
18. Field goal versus PAT block

Thursday Practice (One Hour and 10 Minutes)— Helmet and Shorts

- 2:30: Kicking meeting (overall kicking review)
- 2:45–3:30: Individual position meeting
- 3:35: Practice periods (5 minutes per period)

1. Stretch/agilities
2. Stretch/agilities
3. Kick review
4. Kick review
5. Kick review
6. Kick review
7. Kick review
8. Kick review
9. Team
10. Team
11. Team
12. Team
13. Team
14. Team
15. Weight room (45 to 60 minutes, emphasis on upper body)

Thursday Kick Review

Several different approaches exist with the kicking review period during the Thursday practice. All can be effective if presented properly. The following is a good approach. The coaches and players are on the sideline. The kicking coordinator calls out the particular kicking team he wants on the field; the called kicking team and the appropriate scout team go onto the designated area of the field to execute the particular kick being emphasized. Figure 22-1 depicts the areas on the field for kicking review.

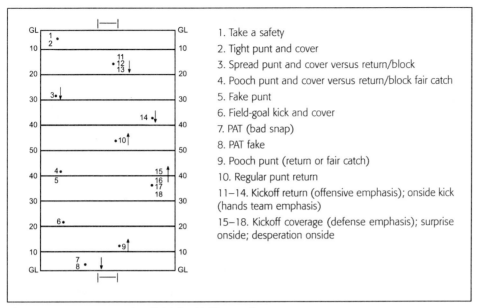

1. Take a safety
2. Tight punt and cover
3. Spread punt and cover versus return/block
4. Pooch punt and cover versus return/block fair catch
5. Fake punt
6. Field-goal kick and cover
7. PAT (bad snap)
8. PAT fake
9. Pooch punt (return or fair catch)
10. Regular punt return
11–14. Kickoff return (offensive emphasis); onside kick (hands team emphasis)
15–18. Kickoff coverage (defense emphasis); surprise onside; desperation onside

Figure 22-1. Areas on the field for kicking review

Thursday Team Review

The defensive team is on the sideline with all the coaches. The players on the field get the defensive call with secondary coverage from the coaches who handle the signals. Start in the goal line to the -10-yard-line zone on the minus end of the field, and progress through each of the field zones to the goal line to the +10-yard-line zone on the plus end of the field (refer to Figure 22-2). The tempo is the same as Tuesday and Wednesday (e.g., high energy and fast paced). Ten plays are scripted in each field zone equally split with five runs and five passes. Managers move the chains according to the down-and-distance situations on the script. A manager is assigned to spot the ball at the appropriate location on the field. The script attempts to duplicate what the opponent has done on various down-and-distances in a particular field zone. For example, if they have run a reverse on first-and-10 on the +30-yard-line, that is put on the script. An attempt is made to make everything as close to game conditions as possible. The team period is completed with a "save-the-game pass" against the designated defense for that situation.

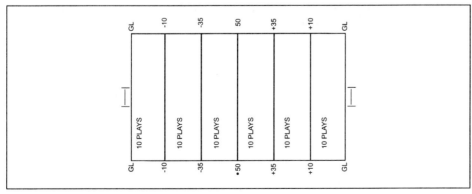

Figure 22-2. Areas on the field for the team review

Helpful Tips and Reminders
to Improve Practice

- Cannot afford to have a quarterback/center fumbled snap. The center has a Nerf® ball, and the quarterback has the ball in his hands, whether he is under the center or in the shotgun. This method saves time by eliminating any snap problems on the part of the offensive scout team.
- Have the proper jersey number placed on the tight ends, wide receivers, and backs so the defensive team can line up quickly and accurately on each play.
- Early in the week, have the scout team look at footage of the opponent's offense so they can imitate splits, stances (whether two-point or three-point), wide receivers' alignments, running backs' mannerisms, and quarterback action under the center or in the shotgun.
- Make defensive players accountable for the defense called, the formation and play being run, and plus or minus performance of the man playing his position.

Friday Schedule (Day Before the Game)

Not having a field workout on Friday of a home game can provide the players with additional rest. However, if it is an away game and the opportunity exists to go to the game site, it is a good idea to acclimate the players to the locker room, playing surface, and so forth. The night-before-the-game meetings include: a 30-minute kicking meeting, followed by 30-minute offensive and defensive meetings. A 5- to 10-play footage/DVD of each kicking unit is shown during the kicking meeting. Players sit together in the defensive meeting with their position coach. The defensive meeting starts with the signal caller going through a quick demonstration of the calls with the defensive team verbally responding with proper calls, checks, and such. The best way to do this part of the meeting is to look at game footage/DVD with the defensive coordinator making a call that correlates with the down-and-distance. The linebackers then make their directional call, and the secondary makes their coverage checks against the formation, motion, and so forth. This meeting should be a quick-moving session with players and coaches communicating with each other. Any last-minute questions can also be addressed at this time.

Richard Bell coached 12 years at the U.S. Air Force Academy overall, including eight years as defensive coordinator. He won the American Football Coaches Association Assistant Coach of the Year Award in 1998. A year prior to that, Bell was nominated by the AFA staff for the Broyles Award as the nation's top assistant coach.

A native of Little Rock, Arkansas, Bell has helped Air Force to four post-season bowl games and coached Chris Gizzi to All-American honors. (Gizzi, a two-time WAC defensive player of the year, developed into one of the finest players ever to wear the blue and silver. He played professionally for the Green Bay Packers.) Bell also turned former Falcon Anthony Schlegel into a big-time college player. (Schlegel, selected to *The Sporting News*' Freshman All-America team in 2001, was a first-team all-conference selection in 2002 before transferring to Ohio State. Schlegel was a third-round draft pick by the New York Jets in 2006.)

Bell came to Air Force from Navy, where he served as defensive coordinator and inside linebackers coach in 1994. Prior to his stint at Navy, Bell spent five seasons at the University of Georgia as the defensive coordinator and secondary coach.

A 1959 graduate of the University of Arkansas, Bell earned a degree in physical education. He earned two letters while playing varsity football for the Razorbacks and later earned a masters degree from the university in 1962. Bell was captain of the 1958 Arkansas team in Frank Broyles' first season.

In Bell's 42 years of coaching at the collegiate level he has coached in 17 post-season bowl games. Bell began his coaching career at Virginia Military Institute as an assistant in 1962-63. He then coached linebackers at Georgia Tech from 1964 to 1967 before becoming defensive coordinator at West Virginia in 1968. After two years with the Mountaineers, Bell moved to Texas Tech as defensive coordinator from 1970 to 1974. In 1975, Bell moved to South Carolina where he was the defensive coordinator from 1971 to 1981 and head coach in 1982. He then coached at Duke (1983 to 1987) and East Carolina (1987-88) as the defensive coordinator before going to Georgia.

Bell has always been involved in his local community. He has been president of the adult group or a sponsor of the Fellowship of Christian Athletes everywhere he's coached. Bell is active in the Colorado Springs community. He volunteers for community projects for his church and is active in Promise Keepers. He's been active in the AFCA, having served on several committees. Most recently, he was on the Assistant Coaches Committee. Bell and his wife, Marilyn, have three daughters, Michelle, Meredith, and Melinda, and one son, Murry. The Bells have six grandchildren: Macy, Daniel, Benjamin, Taylor, Haley, and Alyssa.

About the Author